# Service-Learning Across Cultures:
# Promise and Achievement

# Service-Learning Across Cultures: Promise and Achievement

## A Report to the Ford Foundation

by

Humphrey Tonkin
Susan J. Deeley
Margaret Pusch
Diego Quiroga
Michael J. Siegel
John Whiteley
Robert G. Bringle

edited by

Humphrey Tonkin

The International Partnership for Service-Learning and Leadership
New York, 2004

The International Partnership for Service-Learning and Leadership
815 Second Avenue, Suite 315
New York, NY 10017  USA


© 2004 by
The International Partnership for Service-Learning and Leadership
All rights reserved. Published 2004
Printed in the United States of America




ISBN  0-9701984-8-5
Library of Congress Control Number:  2004114321




This book is printed on acid-free paper.

*To the students, universities and service agencies*
*who have pioneered a new vision of teaching, learning*
*and volunteer service in nations around the world*

# Contents

## Part 4:  How the Partnership Influences Institutions

## Part 5:  Evaluation

## Part 6:  Next Steps

## Appendix

# Foreword

Recently, the *New York Times* published an article by Greg Winter headlined "Colleges Tell Students the Overseas Party's Over." The author describes college and university programs abroad that are short term and superficial, but for which students receive academic credit. Too often students on these junkets behave badly, to the embarrassment of the United States and their home institutions. Now, according to the *Times* article, colleges and universities are cracking down. This is good news for professionals in the field of study abroad, who have seen the Junior Year Abroad reduced to a shadow of its former self. For several years now, the design and quality of study-abroad programs has been the subject of much debate. Most agree that we in academia need to ensure that a study-abroad experience has all the rigor attached to regular studies.

This study, funded by the Ford Foundation and directed by Humphrey Tonkin, examines the effect of programs designed and managed by the International Partnership for Service-Learning and Leadership. It grew out of conversations with Ford Foundation officials who emphasized the need to measure the changes that are brought about by Ford support. In effect, they were saying to the International Partnership, "You maintain that you have made a difference to students and to the communities in which they study and serve. Now prove it."

We welcomed the opportunity. We wanted to examine in a systematic way whether all our time and effort over twenty-two years had indeed borne fruit. We wanted to know what we are doing right. But, as important, we wanted to know what we need to correct, adjust, strengthen, and amplify. We wanted to know what conditions help to produce a high-quality program that truly immerses students in society and culture abroad.

And because our programs combine academic study and community service—a kind of Peace Corps but with study and credit—we needed to look at the effect of the programs not only on the participating students, but also on the universities around the world that host the programs and on the service agencies and communities where the students volunteer.

It has been a gratifying experience for me as president, for the Partnership staff and for the board of trustees. The conclusions indicate that we have generally been headed in the right direction. It has been wonderful to learn of the leadership our alumni have demonstrated in their lives subsequent to participation, of the credit they give to the programs, and of the service they have rendered in so many and varied ways to US society and to other nations and communities around the world. It has been rewarding to learn that host institutions have, to one degree or another, embraced this pedagogy of service-learning for their own students. It is satisfying to learn that those who direct service agencies and the clients who use their services have benefited by the presence of the international service-learning students.

But even more invigorating is the identification of work yet to be done. The study enumerates areas needing further work and poses further questions regarding program effectiveness.

Colleges and universities throughout the world are recognizing three important truths for today's world. First, they know they must educate—truly educate—students about other cultures, since we do indeed live in a global village. Students must learn to understand, appreciate, and work cooperatively with those of different beliefs and values. Second, academic institutions are recognizing that there are many sources of information, methodologies, and epistemologies that must and should be incorporated into academic learning. Books and lectures remain the bedrock of formal study, but experience, especially experience as rich as serving those in need in another country, is a powerful source of knowledge that can be examined critically and reflected upon just as are the sources of traditional study in higher education. Third, the colleges and universities themselves are realizing they cannot stand apart from the problems, issues, and suffering in their own societies or those of the world. They have a responsibility to deploy their resources to address these needs.

International service-learning, as the study shows, can be a powerful means of addressing all three of these issues—but only under certain conditions, only with a well thought-out design and careful management, and above all, only with a clear and compelling vision and sense of responsibility to all who experience the impact of the service-learning program: students, universities, and the communities they serve. The sad truth is that even international service-learning can be superficial, destructive or exploitative.

This study is a beginning effort to ensure that quality prevails in international service-learning, and that by maintaining quality, we can increase the participation of our young people in this important enterprise. The study's conclusions will guide our way over the coming years. We expect to engage in further study of the questions it raises. We hope it is useful to our readers. Above all, we aspire to understand and increasingly implement the elements that give students a rich experience of the host culture and a means for examining in depth their own beliefs and values, which inspire and invigorate the universities hosting the programs and which make communities and our world more humane, more just, and more peaceful.

LINDA A. CHISHOLM
President, The International Partnership for Service-Learning and Leadership

# Preface

This volume is a report on a series of data-gathering and research activities carried out by the International Partnership for Service-Learning with the support of the Ford Foundation in the period 2001–2004. These activities included a report on the characteristics of Partnership alumni, a study of the effects of Partnership programs on students, a study of the impact of the Partnership and of service-learning in general on the agencies where Partnership students work, an assessment of the impact of the Partnership on the colleges and universities hosting the Partnership, and the development of an evaluation protocol for Partnership programs.

These activities reached completion at different stages over the three-year period. The first to be completed was the report on the characteristics of Partnership alumni, finished early in 2002 and contained in chapter 3 (we have done some minor updating, but the report is essentially as it was when we first posted it on the Partnership website and produced a paper version in April 2002). The evaluation protocol was given its final form in December 2002, and the report on the agency study was completed in July 2003. Most of the work on the student study was finished by September 2003, and the final portion of the institutional study was completed in April 2004. Work on preparing this final report began soon thereafter. Some of the chapters are the work of individual authors, as indicated in the table of contents. Unsigned chapters were put in their final form by Humphrey Tonkin in his role as editor and project director, often with the assistance of other members of the team.

Chapter 1 includes materials from Humphrey Tonkin, "Study, Service, and the Self Transformed," in *Study Abroad: A 21st Century Perspective,*

*Volume II: The Changing Landscape,* ed. Martin Tillman (Stamford, CT: American Institute for Foreign Study Foundation, 2003), 22–25, and from "From Diversity to Diversity," a speech given by Tonkin at the Partnership national conference, New York, March 1995. The section on the history of the Partnership is based in part on information collected by Linda Chisholm.

The chapters on the student survey include material presented by Margaret Pusch and Michael J. Siegel in May 2003 at the Conference of NAFSA in Salt Lake City and in October 2003 at the 3rd International Conference on Service-Learning Research, also in Salt Lake City (see Pusch 2003 and Siegel 2003a, 2003b). These chapters, particularly chapter 6, also include material contained in Humphrey Tonkin and Diego Quiroga (2004), "A Qualitative Approach to the Assessment of International Service-Learning," in the journal *Frontiers.*

Thanks are due to Sarah Callahan, Kate Chisholm, Barbara Dessureau, and Molly Shaw for their assistance in preparing and presenting the data contained in the demographic report, and to Jane Durnin for her transcription of student interviews and focus groups. We are most grateful to all of the students who participated in these groups and to the staff members and board members who assisted us by serving as rapporteurs and in numerous other ways. We are grateful, too, to the program directors who interviewed one another for the institution study: Marie Cerna, Irma Guzmán de Torres, Jenny Iles, Brad Blitz, David Woodman, Chantal Thery, Kalyan Ray, Mark Gelber, Carmen Pencle, Geraldene Hodelin, Guadalupe Delgadillo, José Luis Arreguín Romero, Cesar Orsal, Valerian Three Irons, Yuthachai Damrongmanee—and of course Susan Deeley and Diego Quiroga. José Luis Arreguín Romero at Guadalajara, Irma Guzmán de Torres at Guayaquil, and Chantal Thery at Montpellier also assisted us in reviewing and testing the program evaluation protocol.

For numerous favors, assistance, and advice, the authors would like to thank Donn Weinholtz, Ira Harkavy, Frank Johnston, Patrick Love, Florence McCarthy, Nevin Brown, John Gardner, Dwight Giles, Ed Zlotkowski, Maureen McHale, Ilana Golin, Erin Foley, Martha Butt, David Peacock, Stephen Schwartz, Adel Safty, and John Annette. Barbara Wanasek has assisted us in numerous ways, and her unfailing courtesy and efficiency helped make arrangements smooth and information readily available.

Particular thanks for their time and help are due to the staff and service-users in Glasgow and Kingston who participated in the agency study. Thanks also to Carmen Pencle for arranging the interviews in Kingston, Jacqui

Pilkington and Faith Nelson for their administrative assistance, and Carmen Sanguinetti for her hospitality and support.

It is hardly possible to thank all those who assisted with the institutional study, but our special gratitude goes to Cesar Orsal, who made all the arrangements at Trinity College, and Esperanza San Diego, who arranged the agency visits. Brad Blitz kindly performed a similar role in Roehampton and also assisted us in Jamaica. We are especially grateful to President Josefina Sumaya, of Trinity College of Quezon City, and Vice-Chancellor Bernadette Porter, of Roehampton University, for their hospitality and assistance.

Kate Chisholm handled the layout and preparation of the volume for the press with admirable speed, efficiency and good humor. Thanks also to Monika Frey for copy-editing.

The authors wish to declare that they alone are responsible for any errors or omissions that may have crept into their contributions. The editor accepts similar responsibility for all unsigned portions of the volume. And authors and editor are grateful for the comments and suggestions that they have received from many sources—which reduced the errors and increased the felicities in the final texts. Finally, we are all of us most grateful for the ongoing support for this project shown by the Partnership Board of Trustees and for the leadership, support and inspiration provided by President Linda Chisholm.

And, of course, without the support and funding of the Ford Foundation this three-year research project could not possibly have come to fruition. We are deeply grateful.

# 1 Preliminaries

# 1 Researching the Partnership

## Introduction: Service-Learning in an International Setting

*In Zimbabwe, I have also become accustomed to being motionless. Being motionless usually feels good, as when I sat with Amai Kyandere on the kitchen hut floor waiting for the water to boil. Sometimes even waiting for a bus that may never come can feel good. It has to do with acceptance, allowing for a slower pace, and understanding that nothing is really predictable.*

These are the words of an American undergraduate, Perrin Elkind, newly returned from study in Africa. Her story, *Tonderai: Studying Abroad in Zimbabwe* (1998), a moving account of how study in a very different culture can deepen understanding of the self and the world, is a model of what can be achieved at the edges, the frontiers, of American higher education. It serves as a kind of testimony to the flexibility of a system that can expand to include life experiences such as these within its capacious formal structures. These structures are challenged daily as more and more students like Perrin Elkind set out on journeys through mind and space in search of themselves and the world.

Such students are going in new and different directions. More are studying outside the customary European destinations, for example. The once dominant idea of study abroad as a kind of European finishing school has been replaced, at least in part, by a more eclectic pattern, with less emphasis on immersion in traditional western culture and greater emphasis, for instance, on discovering the Americas (the most dramatic increase in numbers relates to Latin America) and on engaging with other, more distant parts of the world (and not just the europeanized environment of Australia and New Zealand, but the countries of Africa and of east, south-east and south Asia). Totals for all US students going to Africa, for example, are up by a factor of six over the past fifteen or so years.

There is plenty of evidence that prolonged study abroad, particularly when it involves a degree of immersion in a culture very different from one's own, is a transforming experience for many. Leaders of study programs abroad point to the ways in which such experiences challenge received assumptions, teach values, and allow students to look at their home-country lives in a different way. We do not need reminding that in the world of tomorrow, with more and more people occupying tighter and tighter physical, intellectual, and emotional space, and with increased mobility and easier communication leading to more and more overlap and layering of cultures, young people (and old ones too) need such perspective.

Yet there are still many students who do not travel abroad. For others the experience of study abroad is little more than a glorified vacation or a visit to a theme park. There remains a substantial problem of rendering study abroad meaningful for the students who pass through it, and making it transformative in their thinking about the world. But at the other end of the scale, there is also a greater sense of adventure on the part of many students, and a determination to immerse themselves in a thoroughly different culture.

Just as more students are traveling to more locations, so they are seeking out a greater range of experiences. The International Partnership for Service-Learning and Leadership (IPSL) operates semester-long and summer programs in some dozen foreign countries and among the Lakota Nation in the United States. These programs are roughly evenly divided between conventional classroom study, generally in a host institution such as the University of Montpellier in France, Ben-Gurion University in Israel, and Trinity College in the Philippines, and community service—in literacy programs, grass-roots community organizations, legal defense programs, social work services, and a host of other activities. Classroom work and community service are linked in a regular seminar or equivalent experience under the leadership of an experienced mentor who helps students process their experiences in the field and relate their classroom learning to their community work.

# The Partnership Experience

- Fifteen to twenty hours of service per week

- Full semester programs in most cases

- Academic courses taught by in-country faculty members trained by Partnership personnel and in most cases including the course "Institutions in Society," adapted to the host country

- Emphasis on reflection, linking practical experience in the field with theoretical knowledge in the classroom

- Journal writing (assisted by Chisholm's *Charting a Hero's Journey*)

- Individualized placements in established agencies engaged in direct human care

- Language learning where appropriate

- Maximum immersion in the host culture through homestays, in-country faculty and program directors, and individual placements

- Credit for academic work, with a transcript from the host institution

The service-learning movement, of which the Partnership is a major manifestation, began primarily as an offshoot of the experiential education movement[1] some thirty or forty years ago—a movement allied with the educational theories of John Dewey (Hatcher 1997) and given currency

---

[1] On connections between service-learning and experiential education, see Stanton, Giles and Cruz 1999. But note also the early efforts of Dickson and others in Britain, going back to the 1950s, to develop the concept of study service (Dickson 1976, 1980; Goodlad 1982).

in part by the radical reforms in higher education in the late 1960s and 1970s. Service-learning is rooted in the belief that students learn best (or learn certain subjects best: different thinkers hold different views) when they can link direct experience to classroom learning—when they can check theory against practice, and when they can analyze practice to formulate theory.[2]

With the vast expansion of American higher education in the 1960s and 1970s—in an atmosphere increasingly politically and ideologically charged—many teachers were looking for ways to engage students in learning, and they believed that the linkage of action and reflection in this way would help engage students.[3] But their intentions went further. By having the students engage in community service, they were allowing them to experience cultural difference—and cultural dissonance—in their own backyards: many students coming to American colleges knew little or nothing about the lives of the poor or the experiences of those less fortunate than themselves. Service-learning brought these other subcultures to the attention of students, and the students in turn contributed their newly acquired skills for the good of the community. Today, though it is still somewhat marginal at many institutions and not accepted by all faculty members, service-learning is fairly well established across the country, and it is a rare college or university that does not have some service-learning activity somewhere in its curriculum (even discounting the fact that the term "service-learning" is often misused to cover non-credit community service; our use of the term here refers to credit-bearing activity in the curricular mainstream).[4]

---

[2] Dewey's emphasis on the importance of learning through reflection on experience is central to the pedagogy of service-learning. For a statement of Dewey's views on reflection, see, for example, his chapter on "Experience and Thinking" in *Democracy and Education* (1916). See also Ehrlich 1997 on the debate between Dewey and the reformist president of the University of Chicago, Robert Maynard Hutchins.

[3] Bringle & Hatcher 1995 (and 2000) define service-learning as a "course-based, credit-bearing educational experience in which students (a) participate in an organized service activity that meets identified community needs and (b) reflect on the service activity in such a way as to gain further understanding of course content, a broader appreciation of the discipline, and an enhanced sense of civic responsibility." On the definition of service-learning, see, among numerous examples, Sigmon 1996. On reflection, see Bringle & Hatcher 1999, Moon 2001.

[4] At the University of Pennsylvania, in part in order to avoid the negative connotations of the term "service-learning," such courses are defined as Academically Based Community Service. See Benson & Harkavy 2002, Lawson 2002.

Service-learning has expanded its currency in part through such organizations as Campus Compact (www.compact.org), whose initial aim was to persuade more students at conventional liberal arts colleges and universities to get involved in volunteer work in the communities around their institutions. But, while it builds on the ethic of community service, its goals are at once deeper and more ambitious: it seeks to make community service not an adjunct but an integral part of formal study. Many of the member institutions of Campus Compact now have their service-learning programs, in which they encourage faculty members to develop teaching programs linked to the community and assist them in making the connections. Service-learning has also gained broad currency in elementary and secondary schools, though in many cases the zeal of local school boards to inculcate in young people a sense of citizenship and responsibility has not been matched by corresponding curricular adaptation, and "service-learning" is often little more than occasional community service.

The service-learning movement has grown in strength in recent years, in part, as we have seen, in response to educators' expanding realization that uniting theory and practice benefits both sides of the equation: students learn to derive theory from practice and to test theory through practical observation. The net result is that a generation of students less adapted to the traditional ways of acquiring knowledge through passive absorption learns in a new way, and perhaps in the process advances its own moral development and the ethic of service to fellow human beings.

Community service, too, can be a transforming experience. Many students, growing up in middle-class homes in suburban neighborhoods, have had little to do with the world revealed to them when they embark on programs taking them into social-service organizations, hospitals, and inner-city schools, and they can derive deep satisfaction from combining their own studies with the well-being of their communities. They can also learn new ways of looking at the world and, through the formal learning process, share their experiences with others. Furthermore, while so much of classroom learning is based on competition, community service revolves around cooperation: such service puts students in situations in which they maximize their productivity by working effectively with others.

It is perhaps worth emphasizing that the idea behind service-learning, of linking the classroom with the larger world, theory with practice, is an idea of worldwide potency. While we can find some of its roots in the long-established American belief in volunteer service, an idea fostered and promoted by enlightened liberal arts institutions over many years—or in the conjunction of education and practice that lies behind the land-grant colleges of the nineteenth century—it has many genealogies in many traditions across the world. In 1998, a group of educators and representatives of non-governmental organizations from the United States and fifteen countries around the world met at the Wingspread Conference Center in Racine, Wisconsin, to review the progress of service-learning initiatives in the United States and abroad. A report published by the Partnership the following year, *Service-Learning in Higher Education Around the World* (Berry and Chisholm 1999), described service-learning programs in these countries and fifteen others—programs linked with teaching (in Indonesia, Israel, Ecuador, the Czech Republic, for example), health care (in Japan, Jamaica, Liberia, France . . .), community development (the Philippines, Mexico, Kyrgyzstan, Korea . . .), and so on. These programs include those of individual professors or institutions and also nationwide and region-wide efforts. Service-learning, in short, has become an important element in the higher education systems of many countries and in the academic programs of numerous individual institutions. "I would like not only to study at my desk but also to go to the place, to touch and feel," writes Miyuki Araki in the IPSL report (p. 22). "Service-learning gives me first-hand experience of team work and brings me in contact with people, especially children," adds Ifeoma Nnaji of Nigeria; "I consider this vital because I want to be a doctor."

One reason for convening the Wingspread conference was to explore international cooperation in service-learning. When service-learning and study abroad are brought together, they form a powerful combination. Students find themselves studying in settings very different from those of their home country, which call forth all the adaptation skills that we associate with study abroad: learning a new culture while attending to the ordinary needs of daily living, participating in a dialogue with those around them in a different idiom or a different language. But this challenge to their sense of self is not simply a journey of self-discovery, not simply an adaptation that, once embarked upon, benefits them and them alone: it is a means to an end. Students in service-learning programs adapt to their surroundings not simply to advance their own agenda but to enter into a partnership, a compact, with a community needing their services. So there is a collectively recognizable goal and purpose to their adaptation, and the effort that they expend on it has its rewards not only for them but also for the people they serve. The willingness to serve and the desire to do it well are powerful motivators, hastening an adaptation that, once a threshold has been crossed, allows students to benefit most fully from the cultural experience. In the course of the research that we carried out for the present study, we discovered that one reason why international service-learning is so effective is the fact that students are put in positions in which they have to adapt fast, and in which strong supportive mechanisms are in place to hasten the adaptation.

A few years ago, asked to speak to an audience of specialists in international service-learning about my own sense of why such learning works, I enumerated a series of points that perhaps bear repeating. Abstract learning, I declared (and as I have suggested above), is easier to grasp when it is rooted in practical experience, and the experience itself is enriched when it is linked directly with learning. There are those who argue that we sacrifice objectivity when we allow the practical or the here-and-now to intrude into the classroom, but the objectivity that we allegedly sacrifice may be the objectivity of the status quo, the ideology of the powerful. A classroom in which real-life experiences are analyzed, and in which guidance is provided for dealing with such real-life experiences, may be a messier place than the antiseptic environment of clinical objectivity, and it may wreak havoc with test-taking and unambiguous competition for grades— but, as my very examples imply, education is never value-free. I might add that it doesn't always work, and a system that encourages tempered self-worth may be a better teaching environment than one that simply sorts, rewards, and punishes. Teachers working in a service-learning environment may become better teachers of students (as opposed to machines for the unerring separation of sheep from goats) and better observers of societies and cultures.

Far from value-free, education is in fact a journey with maps and compasses: namely the values of the teacher, and the collective and individual values of the students themselves. The best way to learn the values of sharing and service is by deriving them from concrete, unambiguous situations, where the human need to cooperate is made incontrovertibly clear. The right way to learn self-worth is by observing one's ability to better the self-worth of others.

But, of course, there is more to *international* service-learning than this, since participants find themselves living in another country, in a minority. The very rendering of service raises a host of complex issues, beginning with a sense on the part of students that they are simply doing what Americans so often do—trying to make other people more like themselves, and exercising their sense of generosity by bestowing it on those they regard as less fortunate. But such delusions of social beneficence are rapidly countered by the discovery of value systems that reshuffle the priorities or build other assumptions into family and community. With good guidance, particularly from in-country specialists, students learn to serve on other terms than their own, and it is this, perhaps more than anything else, that they take with them when they leave. Living in another culture and critically absorbing its values may be the best way to prepare young people for the multicultural and globalized world of today and tomorrow—a world in which, despite the rather frequent assertions of our leaders, we cannot expect to live by one standard and have others live by another.

There is a further value to be associated with international service-learning: when the students leave their hosts to return home, they leave something behind. The International Partnership, for example, is not simply engaged in providing students with a collection of opportunities: it is also embarked on helping a range of institutions work better and deliver better services—an orphanage in Kingston, Jamaica, a kindergarten in Guadalajara, a literacy program in Quito, and so on. One measure of the Partnership's success is the success of the agencies it serves, and so it takes these connections very seriously. It is significant that many of the students who pass through its programs develop lasting friendships with those they serve and with their fellow workers. Many return to their host countries at a later date, sometimes to continue volunteer service. Some go into the master's program in International Service run jointly by the Partnership and universities in Britain, Jamaica and Mexico.

Recently, Linda Chisholm prepared a manual, *Charting a Hero's Journey*, designed, through a series of readings and exercises, to assist students in keeping journals and in reflecting on their experience abroad or in community service, or in the combination of the two that is the Partnership's particular mission. This wonderfully practical and intelligent volume contains excerpts from published journals spanning two hundred years—journals which tell us both that the anxieties of travel and of service have always been with us, and that others went before us, into an often far more mysterious world. James Boswell and Dr. Johnson led the way, trudging through the Outer Hebrides, but Jane Addams, Mary Kingsley, Octavio

Paz and others told their stories too, and do so again in Linda Chisholm's book. Of all the excerpts, I think I like best the ones by Langston Hughes, who at one point observes, acerbically,

> Six months anywhere is enough to begin to complicate life. By that time, if you stay in one place, you are bound to know people too well for things to be any longer simple.

That is what Perrin Elkind discovered. And she returned transformed.[5]

## The Partnership

In the sections of this chapter that follow, we will first lay out the history and present condition of the International Partnership for Service-Learning, then discuss the nature of the Partnership experience, and finally describe the goals of our study. This introduction will prepare us to examine the research program in greater detail in chapter 2, and then the various phases of the research itself in the chapters that form the bulk of this volume.

The Partnership began over twenty years ago, in 1981, when a pilot service-learning project was co-sponsored by the Presbyterian Church, USA, and Rockland Community College to help disadvantaged African-American students recover their African heritage. The program was developed by Howard A. Berry, of Rockland, and the Reverend Walter Graig.

The following year, service-learning programs were added in England and Kenya, and a task force was set up, under the direction of Howard Berry, who was chair of the department of international studies at Rockland, and Linda A. Chisholm, executive assistant to the president. The task force's charge was to consider how to advance the pedagogy of service-learning and to explore the feasibility of establishing a national organization to promote it. The task force met regularly over a three-year period. In the academic year 1983–84, the groundwork for the foundation of the Partnership for Service-Learning was laid, and the new organization gradually became fully operational. The president of Rockland Community

---

[5] Perrin Elkind went abroad through the Study Abroad program of the School for International Training. SIT, based in Brattleboro, Vermont, is a pioneer in the creation of challenging study-abroad experiences and maintains a network of study-abroad sites across the world.

College, Seymour Eskow, was selected as the first chair of the Board of Trustees and gave his support to the creation of service-learning programs for US students in England and Ecuador. When Eskow retired from Rockland in 1984, his successor, Thomas F. Clark, briefly served as chair of the board.

The new organization applied for and was awarded a planning grant by the Ford Foundation to lay out a five-year plan for the development of the Partnership. The plan, directed by consultant Sven Groennings, former executive director of the Fund for the Improvement of Postsecondary Education, called for the Partnership to become an independent educational organization supported by fees from its student programs and additional funding from grants. Ford then awarded the Partnership a further three-year grant aimed at making it self-sustaining.

Linda Chisholm left her position at Rockland Community College to become the president of the Association of Episcopal Colleges (AEC), with an office in the national headquarters of the Episcopal Church on Second Avenue in New York City. The AEC board of trustees included in her portfolio the development of the Partnership and service-learning programs from which AEC students could benefit. Howard Berry left his position at Rockland to become co-director of the now independent Partnership, which received not-for-profit status from the State of New York as an independent organization in 1986–87. The headquarters were transferred to Second Avenue, in a cooperative arrangement with AEC, which has continued to this day. By-laws were drawn up, calling for a board of trustees, initially led by Dr. Margaret Gwynne, vice-president of Brookdale College, as chair of the board. She was succeeded by Dr. Humphrey Tonkin, president of Potsdam College of the State University of New York and subsequently of the University of Hartford. Berry was named first president of the Partnership and Chisholm executive vice-president.

The organization has blossomed and expanded over the years, moving into a major advocacy role and embracing service-learning activities around the globe. From its early beginnings in England, Ecuador and Jamaica, it has established undergraduate service-learning programs of several weeks' or a semester's duration primarily for American undergraduates in a dozen or more locations around the world, including France, the Philippines, Liberia, India, Israel, Scotland, the Lakota Nation of South Dakota, Mexico, Russia, the Czech Republic, and, most recently, Thailand. These programs were made possible by affiliations with a university in each of the locations, which issued a transcript for the academic study and whose faculty carried out the teaching according to principles agreed upon with the Partnership. The program director in-country, usually a member of the university staff, arranged the service placement for each student. Through annual meetings of the program directors, programs were adjusted and refined as best practices emerged and were incorporated into the programs at each location. The addition of a course called *Institutions in Society*, adapted country-by-country to reflect issues encountered by students in the field and to link them with the institutional and cultural structures in the country and region in question, greatly strengthened the programs and helped advance the action-reflection process at the core of the educational experience. Although the AEC institutions were initially the major sending institutions, the program rapidly spread beyond these colleges and soon students from literally hundreds of American colleges found their way to Partnership programs (see below). Over the years, the locations of Partnership programs have remained relatively constant, with additions from time to time, but relatively few omissions (the most notable exception is the Partnership's collaboration with Cuttington College, Liberia, discontinued because of that country's prolonged and tragic civil war).

To advance the goal of fostering service-learning, the Partnership expanded its annual meeting to become a national conference on service-learning, held for the first few years in Washington, DC, and then at a different US city each year. The newsletter *Action/Reflection* was launched and distributed nationally, and a book, *How to Learn and Serve Abroad Effectively: Students Tell Students* was published with the support of a NAFSA Co-op Grant.

While its core programmatic activity remains the operation of undergraduate service-learning programs, the Partnership now also operates a full-year master's program in international service-learning, with a degree offered through Roehampton University (formerly University of Surrey Roehampton, UK), in cooperation with the University of Technology Jamaica and the Autonomous University of Guadalajara, Mexico. Students spend the first half of the year in either Mexico or Jamaica, and then, after a short study visit to New York for visits to nongovernmental organizations and United Nations agencies, they go to Britain, where they complete their coursework and write their master's thesis. The program prepares students for careers in international relief and development work, primarily in NGOs (nongovernmental organizations). In addition, for the past several years the Partnership has run special service-learning programs for particular purposes in various locations, particularly in Southeast Asia. Thus, the undergraduate programs have become somewhat smaller as the graduate program and the special programs have expanded. The present survey is concerned primarily with the regular undergraduate offerings.

The development and expansion of the master's program (located at three institutions, all of them outside the United States, and with a student body drawn from many countries) and the growth of special programs (including programs tailored to the needs of non-US institutions as well as of individual institutions in the US seeking cooperation overseas) are indicative of the Partnership's expansion beyond its US location and focus to become a fully internationalized organization. A decision was made in the mid-1990s to add the word "international" to its title, and the *International* Partnership for Service-Learning soon became an organization with two clear and interlinked missions: the operation of programs, primarily for, but not exclusively for, American students; and the advocacy of service-learning across the world, particularly in countries outside the United States (in the United States, numbers of other organizations, among them Campus Compact, were performing the role of advocates, and in any case the interest of the Partnership remained strongly cross-cultural and international).

The conference convened by the Partnership at Wingspread in May 1998 developed a plan to promote service-learning in colleges and universities around the world. The conference marked a turning-point in the Partnership's role as an advocacy organization. "For some years now," the conference declared in its closing statement, "universities and colleges of higher education around the world have been developing programs for their students that link formal learning and volunteer service. Although diverse in history, location, curricula, student bodies and resources, these institutions are using the pedagogy of service-learning to re-connect their institutions to the needs of their community by working cooperatively with community organizations. They have discovered that service-learning has the power to reform education, transform students, and address human and social needs."

In identifying their activities in this way, the Wingspread participants allied their activities with those of another growing movement—the trend towards civic engagement and democracy-building on the part of growing numbers of universities around the world.[6] These interests, long the philosophical mainstays of Campus Compact and given focus in the work of Ernest Boyer and the Carnegie Foundation for the Advancement of Teaching (Boyer 1996), were gaining greater and greater currency not only in countries where higher education systems had long made explicit their commitment to nation-building and capacity-building, but even among more traditional institutions, for example in Europe.[7] One such recent effort, the International Consortium on Higher Education, Civic Responsibility and Democracy, was jointly sponsored in the United States by the National Science Foundation and in Europe by the Council of Europe. The Wingspread participants went on to propose that

> because the major challenges facing human societies at the dawn of the third millennium are largely shared, and institutions of higher education, from their positions of relative privilege and influence, ought properly to be committed to the relief of human suffering and the enhancement of quality of life for all, and the idealism and energy, especially among the young, motivate people to seek social change and the creation of a better world, and the value of experiential learning at higher education level is now widely recognized, and societies across the world depend to a greater or lesser extent on the voluntary principle to provide care and support for their members . . . we, as representatives of universities and colleges of higher education and of social service organizations from across the world with an existing commitment to the continued development of learning through service, seek continuing association in a spirit of mutual respect, cooperation, affirmation and support.

---

[6] See, for example, Lawson 2002, and the essays in Orrill 1997, Ehrlich 2000, and Kenny & others 2002.

[7] In Britain, the Dearing Report (Dearing 1997) is quite explicit in stating that one of the main aims of higher education is "to play a major role in shaping a democratic, civilised and inclusive society." See also Annette 2002; Battistoni 2002; Lockyer, Crick & Annette 2003.

It was agreed that the International Partnership should serve as coordinator and secretariat for this new effort, whose purpose would be to

- enable students from across the world to benefit from the advantages and programs of service-learning;
- encourage, in cooperation with communities, the continued development of service-learning in institutions of higher education and in service agencies across the world;
- enable an international sharing of experience and good practice in the field;
- achieve a wider dissemination of the values and ideals of learning through service;
- encourage institutions of higher learning to play their rightful role in both addressing local and global challenges and seeking to meet human and social needs;
- promote a sense of community and civic responsibility;
- advance the common purpose of building a new generation of leaders through service-learning;
- encourage public policies which initiate and support opportunities for community service linked to the education of students.

These purposes were to be advanced through "the development of a broad network of contacts" among institutions, the development of "communication strategies," the organization of "conferences and training opportunities," "curricular development," local and international service-learning programs, and the encouragement of service-learning research. Participants called for the development of a statement of the nature and intent of service-learning, a worldwide survey of existing models, and an effort to raise further funds.

The Wingspread conference served as an important catalyst for the Partnership, which increasingly assumed the role of coordinator of this international effort. Howard Berry and Linda Chisholm carried out the survey of international models called for by the conference,[8] the Partnership's communication network was expanded (soon with the addition of Web capacity), and new training opportunities and conferences were launched.

---

[8] Berry & Chisholm 1999. This volume also contains the full text of the Wingspread recommendations.

Among its initiatives was the founding of a system of so-called Distinguished Partners (Berry & Chisholm 1999:117–120, and see the Partnership website www.ipsl.org), institutions across the world that accept the principles of service-learning as laid down by the Partnership and seek to promote it within their own campuses and communities. Each Distinguished Partner has to be approved by the Partnership board. Such approval, while it bestows no specific rights or privileges on individual institutions, can serve as a powerful stimulus to the development and approval of service-learning on the campuses in question. The program also offers a way in which institutions running their own service-learning programs can become affiliated with the Partnership, and so it extends the network beyond the dozen-or-so institutions at which the Partnership has formal student programs. Institutions in various parts of the world are now recognized as Distinguished Partners, including numbers of institutions in developing countries, which have come to service-learning through Partnership programs and initiatives (for a list, see the Partnership's website www.ipsl.org).

Following the Wingspread Conference, the composition of the Partnership's board shifted to reflect its broadened interests, and trustees from other countries were added (currently one-third of the board is from outside the United States and the intention of the Partnership is to maintain or increase this number). The Partnership decided (in a move endorsed by the Wingspread participants) to shift to a pattern of biennial conferences at various locations around the world (Mexico 1996, Jamaica 1998, Ecuador 2000, Czech Republic 2002, Thailand 2004) and sought to involve educators on a worldwide basis (the Thailand conference, for example, convened representatives from Mainland China (including Hong Kong), Taiwan, Korea, Singapore, Turkey, Vietnam, Myanmar, Indonesia, Japan, South Africa, American Samoa, Belarus, and Australia, in addition to those countries where the Partnership has programs). A grant from the Luce Foundation allowed the Partnership to begin its special programs in the Philippines, which brought together students from twelve Asian nations and the United States and helped build a practical and theoretical framework for the development of Asian service-learning programs. A faculty training seminar for representatives from eighteen institutions of higher education in Asia, sponsored by the United Board for Christian Higher Education in Asia, was organized to help these institutions develop local service-learning programs. The seminar was followed by the awarding of a small grant to each institution for program design and implementation. On behalf of the Partnership, Dr. Florence McCarthy visited each of these colleges and universities over the following two years to aid in their work. All institutions successfully initiated and have sustained and further developed their service-learning programs. Florence McCarthy, named a visiting lecturer at International Christian University, in Tokyo, was also appointed by the Partnership as its vice-president for Asia in order to continue her work.

During these years, Louis Albert, of the American Association for Higher Education, now president of Pima Community College West, Arizona, headed the board. When grants of $650,000 from the Ford Foundation and $300,000 from the Luce Foundation enabled the Partnership to move forward with programs, advocacy, and organization development, Humphrey Tonkin, former board chair and now president emeritus at the University of Hartford, was named vice-president for evaluation and research, on a part-time basis. Margaret Pusch, of the Intercultural Communication Institute (Portland, Oregon), former chair of the board of NAFSA, became board chair.

In January 2001, Linda Chisholm retired as president of the Association of Episcopal Colleges to devote herself full time to the work of the Partnership. In January 2002, Howard Berry died suddenly and unexpectedly, and the board moved quickly to appoint Dr. Chisholm as president of the Partnership. With the loss of Howard Berry, the board lost not only a major link to its origins but also one of the sharpest minds in the theory and practice of service-learning and a devoted adherent to its educational philosophy. His death was a significant setback. Eighteen months later, Nevin Brown was appointed Dean of Academic Programs and moved ahead energetically to rebuild the Partnership's programs and further expand its base.

Among the most significant arguments for the promotion of service-learning contained in the recommendations of the Wingspread conference was the advancement of "the common purpose of building a new generation of leaders through service-learning." This was the first explicit mention in the context of the Partnership of a principle that had been implicit in its work for a number of years. Not only was service-learning dedicated to the principle of service to the community, but increasingly it was seen as a means of community empowerment by encouraging community members to take charge of their lives for the common good, and by inculcating such principles also in the service-learners themselves. Service-learning, it was felt, was inevitably linked with the development of collective leadership and leadership for change. Here, too, its ideas intersected with the civic engagement movement. It was the hope and desire of educators engaged in service-learning that their charges play an active role in the life of the community, not only as followers but also as leaders.

Accordingly, the Partnership decided to add "leadership" to its title and to begin to incorporate ideas of leadership education into its programs. The idea, according to Partnership president Linda Chisholm, was "to incorporate the concept of leadership education since the quality of leadership at all levels and in all institutions of a society is generally agreed to be the single most important determinant of the well-being of a society and critical to achieving a 'culture of peace' among peoples and nations." And thus the International Partnership for Service-Learning and Leadership came into being and work began not only on the integration of leadership principles into all of the Partnership's programs, but also on the development of a new international master's program, still in the planning stages, in leadership education and service-learning (see Safty 2004).

## The Partnership Experience

The service-learning programs of the Partnership for Service-Learning are different from those of many other organizations because they transport the student out of his or her day-to-day world and into another, entirely different environment. Most service-learning programs involve a crossing of divisions defined by economic class, and most study-abroad programs involve a crossing of divisions defined by geography and culture and, frequently, language. But the programs of the Partnership aim to do both—by changing the cultural and the economic contexts at one and the same time.

Service-learning, whether conducted in a different country or here at home, is, according to its practitioners and supporters, a transforming experience. We observe its effects regularly among students returning from Partnership programs around the world, but it is evident in domestic programs as well. It forces the student (and the professor) to re-examine the relationship between theory and practice—between what is learned through experience and the theoretical context in which such experiential learning can be made to take place. Service-learning tends to propel the student from practice to theory, and to vest theory with meaning; but it also creates a kind of feedback loop in which theory and practice are brought into a dynamic relationship as the one reinforces the other.

At the same time, the student's talents are harnessed to provide service, by taking the student out of his or her immediate and self-centered concerns to address the needs of others. Many educators have come to believe that this ingredient is too frequently lacking in undergraduate education, where the emphasis is often all on self-improvement, not on cooperation, and certainly not on putting aside one's own immediate needs in favor of those of others. An educational system based primarily on competition leaves little room for experiences that derive from cooperation, yet such experiences are a crucially important part of learning to live in the world of today and tomorrow.

A different kind of transformation takes place as a result of study abroad, but it is potentially equally radical. Proponents of study abroad frequently use the same vocabulary as service-learning proponents use. They talk about how the experience obliges students to step outside their own concerns, to look at the world in a new way, but also to confront certain things about themselves that they might otherwise not be aware of. The vocabulary of distance and separation, of objectivity and apartness, is supplemented and complemented by the vocabulary of engagement and confrontation.

So service-learning of the kind proposed by the Partnership is based on the assumption that a student learns through a self-induced and self-motivated process of accommodation to the larger environment. Changes in that environment must be processed and understood. In one sense learning comes easily under such circumstances: motivation is seldom a problem when the student is confronted with a new culture and a job to be done. More to the point: such learning *belongs* to the student and comes from within.

So far, such argument is conventional enough. Through twenty years of planning and practice the Partnership has developed its programs, and the goals and methods that it espouses are reasonably well understood, at least by its most active participants.

But what we may not fully comprehend is the extent to which, over this period, the world itself has changed, and that these changes are destined to continue. The old model of study abroad, made popular a quarter-century ago, has the student moving from known to unknown, from a homogeneous and well understood environment to an environment different and more complex. Traditional notions of service-learning work with similar assumptions: the conventional, middle-class, protected student must suddenly deal with complexity and with the imperative of serving others.

While such notions are still expressive of certain realities of our world, we should recognize that neither country of origin nor country of destination is as separate and distinct as it once was. Similarities and differences are more subtle and unexpected, the cultural values of America are increasingly permeating other parts of the world, and these "other parts of the world" are increasingly permeating American society, in part through immigration, in part through ease of travel and general mobility, in part through rapid advances in electronic communication.

It is not, then, that young Americans will be condemned to living a life of suburban complacency if we do not drop them down in inner-city Kingston or the squatters' communities of Manila. The Eisenhower years are long over. It is that the problems and values of such communities are increasingly mere variations of our own problems and values, and that humankind's capacity to understand these differences is outstripped by the complexity and rapidity of their occurrence. In short, if our young people do not learn about other societies, they may well be unable to cope with the complexities of their own.

One reaction to this rising tide of human change is to retreat into ourselves, to throw up barriers to change and to stigmatize difference—of race, ethnicity, religion—as the enemy of community. Paradoxically, ease of electronic communication and human mobility lead directly to tragedies like the situation in Bosnia, as peoples react sharply to fear of change and try to resist the alienation that it brings, by forcibly shutting out alien influences—or to the current terrorist emergency, which has brought to the fore a new kind of organized political crime, aided by advanced technology that reaches out across the world, but based on old grudges stretching back to the earliest conflicts of ideologies.

As we enter the twenty-first century, we face many problems, but arguably the greatest imperative for humankind is the management of difference. Our society at home is increasingly diverse, and societies abroad are subjected to increasing pressures from outside. Our young people move, through programs such as the Partnership, not from a homogeneous society to a diverse one, but from diversity to diversity.

So the most important discovery for Partnership students is not that the world is diverse, but that societies handle difference with varying degrees of success. The best lesson that they can learn and absorb has to do with how others manage difference, and how others equip themselves to deal with change. Along the way they may also learn to question some of the assumptions of our own society—the inequalities it creates, the sense of hopelessness it breeds among many, as well as the challenges it offers and the opportunities for self-betterment that it provides.

Such knowledge and understanding, so vitally important to the students who experience it, is not easily brought back to enrich our own society. Study and work abroad, while personally rewarding, may (as we shall see) actually induce a certain sense of alienation in the returnee, especially when the returnee is faced with the conventionalities of the American classroom; but we might hope that the Partnership's brand of teaching and learning, which stresses providing the student with the resources he or she needs to process experience, may help the student overcome this obstacle and adapt what he or she has learned to practical use in participation and leadership at home.

This brand of learning is what makes the Partnership unique. Patterns of teaching and learning are changing around us quite rapidly—even if some of our colleagues have yet to realize it—and the old notions of separation between theory and practice are beginning to recede, to be replaced by a more dynamic sense of how the one can be used to reinforce or challenge the other, and how efforts to address real-life problems need not be separated from formal learning. For too long we have isolated formal education from the processes of personal development. The success that service-learning programs are enjoying, in many highly diverse contexts, shows how effective the linkage of the two can be. In a society that seems increasingly to have lost its sense of intellectual direction, such programs offer an opportunity for a new educational synthesis, capable of motivating student and professor and capable of creating a new sense of cooperation to address some of the problems that beset our society.

In putting these programs into operation, and in bringing them to the attention of our colleagues, the Partnership and its allies face certain fundamental challenges. Though its mode of teaching may be the wave of the future, and though the emphasis on intercultural experience and service experience may become increasingly important to those who design and lead undergraduate education, we should recognize that the future, by definition, has not yet arrived. Those in the Partnership are still pioneers and are faced with structural and substantive obstacles to the general acceptance of their programs. The capaciousness of the American higher education system may be a reality, but fitting such experiences as service-learning within it can still prove difficult.

Some years ago, at the annual conference of the Partnership in New York City (March 1995), I laid out a brief agenda for the general acceptance of Partnership activities. It remains largely current today. "We must make it easier," I wrote, "to classify our programs as conventional study-abroad offerings, so students will not run into difficulty in enrolling from their home institutions." My suggestion was not to disguise what actually goes on in international service-learning, but to interpret it in terms readily understood by faculty members concerned about the academic quality and nature of the experience. Indeed, I added, "We must help our colleagues understand how service-learning works and how they can apply it in their own teaching." My concern, then, was to address the question of academic quality head-on.

But, I added, "We must remind our more conservative colleagues that practical experience is not necessarily a challenge to objectivity—indeed that it is possible to have students engage in community service without advancing a specific political agenda, especially if, as is the case with the Partnership, emphasis falls on raising the right *questions*, rather than providing the right answers—on opening, rather than closing, minds." Any activity that is based on direct intervention in the daily lives and community existence of people half the world away can easily be interpreted as ideologically or politically biased. As I have suggested elsewhere, such bias may in fact be an element in all that goes on in the classroom, wherever that classroom may be; but, given that reality, it is a commonly held belief by those engaged in the Partnership that, if anything, Americans are too quick to move to answers, too uncomfortable with open-ended questions. The goal of the international service-learning experience should be to cultivate or awaken in the student a certain tolerance of ambiguity and an awareness that there are no easy answers.

To these three suggestions I added three more:

- We must encourage colleges to provide support for faculty and students to get involved in service-learning activities;

- We must get the word out about what we do—in better publicity for our programs and promotion of our methods of teaching and learning;

- We must institute more rigorous program review, so that we can satisfy our most demanding client institutions and gain credibility for our programs.

All three of these priorities have emerged in the recent work of the Partnership. "We have talked often in our conferences and elsewhere about getting the Partnership and its ideals into the mainstream of higher education," I added. "It is time we moved on this agenda and made it our primary goal." The Partnership has made much progress in the intervening years, but challenges remain. The present study is designed to examine the strength of our claims, the criteria for success, and the impact of international service-learning on its various constituencies.

## The Goals and Focus of the Study

In 2001, as we have noted, the International Partnership for Service-Learning received a grant from the Ford Foundation to strengthen its own operations and also to carry out an extensive study of the effectiveness of its programs. As a long-term board member and former chair of the board of the Partnership, I was asked to assume responsibility for the coordination of the research effort, and in the fall of 2001, after consultation with many people within and beyond the Partnership itself, I prepared a research plan that was subsequently adopted by the Partnership board and is now being implemented.

I should stress at the outset that, while we were eager to obtain an objective assessment of our programs and to contribute to the research effort in service-learning, our primary interest was, and remains, the improvement of the Partnership's activities and those of others engaged in service-learning: our research is therefore targeted, outcomes-oriented, and designed to yield usable information.

The Partnership's work, by involving both the service-learning experience and the international and intercultural experience, cuts across two major areas of research: study abroad (particularly the impact of study abroad on students)[9] and service-learning (particularly the educational

---

[9] On assessment of the effect of study abroad on students, see the annotated (Internet) bibliographies by Burn, Carlson and others, and by Chao. See also Carlson, Burn and others 1990, and Gillespie, Braskamp & Braskamp 1999. Several research programs for the assessment

value of linking community service and the curriculum—for the students, for the process of learning, and for the institutions in which the learning takes place).[10]

Partnership programs, by their nature cross cultural divides between one nation or culture and another, socio-economic divides between the advantaged and the disadvantaged, and also pedagogical divides between conventional pedagogy and the pedagogy of action and reflection.[11]

Throughout its history of over twenty years, the Partnership has been influential both as an advocate and as an agent of change. Many of those now actively involved in service-learning in this country and abroad were inspired to make that commitment through the work of the Partnership and the example of some of its early leaders, such as Alec Dickson, the founder of Voluntary Service Overseas in Britain and a strong supporter of the Partnership's work,[12] and Howard Berry, the partnership's first President. Indeed, the influence of the Partnership has been out of all proportion to its relatively modest organizational structure and programmatic activity. The Partnership is not intended as a mere service for institutions of higher education, but as a transforming agent, shaping students' lives, determining

---

of student outcomes of study abroad are currently ongoing, including a consortial effort led by Georgetown University (Michael J. Vande Berg), the IES program mentioned above, and a study by the Council on International Educational Exchange.

[10] On assessment of the effect of service-learning on students, see Driscoll and others 1998, Eyler & Giles 1999, and Eyler, Giles, Stenson & Gray. The Policy Center on the First Year of College (Brevard, NC) and the Higher Education Research Institute at UCLA have developed a survey designed as a follow-up (pretest/posttest measure) to the Cooperative Institutional Research Program (CIRP) Freshman Survey, a national survey administered annually to thousands of entering college students around the country (Gardner, Siegel & Cutright 2001). This survey measures the degree to which students change during the first year on several behavioral and cognitive domains. Analysis of results of the 2002 survey revealed that students who participated in some type of volunteer work during their first year reported higher levels of success with various aspects of the first college year. Further assessment initiatives to learn more about the impact of international service on students and the gains students make in their moral and intellectual development, their sense of citizenship and engagement, and their cultural awareness are needed. Also still to be addressed is the relative impact of service-learning as opposed to service alone. See also Zlotkowski 2002 and particularly Vogelgesang, Ikeda, Gilmartin & Keup 2002. On experiential elements in the overseas experience, see Montrose 2002.

[11] On navigating these divides, see Chisholm 2000.

[12] See, for example, Alec Dickson 1976, Mora Dickson 2004.

the priorities of institutions, reforming educational practice, building better communities, and developing future leaders.[13]

My early discussions in 2001 with board members, sending institutions in the US, directors of our programs overseas, and various others, identified three areas where our activities have been particularly influential and that warranted further research.[14] They also defined two additional needs related to the research effort.

The three areas identified for further attention were: (1) the effects of our programs on students, (2) the role of the Partnership as an agent of institutional change, and (3) the impact of our programs on social service agencies and the clients and communities they serve. We adopted three working hypotheses as we designed our research in these three areas.

### Students

First, the effect of our programs on students. The Partnership's pedagogies of engagement seem to have caused students to learn to look at other cultures with new eyes, to examine their own culture and assumptions with a newly critical regard, and to appreciate the importance of cooperation and of service to others. The processes associated with service-learning, in other words, seem to have led to a degree of engagement with another culture that goes beyond what we normally associate with the nonetheless transformative experience of study abroad. The pedagogy of action/reflection, the direct interaction with another culture through the service component of the program, and the architecture of Partnership programs with its stress on the use of in-country personnel and its emphasis on self-reliance seem to be the distinguishing features of the Partnership experience. We have extensive written materials—questionnaires, journals and the like—from students that testify to these transformations, but we are

---

[13] For a statement on the goals of the Partnership and its pedagogy, see the Partnership's website, www.ipsl.org. See also Berry 1990. Of late, the Partnership has put increasing emphasis on the need to develop new paradigms of leadership through service in a globalized society (see, for example, Aquino 2001). On the mechanics of setting up international service-learning programs, see Chisholm 2003, McCarthy 2002. On the nature of international service-learning, see Tonkin 1999 and 2001.

[14] On research on service-learning's effects in general, see the comprehensive annotated bibliography by Eyler, Giles, Stenson & Gray at http://www.compact.org/resource/aag.pdf.; Driscoll, Holland, Gerlmon & Kerrigan 1996; and several of the essays in Billig & Furco 2002.

interested in examining the relationship between such testimony and the actual lifetime experience, behavior and life choices of our alumni—and the extent to which such experience and behavior can be linked with the Partnership's programs.

## Institutions

Second, the influence of the Partnership on institutions. The Partnership's work as an advocate and practicioner of service-learning appears to have changed the priorities and programs at numbers of institutions of higher education. We can point to several examples of institutions that, serving as hosts of the Partnership when we first got started in the 1980s, are now requiring community service or service-learning of all their students.[15] We do not know how influential the Partnership and its ideas were in that process, nor do we know with any clarity what factors impeded or advanced the shift toward service-learning: this is what we wish to investigate.[16]

## Agencies and communities

Third, the influence of the Partnership on agencies and communities. Working with social service organizations, Partnership programs have assisted communities in addressing their needs, often in powerful ways. A close relationship has developed between the programs and the agencies to which they send students. Since Partnership pedagogies emphasize long-term human commitment to community service, and since they are process-oriented rather than specifically outcomes-oriented, assessing the influence of the Partnership will be particularly difficult: we cannot point to so many houses built, or so many wells dug, because the Partnership focuses on people and on the process of service rather than on material outcomes. However, this third area of research is particularly important: service-learning is so often conceived as something that is "good for" students, in that it builds a sense of citizenship and altruism, that we give little or no

---

[15] On service-learning internationally, see Berry & Chisholm 1999, Yamamoto 2002, Annette 2002, Showalter 1989.

[16] On the institutionalization of service-learning, see, for example, Bringle & Hatcher 1997, Ward 1996.

attention to what actually happens to the people at whom the service is directed.[17] Is our objective better education, better communities, or both?

### Qualitative vs. quantitative research

Even with the substantial Ford Foundation grant, our resources were too limited to carry out a fully comprehensive, quantitative study—though one of our objectives is to encourage further work following the start that we are now making,[18] and we are beginning to recruit interest from researchers in need of good research materials and clearly defined and limited subject groups. Indeed, there are entire areas (for example language learning) that are not part of the present study. So our research is not wholly comprehensive, and is in some instances qualitative and anecdotal rather than quantitative and comparative, though based on solid evidence and verifiable data.

Our efforts began with the drawing up of a comprehensive Research Plan, divided into seven "phases" on a three-year time-scale. Each of the phases involved certain specific steps, with each step verifiable in relation to specific outcomes. A budget was drawn up to accompany the plan. As each phase was completed, I filed a report with the Partnership and revisited both plan and budget to make modifications as needed. The details of the plan are the subject of our next chapter.

---

[17] "Are we and our students exploiting the community for learning purposes as we engage in service-learning endeavors," asks Barbara L. Rich, of the University of Southern Maine (Rich 2002). On the problem of assessing the community impact of service-learning, see Cruz & Giles 2000. In their collection on service-learning Kenny and others 2002 include several chapters written from an agency point of view.

[18] See, for example, Kathia Monard's recent University of Pittsburgh dissertation *Nurturing Senses of Care, Justice and Reciprocity through International Service-Learning,* on the Partnership's Ecuador program (Monard 2002; see also Porter & Monard 2001).

# 2 The Research Plan

## Introduction

As a reform movement in higher education, service-learning on many college campuses has served as both testing ground and launching pad for innovative programming, creative new pedagogies, curricular change and reform, and fruitful partnerships between faculty and student affairs personnel. Like other educational reform movements, service-learning is generally confined to the margins at those institutions where it is practiced, and we still know relatively little about how to make such opportunities part of the mainstream in collegiate education. It is a primary goal of service-learning to help institutions of higher education, students, faculty, staff, and communities at large create useful and meaningful partnerships, academic in nature, in the spirit of civic engagement and awareness. Here too, we know relatively little about its long-term effects on students, agencies, and institutions.

Less prominent on the agenda, but equally important, is the question of whether service-learning also achieves its *service* objectives. It may be good for educational institutions and educationally effective for students, but is it meeting a need in the communities where students serve? Are service agencies full-fledged partners with the colleges and universities offering service-learning? The question raises important ethical and practical issues.

Finally, most service-learning programs are designed to link institutions and their immediate communities. But what if the entire world is seen as a potential location for service-learning? What if it becomes part of an effort at global education and cross-cultural understanding?

The research begun in 2001 and described in this report was, then, an attempt to address international service-learning along three dimensions: student response to international service-learning, the impact of student service on agencies and their clients, and institutional adaptation to service-learning.

## The Plan

As we have noted in chapter 1, the research plan drawn up in the fall of 2001 pointed out as a preliminary rationale the fact that the programs of the Partnership in various parts of the world have been influential in three particular ways:

1. They have had a major impact on the educational and moral development of young people from the United States and elsewhere. The Partnership's pedagogies of engagement have caused students passing through Partnership programs to learn to look at other cultures with new eyes, to examine their own culture and assumptions with a newly critical regard, and to appreciate the importance of cooperation and of service to others.

2. By virtue of their ongoing support for social service organizations, Partnership programs have helped transform communities in many parts of the world. A close relationship has grown up between programs and agencies.

3. The Partnership's involvement in, and advocacy of, service-learning programs in various parts of the world and its encouragement of institutional participation has had a transforming effect on the programs and priorities of numbers of institutions of higher education.

Evidence to support these contentions, the report pointed out, was nonetheless largely anecdotal: the Partnership had not had the resources to document such transformations. The new funding from the Ford Foundation would make it possible to carry out research in these areas and to assemble evidence that, depending on the outcomes, might make the Partnership's case considerably more powerful, and at the same time point to areas for improvement.

Furthermore, as the research plan pointed out, when the Partnership began its work in the early 1980s, its focus was almost exclusively on running programs abroad for US students. Today, as the *International* Partnership for Service-Learning, it has connections all over the world, it is linked with numbers of service-learning activities that touch the US only peripherally, and it has shifted its emphasis from programming alone to programming *and* advocacy.

Accordingly, the plan singled out two fundamental groups of questions to be answered:

1. How effective are the Partnership's programs, and what can be done to strengthen them?

2. How has the Partnership's advocacy of international service-learning, and its work with other institutions and individuals, had an impact? What can be done to increase this impact?

The purpose in asking these questions was not simply academic: the goal was improvement of the Partnership's activities. What works well and what works less well? Are there ways of increasing the Partnership's impact? Are there elements in its programming, or in its advocacy of international service-learning, that should be improved or changed? Are opportunities being missed?

One very important product of such attention to outcomes would be the development of better criteria for evaluating the success of individual in-country programs. Such evaluation must be a collective undertaking, in which the directors and faculty in individual programs are fully engaged, both in the assessment of their own in-country programs and in an ongoing professional dialogue with their peers in other programs, aimed at strengthening consensus in the Partnership and fully exploiting new developments in the field. For example, the research plan explained that the Partnership wished to strengthen its programs by building on work already being done, within the Partnership and beyond, in the creation of learning communities and in pedagogies of engagement.

Accordingly, the Partnership wished to establish a systematic program of assessment and self-improvement, designed to help programs and their directors serve the needs of the students and the community-service agencies more effectively, and to assure the sending institutions that the work the students are doing is fully credit-worthy and intellectually fully engaging. Such assessment, the research plan suggested, might include regular peer evaluation of programs, with the active involvement of sending institutions. The existence of such a system of self-improvement and self-assessment would help to raise the profile and credibility of the Partnership and its programs—credibility not only as a programming organization but also as an advocate for international service-learning. Thus, internal strength would translate into external credibility.

The Partnership's new Office of Research set for itself five program objectives:

### 1. Statistical Survey and Ongoing Data Collection
To assemble a demographic profile of past and present students in the program, with information on their sending institutions, their majors, and any other evidence that can be obtained from existing records. In addition, new data-gathering instruments will be put in place to provide additional longitudinal data in future years. The scope of this preliminary study will be largely determined by the extent of the retrievable information now in student files.

### 2. Impact Assessment
To carry out research and data-gathering on past and present students, their opinions, their career patterns, their experiences, through contact not only with the students themselves, but also with parents, home institution faculty members, advisors, program directors, and others. This study will focus particularly on student goals and attitudes. If possible, it will include some data comparing students who have passed through the Partnership's programs with students who have not.

### 3. Study of Institutional Change
To carry out a four- or five-institution study of institutional change at colleges and universities that have integrated Partnership-style service-learning into their educational and developmental programs. Who have been the principal agents of change? How have the stated priorities

and missions of the institutions changed? What impact have the philosophy and practices of service-learning had on faculty, staff, students, service agencies? To what extent has the Partnership's involvement been the determining factor, or one in a number of factors, influencing changes in policy and practice? The study, to be carried out by a small team, will draw on any research or data within the institutions themselves, might be linked to funding for follow-up projects, and might include recommendations on institutional integration of service-learning. Most, or all, of the institutions involved will be in countries outside the United States. One of the purposes of the study will be to explore the applicability of their experiences to US institutions.

### 4. Impact on Agencies

To carry out a study of social service organizations that have worked with the Partnership and its receiving institutions over a number of years, including the development of profiles of these organizations and of the Partnership's impact (a) on the agencies themselves and (b) on the transformation of the communities they serve. The study will also examine the importance of the university/agency connection.

### 5. Program Evaluation

To establish an ongoing evaluation procedure for Partnership programs, to put it into effect, and to disseminate it as a model for others; also to examine these programs to assess their effectiveness as learning communities.

These initial plans inevitably underwent some modification as the research activities moved forward. The statistical survey was completed in good order, but the new instruments for data-gathering are only now moving to completion and are not yet fully in place. The student study, while it has included contact with numbers of other actors than those described in this report, was not triangulated as we had hoped, and this aspect of the study will have to be incorporated in future efforts. The agency study, while largely completed in accordance with the original plan, has demonstrated how elusive is the measurement of students' collective effectiveness in the field, in part because of the intentionally scattered nature of student placements (as a matter of policy, the Partnership avoids placing multiple students in single agencies in any one semester). On the other hand, isolated examples of student effectiveness are easy to document. Also disappointing was our inability to involve all parties in the research in Kingston, Jamaica: our original plan called for the engagement of researchers at University of Technology, Jamaica, who could then go on to do further research at a third location, but we were unable to locate suitable individuals in the time available. As for program evaluation, the first full-blown on-site evaluations will take place at three locations in the fall of 2004, too late for documentation here. All other aspects of the evaluation project were successfully carried out.

The research plan also detailed procedures for publishing and disseminating the results of the various research activities, identifying a number of audiences, among them:

- The Partnership itself. To strengthen its programs and to make its case, the Partnership needs to know more about itself. Such knowledge will benefit program directors, others associated with programs in the field, the staff in New York, and the Board of Trustees.

- Sending personnel, including study-abroad advisors, and faculty members.

- Students, who will have a better sense of the Partnership's programs and a better understanding of service-learning.

- Agencies and others interested in involving students in community service.

- Educational planners, particularly those involved in curricular planning, and those eager to evaluate the strengths of experiential learning and pedagogies of engagement.

- Educational reformers, particularly those in the service-learning community.

- Advocates of service-learning in the United States and abroad.

- NGO leaders and others involved in international development.

Each of these audiences is now being engaged in various ways. Researchers involved in the student study have given four conference presentations, one article has been accepted, and a second is under review. Material from the study has been posted on the Partnership's website, the demographic report has been published separately, and further initiatives will be taken in the year 2005.

Perhaps the biggest setback to the research effort came in the early months of the project with the death of the president of the Partnership, Howard Berry. As an important part of the collective memory of the Partnership and as the person perhaps most closely acquainted with the day-to-day operations, Howard Berry was a major inspiration for the effort—and his death also meant that much of the time initially set aside for research was consumed by the need to reassign the routine operations of the office and, in a painful and prolonged effort, to recruit staff to carry on this work.

## Timeline

### *Phase One: Preliminaries*

The timeline for the research plan was divided into seven phases. The first, from September to November 2001, called for setting up a group of advisors to work with the director of the project and to provide ongoing advice: "The group will consist of experts in the field of service-learning and individuals familiar with this type of research. Most of its business will be conducted by e-mail." A loosely structured group was duly formed, consisting of established researchers across the United States and beyond, the Partnership board of trustees, and several of the program directors. Plans were shared with them, and their advice was sought on the various phases and aspects of the plan. Also a part of this first phase was solicitation of the views of the Partnership board on the five objectives and modification and refinement as needed. Such advice was sought and received, and a similar process was followed, during these months and the months ahead, with program directors, particularly asking them to identify activities that would be directly useful to them.

A third activity during this first phase was to conduct a review of the student data currently available in the office and to make decisions on how this information would be assessed and presented. Finally, a fourth activity was to investigate the question of quality control of study-abroad programs, particularly the procedures used by major senders to multiple locations, and any information available from accrediting organizations. Although some senders were reluctant to share details of how they carried out internal assessment, enough information was assembled to begin work on a program evaluation system, not least because evaluation and assessment has become a burning topic in study-abroad circles and numbers of researchers were eager to discuss the topic.

For each phase, a list of products or procedures was provided as "evidence of completion" of the phase.

### Phase Two: Short-Term Steps

The second phase extended from December 2001 to May 2002. During this phase, nine steps were envisioned:

1. "With the help of Partnership staff, assemble statistical data and other information from Partnership files. Develop an initial profile of the Partnership student. Prepare a demographic/statistical report based on this information." This report was completed ahead of time and published in paper form in April 2002 and made available on the Partnership's website.

2. "Assess the strengths and weaknesses of the current student data and begin to prepare and put in place procedures for gathering more focused or comprehensive student information from present and future classes." Significant improvements were made in the data base and in data entry, and an initial effort was made at designing new data-gathering instruments, but changes in personnel during 2002 and 2003 delayed the project, which has yet to be fully completed.

3. "Identify, and plan in advance, time at the Prague conference (April 2002) for consultations with program directors, focus groups, and similar activities." Several sessions were organized and completed in Prague, allowing for extensive consultation with program directors and other conference participants, and resulting in the collection

of numerous good ideas and in the improvement of the research design.

4. "Establish consultative advisors for each research study and the evaluation study. Exchange ideas regarding purpose, focus, operations, etc. for each major endeavor." Such advisors were duly identified, and dialogue with them has continued throughout the project.

5. "Seek input from program directors, study-abroad advisers, faculty members and others on the question of program evaluation." Such input was duly gathered. The program directors, particularly, were invited to contribute their ideas on program evaluation—an important part of the process, since their investment in the success of the process was crucially important.

6. "On the basis of advice received from program directors and others, information on evaluation procedures used by other sending organizations, etc., draft a list of criteria to be used for program evaluation." The draft was duly drawn up and resubmitted both to the program directors and to the board for further refinement. Two extended discussions of the draft were arranged for Prague, involving program directors in one case and the Partnership board in the other.

In addition, a detailed budget was drawn up for the project which was revised and updated at intervals throughout the project (7), efforts were made to identify additional funding where appropriate (8), and regular revision of the research plan was undertaken upon completion of each phase (9).

### Phase Three: Medium-Term Steps

The third phase covered the balance of the year 2002, from June to December, and involved seven steps.

1. "If the statistical (demographic) report provides useful information, disseminate the findings of the report in appropriate ways." The

report was made available in paper form and also posted on the Partnership's website. It formed the basis for a session at the May 2003 NAFSA conference and was one of the elements included in a presentation at the International Service-Learning Research Conference in October 2003.

2. "Continue the process of data-gathering for the study of student goals and attitudes."

3. "Develop a more detailed description of the study of student goals." This and the previous item involved consultation with numbers of scholars and researchers and the drawing up of general description of the plans for the student study, centered on a focus-group approach. Four researchers were chosen to conduct the study: Michael Siegel, Margaret Pusch, Diego Quiroga, and John Whiteley. Each had a different set of skills to bring to the process, two (Pusch and Quiroga) knew the Partnership well, and two (Siegel and Whiteley) had had little previous experience with it (for more details, see the chapters below).

4. "Develop a description of the study of institutional change and a procedure for selecting the institutions and the authors of the study." After consultation with numbers of individuals within and outside the Partnership, it was decided to begin the process by asking the directors of all programs to contribute observations on their own institutions and the way in which these institutions became associated with the Partnereship. Plans were put in place for interviews with all directors and for the selection of institutions on the basis of their responses. The selection would depend on several features: depth and duration of the association with the Partnership, variations among institutions (size, location, configuration of programs), and the likelihood that short visits would yield rich results (high turnover of personnel, for example, would constitute an obstacle). Budgetary considerations and availability of researchers were also matters of concern (see chapter 11).

5. "Develop a description of the study of impact on agencies and a procedure for selecting the agencies and the authors of the study." A description was drawn up and reviewed with numbers of

individuals, one of whom, the Partnership director at the University of Glasgow, Dr. Susan Deeley, seemed particularly qualified to carry out the study. Plans were made for her to conduct a series of interviews in Glasgow and to work with other researchers at the University of Technology Jamaica.

6. "Develop a specific plan of action with precise timelines and budget for each research activity." These plans were duly prepared.

7. "Issue the program evaluation criteria and identify 2–3 programs willing to conduct a self-assessment based on these criteria." The criteria were duly completed, and three programs were identified to conduct a dry run of the criteria: Montpellier (France), Guadalajara (Mexico), and Guayaquil (Ecuador).

### Phase Four: Initial Implementation

Seven steps were identified for this phase, running from the end of the year 2002 to April 2003.

1. "Select the institutions to be covered in the study of institutional change and identify the authors of the study." After reviewing the budget and the availability of researchers, it was decided to have the project director, Humphrey Tonkin, carry out the visits personally, relying on support from the program directors at each site. The three sites selected for visits were Trinity College of the Philippines, University of Technology Jamaica, and University of Surrey Roehampton (now Roehampton University, London). As we explain below, they were selected in part because of their extreme differences: Trinity, a small, suburban American-type religious-affiliated college that has become a city institution in a difficult urban environment; UTech Jamaica, a technical institution in the capital city that has now become a university; Roehampton, a new well-funded secular university in an affluent suburban setting that has grown out of the merger of three sectarian teacher colleges. Visits took place to Trinity in August 2003 and to Roehampton in February 2004. In the event, Tonkin was prevented from visiting Jamaica and interviews were conducted there in September 2003 by Brad Blitz of Roehampton and Nevin Brown of the Partnership staff.

2. "Select the agencies to be covered in the agency study and identify the authors of the study." Dr. Susan Deeley (see p. 37) arranged to carry out interviews and conduct focus groups in her home city of Glasgow, thereby developing a research model that she could then apply in Kingston, Jamaica.

3. "Continue the process of data-gathering for the study of student goals and attitudes." The four researchers chosen to conduct the study began correspondence and telephone communication, drafting protocols for the content and conduct of interviews and focus groups. A date in April was identified for the exercise, corresponding with a period when both the Partnership board and the program directors would be meeting in New York. Members of the office staff who worked with alumni were asked to identify likely participants for the focus groups, and invitations were issued to them.

4. "Work with the institutions selected for the institutional study on data-gathering and preparations for the site visit." The meeting of the program directors in New York in April provided a good opportunity for preliminary discussions.

5. "Work with the agencies selected for the agency study and the program directors in the countries in question on preparations for the site visit." Susan Deeley began her agency interviews in Glasgow early in the year and, after preparing a preliminary report on the Glasgow visits and gathering feedback, visited Jamaica in April.

6. "Conduct 2–3 program self-assessments using the program evaluation criteria." Despite the offer of money to cover the costs of a thorough self-assessment, the three sites all chose essentially to conduct a review of the criteria themselves through focus groups, using on-site students and faculty members. This process yielded useful results but lacked the thoroughness originally sought.

7. "Select a program or programs for an initial experimental program evaluation and prepare them [the programs] for the visit." Lack of resources for the visits led to delay in carrying out the selection until July 2004, when Guadalajara, Mexico, and Guayaquil, Ecuador, were selected for visits in October and November 2004.

## *Phase Five: Site-Visit Implementation*

This phase, set for April to August 2003, was a time of extreme activity. The following steps were anticipated:

1. "Complete study of student goals and attitudes and present main findings."
2. "Carry out the site visits for the institutional study."
3. "Carry out the site visits for the agency study."
4. "Carry out the initial experimental program evaluation."

The interviews and focus groups associated with the student study were carried out by the four researchers in April, and in that same month Susan Deeley conducted her on-site interviews for the agency study in Jamaica. The first of Tonkin's institutional site visits took place in the Philippines in August.

Preliminary findings of the student study were presented at the NAFSA conference in May by Siegel and Pusch. For reasons explained above, the initial experimental program evaluation was delayed until the following year.

## *Phase Six: Reporting*

This phase, anticipated for August 2003 to January 2004, had to be extended to April 2004 primarily because of growing pressure on Tonkin's time from forces having little to do with his work for the Partnership. The phase involved four steps, the first of which ("Assess results of the initial experimental program evaluation, make changes in the criteria, institutionalize the procedure, and determine a schedule for evaluation") was still delayed. The other three steps were as follows.

2. "Complete the final report on student goals and attitudes and plan its dissemination." Each of the four researchers wrote his/her own report on the interviews and groups he/she was involved in, and the reports were shared among the group and with Tonkin in his role as project director. The reports were discussed and reviewed in various ways among the five. The results are presented in the present report.

3. "Complete the institutional study and plan its dissemination."
The Partnership conference in Thailand in January 2004 provided
opportunities for further follow-up conversations with representatives of Trinity College (Philippines) and University of
Technology Jamaica. Data-gathering for the study was completed
in February 2004 with Tonkin's visit to Roehampton, and the
preparation of the final report, contained in the present document,
began.

4. "Complete the agency study and plan its dissemination." The
agency study was completed and submitted to Tonkin in July 2003.
An article on the subject is now under review.

### Phase Seven: Institutionalization

The seventh phase, originally planned for February–July 2004 and
now extended to November 2004, calls for the following steps and is still
in progress at the time of writing.

1. "Begin implementation of the evaluation procedure."
2. "Publish and disseminate the final report on student goals and
attitudes."
3. "Publish and disseminate the institutional study."
4. "Publish and disseminate the agency study."

A note in the Research Plan states that "The nature of publication in
each case will be determined by the quality and interest of the results." It
was decided to prepare a comprehensive report on the entire project in
book form. The present volume is the result. A panel at the October 2004
International Conference on Service-Learning Research, in Greenville, South
Carolina, will address the question of a research agenda for international
service-learning, modeled on the contribution of Bringle and Tonkin to
the present volume. Discussion and planning on this topic commenced in
the final months of 2003, when Bringle and Tonkin began preparations for
a workshop on service-learning research that they conducted in Chiang
Mai, Thailand, in January 2004 at the Partnership's biennial conference.

## Next Steps

The purpose of the Chiang Mai workshop was to introduce participants to research on service-learning and to provide guidance for those engaged in work in the field—with the ultimate goal of broadening and deepening the work carried out through the Ford Foundation grant to the Partnership. The research agenda outlined in chapter 15 of the present volume is a first step in that direction. It includes also questions that have arisen in the course of the present study.

No research plan is likely to remain unchanged over a three-year period. Conditions change, opportunities look more promising or less so over time, and professional expertise is not always available on schedule. In the present instance, it proved possible to keep fairly closely to schedule and even to expectations (and in some cases to exceed them), though the initial plan for the student study proved over-ambitious and had to be somewhat reduced. However, in the course of the three-year period several new questions began to emerge, most of which we outline in chapter 15 and which form the beginning for a future research agenda.

But let us mention a couple of issues here, because they will color our discussion in later chapters. First, the question of the ethics of service-learning. After many years of relative complacency on such matters, the service-learning community is becoming increasingly concerned about the ethical dimensions of the service connected to service-learning (Langseth 2000, Aquino 2001, Rich 2002, Schaffer, Paris & Williams 2003), and, indeed, the effects of service-learning on agencies in general are gaining greater attention from those who make policy in higher education and the researchers who work with them (Sigmon 1998, Cruz & Giles 2000, Clarke 2003).

All too often, service-learning is conceived as something designed to benefit students rather than agencies, as though the service itself has become commodified and is merely an ingredient in the economy of learning. But, while the relationship between institutions and agencies is largely mediated by students and their professors, at the end of the continuum are clients of the service agencies and real-life problems and policies. If service-learning is intended to inculcate in the student a certain kind of altruism and devotion to the community, it is surely incumbent upon the institutional actors who initiate the process to show a similar sense of altruism and community devotion regarding the recipients of the largesse supposedly provided by the students. What of the orphaned child whose life is brightened by the continued ministrations of a student over a twelve-week period only to have that student suddenly disappear back to his or her home country? What of the elderly man or woman who finds a companion in a young visitor from far away when that visitor returns home? The Partnership stresses the importance of human communication in the service practiced by its students: hence it is less interested in what might be called technical development projects (digging wells, building schools) and more involved in the human dimension (public health projects, teaching and caring for the destitute). But that makes such ethical questions all the more urgent and important.

One of the discoveries that came from our student study was that many Partnership alumni maintain contact with their agencies after their return—but this is hardly the pattern, it would seem, for service-learning programs in general, either in the United States or abroad. And the forging of bonds only to have them broken may be no more than a reinforcement of the sense of isolation that many of those touched by such service have experienced so many times before.

Furthermore, these ethical questions intersect with two other concerns raised in this report: the fact that the Partnership pedagogy stresses the asking of questions rather than the discovery of easy answers (a service assignment from which all the ambiguities have been somehow extracted is less educationally compelling than one where the student must confront such ambiguities) but the apparently contradictory fact that, if the Partnership is serious about the service portion of its work, it ought to be interested in practical outcomes—about doing something useful for the people among whom the service is conducted.

Secondly, we should also say a word about academic achievement. While it is quite understandable that a project investigating service-learning should choose to examine those characteristics of the pedagogy that are unique, there is an increasingly urgent need for assessment of the entirely conventional aspects of student learning in international service-learning. To what extent do students acquire academic knowledge (however that is defined) in service-learning situations? Do they do so at a speed or with a thoroughness comparable to the speed and thoroughness of conventional study abroad (again, however that is defined) and comparable to the process of knowledge acquisition if they were to remain on their home campuses engaged in conventional study? The present study gives limited consideration to academic aspects of the international service-learning experience and clearly more is needed.

Finally, our present findings would benefit from being passed through the filter of parent perceptions and the perceptions of the students' advisors and professors. As the reader will discover from our concluding chapters, we remain mindful of this need and hope to pursue it further. Indeed, it is important that the present volume be seen not as the culmination of a research project but as the beginning of what will become an ongoing effort and a permanent feature of the work of the Partnership. We are pleased with our progress, but there is more to be done.

Let us turn now to the substance of our study.

# 3 The Partnership Participants: A Portrait of the Undergraduate Programs

## Humphrey Tonkin

## Introduction

When the research project on the undergraduate programs of the International Partnership for Service-Learning was launched in the fall of 2001, the first step undertaken was a review of the existing data on Partnership participation and demographics. This initial stage required a certain amount of data entry and the manipulation of existing data, but for the most part it was based on readily accessible, already existing information. This part of the project was begun in September 2001 and published in its present form as a Partnership report in April 2002.[1]

Because the Partnership came into being over a number of years, initially under the auspices of Rockland Community College and only later as a fully independent organization, as our earlier chapter has explained, student records for the initial years are often incomplete. While it is possible to give reasonably accurate aggregate numbers for the Partnership's programs as of the move to New York City in 1986, the present survey is largely limited to the period after 1990, when the records are more complete and are, for the most part, available in electronic form. Readers will note some discrepancies in numbers. These are due to missing information in some cases, and to differences between published figures, which were gathered from old reports, and actual student records in the data base.

---

[1] Humphrey Tonkin, *The International Partnership for Service-Learning: A Review of the Demographics of the Undergraduate Programs* (New York: International Partnership for Service-Learning, 2002).

When they apply for admission to the program, students fill out an application form, some of whose information is routinely computerized, though some is not. To carry out the present survey, some data had to be newly entered (these new data categories will be maintained into the future). For the purposes of longitudinal comparison, we decided to focus on two years early in the decade—1991 and 1992—and two more recent years—1999 and 2000—and data were entered accordingly. (We chose two-year blocks to make the numbers statistically significant and to compensate for annual fluctuations.) We did not try to gather entirely new data, and so our results are limited by the information that was available to us, and by the degree of completeness of application forms and the data base. We did, however, check data for 1991+92 and 1999+2000 particularly carefully; for other years there could be inaccuracies or missing data.

Even with these caveats, the survey does provide an interesting and suggestive profile of the Partnership and its students over an extended period.

The Partnership has been sending students abroad for semester-long and summer programs that combine formal college instruction with community service for the past twenty years. This study looks at who goes on such programs, where they come from, and when and where they go. The Partnership, as we have already noted, operates, or has operated, undergraduate programs at seventeen locations in Africa, Asia, the Caribbean, Latin America, and Europe, and at two locations in the United States.[2] Over the fifteen-year period from 1985 to 2000, some 2,000 students have participated in these programs, with the largest numbers going to Ecuador, England, France, Jamaica, and Mexico. About half of these students are in their third year of college. They come from all parts of the United States and several foreign countries.

Female students account for 80.08% of the total—a higher proportion than in study-abroad programs generally and a particularly high proportion for destinations outside Europe. Their racial profile appears to match that of study-abroad students in general, and they come from a wide range of religious backgrounds. They are getting younger: the average age of undergraduates participating in Partnership programs has fallen from 21.83 in the early 1990s to 20.69 today. Language, area, and cultural studies

---

[2] Liberia has been discontinued, as was an incipient program in the Appalachian Mountains (launched in 1993 and judged too far out of the focus of the Partnership). New programs, too late for consideration here, have been launched in Thailand and the Galápagos.

constitutes the most popular group of majors, but significant numbers of majors in psychology and the cognitive sciences, and in biology and life sciences, also participate.

Most Partnership students come from small institutions. Although research universities account for 54.8% of undergraduates from the United States studying abroad, only 35.63% of Partnership students come from such institutions. Most (61.69%) Partnership students come from small colleges and other largely undergraduate institutions (nationally, these account for only 40.8% of undergraduates studying abroad).

The average Partnership student is female, approaching her twenty-first birthday, and perhaps studying in Latin America. She probably comes from a liberal-arts college and is in her third year of study.

### Students by Academic Year

Almost 2000 students have passed through the International Partnership's regular undergraduate programs between 1986 and 2001. They have been distributed over a total of fifteen programs. Some of these programs, such as those in Ecuador (Guayaquil and Quito), England, France, India, Jamaica, and Mexico, draw substantial numbers of students. Others (the Czech Republic, Israel, the Philippines, Scotland) have always catered to small numbers. Some have experienced ups and downs for political reasons (Israel, Liberia) or because of natural disasters (Quito).

One of the International Partnership's programs is in the United States, at South Dakota State University, where students work among the Sioux Nation. This program, founded in 1990, has attracted a steady stream of students each year. In 1993, the International Partnership launched, experimentally, a domestic service-learning program in Appalachia, which was not successful. The program was discontinued after one year, and the International Partnership returned to its concentration on cross-cultural experiences.

As for total enrollment, after steady growth in the early years the year 1992–93 brought a sudden increase to 184 enrollees, primarily because of a sharp rise in the numbers going to Jamaica in the fall of 1992. Enrollment peaked in 1996–97. Subsequent years have shown declines in enrollment as the International Partnership's attention and resources have shifted somewhat to its special programs and to the master's program (see chapter 1), though the years 2003 and 2004 have shown significant increases again.

These numbers are based on the published enrollment figures, prepared each year for reporting purposes and contained in the International Partnership's reports. Table 1 shows the total number of students participating in the program from 1986 to the present, by academic year, showing programs in operation. Figure 1 gives this same information in graph form. Table 2 shows the academic years of operation of the International Partnership's various programs.

## Table 1. Students by Academic Year

| Year | Locations | Total Students |
|------|-----------|----------------|
| 1986-1987 | Ecuador (Guayaquil), England, Jamaica | 29 |
| 1987-1988 | As above | 58 |
| 1988-1989 | As above, plus France, Liberia, Philippines | 63 |
| 1989-1990 | As above | 93 |
| 1990-1991 | As above, plus India, Mexico, S. Dakota, minus Liberia | 149 |
| 1991-1992 | As above | 131 |
| 1992-1993 | As above, plus Scotland | 184 |
| 1993-1994 | As above, plus Appalachia | 153 |
| 1994-1995 | As above, plus Ecuador (Quito), Israel, minus Appalachia | 158 |
| 1995-1996 | As above, plus Czech Republic | 161 |
| 1996-1997 | As above | 185 |
| 1997-1998 | As above | 175 |
| 1998-1999 | As above, minus Czech Republic, Ecuador (Quito), Israel | 184 |
| 1999-2000 | As above, plus Czech Republic, Ecuador (Quito), Israel | 135 |
| 2000-2001 | As above | 106 |
| **Total Regular Undergraduate Programs 1986 –2001** | | **1964** |

## Figure 1. Number of Students by Academic Year

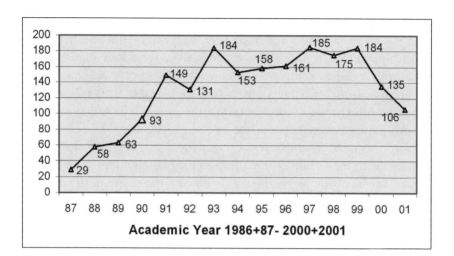

**Academic Year 1986+87- 2000+2001**

## Table 2. Students by Program by Academic Year

| | 86-87 | 87-88 | 88-89 | 89-90* | 90-91 | 91-92 | 92-93 | 93-94 | 94-95 | 95-96 | 96-97 | 97-98 | 98-99 | 99-00 | 00-01 |
|---|---|---|---|---|---|---|---|---|---|---|---|---|---|---|---|
| Appalachia | | | | | | | | 1 | | | | | | | |
| Czech Republic | | | | | | | | | | 1 | 10 | 7 | | 4 | 0 |
| Ecuador - Guayaquil | 1 | 6 | 11 | ? | 27 | 31 | 38 | 41 | 38 | 28 | 19 | 22 | 38 | 10 | 18 |
| Ecuador - Quito | | | | | | | | | 11 | 15 | 25 | 28 | | 16 | 17 |
| England | 20 | 39 | 21 | ? | 28 | 23 | 32 | 16 | 11 | 10 | 15 | 20 | 32 | 9 | 8 |
| France | | | 3 | ? | 29 | 18 | 19 | 17 | 16 | 19 | 17 | 15 | 19 | 15 | 11 |
| India | | | | | 7 | 7 | 7 | 14 | 11 | 12 | 21 | 28 | 7 | 15 | 16 |
| Israel | | | | | | | | | 2 | 3 | 4 | 1 | | 7 | 2 |
| Jamaica | 8 | 13 | 20 | ? | 27 | 12 | 38 | 31 | 23 | 21 | 19 | 17 | 38 | 17 | 11 |
| Liberia | | | 7 | ? | | | | | | | | | | | |
| Mexico | | | | | 18 | 23 | 26 | 16 | 26 | 27 | 27 | 18 | 26 | 28 | 11 |
| Philippines | | | 1 | ? | 2 | 3 | 1 | 1 | 4 | 6 | 5 | 3 | 1 | 1 | 3 |
| Russia | | | | | | | | | | | | | | | |
| Scotland | | | | | | | 3 | 0 | 2 | 6 | 4 | 5 | 3 | 4 | 2 |
| S. Dakota | | | | | 11 | 14 | 20 | 16 | 14 | 13 | 19 | 11 | 20 | 9 | 7 |
| **Total** | 29 | 58 | 63 | 93 | 149 | 131 | 184 | 153 | 158 | 161 | 185 | 175 | 184 | 135 | 106 |

* Program totals unavailable for this year.

## Students by Calendar Year

These numbers are based on actual student records. They are somewhat lower than the numbers reported year by year in the International Partnership's annual reports and elsewhere, since they omit students who withdrew or failed to complete programs, for whatever reason, and since they are based on verifiable student records available in the New York office. Accordingly, they probably err on the minus side: actual numbers may well be somewhere between the two sets of figures.

Table 3 shows the totals year by year (note that they will not match the numbers in the section on the previous page because they are based on *calendar* not *academic* years). Figure 2 presents the same information in graph form.

**Table 3. Students by Calendar Year**

| Calendar Year | Total Students |
|:---:|:---:|
| 1986 | 8 |
| 1987 | 22 |
| 1988 | 51 |
| 1989 | 56 |
| 1990 | 136 |
| 1991 | 129 |
| 1992 | 164 |
| 1993 | 121 |
| 1994 | 157 |
| 1995 | 146 |
| 1996 | 179 |
| 1997 | 159 |
| 1998 | 154 |
| 1999 | 143 |
| 2000 | 125 |

**Figure 2. Students by Calendar Year**

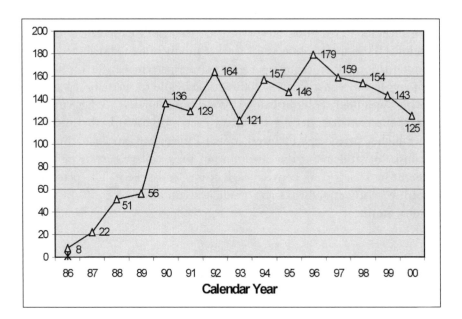

## Students by Year in College

A comparison of the totals for calendar years 1991 and 1992 with those for 1999 and 2000 (Table 4 and Figure 3) shows no significant change in the number of students by year in college. The totals for 1991 and 1992 show a large number of students in the "Other" category, some of whom are probably college graduates or fifth-year students. Indeed, a rather larger number of students beyond the undergraduate years participated in 1991 and 1992 than in 1999 and 2000, including two college faculty members and two students who had completed a graduate degree. Perhaps the higher numbers in the earlier years reflect the condition of the economy during that period, when jobs were scarce and college graduates were looking for alternatives.

The later years show a shift towards the conventional: a higher percentage of students, in fact almost fifty percent, were regular third-year college students, most of them no doubt coming to the International Partnership through the conventional channels of study-abroad offices in the various sending institutions and, increasingly, through the Web.

We have added recent percentages for the four college years from *Open Doors*, the annual survey of international educational exchange prepared by the Institute of International Education (IIE). Note, however, that *Open Doors* includes 15.6% in a category called "Bachelor's Unspecified" and an additional 0.9% under "Associate." If these numbers are redistributed across the International Partnership's percentages, the percentages for the second, third and fourth years in 1999+2000 are very close to the national average (see the "weighted" column below). We should, however, take particular note of the fact that, despite the trend over time towards the middle, a rather higher percentage of International Partnership enrollees continues to consist of students at the beginning of their college careers or taking time out in a "gap year" between high school and college. The percentage of fifth-year undergraduates and graduates continues to conform to the national norm.

**Table 4. Students by Year in College During Program**
[*Open Doors* norm 1999/2000 in brackets]

| | 1991 + 1992 | | *Open Doors* 1999/2000 | | 1999 + 2000 | |
|---|---|---|---|---|---|---|
| | No. | % | Actual | Weighted | No. | % |
| 1st year and high-school graduate | 15 | 5.12 | [3.2%] | [3.9%] | 15 | 5.60 |
| 2nd year | 58 | 19.80 | [13.6%] | [16.6%] | 44 | 16.42 |
| 3rd year | 121 | 41.30 | [39.8%] | [48.6%] | 129 | 48.13 |
| 4th year | 49 | 16.72 | [17.7%] | [21.6%] | 53 | 19.78 |
| 5th year or college graduate | 26 | 8.88 | [7.7%] | [8.9%] | 21 | 7.84 |
| Other | 24 | 8.20 | | | 6 | 2.24 |
| Total | 293 | | | | 268 | |

**Figure 3. Students by Year in College During Program**

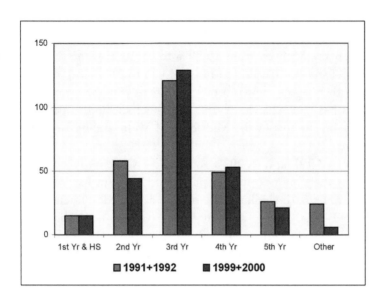

## Number of Students by Home Country and State

Every state in the Union and many foreign countries have contributed students to the Partnership's programs over the years. Table 5 lists the states represented in Partnership programs from 1991 to 2000, arranged alphabetically, along with breakdowns for 1991+1992 and 1999+2000.

Table 6 offers a list of the ten leading states in 1991+1992 and 1999+2000. It is striking that in 1991+1992 a large percentage of students came from the East and West Coasts, particularly the East. By 1999+2000, the numbers have shifted: there are more students from the Midwest (Ohio, Colorado and Minnesota account for one quarter of the students from the top ten states), more from the West (a total of 51 from Washington and California, compared to 36 in 1991+1992), and relatively fewer from the East and South (70, from an assortment of states, compared to 115 in 1991+1992). Connecticut and Florida drop out of the top ten between the early 1990s and the end of the decade, and Colorado and Minnesota come in (Ohio replaces Illinois).

Table 7 provides more precise figures on numbers of students per region. We have divided the United States into four regions: East, Midwest, West (incl. Alaska and Hawaii), and South. The resulting numbers confirm the above observations: the West has seen an increase from 22.05% to 29.84% and the Midwest from 15.59% to 25.58%, while the percentage of East Coast students has dropped from 43.35 to 31.78 and the percentage for the South has gone down from 19.01 to 12.79. The primary factor in these shifts has been changes in the pattern of sending institutions, with certain key institutions in the Midwest and West sending larger numbers than before.

Between 1991 and 2000, a total of 34 students listed 17 foreign countries as their home countries, including 11 from Canada. In 1991+ 1992, 10 students (including 2 from Canada) listed 7 foreign countries, but in 1999+2000 only 4 students were so listed (including one from Canada). Clearly the International Partnership programs are less appealing to students living in, or from, other countries than they were in the early 1990s.

When asked their nationalities, 16 students in 1991+1992 indicated that they were citizens of other countries than the US (Canada, 4; Australia, Israel, Jamaica and Spain, 2; Cyprus, Guatemala, Japan, and the UK, 1), but in 1999+2000, there were only 8 (2 from Japan, and 1 each from France, India, Iran, Israel, Jamaica, and Mexico).

Table 8 lists students by nationality, between 1991 and 2000; 21 nationalities are listed, none of them providing a significant number, except perhaps Canada (with 12 students). Note that a very large number of students did not specify their nationality: the question is asked primarily in connection with immigration regulation. We can probably assume that they were US citizens or dual nationals with US citizenship.

## Table 5. Students by Home State 1991–2000 and Representative Years

| State | 1991+ 1992 | 1999+ 2000 | 1991- 2000 | State | 1991+ 1992 | 1999+ 2000 | 1991- 2000 |
|-------|-----------|-----------|-----------|-------|-----------|-----------|-----------|
| AK | 1 | 2 | 6 | NC | 8 | 2 | 42 |
| AL | 1 | 2 | 5 | ND | 0 | 0 | 1 |
| AR | 2 | 0 | 2 | NE | 3 | 1 | 13 |
| AZ | 4 | 1 | 13 | NH | 4 | 3 | 16 |
| CA | 25 | 19 | 120 | NJ | 12 | 10 | 57 |
| CO | 3 | 11 | 28 | NM | 1 | 1 | 4 |
| CT | 11 | 6 | 33 | NV | 1 | 0 | 6 |
| DC | 3 | 1 | 15 | NY | 36 | 22 | 137 |
| DE | 0 | 0 | 1 | OH | 7 | 20 | 64 |
| FL | 10 | 2 | 29 | OK | 2 | 2 | 5 |
| GA | 3 | 3 | 13 | OR | 7 | 8 | 53 |
| HI | 0 | 0 | 2 | PA | 9 | 15 | 70 |
| IA | 2 | 3 | 12 | RI | 1 | 1 | 9 |
| ID | 2 | 0 | 8 | SC | 1 | 5 | 12 |
| IL | 9 | 8 | 48 | SD | 0 | 1 | 5 |
| IN | 2 | 3 | 17 | TN | 1 | 5 | 17 |
| KS | 0 | 0 | 4 | TX | 6 | 4 | 24 |
| KY | 1 | 0 | 8 | UT | 0 | 0 | 3 |
| LA | 2 | 0 | 6 | VA | 10 | 8 | 60 |
| MA | 27 | 15 | 103 | VT | 1 | 2 | 15 |
| MD | 8 | 6 | 32 | WA | 11 | 32 | 127 |
| ME | 2 | 1 | 16 | WI | 2 | 6 | 26 |
| MI | 6 | 8 | 32 | WV | 2 | 0 | 6 |
| MN | 3 | 9 | 26 | WY | 0 | 0 | 2 |
| MO | 7 | 7 | 28 | Unspecified | 20 | 6 | 47 |
| MS | 1 | 0 | 2 | Other Countries | 10 | 4 | 34 |
| MT | 3 | 3 | 12 | | | | |

| Totals | | |
|--------|--------|--------|
| 1991+1992 | 1999+2000 | 1991-2000 |
| 293 | 268 | 1477 |
| *44 states** | *38 states** | *51 states** |

*incl. District of Columbia*

## Table 6. States with the Largest Numbers of Participants 1991+1992 and 1999+2000

| 1991+1992 | | 1999+2000 | |
| --- | --- | --- | --- |
| State | Participants | State | Participants |
| 1. New York | 36 | 1. Washington | 32 |
| 2. Massachusetts | 27 | 2. New York | 22 |
| 3. California | 25 | 3. Ohio | 20 |
| 4. New Jersey | 12 | 4. California | 19 |
| 5. Washington | 11 | 5. Pennsylvania | 15 |
| 6. Connecticut | 11 | 6. Massachusetts | 15 |
| 7. Virginia | 10 | 7. Colorado | 11 |
| 8. Florida | 10 | 8. New Jersey | 10 |
| 9. Pennsylvania | 9 | 9. Minnesota | 9 |
| 10. Illinois | 9 | 10. Virginia | 8 |
| Totals from ten leading States | 160 | | 161 |
| % of total students | 56.5 | | 60.99 |
| Total students | 283 | | 264 |

## Table 7. Students by Region* (All states and D.C.) 1991–2000 Representative Years

| | 1991+ 1992 | % | 1999+ 2000 | % | 1991- 2000 | % |
| --- | --- | --- | --- | --- | --- | --- |
| East | 114 | 43.35 | 82 | 31.78 | 505 | 36.17 |
| Midwest | 41 | 15.59 | 66 | 25.58 | 276 | 19.77 |
| West | 58 | 22.05 | 77 | 29.84 | 384 | 27.51 |
| South | 50 | 19.01 | 33 | 12.79 | 231 | 16.55 |
| All | 263 | | 258 | | 1396 | |

*Regions:

| | |
| --- | --- |
| East | CT, DC, DE, MA, MD, ME, NH, NJ, NY, PA, RI, VT |
| Midwest | IA, IL, IN, KS, MI, MN, MO, ND, NE, OH, SD, WI |
| West | AK, AR, AZ, CA, CO, HI, ID, MT, NM, NV, OR, UT, WA, WY |
| South | AL, AR, FL, GA, KY, LA, MS, NC, OK, SC, TN, TX, VA, WV |

## Table 8. Students Specifying Nationality 1991–2000

| | |
|---|---|
| Afghanistan | 1 |
| Australia | 2 |
| Bahamas | 1 |
| Canada | 12 |
| Cyprus | 1 |
| Ecuador | 1 |
| France | 1 |
| Germany | 1 |
| Guatemala | 1 |
| Hungary | 1 |
| India | 1 |
| Indonesia | 1 |
| Iran | 1 |
| Israel | 3 |
| Jamaica | 3 |
| Japan | 5 |
| Mexico | 2 |
| Philippines | 1 |
| Spain | 2 |
| Sweden | 1 |
| United Kingdom | 1 |
| USA | 534 |
| (Unspecified | 900) |

## Students by Gender

From 1986 to the present, of 1,894 participating students, 1,516 (80.1%) were female and 377 (19.9%) were male. This strong female emphasis remains more or less constant from year to year, with a female/male ratio of about 4:1. Table 9 gives totals and percentages for the entire period and for 1991+1992 and 1999+2000. The comparative data indicate a slight shift in the direction of still greater female participation and a corresponding drop in the percentage of males. Figure 4 provides totals and percentages.

Program-by-program, a comparison of 1991+1992 and 1999+2000, shows little change, though it does indicate that some programs attract more males than others (we should note that the totals are extremely small, and hence ratios can vary considerably from year to year). In no program, however, do males exceed females in absolute numbers. Table 10 compares the approximate male/female ratio in 1991+1992 and 1999+2000 for the larger programs. Only South Dakota and Jamaica stand out as marginally more attractive to males than other programs; Guayaquil is heavily female; India is now attracting more male students than when it first started.

Even in comparison with national figures for study abroad, these numbers are unusual. According to IIE's annual survey *Open Doors,* more females than males choose to study abroad: in 1999–2000, a total of 92,725 females and 50,865 males engaged in foreign study—a ratio of almost two to one. But the International Partnership's female/male ratio is over twice as high. What makes these numbers still more extraordinary is that, in general, the female/male ratio for Americans studying abroad tends to be somewhat higher for students studying in Europe than for those studying in other parts of the world, where male percentages are closer to female ones. But a large percentage of International Partnership students study outside Europe (189 in 1999+2000, compared with 67 in Europe and 12 in the US), and even in these countries International Partnership females outnumber International Partnership males. And European International Partnership programs are attracting fewer and fewer males. Table 11 gives comparative data for 1991+1992 and 1999+2000.

In short, international service-learning, at least as practiced by the International Partnership, is overwhelmingly more attractive to female students than to males, and this trend seems to be intensifying.

## Table 9. Gender 1986–2000, and Representative Years

|  | Female | | Male | |
|---|---|---|---|---|
|  | No. | % | No. | % |
| 1986-2000 | 1516 | 80.08 | 377 | 19.92 |
| 1991+1992 | 228 | 77.82 | 65 | 22.18 |
| 1999+2000 | 215 | 80.22 | 53 | 19.78 |

## Figure 4. Gender 1986–2000, and Representative Years

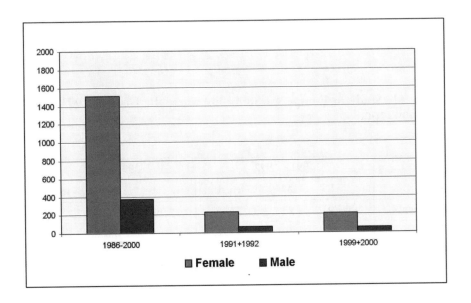

Table 10. Approximate Gender Ratios, Selected Programs 1991+1992 and 1999+2000

|  | 1991 + 1992 | | | 1999 + 2000 | | |
|---|---|---|---|---|---|---|
|  | F | M | Ratio | F | M | Ratio |
| Ecuador (Guayaquil) | 49 | 11 | 4 ½ : 1 | 22 | 4 | 5 ½ : 1 |
| England | 44 | 13 | 3 ½ : 1 | 15 | 3 | 5 : 1 |
| France | 33 | 9 | 4 : 1 | 27 | 2 | 13 : 1 |
| India | 14 | 0 |  | 30 | 10 | 3 : 1 |
| Jamaica | 23 | 8 | 3 : 1 | 24 | 12 | 2 : 1 |
| Mexico | 36 | 10 | 3 ½ : 1 | 29 | 8 | 3 ½ : 1 |
| South Dakota | 23 | 10 | 2 ½ : 1 | 9 | 3 | 3 : 1 |
| Totals, all programs | 222 | 61 | 4 : 1 | 156 | 42 | 4 : 1 |

Table 11. Study in Europe vs. Study Elsewhere, by Gender, 1991+1992 & 1999+2000

|  | 1991 + 1992 | | | 1999 + 2000 | | |
|---|---|---|---|---|---|---|
|  | F | M | % female | F | M | % female |
| Europe | 79 | 23 | 77.45 | 60 | 7 | 89.55 |
| US | 23 | 10 | 69.70 | 9 | 3 | 75.00 |
| Elsewhere | 126 | 32 | 79.75 | 146 | 43 | 77.25 |

## Students by Race

At the time of their enrollment, students are asked to specify their race on the personal data form, though they of course have the option of not doing so. Many exercise this option. The fact that the categories on the application form have for the most part not been changed over a ten-year period would suggest that the numbers might be roughly comparable year by year, but unfortunately data collection by race has also been hampered by a system of classification that is both outdated and confusing—sufficiently confusing to make even year-by-year comparisons questionable.

Nine categories are listed in the personal data form, as follows: Asian-American, Black, Mexican-American, Multi-ethnic, Native American, Non-US citizen, Spanish surname, White, and Not listed. "Asian-American" can of course be construed as covering South Asians as well as East Asians. The category "Spanish surname" is obviously unsatisfactory, as is the category "multi-ethnic" (race and ethnicity are, after all, different things, though American definitions of such categories are, at the best of times, muddled). It is also of course quite unclear as to why students might choose the "not listed" category.

Some twenty percent of students choose not to complete this item. For this reason, and given the idiosyncratic classification system, the data reveal relatively little about the racial composition of International Partnership students.

Table 12 gives the aggregate data for the period 1991–2000, taken directly from the personal data form.

In Table 13 we present the minimum picture, counting only those students who have clearly identified themselves as members of minority groups. To do so, we have eliminated from our totals all students who did not answer this question at all, plus all who listed themselves as "non-US citizen," "multi-ethnic" or "not listed." We have added "Mexican-American" and "Spanish surname" together to create a (probably underestimated) Latino category.

For purposes of comparison, we also show the 1999/2000 percentages for all American students studying abroad, as published in the IIE publication *Open Doors*, and for the sake of clarity we use the same racial descriptors as IIE uses. While IIE's numbers seem much cleaner and clearer than ours, they are dependent on data-gathering at the program level that may not be much superior to that of the International Partnership. This may be an area in which we know less than we think we know.

In Table 14 we take the same data and add the "not listed" and "multi-ethnic" figures to our totals, assuming that students are likely to use "not listed" if, for example, they are Hispanic Americans but not of Mexican ancestry (e.g. from Puerto Rico or Cuba), and that they are likely to use the "multi-ethnic" category if they regard themselves as multi-racial. If we assume, then, that those identifying themselves with these categories are members of minority groups, the percentages change significantly.

Figures 5 and 6 present the same data as Tables 13 and 14, but in graphic form.

A comparison of Table 13 and Table 14 shows that, according to the narrow classification, International Partnership programs have *lower minority representation* than in study programs abroad in general (12.31% as compared with 15.00%), and according to the broad classification they have *higher minority representation* (17.26% as compared with 15.00%). It would seem reasonable to conclude that International Partnership programs do not in fact depart significantly from the national norms.

Table 15 provides comparative data for 1991+1992 and 1999+2000 omitting the "multi-ethnic" and "not listed" categories. They would seem to suggest that the minority population in International Partnership programs is actually *declining* quite sharply (down from 14.44% to 10.31%). However, Table 16, in which "multi-ethnic" and "not listed" are included, shows exactly the opposite trend, with impressive minority participation in both time periods and with *rising* numbers (19.51% rising to 22.48%, well above the norm of 15%). In short, the results are inconclusive.

An examination of the racial data program by program, using our narrow definition, indicates that certain programs draw particular minority groups better than others: clearly heritage is a factor in the decisions students make. In the period 1991–2000, of 47 self-declared Asian-American students, 11 went to the Philippines, 8 to India, 8 to Ecuador (Guayaquil), and 7 to Mexico, leaving only 13 scattered across the other programs. In this same period, 13 African Americans went to England, 12 to Ecuador (Guayaquil), 10 to Jamaica, and 8 to France, leaving 9 in all of the other programs. Of 35 Hispanic Americans, 13 went to Mexico, 9 went to Ecuador (Guayaquil), and 7 to France, with only 6 going to other destinations. The 4 Native Americans in the International Partnership during this period went to four different locations: Ecuador (Guayaquil), England, India, and Mexico. While the racial concentration in certain programs seems real enough, we should remember that these numbers do not include students in the "multi-ethnic" and "not listed" categories.

**Table 12. Data on Race, as Collected, 1991–2000**

| | |
|---|---|
| Asian American | 47 |
| Black | 52 |
| Mexican American | 1 |
| Multi-ethnic | 19 |
| Native American | 4 |
| Non-US Citizen | 18 |
| Not Listed | 48 |
| Spanish Surname | 34 |
| White | 983 |
| Undeclared | 271 |
| **Total** | **1477** |

Table 13. Race by Category, 1991–2000

| Race | No. | % | Open Doors 1999-2000 % |
|---|---|---|---|
| Asian American | 47 | 4.19 | [4.9] |
| African-American | 52 | 4.64 | [3.5] |
| Hispanic-American | 35 | 3.12 | [5.1] |
| Native American | 4 | 0.36 | [0.5] |
| Total Minority | 138 | 12.31 | [15.0] |
| Caucasian | 983 | 87.69 | [85.1] |
| Total | 1121 | | |
| Unspecified or non-US | 356 | | |
| Total Students 1991–2000 | 1477 | | |

Figure 5. Race by Category (%) 1991–2000

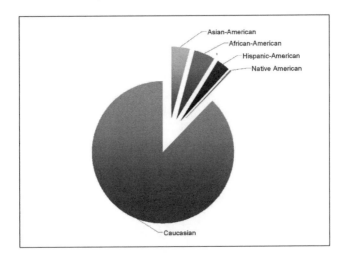

## Table 14. Race, by Broad Category, 1991–2000
("multi-ethnic" and "not listed" included)
[Descriptors as in *Open Doors 2001*]

| Race | No. | % | *Open Doors* 1999-2000 % |
|---|---|---|---|
| Asian American | 47 | 4.19 | [4.9] |
| African-American | 52 | 4.64 | [3.5] |
| Hispanic-American | 35 | 3.12 | [5.1] |
| Native American | 4 | 0.36 | [0.5] |
| *Multi-ethnic* | 19 | | |
| *Not listed* | 48 | | |
| Total Minority | 205 | 17.26 | [15.0] |
| Caucasian | 983 | 82.74 | [85.1] |
| Total | 1188 | | |
| Unspecified or non-US | 289 | | |
| Total Students 1991–2000 | 1477 | | |

Figure 6. Race by Broad Category (%) 1991–2000

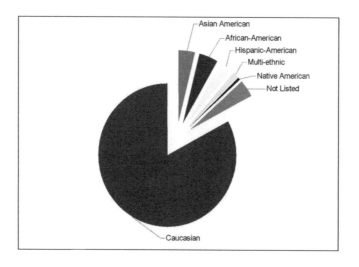

## Table 15. Race by Category, omitting "multi-ethnic" and "not listed"

| Race | Open Doors 1999-2000 % | 1991+1992 | % | 1999+2000 | % |
|---|---|---|---|---|---|
| Asian American | [4.9] | 14 | 5.19 | 8 | 3.59 |
| African-American | [3.5] | 16 | 5.92 | 8 | 3.59 |
| Hispanic-American | [5.1] | 6 | 2.22 | 7 | 3.14 |
| Native American | [0.5] | 3 | 1.11 | 0 | |
| Total Minority | [15.0] | 39 | 14.44 | 23 | 10.31 |
| Caucasian | [85.1] | 231 | 85.56 | 200 | 89.69 |
| Total | | 270 | | 223 | |
| Unspecified or non-US | | 23 | | 45 | |
| Total Students | | 293 | | 268 | |

## Table16. Race by Category, "multi-ethnic" and "not listed" included

| Race | Open Doors 1999-2000 % | 1991+1992 | % | 1999+2000 | % |
|---|---|---|---|---|---|
| Asian American | [4.8] | 14 | 5.19 | 8 | 3.59 |
| African-American | [3.8] | 16 | 5.92 | 8 | 3.59 |
| Hispanic-American | [5.5] | 6 | 2.22 | 7 | 3.14 |
| Native American | [0.6] | 3 | 1.11 | 0 | |
| Multi-ethnic | | 0 | | 13 | |
| Not listed | | 17 | | 22 | |
| Total Minority | [15.0] | 56 | 14.44 | 58 | 22.48 |
| Caucasian | [85.1] | 231 | 80.49 | 200 | 77.52 |
| Total | | 287 | | 258 | |
| Unspecified or non-US | | 6 | | 10 | |
| Total Students | | 293 | | 268 | |

## Students by Religion

Students are asked about their religious affiliation and about their level of religious activity. This information is helpful in placing them in the field. They are free to use whatever designation they wish: there is no predetermined list of categories. As a result, it is hard to compile any very meaningful data. Accordingly, we selected only those denominations with significant numbers, using our judgment in some cases (combining Episcopalian and Anglican, for example, and Methodist and United Methodist). The results are shown in Table 17. About one quarter of the students list no religion (the percentage of the total is slightly up from the beginning of the decade to the end). The number of Episcopalians has dropped quite sharply as the International Partnership has moved out beyond some of its initial sending institutions, where Episcopalian colleges dominated. Roman Catholics remain strong, and the Jewish percentage has increased. Non-Judeo-Christian denominations remain extremely small.

**Table 17. Religion by Major Category, 1991+1992, 1999+2000**

|  | 1991 + 1992 | | 1999 + 2000 | |
|---|---|---|---|---|
|  | No. | % of total | No. | % of total |
| Roman Catholic | 69 | 29% | 52 | 25% |
| Episcopalian | 39 | 16% | 14 | 7% |
| Presbyterian | 22 | 9% | 10 | 5% |
| Jewish | 21 | 9% | 27 | 13% |
| Lutheran | 12 | 5% | 12 | 6% |
| Methodist | 5 | 2% | 16 | 8% |
| None/Not Listed | 72 | 30% | 75 | 36% |
| TOTAL | 240 | | 206 | |

## Students by Age

The following provides information on the ages of students at the time when they began their programs. The years covered are 1991+1992 and 1999+2000. Table 18 gives numbers and percentages. Figure 7 provides the same information in graph form.

Over the decade, there have been significant shifts in the age of participants in the International Partnership's programs. By adding the numbers year by year, we see that, while at the beginning of the decade only 14.32% were 19 or younger, this percentage had grown to 18.65 by the end of the decade. Some 45.04% were aged 20 or younger at the beginning of the decade, but at the end of the decade the percentage had grown to 58.57. The percentage of participants aged 19 was up by 3 points and those aged 22 were down by 5 points—a marked shift in age distribution.

At the other end of the age range, the 12 participants aged 30 and over in 1991+1992 were down to a single participant in this age group in 1999+2000. Those aged 22 and over constituted 28.67% at the beginning of the decade and only 17.92% at the end.

In fact, the average age of participants in 1991+1992 was 21.83, probably significantly above the average for traditional study-abroad students. By 1999+2000 it had dropped to 20.69. Even if we eliminate all participants aged 30 or over, still there is an appreciable drop in age, from 20.83 in 1991+1992 to 20.57 in 1999+2000.

Interestingly, there has been little corresponding shift in the students' year in college (see above), with 41.3% in their third year in 1991+1992 and 48.13% in 1999+2000, and even a slight shift in the direction of the third and fourth years as opposed to the first and second. However, the higher age cohorts have almost entirely disappeared. The shift to third and fourth years is a reflection of the norm for study abroad: International Partnership programs have moved significantly towards that norm.

The loss of older students more than accounts for the decline in total enrollment between the beginning and the end of the decade: students aged 22 and younger totaled 84 in 1991+1992 and 47 in 1999+2000, but the numbers for those 23 and over were 44 at the beginning of the decade and a mere 23 at the end. A partial explanation for this drop-off in older students is the creation of the Master's program.

**Table 18. Students by Age 1991+1992 and 1999+2000**

|  | 1991 + 1992 | | 1999 + 2000 | |
|---|---|---|---|---|
| Age | No. | % | No. | % |
| 17 | 1 | 0.34 | 4 | 1.50 |
| 18 | 11 | 3.75 | 14 | 5.17 |
| 19 | 30 | 10.23 | 36 | 13.29 |
| 20 | 90 | 30.72 | 107 | 39.48 |
| 21 | 74 | 25.26 | 58 | 21.40 |
| 22 | 40 | 13.65 | 24 | 8.86 |
| 23 | 19 | 6.48 | 8 | 2.95 |
| 24 | 6 | 2.05 | 6 | 2.21 |
| 25-29 | 7 | 2.39 | 9 | 3.32 |
| 30 and over | 12 | 4.10 | 1 | 0.37 |
| Unknown | 3 | 1.02 | 4 | 1.50 |
| Total | 293 | | 271 | |

**Figure 7. Students by Age 1991+1992 and 1999+2000**

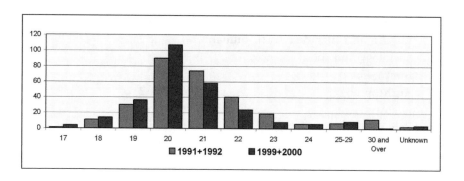

## Student Majors

Students are asked to indicate their majors. Not all of them do so, and many are undecided at the time they embark on an International Partnership program. As a result, our data are not complete. A review of the data base back to 1986 provided us with information on 918 students.

Given the variety of the institutions from which International Partnership students come, and given the increasing tendency of all institutions to come up with new titles and new combinations of fields, student responses are richly various. Furthermore, a response like "History and Government" or "Education/Philosophy" may indicate a single program or a double major.

Accordingly, we have reviewed the entire list in search of concentrations of interest. The following statistics are based on counts of references to a given field or related fields. These counts are inevitably somewhat subjective and inexact. If students have indicated, say, History and French, we have counted them in both areas. These fields are, however, exclusive of one another: we have not counted a given discipline in more than one field. Thus the following statistics tell us approximately how many students over the years, among the 918 on whom we have data, have evinced an academic interest in a given field.

Within these limitations, the data are quite revealing. A dozen areas of interest emerge as major preoccupations of International Partnership students. They are, in descending order of student numbers.

| | |
|---|---|
| Language, area and cultural studies (esp. Spanish and Latin American studies) | 101 |
| Psychology and cognitive sciences | 87 |
| English and literature (incl. humanities) | 82 |
| Sociology and social sciences | 80 |
| International studies | 71 |
| Anthropology | 62 |
| History | 52 |
| Politics and government | 51 |
| Social work and human services | 51 |
| Biology and life sciences | 49 |
| Business and economics | 48 |
| Education | 42 |

The dominance of languages and area studies is understandable, given the presence of several International Partnership programs in non-English-speaking countries (particularly Mexico, Ecuador and France). The International Partnership's programs outside Europe understandably attract large numbers of anthropologists. It is encouraging to see the large concentrations of students in social work and in the biological sciences, the latter often involving tight sequential programs that are not easily adapted to study abroad.

## Students by Type of Sending Institution

The International Partnership's programs are notable for the wide range of institutions from which they attract students. In the period 1991–2000, 1,457 students with institutional affiliations at 423 US and foreign institutions have participated, an average of 0.34 students per institution per year. While there are a few institutions with which the International Partnership has close ties and which are regular suppliers of students in appreciable numbers, numerous students in a given year are the only students to apply from their colleges. In the period 1991+1992, 293 students came from 164 institutions, and in 1999+2000, 268 students came from 145 institutions.

The US institutions represented all categories of American colleges and universities according to the Carnegie Classification of higher education institutions. Recently the Carnegie Classification has undergone some significant changes, so that it is difficult to make good comparisons over time. We created a master list of institutions for the entire ten-year period and classified them according to their current (2002) standing in the Carnegie Classification. Table 19 shows the number of students from each institution type for the period 1991–2000 and for the years 1991+1992 and 1999+2000, with percentages. We also provide comparable data for all US students studying abroad in 1998–99, from *Open Doors*.

Table 19. Enrollment by Institutional Type, 1991–2000 and
Representative Years

|  | 1991-2000 | % | 1991 +1992 | % | 1999 +2000 | % | *Open Doors* % |
|---|---|---|---|---|---|---|---|
| Research I & II | 548 | 37.98 | 115 | 40.21 | 93 | 35.63 | [54.8] |
| Masters I & II | 402 | 27.86 | 69 | 24.13 | 83 | 31.80 | [20.3] |
| Baccalaureate I & II | 458 | 31.74 | 91 | 31.82 | 78 | 29.89 | [20.5] |
| Associate | 29 | 2.01 | 11 | 3.85 | 6 | 2.30 | [2.7] |
| Other | 6 | 0.42 | 0 | 0 | 1 | 0.38 | [1.7] |
| Total students | 1443 |  | 286 |  | 261 |  |  |

The data show that a rather higher percentage of International Partnership students come from smaller, primarily undergraduate institutions (some 60%, as opposed to 40% for all students studying abroad), and a rather lower percentage from the large research universities. This trend is increasing (from 55.95% in 1991+1992 to 61.69% in 1999+2000; the intake from larger institutions has dropped from 40.21% to 35.63%).

The percentages from *Open Doors* relate to students *studying* abroad. International Partnership students, of course, also do more: they are engaged in work in the community. *Open Doors* also contains information on the number of students engaged in for-credit internships or work abroad. International Partnership students fit this category as well. Here there is again a quite sharp discrepancy between the overall distribution among institution types and the International Partnership's distribution, as the following table shows.

Table 20. Enrollment by Institutional Type 1999+2000, and *Open Doors* percentages for students engaged in for-credit internships or work abroad in 1999–2000

|  | 1999 + 2000 | % | *Open Doors* % |
|---|---|---|---|
| Research I & II | 93 | 35.63 | [54.3] |
| Masters I & II | 83 | 31.80 | [18.5] |
| Baccalaureate I & II | 78 | 29.89 | [22.4] |
| Associate | 6 | 2.30 | [1.3] |
| Other | 1 | 0.38 | [3.4] |
| Total students | 261 |  |  |

## Leading Sending Institutions

We have already noted the large number of sending institutions. Table 21 recapitulates this information.

Table 22 lists the top 16 sending institutions for the ten-year period 1991–2000, with their student numbers for 1991+1992 and 1999+2000. This table shows that several of the institutions that were significant senders in the early 1990s have dropped off in numbers (notably Cornell, Bard, Hobart and William Smith, and Suffolk), while others have grown to take their places (Washington State, Colorado College). There is clearly a need, however, to cultivate a few major senders to build the overall enrollment.

In Table 23 the top sending institutions in 1991+1992 are compared with the top sending institutions in 1999+2000. The comparison underlines the lack of continuity among the leading sending institutions: only two institutions, Pacific Lutheran and Kenyon, appear on both lists. In fact, 7 of the 10 leading senders in 1991+1992 do not appear among the top 24 in 1999+2000 (Cornell, Bard, Suffolk, Hobart and William Smith, Virginia, Hampshire College, and American University). Of the top 9 senders in 1999+2000, 6 were not among the top 23 in 1991+1992 (Washington State, Colorado College, Bates, Oberlin, Middlebury, and Evergreen State).

Four of the top 10 in 1991+1992 are Research I universities; 2 of the top 9 are in that category in 1999+2000. Four of the top 10 in 1991+1992 are baccalaureate institutions, and 6 of the top 9 in 1999+2000. This is further confirmation of the enrollment shift away from large research universities toward liberal-arts colleges.

**Table 21. Number of Students and Number of Sending Institutions, 1991–2000 and Representative Years**

|  | 1991 - 2000 | 1991 + 1992 | 1999 + 2000 |
|---|---|---|---|
| Students from US and foreign institutions | 1457 | 293 | 268 |
| Sending institutions | 423 | 164 | 145 |
| Avg. students per institution | 3.40 | 1.79 | 1.85 |

**Table 22. Top Sending Institutions 1991–2000, with student numbers for 1991+1992 and 1999+2000**

| Rank | Institution | Carnegie | 1991 - 2000 | 1991+ 1992 | 1999+ 2000 |
|---|---|---|---|---|---|
| 1 | Pacific Lutheran U | Master's I | 144 | 18 | 24 |
| 2 | Kenyon College | Baccalaureate | 40 | 4 | 6 |
| 3 | Stanford U | Rech I | 31 | 3 | 5 |
| 4 | Cornell U | Research I | 30 | 13 | 2 |
| 5 | Washington State U | Research I | 27 | 1 | 7 |
| 6 | Bard College | Baccalaureate | 27 | 13 | 2 |
| 7 | U of Vermont | Research I | 22 | 6 | 3 |
| 8 | Saint Augustine's C | Baccalaureate | 17 | 3 | 0 |
| 9 | Hobart & Wm Smith C | Baccalaureate | 16 | 8 | 0 |
| 10 | Suffolk U | Master's I | 14 | 8 | 0 |
| 11 | Colorado College | Baccalaureate | 14 | 1 | 5 |
| 12 | Penn. State U | Research I | 13 | 1 | 2 |
| 13 | Miami U of Ohio | Research II | 13 | 3 | 2 |
| 14 | U of the South | Baccalaureate | 12 | 0 | 2 |
| 15 | U of Colorado | Research I | 12 | 3 | 0 |
| 16 | American U | Research I | 12 | 4 | 2 |

## Table 23. Top Sending Institutions 1991+1992 and 1999+2000

| 1991+1992 | | 1999+2000 | |
|---|---|---|---|
| 1 | Pacific Lutheran U | 1 | Pacific Lutheran U |
| 2 | *Cornell U\** | 2 | *Washington State U\*\** |
| 3 | *Bard C\** | 3 | Kenyon C |
| 4 | *Suffolk U\** | 4 | *Stanford U* |
| 5 | *Hobart & Wm Smith C\** | 5 | *Colorado C\*\** |
| 6 | *U of Vermont* | 6 | *Bates C\*\** |
| 7 | *U of Virginia\** | 7 | *Oberlin C\*\** |
| 8 | Kenyon C | 8 | *Middlebury C\*\** |
| 9 | *Hampshire C\** | 9 | *Evergreen State C\*\** |
| 10 | *American U\** | | |

[Institutions in bold appear in both lists; institutions in italics appear only in one.]
\* Institutions absent from the top 24 sending institutions in 1999+2000
\*\* Institutions absent from the top 23 sending institutions in 1991+1992

## Conclusion

The average Partnership student is female, approaching her twenty-first birthday, and perhaps studying in Latin America. She might be from any part of the country, though probably from the East or West Coasts. She is probably Caucasian, very possibly Catholic, and she may well be majoring in Spanish or Latin American Studies. She probably comes from a liberal-arts college and is in her third year of study. What is less likely is that our student will be male, older than the average undergraduate, and studying at a large university.[3]

Given the profile of the average Partnership student, two responses are possible: the International Partnership might choose to build on its strengths, by directing its programs to this population and focusing its curriculum-building and marketing, for example, on female students in liberal arts colleges interested in Latin America.

Alternatively, it might choose very specifically to counter this trend, seeking more male students, in institutions capable of sending larger numbers of students on Partnership programs. It might specifically recruit more minority students with a heritage connection to some of the countries in which the Partnership has programs.

These are decisions that will have to be made as the International Partnership plans its future. Careful analysis of this study will, we hope, make the task easier.

There are some ingredients in the decision-making that are still missing. What kinds of community-service work do International Partnership students engage in at the various program locations? What do they find most satisfying? How do they make their decisions to enroll in a International Partnership program and how do they select the program from among the International Partnership's offerings? How do they communicate their experience to fellow students when they return, and how do they evaluate

---

[3] A recent review of the data reveals that little has changed since our survey was completed at the beginning of the present project. Undergraduate enrollment, after dropping in the post-9/11 period, is now at approximately the same level as in 2000 (117 in 2004; 125 in 2000), though graduate enrollment has increased significantly. While various other indicators have remained more or less constant, the male-female ratio has shifted still further, with female enrollment for the years 2003+2004 exceeding 85% (as opposed to just over 80% in 1999+2000). Enrollment in the Spanish-speaking programs (Quito, Guayaquil, Guadalajara) has increased over the year 2000 in both percentage and absolute terms in all three programs.

it? What can we discover about personal growth, skills development (foreign language knowledge, for example), and understanding of their fields of study?

Such questions take us further and further away from the hard data already at our disposal, though there is still a good deal of information that can be gathered from the student data base and from student files if we dig a little—and obviously we should supplement what we have (a) by other methods of data-gathering and analysis, and (b) by the establishment of new ongoing procedures to gather and store data useful for strengthening the programs and evaluating their impact. The data on undergraduate enrollment should of course be compared with, and supplemented by, data on the master's program and on special programs, where appropriate.

Work on the collection of data for the present study has revealed strengths and weaknesses in the Partnership's data collection procedures. The student files themselves provide a unique resource, covering over fifteen years of Partnership history. Not only do they contain basic personal information and information about Partnership programs, but also application essays, written work by students, exit evaluations, and journals. There is a wealth of valuable information that is not electronically available but could be made so: data input should continue so that some of this information can be made more accessible.

Finally, work has begun on the redesign of the application and student data forms to improve data collection and to provide easily comparable items of information for future researchers and planners. It is crucially important that improved data collection become an integral part of the planning process for the International Partnership as a whole.

# 2 How Partnership Programs Affect Students

# 4  The Student Study: Introduction

## The Research Team

Over the past fifteen years, International Partnership for Service-Learning programs have served some 2,000 students, almost all of them from the United States, with the largest numbers going to Ecuador, England, France, Jamaica, and Mexico. About half of these students are in their third year of college. They come from all parts of the United States and several foreign countries. In the previous chapter we looked at the data revealing the characteristics of Partnership students. We discovered also that female students account for 80.08% of the total, noting that this was a higher proportion than in study-abroad programs generally and a particularly high proportion for destinations outside Europe.[1] We did our best to examine the students' racial profile, their average age, and their academic majors. We considered the institutions from which they had come, noting most Partnership students come from small institutions.

---

[1] For statistics on US study abroad, see the annual Institute of International Education publication *Open Doors*. NAFSA, through its Section on US Students Abroad (SECUSSA), has recently launched the SECUSSA Data Collection Initiative to make the Open Doors survey more comprehensive: the Open Doors survey is based on numbers gathered from colleges and universities and covers those students given credit by their home institutions for academic work outside the United States. Many students, however, may enroll with a third-party provider and may not show up in home institution statistics. Kathleen Sideli (Indiana University) chairs the Data Collection Working Group, which is currently conducting a survey of study-abroad providers as a part of the SECUSSA effort.

This preliminary demographic study made no attempt to explain these numbers. We can speculate (a) that smaller colleges are unable to offer programs of the kind or quality that the Partnership offers and, therefore, their students gravitate to the Partnership, (b) that women are attracted to Partnership programs because they seek to provide practical help to communities and many programs require foreign language (more women than men study languages in college), and (c) that students in the undergraduate programs are getting younger because the Partnership now offers a separate master's degree. But the data give us few firm answers on these questions. Indeed they tell us very little about student choices, beliefs, or motivations.

A full-blown quantitative study of these less data-driven questions was beyond the scope or capabilities of the Partnership in its present condition. While there is a good base of student data going back many years, large numbers of former Partnership students are essentially lost to the Partnership as matters now stand: their addresses have changed, and it is only in the past couple of years that the Partnership has begun to breathe life into its alumni activities and started to gather up-to-date information and addresses for its former students. Current students certainly could have been canvassed, but such an effort would have used up much of the resources available and would not have allowed for any kind of in-depth follow-up. Accordingly, it was decided that a narrower but deeper qualitative study should be carried out.

According to the Research Plan, the stated goal of the student study was "to carry out research and data-gathering on past and present students, their opinions, their career patterns, [and] their experiences," by concentrating on "student goals and attitudes." Following numerous discussions between Humphrey Tonkin, in his role as director of the research effort, and specialists in student development and student attitudes, in study abroad, and in service-learning, a decision was made to conduct a series of interviews and focus groups with a small group of Partnership alumni. The interviews and focus groups would be conducted by specialists in relevant fields, such as developmental psychology, intercultural communication, and student development.[2] Four researchers were chosen and provided with small honoraria for their work:

---

[2] On the strengths and weaknesses of focus groups as a mode of inquiry and data-gathering, see Patton 1990:335–337. Our decision to choose researchers used to working in such a context resulted in particularly rich material.

**Margaret D. Pusch,** associate director of the Intercultural Communication Institute, Portland, Oregon. Among other activities, in her capacity as associate director she conducts two or three intensive workshops each year for professionals in the field of intercultural communication. She has also served as leader/trainer for the European Association of International Education and was for many years president of Intercultural Press. In 1995–96 she served as president of NAFSA: Association of International Educators.

**Diego Quiroga,** successively dean of social sciences, dean of academic affairs, and dean of the graduate school, at Universidad San Francisco de Quito. He holds a Ph.D. in anthropology from the University of Illinois and teaches courses in such fields as ethnography, Andean anthropology, and medical anthropology. He is co-director of the Galápagos Academic Institute for the Arts and Sciences (GAIAS) and has conducted extensive research on community health in the Upper Amazon Basin and the Ecuadorian Highlands.

**Michael J. Siegel,** research fellow at the Policy Center on the First Year of College, Brevard, North Carolina. He holds a Ph.D. in higher education from Indiana University and degrees also in psychology and in counseling. He has done extensive work in survey instrument design, assessment, and related activities, and has coordinated inter-institutional cooperative efforts aimed at improving the college experience for students, particularly in the first year.

**John M. Whiteley,** professor of social ecology at the University of California Irvine. He holds a doctorate in education from Harvard University and is particularly interested in the moral development of young people. His published work includes essays and books on character development in college students, on counseling psychology, and on peace studies. He is currently conducting research on conflict prevention in the Caucasus region of the former Soviet Union.

Pusch was familiar with the work of the Partnership, having served on its board for a number of years, and having recently been elected chair of the board. Quiroga, in addition to his work as dean at his university in Quito, serves as program director for the Partnership's Ecuador program in Quito and was thus familiar with most facets of the Partnership's activities.

Siegel's knowledge of the Partnership was far slighter, his only connection being the fact that he was part of the same research operation as then Partnership board member John Gardner. Whiteley had no direct connection with the Partnership and was relatively new to service-learning.

## The Student Participants

The alumni were chosen not because they could be described as typical Partnership students (defining typicality would be hard under any circumstances), but on (1) the likelihood that they would have articulate things to say about their experiences, (2) their diversity (both with respect to characteristics external to the programs, like gender and race and profession, and with respect to internal characteristics, like their year of study and their destination). Neither of these characteristics, of course, could be said to reinforce typicality, not even the second. Indeed the first might raise questions about a bias toward students likely to have positive things to say, and a consequent suppression of the negative.

The selection of students was a collective effort, involving staff members, the four researchers, and program directors. A list of names was drawn up, through conversation among these parties, and most of those on the list were approached by letter, phone call or e-mail. Barbara Wanasek, of the Partnership staff, was largely responsible for the contacts. Those approached were invited to come to New York for a day's intensive program of interviews and focus groups. They were told (though not necessarily in these words) that the purpose was a study of the attitudes and behavior of former Partnership students, and they were informed that their travel and accommodation costs would be covered by the Partnership. There was no attempt to conceal from any of the alumni participants the true purpose of the research. Indeed, the notice laying out the plan of activities for the New York visit, e-mailed to the alumni by Barbara Wanasek on February 11, explained: "You will be meeting with a small number of IPSL alumni and experts who will assess the effectiveness of the programs and their impact on students in such fields as cross-cultural communication, moral and ethical development, and critical thinking." The alumni were asked to sign a release upon arrival, specifying the purpose of the study and giving permission to the researchers (and the Partnership) to record, transcribe and quote student statements for the purpose of research, but on condition of anonymity. It was made clear that the release related only to research: the Partnership would have to ask students' permission to quote them in any other context, such as in promotional materials.

The alumni who tend to stay in touch with the Partnership staff and the programs are likely to be those who have been most stimulated by their experience and who care most about the work of the Partnership. Those for whom the Partnership experience has figured less prominently are less likely to remain in contact with the organization. While there may well be those who, having been touched by the experience, are now pursuing their lives with such intensity that they fail to stay in touch with the Partnership, the very selection mechanism is likely to produce a favorable bias. So the student study tells us relatively little about what the "typical" Partnership student thinks or feels, or how he or she behaves, but a great deal about those for whom the experience has been significant and life-changing. The study tells us more about the possibilities of the Partnership, about what can happen when it is well matched with the student, than about what normally or typically happens. Indeed, we were interested in the relationship between what might be described as the typical Partnership narrative and the actual behavior of students, and in the shape of the experience among those whom it has influenced significantly.

Though the alumni invited to New York were personally known to members of staff or program directors, the staff made an effort to create a diverse group, in terms of age and program year, program participated in, race and ethnicity, type of home institution (large, small, secular, denominational) and gender. The ratio of thirteen women to four men was a good reflection of the Partnership's demographics over the years, and the presence of five minority-group members (2 African American, 2 Indian American, 1 Filipino American) also introduced an element of balance. While no formal attempt was made to balance socio-economic backgrounds, it transpired that the diversity of the group was considerable. Nine of the Partnership's programs were represented: Ecuador (Guayaquil), Ecuador (Quito), England, France, India, Jamaica, Mexico, the Philippines, and South Dakota (the Lakota Nation). There were three heritage students (India and the Philippines) in the group.[3]

---

[3] Glesne 1998:29, drawing on the rather more complex taxonomy employed by Patton 1990:182–183, describes six possible selection strategies for participants in a qualitative study: (1) typical case sampling, (2) extreme or deviant case sampling, (3) homogeneous sampling, (4) maximum variation sampling, (5) snowball, chain, or network sampling, (6) convenience

The day of interviews and focus groups was scheduled for April 5, 2003, and the meetings were to take place at the Partnership's offices and in adjacent conference rooms beginning at 8:30 a.m. and ending at 5:00 p.m. Plans were made to invite 16 alumni to attend. Most of those approached accepted the invitation, and, ultimately, because of a minor mix-up, a total of 17 alumni participated (we have chosen fictitious names to identify them: the information summarized here was provided through a request for resumés in advance of their arrival on April 5, and these resumés were made available to the researchers):

**Anita.** Ecuador (Guayaquil) 1991. While on the Partnership program, taught in a school for special education. Now a vocational rehabilitation counselor for the State of Connecticut, with extensive experience in working with the disabled, in both professional and volunteer roles, over a ten-year period. Majored in Latin American studies at the University of Vermont; recently completed a master's degree in rehabilitation counseling in Massachusetts. Did a one-year student exchange with the American Field Service in Brazil.

**Ashley.** Ecuador (Guayaquil) 1990. Faculty advisor for an international education NGO based in Washington and New York. Spent academic year abroad as a high school student in France. BA in international and Latin American studies 1992. MAT 1997. After Ecuador, did additional foreign study in Canada. Volunteered for an agricultural work brigade in Guatemala in 1994, served as a relief worker among Cuban refugees at Guantanamo Bay in 1995, engaged in other professional and volunteer work in Britain, Benin, Ecuador, and Kosovo. Fluent in Spanish and French.

**Bill.** Mexico 1992. After graduating with a BS in finance, ran a successful catering business in California for a number of years; now employed as a high-school Spanish teacher. Before going to Mexico, served in the Big Brother Program and was an Eagle Scout.

---

sampling. Convenience sampling she suggests, is the least acceptable. Our selection strategy combined elements of maximum variation sampling (we did not design a maximum-variation matrix and then populate it, but we did seek maximum variety among our participants) and snowball, chain, or network sampling.

**Courtney**. France 1998. Working for a master's degree in elementary education. BA in religious studies, Lewis & Clark. Study abroad in Turkey. After graduating, employed for two years as an English teacher in Japan, then as an ESL instructor in the United States.

**David**. Jamaica 1991–1992. Ph.D. candidate in ethnomusicology at Indiana University, writing on the arts in Jamaica. BA in cultural anthropology. Currently employed as an instructor at Indiana University and formerly as a "cultural broker and producer" promoting lectures, workshops and performances focusing on Jamaican expressive culture. Creative and scholarly writer with several publication including books of poetry; oboe player; painter.

**Elizabeth**. South Dakota (Lakota Nation) 2001. Currently a NEPA Environmental Protection Specialist in North Dakota, coordinating reviews of environmental impact statements and assisting in the development of tribal environmental policy and resource management. Immediately after graduation from Oberlin College (environmental studies and comparative literature), assisted in the photographic documentation of sacred sites and village sites for a tribal historic preservation office. Served as a tutor for America Reads while in college and as an intern for a local and organic farm support organization in Vermont during the summer before going to South Dakota. Strong interest in sustainable agriculture.

**Gabriel**. India 1997–1998. After working as a stockbroker and benefits consultant, took an undergraduate degree from Excelsior College (formerly Regents College), an institution operated by the New York State Regents to make degrees more accessible to working adults. Expecting to graduate from Syracuse University College of Law in 2005. Before going to India, he volunteered in Brooklyn as an emergency medical technician. A year after his work in India, he worked for a time as an English teacher in Tanzania with the Global Volunteers of St. Paul, Minn.

**Heather**. Ecuador (Quito) and Mexico 2001. Graduated in Spanish, with political science and global studies minors. Volunteer and professional work for the Make-A-Wish Foundation, for a library ESL program, for the Student Global AIDS Campaign, the House of Bread (Hartford, CT), etc. For the Partnership, organized basic skills courses for street children in Mexico and cared for toddlers in an orphanage in Ecuador.

**Jeanne**. Mexico 1997. BA in anthropology, University of the South; recent MA in Latin American studies, George Washington University; now employed at the university in an administrative position. Volunteer for Oxfam America. In Mexico, worked in a home for abused and abandoned girls. Later, returned to Mexico for a program at the Institute for International Mediation and Conflict Resolution, Monterrey.

**Jen**. Ecuador 1994. Interviewer for a study on welfare and health utilization at Columbia University: she is responsible for interviews in Spanish in New York City and San Antonio. Extensive history as a community health researcher, with an extensive list of presentations and publications. Double BAs from University of Rochester in psychology and in health in society.

**Jeremy**. Ecuador (Guayaquil) 1986. BA in English literature and Latin American studies from Hamilton College, MBA from INSEAD (France). Vice-president for mergers and acquisitions for a consulting company in Paris. Bilingual in French and English, with a working knowledge of Arabic and Spanish. Active in student journalism while in college. Went on the Partnership program before beginning college.

**Laurel**. India 1999. Educated at Humboldt State University. Adolescent health outreach coordinator working for a community organization in California. Previously she served as an advocate for mental health services for a local high school district, also in California. She has had extensive experience in working with children, in both paid and unpaid positions. In India she worked in an orphanage in Calcutta, learning some Bengali to communicate with her charges.

**Marie**. Philippines 2001–2002. She went on the Partnership program after graduating from the University of California San Diego with a degree and teaching certificate in mathematics. Now a middle-school math teacher. In the Philippines, volunteered as a math tutor both at the high school level and for neglected, abused or abandoned elementary-aged boys.

**Maxine**. Mexico 1999, France 1999. Degrees in French & Spanish and in elementary education from the University of South Carolina. Currently employed as an elementary Spanish teacher (Teacher of the Year 2003). Participated in the teacher study program, Guatemala, in the summer of 2002.

**Paula**. India, South Dakota 1997–1998. BA Kenyon College. Returned to the Partnership in 1999 to do the one-year MA program in international service (graduated October 2000), based in Jamaica, where she carried out her service as instructor and researcher in a government-funded detention center for adolescent girls. Completed University of Maryland School of Law in 2004. Volunteered as a youth mentor for the Network of South Asian Professionals, as a Crisis Hotline Listener for Crisislink, and as a Volunteer Judge in the Barbara Jordan Youth Debates. Intermediate Czech and French, basic German and Punjabi.

**Shreela**. India 2000. Graduated in microbiology from UCLA. Currently working in investment planning and tax preparing while volunteering as a clinical researcher in oncology. Also volunteering in Best Buddies UCLA. Previously, she was involved in a number of health-related volunteer activities. Two research publications, one as principal author. Roller-skating champion. About to enter medical school.

**Tamara**. England 1988. Graduated from St. Augustine's, Raleigh, NC, in 1990, going on to UNC for a medical degree. Served for several years as a staff physician in the emergency room of a large medical center and simultaneously as a university instructor in emergency medicine. Now in regular practice.

## The Protocol

At about the same time as the invitations went out, the research team, coordinated by Siegel, was exchanging e-mail messages and phone calls in an effort to develop a protocol of questions and issues to guide the discussion in April. The process began with a memorandum from Tonkin on February 13, aimed at stimulating discussion among the team members. "As I see it," he wrote, "we are interested in several groups of issues." He mentioned the following as a possible framework for the question protocol to be used in focus groups and interviews:

### 1. Students' intellectual development

Did their experience with the Partnership help not only to increase their knowledge but also increase their ability to process that knowledge, and to relate knowledge to practical experience?

Was their ability to think sharpened?

Was their global awareness (i.e. their awareness of the larger world beyond the US) enhanced, and how?

Did the experience enhance their communication skills (including knowledge of foreign languages, where appropriate)?

Did this experience have a longer-term effect, perhaps redirecting their aspirations upon their return to the US, influencing the subjects they studied and the career choices they made?

### 2. Students' affective and moral development

How does time with the Partnership help develop in students an ability to empathize and sympathize?

Did it break down or confirm stereotypical views (about other countries, about the poor and disadvantaged, about other societies)?

Did service to the community cause them to reflect on themselves and their aspirations?

Did such service heighten their sense of compassion, their sense of social justice, their awareness of the values of service without material reward, their spiritual awareness?

### 3. Definitions of service

How (if at all) did the Partnership experience cause students to rethink the idea of service to the community (many have done such service already, but perhaps the Partnership experience changed their views of it)?

Has the Partnership had a lasting effect on students' civic awareness, personal commitment to service, and actual behavior in this regard?

### 4. Cross-cultural awareness

(and not just different cultures, but also differences of social class, political and economic organization, religion, etc.)

Has this awareness had an effect also on students' subsequent behavior?

Have they maintained links in the country in question, or made new links in other parts of the world?

### 5. Social integration

To what extent has the Partnership experience changed students' attitudes to college education in general?

Were they better able to integrate themselves into the community after the experience or before?

How has the Partnership experience changed their attitudes to friendship, authority, family, teachers, sexual attachments, sense of teamwork?

How has their sense of themselves as leaders been strengthened, weakened, redefined?

### 6. Assessment of the experience

What are the strengths and weaknesses of the Partnership and its experience?

What are its prospects for the future?

What needs fixing?

The six areas that Tonkin singled out were not entirely his own, but sprang out of earlier informal discussion with individual members of the team and consultations beyond the group. He stressed, however, that he wrote as a layman, that his purpose was to move the discussion along, and that he assumed that the four researchers themselves would take the initiative from then on. This is indeed largely what happened. The researchers consulted among themselves, agreed with Tonkin's division of the field of discussion into six areas, and assigned one of their number to each of these six areas:

**Students' intellectual development.** Whiteley
**Students' affective and moral development.** Whiteley
**Definitions of service.** Siegel
**Cross-cultural awareness.** Pusch
**Social integration.** Quiroga
**Assessment of the experience.** Siegel.

By early April, and following further discussions among the four and the circulation of drafts, Siegel distributed to the researchers a complete list of questions agreed upon by the group (with some final additions of his own), intended simply as a guide and stimulant to discussion rather than an itemized and precise list. In essence, the question protocol was intended to be semi-structured. Siegel also invited Tonkin and Partnership president Linda Chisholm to comment. The resulting document, labeled "Areas of Discussion and Guiding Questions" and bearing the date April 5, 2003, reads as follows:

## 1. Students' intellectual development

(a) Did your experience with the Partnership help not only to increase their knowledge but also increase your ability to process that knowledge, and to relate knowledge to practical experience?

(b) Describe any benefits to your thinking and reasoning that resulted from your Partnership experience (e.g., Was your ability to think sharpened? Has the experience advanced your critical thinking and reasoning skills?). To what do you attribute the changes?

(c) What was your self-described level of global awareness (i.e. your awareness of the larger world beyond the US) before your international experience and how has it changed as a result of that experience?

(d) How did the experience enhance your communication skills (including knowledge of foreign languages, confidence in interacting with people from different backgrounds and of different language orientations)?

(e) Did this experience have a longer-term effect, perhaps redirecting your aspirations upon their return to the US, influencing the subjects you studied, major you chose, and other career choices you have made?

## 2. Students' affective and moral development

(a) How has the time with the Partnership helped you develop an ability to empathize and sympathize?

(b) Did the Partnership experience break down or confirm stereotypical views (about other countries, about the poor and disadvantaged, about other societies)?

(c) In what way did your involvement with the communities in which you served cause you to reflect on yourself and your aspirations?

(d) Describe whether, and how much, the service experience heightened your sense of compassion, your sense of social justice, your awareness of the values of service without material reward, and spiritual awareness.

(John [Whiteley] suggested a two-part question on values)

(a) Describe any values represented by your host country that were different than what you observe to be characteristic values of America. How are they different?

(b) How did the experience above impact your own values?

(Question about how moral and character issues differ from society to society; difference between moral values in workplace and values in family—how acceptable moral behavior in the workplace might be different than acceptable family values)

## 3. Definitions of service

(a) How (if at all) did the Partnership experience cause you to rethink the idea of service to the community?

(b) How have your notions of service, and more specifically international service, changed as a result of your experience?

(c) Describe any lasting effects the Partnership and the service experience have had on your civic awareness, personal commitment to service, and actual behavior in this regard?

(d) What are the key differences between domestic service experiences in the United States and international service experiences elsewhere around the world?

(e) How did you define "service" before you participated in the international Partnership experience? Do you define it differently now, and if so, how much of the change in definition is related to your service experience?

### 4. Cross-cultural awareness

(a) Describe changes in your cross-cultural awareness as a result of the Partnership experience. Talk about your awareness of not only different cultures but of differences of social class, political and economic organization, religion, etc.

(b) Has this awareness had an effect on your subsequent behavior?

(c) Have you maintained a connection or link with the country in question, or made new links in other parts of the world?

(d) When did you feel comfortable and confident in the host culture?

(e) What contributed most to that feeling of "fitting in" or "understanding"?

(f) What new ideals or values did you adopt while living in the host culture?

(g) What were the most surprising differences between your home and host cultures?

(h) What were the greatest contrasts between your home and host cultures?

(i) What differences were most difficult to accept or adapt to? What were the easiest to accept?

(j) How many of those values and behaviors that you adapted have remained part of your continuing life style?

(k) What did you miss the most about home while you were away?

(l) What was your immediate reaction to returning to the United States and your college or university? Can you remember?

(m) What was most comforting about coming home?

(n) When did you to feel comfortable in your home environment? What made you feel comfortable?

(o) What was most challenging or disconcerting about coming home?

(p) Do you feel as if you fit right back into your home culture? If not, why not? How would you describe yourself culturally now?

(q) How did your experience with IPSL influence your relationships with friends and family at home? With the manner in which you approached your studies? With your choices in how to live your life?

(r) How did your relationships with the people at home change?

(s) Have you maintained links with people in your host country, or made new links in other parts of the world?

(t) How did you think about the war in Iraq? (Not "what" but "how.")

(u) What do you miss the most about your host culture?

## 5. Social integration

(a) Describe the extent to which the Partnership experience changed your attitudes to college education in general.

(b) Were you better able to integrate into the community after the experience or before?

(c) Describe the ways in which the Partnership experience changed your attitudes to friendship, authority, family, teachers, sexual attachments, sense of teamwork, and the ways in which your sense of self as leader was strengthened, weakened, redefined.

(d) What is the extent to which the experience helped you deal with a foreign language?

(e) It might be also interesting to ask the participants about whether the experience helped them reflect about their own culture, identity and nationality.

## 6. Assessment of the experience

(a) What are the strengths of the Partnership and its experience? Weaknesses? Prospects for the future? Things that need fixing?

(b) What elements of your experience do you feel were unique to the Partnership program (e.g., benefits and experiences unique to IPSL experience that you would likely not receive from another program, etc.)?

(c) What is missing from the Partnership experience?

(d) If you had the opportunity to make suggestions about changes to the Partnership and/or the international experience, what would they be?

(e) What do you see as the future role of the Partnership (reach more countries, have greater number of experiences in fewer countries, etc.)?

(f) How likely would you be to recommend this experience to your friends and colleagues? What advice would you give them?

Whiteley's comments about a question on values, alluded to in the above document, pointed to a strategy: "The value question can be simply put by asking two interrelated questions. The first question is to ask what values were held by the culture in which they [the interviewees] worked and studied that were different from the values they had observed in their own culture. Then I would ask them what impact this experience of observing differing values had on their own." Whiteley added, "With respect to the moral reasoning question, [I] would ask two interrelated questions about moral reasoning in the work environment, how they thought it differed from America and what impact it had on their own moral reasoning. I would ask the same question about moral reasoning in the personal domain. . . . This will ultimately show the impact of the experience on the individual but will also allow a demonstration of their understanding of the culture they learned in as well as their own."

Tonkin, when asked for his comments on the questions, focused most particularly on the actual behavior of the alumni before and after the Partnership experience down to the present day. "Deciding whether an experience like this has actually changed an individual is difficult indeed," he pointed out, "but it would be nice to know whether the interviewees currently engage in community service, whether they have what might be described as active spiritual lives, whether they manifest altruistic tendencies in their everyday lives, whether they are politically engaged." He wanted the team to "be able to map interviewees' lives in a quite factual way: how they allocate their time, what they do with it, how they choose their friends, how they behave as social and political beings, what kind of work they do and how they spend their leisure time."

Tonkin also stressed that it was important "to know whether the Partnership experience was unlike anything else that an interviewee has done, or whether it is part of a pattern of service, curiosity about other cultures, interest in engaging with the poor or the disadvantaged." In the event, this varied widely from individual to individual, as the team discovered. Tonkin suggested that the interviewers could usefully get interviewees "to talk about their aspirations and family and educational backgrounds," and, finally, he reminded the interviewers of some emerging directions for the Partnership when he called for "questions about leadership and ways in which the Partnership experience has added to people's ideas of leadership and their own practices as leaders."

Chisholm urged the need for an open-ended question about the interviewees' overall experience: "What troubling questions remain for you?" Like Tonkin, she also emphasized the importance of the leadership issue: "Did they observe and were they exposed to community leaders, good and bad? What qualities did they possess? Did they meet agency supervisors and/or university leaders, for example, who recognized a problem, conceived of ways of addressing it, were able to communicate a vision to others, built community support, and developed organizational structures to sustain their efforts? Or did they encounter leaders who were unable to sustain their vision and programs? Why?" And on a broader basis, "What did they learn about leaders in the host nation's history? What in the culture encourages or retards the development of leadership at the grass-roots level? Is leadership in the nation widely shared or held by only a few? Is it shared between the sexes and among the groups in the society or are some groups (tribes, castes, classes) excluded? And what, if any, leadership skills did they possess that they were able to put to use and further develop? When they returned home, were they perceived by others to be leaders in ways they were not so perceived before participating in the program?"

The interviewers could be forgiven if they felt that they had enough material and enough separate issues for a month's discussion, rather than a day's. But the abundance of good material seemed to generate good responses, and, as it turned out, the day proved remarkably productive.

## The Meetings

Everything was now set for the arrival of the alumni in New York. They were invited to arrive in time for a welcoming reception and dinner on the evening of Friday, April 4, when they were joined by the program directors, meeting in New York at that time, members of the New York staff, and any members of the Partnership's board who might have already arrived in town for Sunday's board meeting. The three days were so arranged that on the first, Friday, the program directors met and on the second, Saturday, the focus groups took place. On the third, Sunday, the board had its spring meeting, and simultaneously an alumni meeting, involving most of those interviewed and others, took place. The interviewees were also joined at the Friday dinner by the four researchers. The event was intended as a social occasion and seems to have been treated largely as such, but inevitably there were conversations, particularly involving the program directors, about students' experiences with the Partnership. While this contact among the interviewees on the previous evening may have colored their responses the following morning, the advantages of informal communication in advance of the formal interviews and focus groups were judged by the team to outweigh the disadvantages, since they were likely to contribute to a relaxed and easy atmosphere. The dinner also provided an opportunity for a short briefing on the following day's activities. Some of the alumni were booked into a hotel by the Partnership, some stayed at home, and some with friends. They arrived in the Partnership office at 8:30 on Saturday, April 5, to begin the day's proceedings with a light breakfast and further briefing on the logistics for the day (8:30–9:00).

The program for the day was designed to minimize cross-communication (and thus standardization of narratives) among the participants in the early stages and to maximize it at the end: the day began with one-on-one interviews and proceeded through larger and larger groups, until in the final session all interviewers and interviewees were brought together into a single session.

Interviews with individual alumni were conducted by individual team members at forty-minute intervals over the three hours following breakfast (9:00–12:00), on the following schedules:

**Michael Siegel:** Bill, Jen, Laurel, Tamara
**Margaret Pusch:** Shreela, Anita, Elizabeth, Heather
**Diego Quiroga:** Courtney, Gabriel, Jeanne, Marie
**John Whiteley:** Maxine, Jeremy, Paula, Ashley
David *was interviewed jointly by Pusch and Quiroga the previous evening.*

The interviewers were provided with tape recorders and cassettes, and each interview was recorded on a separate cassette. An effort was made to diversify each interviewer's interviewees. In his report, for example, Siegel points out that he interviewed on an individual basis students representing international service in four different countries—Ecuador, England, India, and Mexico—and in four different time periods—1988, 1992, 1994, and 1999. When alumni were not in their interviews, they were encouraged to go out into the city (the Partnership office is in midtown Manhattan). Then most of them reassembled for lunch (12:00–1:00), at which Tonkin and members of the staff were also present. The four researchers ate in a separate room, where they could discuss the morning's interviews and plan the afternoon's focus groups.

From 1:00 to 2:00 p.m., each of the researchers met with groups of four (or, in one case, five) alumni different from those he/she had interviewed in the morning. From 2:15 to 3:15 p.m., the alumni were brought together into two groups of eight or nine, with Pusch and Quiroga meeting with one group and Siegel and Whiteley with the other. There was a half-hour break from 3:15 to 3:45, giving the team a chance to spend some time together to discuss the proceedings so far and plan the final session. This final session, at which all interviewers and interviewees were present, ran from 3:45 to 5:00, completing the day. Most of the students stayed on for the alumni meetings the following morning. The two nights surrounding the focus-group day were paid for by the Partnership, which also covered the cost of travel (the alumni received no other compensation for their participation).

All sessions were audiotaped, and in addition to the taping, all sessions (except of course the one-on-one interviews in the morning) were attended by a rapporteur (a member of the staff or in a couple of cases the board) who noted, for the purposes of identification, who spoke when, and in some cases took additional notes that were shared with the team. During the weeks following the event, the interview tapes (i.e. those from the morning session) were transcribed, and the transcriptions were delivered to the team members. The interviewers also received a complete set of tapes for all afternoon sessions.

It was agreed that each researcher would provide an extensive written report. The reports prepared by Pusch, Quiroga and Siegel are presented in the next three chapters, and parts of Whiteley's report are incorporated into an additional chapter, in which we sum up the findings of the study. There was no formal process of consultation instituted following the New York meetings, but a good deal of informal contact took place among the four interviewers and with Tonkin in his role both as project director and as editor.

A careful comparison of the tapes themselves with the reports prepared by the interviewers would likely reveal a fair and accurate assessment of the day's activities on the part of the interviewers, but the sheer richness of the material gathered, and the sheer willingness of this group of articulate alumni to talk and listen, meant that many topics were touched upon and pursued, some of which do not emerge in the reports. We hope that there will be further opportunities to conduct further analysis of the material gathered, perhaps in further phases of the Partnership's research. It is clear that the student study is simply the beginning of what we hope will prove to be an ongoing process. As for the reports themselves, we have edited them slightly, but for the most part they are presented as written: we were eager to have them reflect the assessment of the researchers in the months immediately following the meetings. Both Pusch and Siegel produced more polished but abbreviated statements for their presentations at the International Conference on Service-Learning Research in the fall of 2003, and Quiroga did the same in an article co-authored with Tonkin (Tonkin & Quiroga 2004).

# 5 A Cross-Cultural Perspective

## Margaret Pusch

The opportunity to meet with alumni of International Partnership for Service-Learning programs and discuss their experience with the Partnership programs and the impact of those programs on subsequent life decisions produced rich contextual information about how students fared during and after their period abroad. The discussions were valuable to the alumni because they allowed them to remember and reconceptualize their experiences, to share and connect with each other, and to put the Partnership experience in perspective with their subsequent lives. They were valuable for the Partnership because they allowed a discovery of the long- term impact of international service-learning programs on at least one cross-section of former students. In some ways this was rewarding and encouraging; in others ways, it caused dismay. Both are important to know.

During the various interviews, the uniqueness of each student was striking as was the commonality of their values and goals. It seems, although it cannot be proved, that this particular overseas study experience attracts a set of very diverse people in terms both of life experience and of motivations, but that they share an interest in combining service with learning and gain a great deal of satisfaction from contributing to the welfare of others. Students who decide to study abroad tend to be the exception rather than the rule among college students, and students who select service-learning programs of the kind that the Partnership offers tend to be the exception within an exception. In other words, they are a minority among their study-abroad student peers. However, more students with an interest in service and, more importantly, connecting learning and service, are attending colleges and universities, and the challenge to the Partnership is to reach and bring them into the programs.

The alumni interviewed individually were Shreela, Anita, Elizabeth, Heather and, with Diego Quiroga, David. This chapter relies heavily on those interviews and on the small focus groups that were led by me alone and with Quiroga.

The subjects' motivations for joining this program and their past experiences were explored to discover a starting point in terms of the Developmental Model of Intercultural Sensitivity (DMIS) and how they prepared for adapting to a new culture. This allowed a better understanding of how they changed during the sojourn.

## The Developmental Model of Intercultural Sensitivity

A quick review of the developmental model is essential to understanding comments that will be made in this chapter. The stages in the DMIS are divided into two segments: *Ethnocentrism*, which includes denial, defense, and minimization, and *Ethnorelativism*, which includes acceptance, adaptation, and integration (Bennett 1993).

### Ethnocentric States

*Denial* indicates an inability to construe cultural differences, which may be due to living in isolation in a homogeneous group or due to intentional separation from different others. Any recognition of difference is reduced to broad categories such as "foreigner," "Asian," or "black." Those in *Defense* recognize cultural differences but tend either to denigrate them and engage in defending their own culture from any change that might ensue if there is acceptance of different peoples or to see their own culture as superior to all others. There is the possibility of defense/reversal that can occur when someone becomes deeply involved in another culture and begins to see that culture as superior to his/her own. It is important to note that in both these states, extreme dualistic thinking is common. In reversal, the poles are reversed but the dualism is maintained.

*Minimization* is a state in which there is recognition and acceptance of superficial cultural differences (clothing, food, quaint practices) but in the context of seeing all human beings as essentially the same and having common values. The measure for sameness is being like "us." This sameness can be expressed in terms of physiological similarity (basic needs and the like) or transcendent universalism (everyone is a child of God, whether they know it or not). While *Minimization* is a somewhat more benign form of ethnocentrism, the tendency is still to judge other groups from one's own cultural perspective.

It is generally agreed that moving from ethnocentrism to ethno-relativism, a term devised by Milton Bennett, who created the DMIS, requires a significant experience in an unfamiliar culture. This experience is, of course, provided by participation in Partnership programs.

## Ethnorelative States

*Acceptance* is a state in which people recognize and appreciate differences in behavior and values and see those differences as viable alternative solutions to achieving satisfaction in human existence. It is characterized by an ability to interpret various phenomena within the context in which they occurred and develop categories within which they can be compared. Understanding that behavior exists in a cultural context, one can analyze complex interactions in culture-contrast terms. Similarly, values, beliefs, and other ways of indicating that one is "good" or "bad" are seen within the cultural contexts in which they arose.

*Adaptation* to difference requires the development of communication skills, the use of empathy, or frame of reference shifting that allows one to be understood and to function effectively across cultures. Empathy is an ability to shift into alternative world views and act in culturally appropriate ways but tends to be a temporary, specific situation shift that entails cognitive adaptation. A more sophisticated step is what Bennett terms "pluralism," the internalization of more than one complete world view and the ability to both interpret and respond within that frame with little conscious effort (behavioral adaptation). There is an intentionality to adaptation, which should not be confused with assimilation because it is an expansion of one's capabilities and options for behavior and valuing, not a substitution of one set of cultural behaviors with another.

*Integration* is not only the internalization of bicultural or multicultural frames of reference but seeing oneself as "in process" or "self-creating," and accepting that identity is not based in any one culture. People in this state tend to see themselves as marginal, not primarily based in any one culture. Constructive marginality was as term devised by Janet M. Bennett (1993) to indicate that this is not a pathological state but a way of being that allows one to have rich experiences in any culture rather than having one's reference point always based in a particular culture. These are people who are "at home" anywhere. They can function in ways that are consistent in any culture while maintaining a position of marginality.

The alumni interviewed showed growth in intercultural sensitivity, although they did not all seem to reach the same stage on the continuum. They varied from advanced acceptance to sophisticated adaptation. Most had previous experience that allowed them to enter the program in the state of minimization; one, perhaps two, had already achieved the level of understanding. All of them, by the end of their Partnership experience, had reached the ethnorelativist state of adaptation, several showed signs of pluralism, and one was moving toward, and may now have reached, constructive marginality. Without administering the Intercultural Development Inventory, an instrument that measures the level of intercultural sensitivity, this is difficult to document exactly, but the exploration below will show that they become far more ethnorelative during their participation in the Partnership program.

## Motivation

Students entered the program for a range of personal reasons. Shreela was a heritage student who wanted to discover her cultural identity, since her parents are from India and she has many relatives still there. She wished to explore her culture, religious beliefs, and language, and discover what this meant in terms of her identity. She also wanted to test her ability to be on her own and find out how well she could manage herself in a relatively foreign environment. She had been in India before but only on visits accompanied by her parents. Anita had long planned to study abroad in Latin America during her junior year as an extension, in a sense, of her earlier American Field Service experience in Brazil. However, she was very service-oriented and wanted to be in a program that allowed her to serve in a social service environment, preferably a clinic, coupled with academic study.

This opportunity to combine service and study was the motivation most often shared by the subjects. Elizabeth was strongly motivated by combining academics and service, an extension of her earlier service experience in an elementary school with a large African-American population while a student at her home institution. She wanted to remain in the United States and learn about diversity within her own country and thus chose the South Dakota program. David had been in Jamaica several times, with a church volunteer program and in another study-abroad program, and wanted to return to conduct research as well as engage in service-learning. It appears from other interviews that students do not choose this program unless they are interested in service as a way of being deeply involved in and learning about the culture. David stated this clearly, emphasizing that he did not want to learn culture through language study but by contributing directly to the society, "The combination of service and learning made a lot of sense to me and it still does."

None of these motivations is unusual or unexpected. However, they are driven by individual interests synthesized through the focus on service and culture learning. All of the subjects made mention of the need to experiment, to be involved directly, to connect the experience to theory (or ideas, the term more often used), and for the need to reflect on everything that was being encountered. In this they showed an unconscious tendency to complete the full experiential learning cycle developed by Kolb (1984). Kolb's research shows that experiential learning occurs when a person engages in an activity (concrete experience), reviews this activity critically (reflective observation), abstracts some useful insight from the analysis (abstract conceptualization), and applies the result in a practical situation (active experimentation). Individuals grasp the learning through concrete experience or abstract conceptualization and transform it through reflection or active experimentation. The Partnership students had a strong sense of what they wanted in an educational experience and enough concrete experience to plan how they would go about extracting the learning from the situation they were in. Some, such as Anita and Shreela, spent a lot of time making friends, visiting relatives, hearing stories, and engaging in social activities as a way of learning the culture, and found this to be extremely rewarding. They wanted to connect with people, to learn about the experience of others in this unfamiliar culture. This was not a method used only by these two students, but they were more intentional about it and saw it as the most rewarding part of living in and learning from the new culture.

However, everyone was an explorer both before entering the Partnership and during the program. They also sought clarification about what they were seeing, feeling, and experiencing. Such clarification required reflection and drew on academic sources to explain parts of the society and culture that were puzzling. The academic part of the program was essential to this understanding, and they were uniformly appreciative of the nurturing kind of learning environment that was provided. One person took exception to that, stating that the academic program was not strong enough, and then admitted that in reading her journal, it was clear that she was not taking full advantage of what was being offered. The study tended to rely on reflection to sort out their experience, their own identity, and their sense of what this meant to them in the long term. They then carried what they had learned back into the service but also into their everyday lives, using their social interactions and the process of meeting daily needs as a learning resource. Thus the students used the complete cycle described by Kolb. Ultimately, this led to an internalization of the learning that sometimes had an immediate impact and in other instances took years to realize. David said that something he had begun to learn in 1991 finally came clear when he worked on his dissertation some years later: "I didn't really grasp the weight of [it] until maybe even last year. So there [were] quite a few lessons that I learned there that are still taking a long time to work themselves out." Reflection does not always occur immediately, and the transformative learning that tends to take place in service-learning programs may emerge years after the experience.[1] Anita, unhappy with her agency placement, was frustrated by the lack of attention to her plight and continually asked for help to change her agency assignment or the nature of her work in the placement she had been given. In the end, nothing seemed to work and she remained where she was—only to discover, years later, that it deeply influenced her choice of career when she was prevented from entering medical school.

### The Service

The service experience itself will be covered in other reports, but it is important to note that almost everyone had some complaints about their placement, and their discomfort had an effect on their learning, albeit in ways that were not anticipated. Those complaints included the apparent

---

[1] David is writing a dissertation on artists in Jamaica and sees how they connect everything in their lives. See culture learning in this report.

lack of organization within agencies and an "inability" to use volunteers constructively, the students' difficulty in understanding what they should do and the lack of direction from agency leaders and their failure to provide them with a defined role, the students' inability to make a "real" contribution, and the sense that this portion of the program was too "loose." Over time, the students began to realize that this apparent looseness was itself a cultural immersion experience, that they were learning the culture by sorting things out and finding their way within a structured environment (they would debate that use of "structured," since structure was something they felt they rarely saw). In addition, they took pride in their accomplishments. They cited many examples: helping a young student learn during a placement in a high school (and later returning to attend the young man's wedding); documenting the work of artists in Jamaica and helping them come to the United States to perform; bringing a new perspective into a Tribal Historical Preservation Office and contributing some expertise in environmental studies; finding a role as an assistant cooking instructor for mentally retarded people and getting to know the pupils. As these stories were relayed, there was a tendency on the part of the students to deny that they had made any lasting contributions. By talking about what they did and how they felt about it, however, there was a realization that, indeed, they had made important contributions that had a long-term effect.

The service provided insights into the culture at many levels, and the academic study gave the students theoretical frameworks within which to understand their experience in the agencies and the other contacts they had in the community. A Latin American understands that complaining is part of the process of learning and relating to others; occasionally Partnership students understood that as well. Even as they complained, they were sorting out and making meaning of the experience that they had had in the Partnership program.

During these interviews, the students began to identify specific points when learning occurred and to appreciate the long-term benefits of such learning. Those points included

- a first exposure to and working directly with someone who has a disability, and later realizing how useful this is professionally

- trying to understand what was going on in Jamaica, its economic and human problems, and later realizing that teaching students and inspiring them to go on and do very interesting work contributed to solving some of those problems

- gaining so much satisfaction from helping in a small way to deliver health care in rural areas of India that entering a career solely devoted to research became intolerable and a new direction was taken into patient-centered work.

The impact students had on those in the host culture took on new meaning, and the impact of the Partnership program on the students' future work became very clear during the interviews.

## Culture Learning and Adaptation

The students adapted to and learned the culture in subtle, practical, and various ways. They reached a high level of acceptance/behavioral relativism (Ethnorelative Stage IV) when they began to comprehend subtle behavioral differences such as a different pace of life. Incorporating these differences into their own behavior, at first consciously and then more unconsciously, they showed an increase in empathy and a high level of adaptation (Ethnorelative Stage V). Most students reached a state of adaptation/pluralism. Able to internalize more than one world view, they were able to shift their behavior using different frames of reference without much conscious effort—but that occurred only after consideration was given to those shifts and differences.

This process was relayed by David when he said,

When you are waiting at a bus stop and you want the bus to stop, there's a kind of—you know, there is a way that Jamaicans hail a bus; . . . it's not the same as a taxi here. So it's the little things you pick up on. Just being on the bus—just being a white person on the bus gave you some respect because you're not in a car, you're in the public transportation, and people would see you. I mean they'd see you taking the bus one day, and they'd see you the next day. So you feel good about that.

David also talked about explaining his situation in Jamaica to Jamaicans:

You know, I'm a light person. I have money. Breaking that stereotype, and saying no, no I'm not a tourist. I'm a student here, I'm studying, you know, Jamaican culture, Jamaican literature. I'm part of a community. And they would leave me alone. I mean, knowing enough to explain to them and feel different, very different from being a tourist, being much more connected with something deeper than that.

David began to acquire the overt patterns of behavior of the Jamaicans, which not only made his life smoother but also made those around him more comfortable and more accepting. Edward T. Hall (1994) talks about his early learning in this regard when he worked with Navaho and Hopi. These are subtle changes in personal behavior that begin with observation, followed by application, and eventually become "natural" (Pusch 1994). "White people move so fast," said David—and that doesn't work in Jamaica. Hall made the same observation: moving fast didn't work on the reservations either. David had to adapt not only to fit in but to make the experience more rewarding. With that behavior shift came a shift in world view: "You switch—your mind switches over."

Shreela was engaged with relatives in India, discovering how they thought about life, about their spiritual beliefs, and why certain goals and behaviors were appropriate in the local seetting:

I had to interact with my aunts and uncles who are much older than me, who are different. . . . You know over here I was running around doing this or that, busy busy according to some schedule. Over there things don't happen that way. They're much less regular; people don't do things on time and you have to get used to it. You know you have to adjust because things will get done, but not according to your schedule.

Life is lived at a slower pace, "I felt just very comfortable with the people there." This shift in sentiment did not occur because of formal instruction. Again, the pattern of observing and adopting new behaviors emerges as does the ability to reflect on one's own behavioral shifts and patterns of thinking. Shreela talked of her insights: ". . . you feel over there a struggle for people to just live, you know—who may not have any sort of opportunity—and they just make the best with what they have. And they find a lot of pleasure in that, and they can find a lot of happiness in that." Her search for her own cultural roots led to "understanding my parents and their struggles a lot better. . . . I understood them better as people and not just as parents." She also focused on learning the language and on study about Indian culture, its religions and its history. Study of the culture was important to providing a framework for learning about how people live on a day-to-day basis.

Elizabeth, in South Dakota, said

> there's been a change in how I relate to people and something that actually is that your spirit recognizes like another spirit kind of instantly. When you meet someone you get a feeling off of them. . . . When I'd go to meetings, the style is just kind of different than mainstream culture . . . in that people are kind of more quiet and you get a lot off of people without having to talk to them all the time.

She indicated that this characteristic of the community was never explained, that she learned a lot of things unconsciously rather than through verbal disclosure. But it was deeper than just being quieter and more than an increased ability to read people non-verbally. She talked about gaining a sense of a "kind of historical trauma," and being impacted by it. She spoke of how little she knew of the history of the Indians and the degree to which American society is rooted in Indian practices. For example, "The Constitution is based after the Iroquois tribe's political arrangement or something like that: I was constantly struck and still am by just how much our institutions are built on, you know, like the American Indian presence is everywhere. It just isn't talked about." She was also impressed by the family structure and how important it is to have "a real concrete sense of which people you come from:"

> I mean [among the Lakota] people qualify their relationship to everyone. . . . And everyone is like your auntie or your grandma or your cousin . . . and immediately kind of looking for what that connection is. . . . it was not until the fifties or something, it was illegal for them to leave the reservation so people have

been in the same place for quite a long time . . . and just to be able to see that history all over—in the landscape. . . . the names of towns and even the chief camps. . . . and that family still sort of lives in that area.

This changed how she looked at and analyzed the world:

Environmentalists always stress the interconnectedness of everything . . . but it put it on a human level, the idea that we are all related . . . taking care of burial grounds and burial places . . . the idea that we need to take care of this place because we love it and learn from it all the time, and need it to still be there to teach us who we are . . . the idea that you're related to and had a responsibility to the people who are in the earth, it really just brought it to a different level for me.

Anita, in Ecuador, valued the relationships she had, and still maintains as much as possible, stating that "there is a lot that goes on [in the Partnership experience], but I think that when I was there for the program," relationships were the most valuable, "because you really got to know the people and the way they saw things and what their situation was in life and their struggles. . . . you can be kind of laid back, and not everybody is all professional or working." Her experience in other cultures started at the age of eight, and the Partnership program gave her an opportunity to hone and sharpen skills she had acquired, by necessity, from spending considerable amounts of time outside her culture for the purpose of receiving medical care. Anita can almost be classified as a "global nomad," someone who from a young age has been crossing cultures and relating to more than one reality. She has become adept at bridging differences between many cultures. She is most attracted to Latin American cultures, however: "I think that [a shift in thinking and world view] happened before Partnership, how I look at the world and other peoples, other cultures, and really a need to be open-minded and not make judgments. But at the same time having the sense of who you are and how you can acclimate or not, and trying to understand why." The Partnership program provided the structure to connect the informal learning she had experienced many times, and was experiencing again, with the more formal, academic study. It allowed a synthesis of the conceptual, emotional, and behavioral.

The recognition of patterns of behavior different from one's own and the ability to make adjustments in one's own behavior emerged over and over again. These kinds of statements indicated a high level of adaptation and an ability to learn from small or everyday behaviors, to gain some level of effectiveness in the culture, and to develop important connections with people and with institutions. Hall (1994:80) talks of the necessity to learn informally and to have a friend who will help you understand the culture: "My tutorial with Sam Yazzie began the first time the two of us climbed into our truck. After I slammed my ill-fitting door, he turned around, looked at his door, and pulled it quietly shut. After I had slammed my door a couple of times and he had pulled his shut quietly, I began to get the point." The students got the point and changed their behaviors.

The new behaviors were an outward manifestation of the slow internalization of a new set of values: a greater orientation to being people-centered rather than task-centered, an increased concern for building and maintaining relationships, a sense of responsibility for the collective, and an ability to change one's own goals and objectives because of new ways of perceiving the world and one's place in it. The students had become more mindful: they learned to withhold judgment, and to be flexible—important intercultural skills. The word "openness" came up again and again in our conversations: openness to the new cultures, ideas, and ways of learning but also openness to what the students were learning about themselves and who they were becoming through these experiences. This would not become clear until they returned home.

In addition, the ability to move beyond empathy to pluralism was evident in these alumni. They had obviously acquired and employed at least a second world view (some acquired more than two) and were able to talk about the shifts they made between them. They continually analyzed situations from more than one cultural perspective, discussed those perspectives, and adapted their behavior, sometimes effortlessly. Elizabeth demonstrated the cognitive shift when she reviewed the land-use patterns prevalent in New England and compared them with those on the reservation:

> In New England, there is a concept of public land being kind of a viable way of being able to protect the environment—a win-win relationship. On the reservation . . . they have to have control of their own land. But also it's been the experience of many Indian tribes, having land taken from them in devious ways, that a lot of

the national parks were part of what was reservation land. The Badlands in South Dakota used to be part of the Pine Ridge Reservation. So it's a direct threat to tribal sovereignty. It's a different consciousness, too. I mean the community that I am in, they're struggling to each have okay family relations and stuff like that . . . it's a much different place.

David stated that

I realized that this experience showed me in one cultural context there are both joys, sorrows, you know, things that are difficult to change, things that were great. . . . the larger realization is that you know, this is going on all over the place. The contexts are different . . . but these types of problems with economics, governments, all these things are going on in other contexts. I've focused on Jamaica but I've always realized it was only one example of a larger picture. . . . some of the things I've learned in Jamaica are applicable in a much larger. . . .

Both were able to behave in ways congruent with their analysis of the overarching issues that were important in the host cultures. They also began to think of those cultures less and less as "hosts."

This level of ethnorelativism was further explored by asking the interviewees to discuss their process of thinking about the war in Iraq— not their opinion of it, but *how* they thought about it. David said, "Yeah, the war. When you get to know people in another culture, you become hesitant to make judgments about other peoples and cultures because the "only way to make an accurate assessment would be to experience those people." Without that experience or knowledge, "I wouldn't want to make a jump to judgment about a political situation. . . . So, I guess I am skeptical about people who rush too quickly to judge." Shreela observed, "You just start to think about the people a lot more who are living in this regime, you know whose families are losing people who are victims. . . . They're struggling. . . . I think I can empathize with them a lot more. . . . You have this desire to help them because you've helped people in dire circumstances. . . . You just have to hope that these political entities aren't going to ruin the development of these basic values. So you think about it that way." Anita stated that she doesn't think about the war much; in fact, she avoids seeing or reading the news. However, when pushed to expand the question to any international issue, she said she would think about the issues differently now because "I know that people come from different frames of reference . . . and when you are considering your stance on situations, you really need to be cognizant of where others are coming from, thinking about the well-being of not only you as the individual, but everybody involved." A tendency to use more than one cultural frame was demonstrated as they discussed this kind of phenomena.

## Culture Shock

It is often difficult to remember the transition process one experienced after becoming adapted to a new culture, especially after some time has passed. This difficulty was apparent in our discussions. Participants often denied that they had suffered from culture shock until asked at what point they felt comfortable in their host cultures and if there were any continuing frustrations. Comfort, a sense of fitting in, was not achieved until they hit their stride in their work with community agencies, became more competent in the use of an unfamiliar language, found ways to become less obvious, and no longer felt they were constantly being thrown into new situations.

Some students were very aware of being a member of a minority group (white in Jamaica, black in London), standing out because of their appearance. This, at least in one case, had a profound impact because it was a new experience. Being in a minority, always feeling "different," can be remarkably difficult. Being comfortable meant "forgetting" that you looked different because you were interacting successfully and being accepted by the host people. This occurred with people the students encountered on a daily basis. It was never possible in the larger community: they always stood out—though even "being noticed" became more comfortable as time went on. As David pointed out,

> I wanted to experience other cultural situations and other people, so I was interested and open to that experience, but being open to that experience is different than actually being in that experience. And I mean, when you are a minority, I mean not *just* the only white person on the bus, it was a powerful experience; it was a scary experience; it was a reflective experience; it was many things for me. . . . When the tables are turned like that, it really makes you think about how other people feel when they are in that experience.

Others (the heritage students) felt they would fit in because they were American-born members of the host culture but quickly learned that appearance is, literally, only skin deep. While they looked like other people, they had different patterns of behavior that made them stand out. Shreela mentioned that she was surprised at how little she knew about herself and where she came from, and how much she had to learn: "It's probably more of a life-long process." In some ways, this discovery of difference was more difficult because these heritage students expected to fit in easily, and members of the culture might have expected them to do so as well. They found they could not.

Class issues loomed for some. They were struck by the gaps between the desperately poor and the affluent. Living with middle- or upper-class families placed them in the position of living well while working with those who were acutely needy. There was some frustration, if not guilt, about their comfortable lives. Shreela, in India, spoke of having so much opportunity and so little struggle to live on a day-to-day basis that there should be no excuse for a lack of appreciation for what you have, while Laurel found being swarmed by beggar children who came close and wanted to hold her hand very disconcerting. Jen, in Ecuador, became closer to the maid than to family members and was excluded from family trips and activities as a result.

Gender issues arose, especially for *gringo* women in a Latin culture. One male subject said he felt it was more difficult for women and he was always impressed at how well they managed the experience in a foreign, often "sexist," culture. In general, women found ways to deal with the attitudes toward women and were less and less impacted by them as time went on.

It should be noted that of the so-called intensity factors for sojourners that Michael Paige (1993)[2] has identified, four emerged in this discussion: the degree of difference between the home and host cultures, the level of cultural immersion, visibility and invisibility due to physically different

---

[2] Paige identifies 10 intensity factors for the living-abroad experience: the degree of cultural difference between host and home cultures, the sojourner's level of ethnocentrism, language difficulties, the level of cultural immersion, the degree to which the sojourner is isolated from his or her own culture group, prior intercultural experience and skills that emerged from it, unrealistic expectations of the host culture, how much the sojourner stands out or fails to be noticeable, loss or gain of status, and the amount of power and control one has over one's own circumstances.

characteristics, ethnocentrism on the part of the sojourner and the hosts, and language. Others, such as power and control over one's own circumstances, may have been present early in the experience but, as time went on, the students gained and felt they had gained control over their lives and control no longer posed a problem.

All in all, the frustrations mentioned were ones to be expected, and the students saw them as something to "get over" as they became more familiar with the culture. They clearly failed to remember the more subtle process of slowly coming to grips with everyday differences and working through them, learning gradually to do the correct thing and enduring psychological adaptation. They remembered what they had learned about the culture but forgot the discomfort of the learning. Most participants in overseas programs tend to forget the times that are painful when they become reasonably adapted to the culture. Anita noted that as she read her diary she was surprised at notes of "boredom" and annoyance: she remembers having a good time.

Most research on study abroad shows that host-sojourner interactions are limited and the greatest complaint from participants is their disappointment in not getting to know members of the host culture (Ward, Bochner & Furnham 2001:142–167). This complaint was never voiced by Partnership students. The Partnership program facilitates interaction between sojourners and hosts to a remarkable degree by embedding students in the community through agency service and local living arrangements in addition to attending local universities. The conditions of those placements have most of the qualifications that Allport (1954) cites as critical to positive relations between hosts and sojourners:

(1) Equal status is enjoyed by everyone in the situation (they may not have equal status in society or in the world but conditions for equal status were established for the situation in which they were together).

(2) Everyone involved is committed to an active, goal-oriented effort.

(3) There is no competition between those involved in the situation.

(4) The contact and conditions of the contact are sanctioned by the "authorities."

While Partnership students do not have "equal status" with those who run agencies or teach at the partner universities, they have pupil status, which conveys a purpose for their presence and an agreed upon position within the service agency. All the conditions that Allport indicated as essential to successful relationships in a cross-cultural situation existed in the Partnership situation to some degree and contributes to success in overcoming the greatest hurdle for study-abroad students, getting to know people in the host culture. These conditions contrast with those of a large number of overseas students who are very ambivalent about their host nationals and often feel they are discriminated against. A review of the contact theory research done since Allport's original work shows that if his conditions are met, contact between host/sojourner is productive and those conditions are rarely met in study abroad (Pettigrew & Tropp 2000). They are, however, key elements in Partnership programs.

Much of the research on study-abroad students has focused on listing the problems they encounter, but the studies are so varied in methodology and research samples that it is hard to compile a firm list of those problems most often experienced and their level of severity. However, it is clear that most are related to the academic environment and the fact that students must simultaneously engage in both culture learning and formal study in an unfamiliar academic system, unsure of what is expected of them (Ward, Bochner & Furnham 2001:166). Although there were some complaints about the academic content and, perhaps, intellectual rigor of academic study in particular areas of the Partnership program, there were no complaints regarding the manner in which the teaching was approached. In fact, the participants were more apt to praise specific professors and to refer to the effort to forge a connection among their service, academic work, and experience in the community.

Longitudinal studies can be matched with the experience of these students—following the psychological and sociological adaptation of students during their entire stay abroad. These show that problems encountered in the beginning of the stay diminish over time, that few if any students anticipate difficulties on return, but that many have problems after they return home. These students showed similar patterns (Ward, Bochner & Furnham 2001:167). Their reentry is explored at greater length below.

Shreela laid out the whole process of adaptation when she said she knew she was nervous about getting along with people and being on her own when she arrived. She knew she had been staying in a comfort zone, eliminating contact with anyone new prior to her departure for India:

> I had become so closed because I was so involved in my research. . . . keeping to my own circle of friends . . . and then it was like they threw me into the lion's den. I did my best to adjust but it wasn't easy at first. I was getting homesick just missing people. And then you question all these things about yourself too, like, gosh, I need to be a little stronger . . . I can't be so dependent on everybody, want e-mails all the time. But you know I think I was able to adjust in terms of the learning curve.[3] I think as I became closer to the teachers and the friends that I made on the program, then I started feeling more like home. And then it made it a lot easier to study and to learn things, just becoming more engaged. My classmates became more engaged too. You know when we stopped talking so much about ourselves or the things we didn't like, like the weather or the mosquitoes, and started talking more about what we were learning and reflected on our experiences, it started becoming more meaningful. But I think the first couple of weeks was hard because you're talking about things you never talk about. You're testing yourself in ways you've never tested yourself in terms of your own character and your own inner resilience and ability to stand certain things.

In the end, did they experience culture shock? Probably, but they were able to deal with their frustrations and adapt well enough to get along effectively in the culture, make friends, and return home to be "shocked" again.

### Reentry to "Home"

Reentry was discussed during the individual interviews but also in a focus group of four additional people. The comments here reflect the

---

[3] She had not heard of the U-curve of adjustment but described it very well, calling it a learning curve, which is exactly what it is.

inclusion of these additional individuals. It is my contention, shared by many of my colleagues, that reentry is the hardest and, for learning, the most productive time of study or, indeed, any stay abroad. It takes the complete cycle of departure/sojourn/return to solidify the learning. This realization lay behind David's observation that he had just reached an important realization about Jamaican culture: among artists in Jamaica "you don't see a clear-cut separation between their work and the other components of their lives." Everything, from the mundane to the philosophical, is connected. That different dimensions of life are interconnected, rather than disconnected, was a profound discovery for him, raised in and accustomed to a culture that compartmentalizes.

This sense of interconnectedness may not be reserved only for Jamaica but David did not grasp the ramifications of that way of life until recently. Elizabeth said something similar about connectedness in American-Indian society, an idea she captured on site. Without the theoretical background for discriminating between high and low context and collective and individualistic cultures, none of these alumni could put a theoretical framework around these discoveries. The important point here is that the learning continues long after their return.

When asked how the return was for them, they were almost uniformly certain that it was the most difficult aspect of the entire program. Bill said he definitely experienced culture shock on return, although he had none in Mexico. He went through a long period of working in Spanish restaurants in the Dallas-Fort Worth areas, letting his hair grow, and being careless about his appearance. This earned him a reputation that he did not particularly like, but it was part of trying to figure out how to fit back in at home. It took him a long time to find his niche.

Laurel said she was overwhelmed by so many white people. At a deeper level, she noticed that poverty seemed to be different in the United States: it was an individual experience. In India, the poor still had cohesive families. She felt the poor in the United States suffered emotional as well as economic poverty.

Tamara noted that her return was fine, in the short run, but after a week or so she was ready to return to England. She felt she needed to make sure everyone was all right at home and then she was ready to go away again. At first, Emily was elated to see her family, but then she was repelled by the materialism in the United States.

Shreela said she was frightened:

I felt like everyone would look at me and know that I was different. . . . you wonder, do they know I've been in India for six months? . . . You wonder, where am I, how am I going to fit back in; and you miss the food and the lifestyle in India. . . . You know even around my own family I was—I didn't feel the same, but you kind of have to like give it some time and allow yourself to assimilate into *that role that you want.* Or even if you don't right away, it will happen eventually.

Anita said, "I know that when Ecuador ended there was a lot of heartbreak. We were really close. I was really close to a lot of people. . . . But you know I was probably ready to come home. I was probably more concerned about what it was going to be like to go back to my roots." And then she came home to the news that her father could not support her during her senior year and that medical school was out. She focused on getting as much credit as possible for her studies in Latin America and finishing in one semester.

Elizabeth remembered that going back was hard. Her return to South Dakota State University after a long time in the field was a kind of culture shock. Going back to her regular college was not as difficult because friends had a lot of questions and were interested in her experience and that made her feel good. Going home was good too: she had a new appreciation for her family, so being able to spend time with them and to explore her family history was a pleasure. Mary used the skills she had employed going into the new culture in negotiating her return, and that was most effective in easing her reentry but also in connecting her American-Indian and non-American-Indian life. She became even more aware, however, of the huge division between Native American Indian and non-Indian communities.

On coming back, David definitely felt some culture shock. At first, it was nice to see his friends: "I was a pretty good letter writer. . . . We still had an affinity because we had similar interests in social justice and change." He was frustrated because it was difficult to keep in touch with people in Jamaica after his return to the States. And it became clear that, although he had an affinity for his friends, they did not fully understand his experience: "My perspective would be a little bit deeper—not that I am necessarily deeper than them but my belief in the idea of culture, that it's really culture that shapes what people do and how they think," was not really understood by his friends.

In general, the reactions of these alumni to returning home is not unusual. Rarely do students (or anyone else) expect to have difficulty returning, and so it is interesting that some of these former students were apprehensive about their return before it happened. The return proved harder than they anticipated, and all of them are still working through their reentry in some way. Reentry tends to be a lifetime event, with a continuing impact: there will always be a "before" and an "after" to the time when they were in another culture. The intense time for dealing with what has come to be called "reverse culture shock" is relatively brief and can occur very quickly. Tamara was ready to go back to London after two weeks. Elizabeth was glad she was in her last semester and would be leaving college soon, although she thoroughly enjoyed her time there. Shreela began to find new ways to relate to and appreciate her parents and set aside her medical studies for a year to stay at home as her mother endured terminal cancer. She also became the interpreter for her younger siblings, helping them understand their parents.

Keeping in touch with people in the host country was indeed an issue, one John brought up quickly. All of the four interviewees have managed to keep in touch. David brought several artists to the US to perform, Anita went back to visit Ecuador for a month and experienced a hard reentry there; it was on that visit that she realized she could not remain in Latin America indefinitely because the cultural differences were so great, and she would be too uncomfortable. Shreela stays in touch with relatives in India, of course, and feels that these relationships are much more meaningful than before her stay there. Elizabeth is working at the agency where she did her service.

Considering the reentry styles (Pusch 1998) of these former students, it becomes apparent that they have found ways to include the Partnership, as well as other experiences abroad, into their lives. Elizabeth, David, Tamara and Laurel accomplished a positive readaptation. They found the best fit between the home culture and the people they became; they continue to change and develop. They keep in touch with world issues and have definite opinions about them. Anita tends toward "detachment" as she carves a life for herself that is comfortable and professionally satisfying, and continues her connections with Latin culture and peoples but keeps some distance between herself and her home culture. Bill came back a "free sprit," somewhat estranged from his home culture, anxious to continue the experience of living in a foreign culture, and behaving in unique ways as he searched for a way to fit in. Eventually, as a Spanish teacher, he was able to integrate the experience, but, as we have seen, it took a while for him to find his niche.

Reentry styles may be phases of settling back into the home culture or a relatively permanent response to the experience of living in another culture. It seems that, for most of the alumni interviewed, the Partnership experience contributed to or had a significant impact on the decisions they made on profession or lifestyle and brought them to some realization of their next life steps. Clearly, Tamara, Bill, Elizabeth and Anita found their career direction through service-learning.

## What was Gained: The Impact of the Partnership on the Lives of Four People

Elizabeth exhibits qualities of integration both in reentry styles and in terms of the DMIS. Having come back from the reservation, she chose to return to it. Strange as it may seem, this is a very adaptive style of integrating the foreign and home experience. The friendships she had developed with her supervisor and with an elder and spiritual advisor were instrumental in her return to the reservation. They made her feel she had friends there. Secondly, she discovered "that this was a place to learn things that I can't learn from books or anywhere else . . . and then there is my interest in environmental issues." There is an alliance between tribal nations and environmental groups that is relatively new and promising. Right now she is learning a lot.

Thus Elizabeth is moving between two distinctly different worlds, and she feels she is "finally getting better at doing [it] and it doesn't seem like juggling, you know. And it's like it is one world and here we all are." Going back to the non-Indian world seems refreshing: there are lots of things she misses when she is on the reservation, "But it's all different. You know, different things are talked about out here [in the non-Indian environment] than there [on the reservation]. And those had been important to me before, so I appreciate that." Her ability to flow between the two worlds is remarkable: she functions with a personal style that is clearly influenced by both, and she exhibits all the qualities of a constructive marginal. One difference that she notices between being on the reservation and being at home is the reverence for life that she has discovered with the Lakota and which has changed and enriched her: "It is spiritual, everything is sort of infused with spirit." This discovery has given her a new perspective on people outside the community. She did not grow up with this understanding and she fears she was a little critical of her family about their lack of spirituality when she returned home. Elizabeth constantly talks about learning—the ways she is learning, how much she is learning, and how important it is to learn. This applies to her exploration of spirituality as much as it applies to land-use customs and the present-day threats to the well-being of the Lakota.

Anita is also very focused, this time on her job, her new home, and relationships. She does not watch television, read newspapers or use Internet—she says she cannot afford them. It is hard to know if her detachment from the "larger" world is recent or started with her serious childhood illness and was influenced by the loss of support for her education. She continually talks of having to focus on "the here and the now." Anita entered her career (she calls it accidental) with some reluctance but has discovered that her work with the handicapped involves enough clinical work to satisfy her urge to practice medicine. Her experience with the Partnership service placement, much as she tried to change it, has proved to be invaluable. Her career choice was certainly influenced by her time in Ecuador. Her attachment to the cultures and peoples of Latin America have not diminished, but a return visit to Ecuador made it clear that she could not live there permanently. She "tends to be rather punctual, efficient, likes to get things done, and has a hard time waiting around." However, she is extremely patient and has found ways to participate socially in Latin activities and maintain relationships with people from Latin countries while keeping her life in order.

David was always committed to anthropology, so his career choice did not change as a result of the Partnership experience. Yet his time and ties in Jamaica continue to influence his life: he is now completing his doctoral dissertation in anthropology, and the subjects of his research are two Jamaican artists.

Shreela will start medical school soon, after the delay to be with her mother. She says she learned that you must "take charge of your own life and realize that in the end you define who you want to be and what you want to do with your life and your skills. . . . then you can keep your spirituality, you know." As the oldest of three children, she has been able to steer her siblings into understanding their background and their parents more clearly—an important factor as they came to terms with the loss of their mother. She is grateful that the Partnership program helped her understand her heritage, bringing her much closer to her mother than might otherwise have been possible: she would not have been able to understand Hindu practices or even how to approach the funeral ceremony. In effect, she learned the lessons her mother had been taught, and those lessons will stay with her and allow her to fulfill her own dreams, hard as this might be. At the time of the interview, she was still grieving, so the impact of the study in India on family relations overshadowed everything. Her career choice has been affected as well: she will be going into patient-centered medicine rather than research.

## Conclusions

Memories, some more than a decade old, are often unreliable resources in evaluating study abroad, or indeed any other, experience. This was especially true with regard to recalling the experience of transition to a new culture, labeled somewhat inaccurately as "culture shock." The period of culture shock is only one part of the full transition process. Given that most of the complaints from the alumni were associated with their service placements, it appears that this may have a connection with reaching the transition point where frustration rules. Anita was a prime, and perhaps an extreme, example: she was probably in serious culture shock during her attempts to get her service assignment changed: she would not have labeled it as such, but it bears all the signs. She remembers the period vividly, and it continues to be an issue for her.

Nearly every one of the interviewees echoed Anita's sentiment in asserting that placement was the most frustrating issue. It makes sense that symptoms of culture shock would emerge in the context of the service portion of the program. It is here that students have the most contact with the local culture and the most difficulty in decoding and adapting to it. Instead of recognizing their discomfort and their demands for change, for more structure, and for assistance as culture shock, the students tended to blame the agencies for being disorganized, unable to use their skills appropriately, or provide them with meaningful work. This discomfort translated into a lack of belief in the value of their contribution and to a feeling that they had no substantive impact on the clients they were serving. It would be useful to train program directors more extensively to recognize signs of culture shock so that they could offer the support needed to make this period less painful by turning it into a learning experience rather than a matter of survival.

Ultimately, however, the students found the service a crucial part of their learning and, when they had either discovered a way or simply endured long enough to feel useful, they found a great deal of satisfaction in the service experience. This indicates that they went through a process of adaptation and culture learning that resulted in a realistic view of the culture, and an ability to function in it, coupled with a greater sense of usefulness. They continue, however, to express their dissatisfaction about their inability to make a lasting and significant contribution to the welfare of the agency clients. An example of support that avoided this kind of free fall into culture shock is Elizabeth's experience at the Standing Rock Reservation. It is hard to say if this was a fortuitous meeting of sensitive individuals or simply a Lakota way of drawing people into a situation that is enormously effective— it may be a combination of both. It would be interesting to compare the experiences of students in similar service situations to determine if there is a pattern of orientation and inclusion that can be attributed to culture.

The inability of the Partnership program participants see the long-term impact of the program and their part in it deserves attention. The contribution of the students in the programs has been eloquently expressed by Victor Maridueña, a Partnership trustee and former director of service agencies in Ecuador, who points to the constant presence of students, year after year, doing small things that mean something to the people with whom they work, making a difference if only by demonstrating that there is a group of people who care. It is the continual presence of Partnership volunteers, not the specific contribution of one individual, that has a lasting and profound impact within the agencies and on the clients.

Signs of culture shock may also be apparent in complaints about academic study. This group had so few complaints about the academic side of the program that it was difficult to see it as a culture shock issue. Again, Anita expressed her dissatisfaction with the academic rigor of the program but quickly noted her resistance to doing the assigned work; her dissatisfaction with her placement perhaps leaked into the academic side of the program. Elizabeth was largely critical of the distance-learning component in her studies and the impediments to discussing with faculty and other program participants how to connect theory with practice. This is inherent in a program whose university and living/serving sites are distant from one another. Otherwise, there was little dissatisfaction with academics.

Reentry, on the other hand, is still an immediate memory because it is a longer-term process for most people. Reentry tends to be a very individual and life-long experience, unlike culture shock, a recognized phenomenon whose symptoms are widely known, although they often go unrecognized by the person in the shock phase of transition (Pusch 2001). Also, it is relatively easy to discover the influence of living abroad in the life of the returnee. Those who return recognize their own change and the impact of other culture experience in their career choices, relationships, attitudes, and assessment of social, political, and economic conditions and events. Their evaluation of these conditions and events reveals new patterns of thinking, critiquing, and reaching judgments. It is clear that the Partnership in general and the service-learning process in particular had an impact on the lives of these former students, but their greatest problem was finding a way to process what they had learned on a continuing basis. Elizabeth was fortunate in having interested friends, in being able to use her skills in culture learning during the return, and, of course, in maintaining contact and returning to the reservation. She is in a constant state of entry and reentry and has learned not only to manage this process but to connect her two worlds. David has been somewhat successful in keeping the experience fresh through continuing contact by means of his dissertation research. He states, however, that by constantly having new experiences with Jamaica, he has "layer upon layer of experience. . . . you can still see through, you see the top and somewhere you can still get through to the bottom."

Further examination of the reentry styles that each individual seems to employ may or may not be useful to the Partnership. It may be enough to know that there is no one pattern and that one cannot expect the same outcome for all students. There is no point in striving for a uniform reentry response.

It is clear that Partnership students become more ethnorelative and some do so at a very sophisticated level. While I have hesitated to label anyone a "constructive marginal," it is possible that Elizabeth and, perhaps, David have reached this state. They are both still actively engaged with the host culture and seem able to live in "dynamic inbetweenness" (Yoshikawa 1987), to flow between cultures, to interpret one to the other, and to be content in both. It would be interesting for the Partnership to begin documenting, using the Intercultural Development Inventory instrument, students pre- and post-program to determine the degree of change that occurs as a result of international service-learning. As noted in the beginning of this report, Partnership students seem to be exceptional in their commitment to and past experience with civic responsibility and may come into the program at a higher level than would be expected of most study-abroad students. Thus, the increase in their *level* of sensitivity and intercultural competence may be less dramatic, but the degree of sophistication achieved may be markedly higher.

In conclusion, it is clear that service-learning as practiced by the Partnership in a "foreign" culture context has a significant impact on the lives of its students in terms of personal and professional development and certainly in terms of intercultural competence and learning. While their commitment to service may be what draws them into the program in the beginning, they clearly become more capable of working with a diverse clientele and delivering service under less than ideal conditions during the program. This capability is useful in many situations, both domestic and international, and we have every reason to believe that they have acquired not only intercultural and organizational skills but the ability to be leaders in whatever they chose to do. Leadership was not specifically explored in my interviews, and I suspect the interviewees would deny being leaders, but they clearly exhibited the ability to take charge of their own experience, find ways to fit into the agencies they served, and develop patterns of service that demonstrated leadership qualities and the potential for leadership roles in professional and community work and organizations.

# 6 Beyond the Comfort Zone

Diego Quiroga

The gathering in New York on April 5, 2003, created an opportunity for alumni to reflect on the different ways the service experience transformed their lives. This space for reflection allowed the attendees to rethink their experiences, narrate their life history and process their memories in the company of other alumni who shared similar experiences. For many, the event presented an opportunity to generate new meanings out of occurrences in their past and to discuss an experience that all saw as an important turning-point in their lives. In this report, I will look at common patterns and trends that came out of the gathering, and the reflections that it generated, in an effort to identify the strengths and weaknesses of the program and suggest changes.

## The Service

The most important and distinctive aspect of the service-learning experience and the main difference between this experience and other exchange programs is the service component. Alumni commented that the service experience was not always easy and agreed that they felt a degree of frustration during their volunteer work. They were frustrated with the language differences, with what they perceived as the lack of organization within the agency and with the pace at which things moved. Most students thought, however, that the agencies were making tremendous efforts to maintain the level of support they provided given the limited resources they had. Many students felt that they learned a lot about the ways in which people can be creative and effective, despite their financial limitations.

Many alumni felt that their experience in the agency transformed their conception of service and their understanding of what it truly means to help others. The ways this service was understood varied from one student to the next. In some cases service was considered to be a religious calling, whereas in other cases, it was more a matter of personal duty. Some of the alumni thought that it was important to make a distinction between service-learning and other types of "charitable" activities, and that their service helped them understand the difference between help on the one hand and social development on the other. They mentioned that the combination of service and learning allowed them to contextualize good service as related to development and empowerment, and they contrasted that with charity.

One of the most valuable aspects of the service experience, emphasized by many, was the fact that service helped the students recognize the limits of their ability to effect change in complex situations. The structures and systems that students encounter in their service work represent enormous challenges that they must be able to face and successfully manage. Students recognized that their agencies were often understaffed, underfunded and disorganized. These problems seemed overwhelming at first, but the very lack of recognizable structure and available resources paradoxically created a uniquely instructive environment, since the challenges that it presented also opened possibilities.

When asked about the impact of their work for their agencies, some students commented that they wished there were more continuity in the agencies so that they could feel they were actually generating some kind of change through their service. At the same time, some also felt that it was unrealistic for students to think a serious impact could be achieved in such a short time. It was better, they thought, to recognize the limitations of what can be accomplished given their experience and the length of their stay and thus learn from the situation. For these individuals an important aspect of personal growth was the fact that they learned about their limitations and shaped their expectations. One student thought that by being in their agencies in a different culture they could understand why many of the solutions that local people have developed are the best given the cultural, political and economic context.

A much-repeated sentiment was the development of a strong sense of commitment and a certain fellow-feeling with people in a distant country. We are so often encouraged to think globally and act locally that we forget the importance of global action too. Many participants commented on the fact that the service component generates a sense of involvement with a situation that before was foreign and distant, a globalization of their feelings and concerns and of their sense of citizenship. This deterritorialization of social commitments and globalization of sensibilities was often reflected in the way students talked about world issues and current politics. It was one of the most striking features of the participants' comments. Many alumni felt a certain link to the place where they served that lasted well beyond the duration of the program. In some cases alumni felt a need to go back to the place where they had served or to other places that they felt had pressing needs.

These returns were not always happy ones; some of the students who went back to visit their agency felt that the place had not improved. For Shreela, who went to India, going back was a sad experience, as she was concerned that the situation of the people she was working with would never improve in the agency where she had been working. She commented that in her agency the conditions were poor because it was so tightly institutional, and she hoped that the agency leaders might relax some of their policies. In many cases, however, students were pleasantly surprised to see that the place where they had been working had indeed improved.

Relationships between the students and the agencies in many cases are maintained over time. I know from my experience in Ecuador that former students many times return to their agencies and contribute their time, or on occasion contribute financially. Despite the important differences in material wealth between them and the poor people in the country, some students, such as Elizabeth, said that they learned about the common humanity shared by people around the globe. Elizabeth added that through her experience she learned how to maintain a dialogue with people and discover similarities and commonalities. The Partnership program helped people understand common concerns. In an ever more globalized world the creation of worldwide service networks might be an important consequence of programs such as that of the Partnership. The transformation of the sensibility of alumni is an important step in that direction.

## Different Cultures, Different Experiences

In the service-learning experience the flexible and loose structure that constitutes our cultural symbolic system is negotiated through the journey to different cultural spaces. These encounters with the other constitute instances of learning and challenges to our cultural centricity. It is during such encounters with the unfamiliar that the familiar is questioned and reexamined and our sense of commonality is reevaluated.

Elizabeth's comments should be read in the context of one of the most unsettling aspects of participants' experience, namely their confrontation with a very different type of social reality where people's lack of formal education and material resources generated a significant cultural distance. As David pointed out in his interview, there are many different negotiations going on during service. These negotiations involve sorting out cultural differences between the students and host parents, the community, the agency, and fellow students. The negotiation of different cultural codes and predispositions comes from the constant interaction between students and the host families, their classmates and the agencies. Such interactions generate an environment of symbolic reflection. It is difficult to think of other situations where students can be involved in such diverse arenas of intercultural negotiations and in such a profound manner as are the Partnership students. Courtney, who had also engaged in conventional study abroad, compared her experience with international service-learning and commented that the Partnership experience provided opportunities to explore the value systems of the target country, an opportunity missing in many study-abroad programs.

Nonetheless, as with conventional study abroad, quite mundane experiences were often among the most important in giving the participants a sense of empowerment and in rising to the challenges inherent in a different culture: being able to use a foreign language, traveling on a bus each day to get to work in an agency, controlling a classroom full of teenagers—and, of course, feeling wanted and needed by an agency.

Some participants talked about the sheer range of their interactions during the Partnership semester—from their contacts with the universities and their host families, who often tend to be from the wealthier sectors of society, to their experiences with the least affluent in the agencies. They pointed out that the academic work that they did in the classroom was vital in allowing them to contextualize and understand their cultural interactions within a more general theoretical framework.

## Leaving the Comfort Zone

The comfort zone is construed by many of the alumni as a space of safety, control and material wellbeing. This construct is generated, reinforced and at the same time transformed through their journey. Such a construct is based on a dualism between the familiar and ordered and the foreign, unfamiliar and uncontrollable. Anthropologist Victor Turner (1974) talks about liminal stages of rituals as those moments in which reversal and antistructure create the opportunity for growth and transformation. Turner's idea of liminality can help us understand the service-learning experience and how it represents a journey to a zone where reversals and inversions can be part of the growing process of students. Such journeys cause worries and fears for the students and their families, and these worries and fears are in part based on the understanding of how the world works.

Participants alluded to some of the positive and negative aspects of leaving the comfort zone. The journey forced many to question various aspects of their culture, such as consumerism, individualism and the linear understanding of progress and success. At the same time that it is a moment of cultural criticism, the liminal experience usually serves to reestablish and consolidate a sense of identity as one's culture is not only questioned but also partially reaffirmed. Gender and racial equality were among the aspects of the liberal discourse that seem to be reinforced. But even when it comes to these basic beliefs, liminality is a reflected reaffirmation, and the service-learning experience apparently transformed participants' understanding of what constitutes equality. Thus a student who went to India expressed the belief that women were actually treated better than in the West: in India roles were better defined and women did not have to do double work as in the West, gender equality must be contextualized.

Particularly disturbing for the students was their confrontation with poverty; they seemed eager to address the question in our sessions and were voluble in their interventions. It was not only the lack of material wealth that they found upsetting but also the way it was understood, transformed, managed and even denied. Many students were in constant contact with poverty in their work and in the agencies, causing them to compare the way in which wealth and poverty are lived and experienced in several cultures. Some who had experienced poverty in the US thought that one of the main differences between developing countries and the United States was the way in which family structure in the developing world helps people deal with scarcity. Although the poor in India or Ecuador might at first seem worst off than in the United States, some agreed that solitude and isolation might mean that the poor in the United States feel more desperate. Social support networks and family structures, they felt, serve to transform the experience of poverty so that it is felt not as a sense of hopelessness and anxiety, but with a certain sense of opportunity and support. Such experiences made them question conventional definitions of poverty based solely in material concerns.

Many students mentioned the fact that one of the most important aspects of their living and serving in a different country was their questioning of their long-established dualism between Us and the Other. The portrayal of the other as dangerous and threatening was an issue that many students felt they had to confront critically during their service experience. Students were surprised to hear that in other countries there was concern about violence and insecurity in the United States. During the Columbine killings, for instance, people suggested to Shreela that she remain in India because going back to the United States would be too dangerous. She was surprised to hear people wondering what was wrong with her country. Cities in the United States, some students learned, are considered by many people in foreign countries to be dangerous and threatening. They were of course aware that not all of the threats are products of the imagination and the mass media. Thus their journey made them reverse the sense of center and periphery and question the all-too-easy duality of Us and Other.


## Being an American, and American Culture

We have already noted the view of many participants that one of the most important aspects of leaving one's comfort zone involves interrogating one's most basic and valued cultural constructs. National identity was one of the foundational cultural constructs that students addressed. Most participants did not feel that being an American while studying and working abroad was a significant problem: Americans were well regarded and, in general, they said that they were treated fairly. Nevertheless, they did find that their experiences caused them to question their national pride and identity and to confront their ethnocentrism. Some of the values that the alumni felt were basic to their cultural system, such as consumerism and individualism, were reexamined and reevaluated.

One of the differences noticed by students had to do with the way tasks are ordered and organized. In the agencies there was a very different idea of how to manage resources and time. One of the alumni mentioned that "in America we are taught to get better." By becoming distanced and critical of these predispositions, the service-learning experience helped construct a new model of how to be a young American. Alumni frequently mentioned the value of communal solidarity, sharing and reciprocity. For many, the chance to experience such contrasting social environments constitutes an important learning process, as it provides an understanding of alternative value systems.

The sense of nationality and the construction of an imagined community is an aspect of our identity that is deeply engrained and based on primordial emotions. This sense of national identity is often challenged when one lives in a different country, and particularly in the context of a service-learning experience. The almost blind admiration that people in many countries feel for Americans and American culture was, for many, problematic and bothersome. Blind admiration, like blind hate, they noted, comes from lack of understanding and real knowledge of a culture. Unfortunately, the two often coexist. I have noticed among my current Partnership students in Ecuador that the new international tensions make it difficult for them to deal with being American. During times of international crisis, there is a tense and ambiguous relation to Americans and American culture in some of the countries where the Partnership has programs. Marie encountered anti-American sentiments when she was doing her service in Manila. After September 11th, the United States was training the military of the Philippines in Mindanao, and she was able to talk about her ideas and express her opinions. Although her parents are from the Philippines, people knew that she was an American and assumed wrongly that she was in favor of the American military. She noticed how people treated her differently once they learned her real position. A similar situation occurred with the Partnership students who took my ethnography class during the start of the war on Iraq. The cognitive dissonance that is created by these types of experiences generates tensions that motivate reflection: observing the effects of the policies and practices of one's own country from abroad generates an external and reflective gaze, which most students never obtain. This effect of traveling is even more acute in the case of service-learning students, since in their work in the agencies their perspective is often constructed in close interaction with those who are adversely affected directly or indirectly by international policies and practices.

One of the reflections that their experience generated and that was mentioned by several alumni was the fact that they could see that people abroad were not judging them on the basis of the actions of their government. This capacity to separate a citizen from his government was something, according to Bill, that was not always true in the case of people who live in the United States, who tend to identify people from a particular country with the policies of that country. Some felt that their experience abroad helped them differentiate the two.

## Reentry

If the move from home institution to study and service in a foreign location is jarring to the sensibilities and challenging to students' ability to adapt, it will come as no surprise to learn that it is the re-entry process that students see as the most difficult, after so radical a challenge to their values and their sense of personal priorities. For many, coming back was more difficult than leaving. Leaving the United States to embark on a semester of service was challenging and inspiring, and for some it was a way of giving their lives as students a sense of direction. A variable in any study of the process of departure and return should surely be a student's frame of mind before departure: several participants felt disengaged and alienated and were seeking a challenge. Having met that challenge, they were perhaps lulled into a false sense of security. As our colleague Margaret Pusch points out, "Problems encountered in the beginning of the stay diminish over time," and "few if any students anticipate difficulties on return." And this was so: participants felt they were not prepared for the experience of reentry and that they had little or no opportunity to talk about and process their feelings, their memories and their new understandings.

Bill told us that when he came back, reluctantly, from Mexico he had long hair and a beard. When his family saw him they did not recognize him. He said that he did not experience culture shock when he departed, but he did when he came back. He was surprised that his friends and family judged him on the basis of his appearance, but he realized that before he had gone to Mexico, he would have done the same thing. He believes that now he is more tolerant of diversity. He was distressed on his return by his family's emphasis on consumerism and the accumulation of material objects: in Mexico he lived with very few material things and learned that many of the so-called essentials were really not so important.

Like Bill, several other participants thought that consumerism was one of the most problematic and difficult issues they had to deal with on returning home. The fact that they had been living with very little, and helping people who had great needs and very few resources made them very critical of what they perceived as unnecessary luxuries. Others were less bothered by such differences and thought that each culture and situation has its particularities. Despite their difficulties, many were glad to return and noted that their stay abroad helped reinforce some of the things they liked about being back. As one of the students noted, "When I came back I was glad to be back. I like Wal-Mart."

In addition to the issue of poverty and wealth, necessity and luxury, participants mentioned several other challenges they faced on return: they could not find people with whom they could share their experiences, they felt cut off from the fate of those they had worked with, they had difficulty contextualizing their experiences in their new reality. In addition to proposing some changes in the Partnership to deal with this issue, several participants remarked that they jumped at the chance to come to New York to talk to people who had gone through the process and to analyze their common experiences. Some had waited years for this opportunity to share experiences. The face-to-face contact with people to whom "they do not have to explain what they went through" was a way to reevaluate the impact and meaning of the Partnership experience and to relate it to their professional and personal development.

Some participants suggested that the Partnership might usefully have its own reentry counselor. The creation of an active alumni association could be helpful by providing a space where students could find a support network and mechanisms to keep in touch with their agencies, to reevaluate their experiences with people who have gone through the same process and to contextualize their learning.

For two students the experience meant going back to their place of origin. It helped Marie, a Filipino American, reformulate her identity. She enjoyed learning more about the language and history of her parents' country, and this discovery made her decide to get a job teaching Filipino children in California. Shreela's time in India helped her understand her parents and their perspectives. Each of them felt that going back to the country of her parents was an important part of her personal growth and a way of learning more about her origins.

## Career choice

The narratives that alumni create about their past order their memories in light of an expected future. In that sense, their autobiographical analysis in New York should be seen not as a "true" account of the past, but rather as a way of making sense of the present by organizing their memories of their service in a meaningful way. The experience changed different participants in different ways. In some cases, the experience was perceived to have had a profound effect on their career choices: they construed it as a "turning point" and mapped their experiences in terms of after and before. Theirs in many ways was a liminal experience and, as with other liminal experiences, it reversed social positions, status and roles. Asked to help people who were old and incapacitated, they reversed ethnic, social and class structures. Such was the case of Tamara, who came to college as an African-American scholarship girl from the South; she said that she became a physician because of her service experience in London. Her interaction with the sick in hospitals in the UK made her decide to spend her life helping others as a physician.

Tamara construed the impact of her service experience on career choice as direct cause and effect, but for others the impact was less direct. Participants now employed in education or in the service sector said that they were already largely decided when they went on the Partnership program, and the experience reinforced their resolve. Bill knew that he did not want a corporate career. He described himself as an idealist and that was why he was now a teacher. He felt that although the experience did not change his life, it set him on a particular track. When he returned to New York his only concern was to discover how he could make a contribution. Gabriel, now a law student, said that his interest in law had to do with integrating service and the law. He was very enthusiastic about working for the poor: "Other programs I have done may not recognize the importance of personal contact; that is why I chose law—because I could provide a service to people." He believes that law will give him the power needed to improve people's situation. David was working for a Ph.D. in anthropology and was bothered by the overly theoretical nature of his studies: he wanted to be more involved in hands-on, applied work. Ashley, who is now working in an international relief agency, said that her life might not have been as difficult without the Partnership experience, but also not as fulfilling: without the Partnership, she would have gone into a less service-oriented aspect of international service. Had she done that, she now thinks she would have felt that she was missing an important part of her experience.

For Jeanne the partnership confirmed an interest in anthropology and in Latin America. While Shreela's interest in medicine was confirmed, she realized that she wanted to be a physician rather than a medical researcher: the Partnership stimulated her interest in empowering people with disabilities and in one-on-one contact with the disabled. Through her work with the Lakota Nation in South Dakota, Elizabeth became interested in legal aspects of American Indian territorial rights and decided that she wanted to pursue these interests in her career. As with several other students in the group, her learning and understanding allowed her to break through the enduring dualisms of the traditional education system and connect the local and the global, the conceptual and the practical.

For all these students, expectations of future education and employment seem to have been shaped in important ways by their service-learning experience. They stressed the need for a certain bi-dimensionality, mirroring the Partnership model: in the same way that an exchange program based on traditional classroom experience would not have been complete for them, they also thought that a job based only on office or academic work would be too removed, while one that was involved only in service and hands-on activities would probably not be reflective enough.

The experience, in the case of many participants, shaped and transformed not only their values but also their expectations and needs. Some compared the experience in their agency to a drug that you get hooked on. For some it created a need to leave the United States occasionally and to experience other countries, while others felt a need to be involved in some kind of social service, or meaningful work that might lead to an improvement in people's lives.

The combination of academic work and work in the local agencies was an important catalytic experience for many of the alumni. The combination was empowering because it helped them put into practice in a challenging manner the ideas and concepts learned in class. But for some the appeal went further. Feeling that service combining academic reflection with practical work is appealing and congenial, they organize their present interests and their expectations of the future on the basis of the Partnership experience. The service component became a metaphor that later guided what they considered to be a proper and significant blending of service and academia or service and office work.

For many participants the experience also meant that they now feel a need to engage in social service. Some are now involved in community work through their jobs. Some said that they feel that their present work is not as oriented toward service as they would like it to be. Even for this last group, who are not as actively involved in service as the others, service-learning has created a need to be more involved with service and community work.

One important transformation that many students thought was the result of the service-learning experience is the need that they consider that it created in them to be involved in activities that they find meaningful. Most of them are critical of a search for purely material rewards and value activities that have a lasting impact in the communities. For some that meant going to a different country to help with development projects where as in other cases it meant looking at activities at home that they feel will have an impact on the more vulnerable sectors of the American society.

For some, growth and maturity came from the fact that their experiences helped them reconsider their own personal values. Courtney compared her experience with service-learning to her participation in other programs abroad and found that many other situations offered no possibility of exploring the value systems of the people she visited. Sometimes the most powerful effects of service-learning came from some of its most mundane aspects: being able to use a foreign language, to catch a bus, or to control a classroom full of teenagers, generated in the students a sense of achievement and empowerment.

## Improving the Program

Many of the suggestions made by participants about ways to improve the program need not concern us here, but three do merit consideration in the context of this article. The first was the question of communication following students' return. Could the establishment of Internet networks help ease the transition back into the mainstream culture of the United

States? Could such communication be used to create a more permanent and meaningful impact on the agencies? Could it be used to bring alumni (from different countries and different years) into contact with students enrolling in Partnership programs before their departure? We might expect this group of students, invited as they were to comment on their experiences, to show solicitude for their agencies and for future students, but the depth of their commitment and willingness to involve themselves seemed unusual: service to agencies might be broadened to include service to the Partnership itself.

Participants also spoke about the need to involve more students in the Partnership and similar programs. Some proposed that more programs be established in the United States for students from other countries, and others stressed the need to integrate service-learning in general into the curriculum in higher education. Some resurrected the original dream of the Partnership, and one that seems to be returning to the agenda, namely the creation of a worldwide network of exchange programs in service-learning with a fully international clientele.

A third and more central issue concerned perceived strengths and weaknesses in the program and mirrored similar debates among study-abroad officers about how much pre-departure information is enough, and how much support after arrival is required to assist students in adapting to their new settings. While there was some discussion about the need to give students and their professors a better idea of the nature of the pedagogical practices of the host country (often quite significantly different from the one students are used to), most attention fell on the service experience. Some participants felt that they needed better information on what to expect from the agency in advance of their arrival, and others spoke of the apparent lack of organization in placements and in the agencies themselves. While circumstances were very different from site to site, and while, as we have already observed, what at first appeared to be disorganization in the agencies often turned out to be differences in perception between student and agency, the question of what students need to know and what they should find out for themselves remained an important issue. If some recognized that these differences and the anxieties that they caused may have been to some extent the result of diverse cultural expectations, others argued that finding out where to catch the bus should not be left to students struggling with bigger and more complex cultural issues. As some participants pointed out, different students have different needs, and finding a balance between telling all and leaving all to the students is likely to vary from student to student and site to site. Structure does provide students who need it with a sense of direction and security, but at the same time a lack of structure allows for more freedom and creativity and can have the effect of giving students a sense of empowerment.

Despite all these inconveniences, many felt that over the longer run the perceived disorganization was not a problem but rather an advantage. Some felt that they would not have learned as much if the service had been more cut-and-dried. Jen mentioned that she had always liked to take risks and valued the Partnership because it gave her the freedom to do so. She felt that lack of information was good to a certain extent because it meant that she had to learn how to do things her own way: it created a sense of self-sufficiency and empowerment for her, reinforced by the fact that her work at the agency was flexible and not structure-bound. Students who went to Jamaica and Ecuador mentioned that they were surprised that after a while they were practically running their agencies despite the fact that they were only twenty years old. The experience developed leadership and initiative in them and forced them to be more organized. In some cases students tried to change procedures in the agencies and some of their ideas were taken into account and implemented—a process requiring not just good ideas but also negotiating skills in a different culture. One participant who worked in a center for adolescent girls described the time she spent in the library learning more about her subject and how, on the basis of this research, she proposed changes in the agency on her own initiative and they were accepted, to her considerable surprise. She told us that it was only then that she felt she could accomplish more.

Participants also pointed out that a strength of the program was the fact that when they had a question there was always someone to help, not least because their academic work was tied to their service and vice versa: classroom interaction was important in order to help them reflect on experiences during their service, and classrooms provided the students not only with a sense of direction and a means for contextualizing their experiences but also a critical support network. This process worked better for some students at some locations than for others, but all agreed that it ought to be a vital part of the Partnership experience.

## Conclusions

Evaluating international service-learning is not easy, for the effects and transformations that it generates in the students are long-lasting and in many cases not immediately obvious. Much of the process of evaluation was based on memories of events that in some cases occurred a decade ago. Memories are not faithful accounts of the past nor are they stable and accurate renditions of events that shape our life: they are dynamic constructs generated out of the past to find meaning in the present. In this sense the gathering in New York became a communal searching for new meanings in shared events long past, and a way of understanding present dispositions and needs in terms of this collective past.

In the process of looking at the past and at the service experience in light of their present activities we have seen that most alumni thought of it as an important and fundamental event, one which transformed them in different and significant ways. They asserted that service shaped or reaffirmed their ideas of what is meaningful and important, and for most it constituted a deep metaphor that guided their search for graduate education and jobs. As a liminal event, the experience of international service-learning generated reflection on, and interrogation of, some of the most enduring values of the participants' culture, such as identity and nationality, conceptions of gender and race, and ideas about time and progress.

Students thought that there were several ways in which the service-learning experience could be improved but there was disagreement as to whether there should be more or less structure. For some, structure helps make the experience more significant; for others a rigid structure stifles creativity. Perhaps the support system provided by the reflective portion of the experience is the best compromise between the two. Most of the participants found service to be an empowering experience in which they were able to face and to handle successfully difficult and at times frustrating challenges.

# 7  Making the Strange Familiar: Dealing with Ambiguity

## Michael J. Siegel

*It was almost like going into a wonderland or a place unknown. . . . imagine yourself standing in the center of some magnificent place—almost like I was standing there holding a little satchel or something—and then there's all this big world around me. That's kind of the way it felt. I knew no one. . . . I had no ties with anyone; there was no one that I could really talk to about things. For a moment it was...earth-shattering. "Where do I go," my mind racing. And then I had to come to grips with it—"Okay, calm down. Everything is going to be okay."*

—Tamara, International Partnership alumna, England

## Introduction

The purpose of the student impact study is to document and develop a better understanding of the effect of international service on students who have undertaken a service-learning experience through the International Partnership for Service-Learning and Leadership, an organization whose mission, in part, is to provide service-abroad experiences primarily for American college and university students around the world. The organization has had an enormous influence on the lives of the students who have utilized its services during the past twenty years, but evidence to support the claims is anecdotal at best, and scant at worst. The Partnership does have an extensive cache of written documents and materials—most notably student journals and other self-report data—that testify to the powerful nature of the service experience, but the information has not been organized in a meaningful way to provide evidence of discernible and verifiable patterns. The present study is a first step toward gaining a better understanding of student motivations and goals.

As noted in earlier chapters, individual interviews and group interviews were conducted during the course of a one-day visit, which lasted approximately nine hours and included individual interview and group interview sessions. Seventeen alumni of the Partnership program, representing a broad range of colleges and universities as well as international service-learning experiences, convened in New York City on April 5th, 2003, to participate in the interviews and focus groups. Both individual and group sessions were conducted by a team of four researchers assembled for the purpose. As one of these researchers, I was responsible for coordinating the logistics of the study, convening the group for conference calls, helping develop the question protocol for the interviews and focus groups, and planning sessions. Each of the four researchers conducted four successive individual interviews during the morning session and a series of group interviews during the afternoon session. We were fortunate as researchers and observers to be able to spend a full day with seventeen individuals on whose lives the Partnership had had a measurable influence. We were attempting not only to discern similarities in the experiences of the seventeen alumni who gathered in New York for the day but also to document their unique experiences.

To facilitate accurate information-gathering, interviews and focus groups were tape-recorded by mutual consent. All tapes of the individual interviews were transcribed following the event; all interviews were sent to all members of the four-person research team, who used them to conduct further analysis. Data from transcribed interviews were analyzed using an inductive process, whereby emerging themes, patterns of behavior, and categories were identified and developed using methods of categorization and unitization.

### Interview and Focus Group Protocol

As we have already noted, a question protocol to be used in the data gathering process was developed by the four research team members, in conjunction with the project director. The protocol was arranged around six major domains, which, taken together represented a broad range of intellectual, social, and cognitive areas relative to the international service experience. With input from the other three researchers, the coordinator drafted and prepared the questionnaire protocol (which was based on an original document provided by the project director). Questions were developed to address students' intellectual development, affective and moral development, definitions of service, cross-cultural awareness, social integration, and their assessment of the experience. Sample questions from each area include:

**Intellectual Development.** Describe any benefits to your thinking and reasoning that resulted from your Partnership experience (e.g., Was your ability to think sharpened? Has the experience advanced your critical thinking and reasoning skills?). To what do you attribute the changes?

**Affective and Moral Development.** Describe whether, and how much, the service experience heightened your sense of compassion, your sense of social justice, your awareness of the values of service without material reward, and spiritual awareness.

**Definitions of Service.** How (if at all) did the Partnership experience cause you to rethink the idea of service to the community? How have your notions of service, and more specifically international service, changed as a result of your experience?

**Cross-Cultural Awareness.** Describe changes in your cross-cultural awareness as a result of the Partnership experience. Talk about your awareness of not only different cultures but of differences of social class, political and economic organization, religion, etc.

**Social Integration.** Describe the extent to which the Partnership experience changed your attitudes towards friendship, authority, family, teachers, sexual attachments, sense of teamwork, etc. Describe the way in which your sense of yourself as a leader was strengthened weakened, redefined.

**Assessment of Experience.** What are the strengths of the Partnership and its experience? Weaknesses? Prospects for the future? Things that need fixing? What elements of your experience do you feel were unique to the Partnership program (e.g., benefits and experiences unique to Partnership experience that you would likely not receive from another program, etc.)?

The full text of the protocol is contained in chapter 4.

The participant interviews that form the basis of this paper were conducted in succession on the morning of April 5, 2003, at the offices of the Partnership. In addition, data collected from group interviews was utilized to supplement and complement the analysis. My interviewees were Bill, Jen, Laurel, and Tamara.

To ask people to reconstruct a historical event or experience is a tricky process. The questions that are intended to facilitate the process must necessarily be drafted in such a way as not to "lead the witness," as those in the legal profession might say. That is, the questions must be objective in nature, value-free, and not suggestive of some appropriate way to answer that might make the response more socially desirable to the research team. So efforts were made to develop a process that would allow the alumni to reflect on their service abroad and give them an opportunity to think critically about their experiences.

The basic methodology is explored in much greater detail elsewhere in this document, but a word here is in order. The team desired first to interview the alumni individually in the morning and then proceed to group discussions and focus groups in the afternoon. During the morning block of time we requested that the students avoid talking to one another about their individual interviews until all the interviews were complete; in that sense, we tried to avoid having one student's impressions and reflections color another student's before he or she had the opportunity to hear questions from the various members of the research team. In addition, we wanted students to know that we were not looking for any particular answer but were very interested in their open and honest reflection about their experience and how they interacted with the various structures and components of the process—the early interface with the Partnership, their placement and visit to the host site or country, and their return home.

This paper has two purposes. First, it will describe and examine the characteristics of this group of students who have participated in the Partnership during the past fifteen years. Second, it will document and describe the impact of the international service-learning experience on the participating students. Although the students I interviewed individually represent international service-learning in four different countries—Ecuador, England, India, and Mexico—and during four different time periods—1988, 1992, 1994, and 1999—the experiences were similar in many ways.

## Emerging Themes

Transcripts and notes from the individual student and focus group interviews were analyzed; from multiple sorts of the data several themes emerged that represent common experiences among the student participants. A caveat is in order about the themes derived from the interviews, focus groups, and notes. As is characteristic of qualitative research—where the sample of individuals involved is typically small—generalizability of the analyses and results to other populations is problematic. The notion of "transferability," however, does apply, which suggests that some elements of commonality among the unique experiences of a small group of people can be identified and have relevance for other individuals.

The themes discovered in this analysis are drawn primarily from four individual interviews, three group interviews, and extensive field notes. Students who participate in international service-learning experiences have several common characteristics, and the primary themes suggest that international service-learning students (a) are comfortable with ambiguity, very adaptable in nature, and motivated self-starters, (b) have a positive and self-confident attitude towards learning and serving in an international context [some were endowed with the trait to begin with and some developed it during, or as a result of, their service term], and (c) have a "civic-minded personality" and a predisposition for service experiences.

In like manner, there are commonalities among the students both in their experiences abroad and in their conduct upon their return to America following their service. The following themes are typical of the international service-learning experience in that (a) many international service-learning students experience "reverse culture shock" upon returning from their service experience; (b) students typically undergo a significant transformation of their moral and intellectual character, and they work through the transformation with considerable reflection; and (c) as a result of the service experience, many students develop a renewed, and often more critical, perspective on American values, norms, behaviors, and beliefs.

*International service-learning students are comfortable with ambiguity and necessarily adaptable to the environment and culture.*

A tolerance for ambiguity is a significant characteristic shared by many of the Partnership program alumni with whom we spoke during the course of the study. Many students noted the relative lack of structure during their service experience and commented on the way in which they took control of the situation, using ambiguity as a motivator for, rather than a deterrent to, their work and involvement with the local culture. Though the Partnership takes care to provide a structured experience within the context of the service, inevitably there is some degree of ambiguity inherent in the system when working with international programs, disparate language groups and communities, and foreign travel and study.

The extent to which the majority of students were adaptable prior to entering the program as opposed to developing a sense of adaptability as a result of their experience, remains unclear. To be sure, there appeared to be elements of both characteristics in many of the students. What is clear, however, is that they used or developed a posture of "adaptability" as a resource for becoming more socialized into their host culture. It was a stance, and a way of thinking and acting, that put them in good stead in confronting any number of situations and scenarios during their service term. It helped them examine more closely and better understand the nature of cultural behavior. Further, it gave them license to "surrender" their notions of control and allowed them to participate more fully in the experience.

As one student remarked, "There was a little bit of disorganization with the framework so a lot of things were left to the students to take care of." Commenting on the impact of the service experience after her return to America, another student said, "I'm more flexible; I can adapt to change, I think, better than I could early on. Everything doesn't have to happen in three years or four years. It doesn't have to happen as society would make you think it has to happen."

Consider the comment by an individual in one of the group interviews, which underscores the extent to which ambiguity is inherent in the system. She remarked, "Non-profit work is all about ambiguity—the [notion] of 'baptism by fire' is good for this work." There is a common understanding among the students we spoke with that suggests that in order to be successful you have to channel the ambiguity in ways that ultimately help create some control over the experience. As another reported, "I feel like the ambiguity of it all made it part of the experience, and so if everything had been laid out ahead of time it would have been a different thing altogether." This participant went on to note that while she would have known what she was "walking into" she would not have had that sense of being self-sufficient. This student described her experience working in an orphanage, noting that she was given little instruction or orientation about the type of work she would be doing, and set about developing her own work routine and being a useful resource in whatever manner possible.

> I really think that I had to make the best out of a bad situation [referring to the lack of structure at her site], but that's why I say . . . it's difficult to determine what was a good experience, to use the word 'good,' because I think I was telling one of the other alumnae last night, I think it's all in what you make it and how well you can adapt. It wasn't that I had such good adaptive skills, but I was there and I was willing to make the most of it, and there came a point where I had to just kick in my heels, suck it in, and you know, make something happen.

### *Positive attitude and self-confidence are significant factors that help foster success in the international service-learning experience*

As a research team, we came to understand that positive self-confidence plays a significant role in the success and work of students on foreign soil, particularly students who are living with native families and faced with the challenge of overcoming daunting language barriers. While some students appear to have been equipped with a certain measure of self-confidence prior to their embarking on the service experience, many discovered a self-confidence in themselves they never knew existed (but which became a part of their personality during the experience and served them well throughout the service term and beyond).

Some looked back at their experience and remarked on the courage they felt at having partaken in the service experience in the first place. As one person noted, "Well . . . looking at it from different angles . . . I would say for me the benefit of having [been involved in the program] . . . I could look back and think that I had the courage to go—not knowing anybody—and to seek it out."

As for the impact of socialization into another culture and traveling and working in a service capacity on foreign soil—far from home for the first time, in many cases—the following remark confirms the powerful influence of the international service experience on measures of self-concept and self-confidence. Service, in short, allows for an enhanced sense of identity and self-esteem.

> I feel like I can go anywhere and survive, and I know that I would not feel that way if I wouldn't have been to India. I just know it. I don't think I would have come to New York [for this interview visit]. Where I live now there's like one little stoplight, you know, it's very small. Everyone thought I was crazy. . . . People don't really understand, and now I'm much more free and I just feel like I can survive, and that's a good feeling. I feel really pretty confident in my ability to get around. . . . I definitely think that's . . . one of the biggest things that I took out of my experience in India—just feeling much more confident in my ability to travel and being able to take more risks because of that.

### International service-learning students have a "civic-minded personality"

Many of the students in the study appear to have a predisposition for service experiences, and in many cases they have a long resumé of experiences that suggests service has been either a prominent feature in their upbringing or a choice they have made in their own lives. In short, the Partnership service-learning experience is not a flash-in-the-pan experience for the students; rather, it is representative of a pattern of service behavior. In several cases, the service-abroad experience introduced students to civic service and engagement and started them on a path of service on which they continue to this day.

To the extent service abroad awakened them to a new lifestyle of civic engagement, the Partnership experience was a catalytic event. That is, it served as a spark and was a major force in both confirming their present service work and encouraging future civic engagement. Many students were already headed in the direction of service, but the actual experience of serving abroad moved them further toward that goal. For some students, there appears to be a direct cause-and-effect relationship between the Partnership experience and the work in which they are currently involved.

> And so for that, you know, it was kind of magnified for me that I wanted to help or be involved or just to be exposed to it. So that kind of openness certainly had that impact, but you know I've always been kind of involved with trying to get out there and do things [engage in service]. In fact, you know I think it was frustrating for me during the internships [that she was involved in during college] because I felt like maybe I wasn't doing enough.

For others, the experience affirmed and enhanced what they were already in the habit and process of doing:

> You know I must have cared about people before I went, otherwise I wouldn't have gone there. And so . . . for research [purposes] it would be really great to say, 'I was this terrible horrible person, then I went to India and I saw the light.' But . . . it wasn't really like that for me. I did learn a lot more, and I did see how other people lived. I hadn't seen poverty like that before, and I hadn't seen things that we take for granted, you know, like just basic medical care, being able to turn on the faucet and drink [from] it...I understood more about America too. I'd say I learned just as much about America as I did about India.

Interestingly, one student commented on the fact that he often longs to go out and engage in service and often plans travel out of the country so that he can get back to service in an international context. He remarked, "It is like a drug to get hooked on service—I have the desire to leave the US when I need to get a fix."

Part of the motivation for getting involved in service revolved around students feeling as if they were "living in a bubble," or leading very sheltered lives, and they wanted to remove themselves—"stretch themselves," as one put it—from the comfort zone that kept them protected. While learning theory in the college classroom was useful grounding for their education, many felt that theory was only part of the equation—they wanted to experience the real action and see if it matched with theory.

### Many international service-learning students experience "reverse culture shock" upon returning

Many students with whom we spoke found it more difficult to return home after a service experience than to leave America in the first place. Upon returning to America, some students found it challenging to transition back into the lives they led prior to the experience, and they reported having difficulty reconciling their lives back at home with the lives they had become used to during the previous several months. For the purposes of this study, refer to this as the "repatriation syndrome," whereby students often find it more challenging to become re-acclimated to their home environment than to initially transition into living and performing service in a foreign country and culture. A common remark heard from students about their homecoming to America was that they experience "reverse culture shock." One student summed it up, remarking when I asked him about his return, that, "It was culture shock. It wasn't culture shock going down there but coming back."

The following comments are revealing about the nature of study and service abroad and the way in which immersion in a foreign country has an appreciable impact on the reflection process upon return.

> I remember being happy about returning to friends and family but obviously feeling disconnected to some degree. I remember being disgusted by the luxurious lifestyle that you could see [here in America]. And I certainly did see some of that in Ecuador, but it just seemed far more luxurious . . . when I came back and moved to a wealthier suburb outside of Boston. And yeah, I really had in mind that I wanted to move right back to a . . . developing country, and I was really intense about it.

This comment echoes the same thoughts, and points to the way in which participants framed their thoughts from the perspective of the people with whom they lived during their service term:

It was harder coming back than going. Much harder. Because I do well in crisis . . . and when I was there, there was a lot going on and I didn't know what I was doing—I did well because I'm strong in those periods. When I came back and everything was fine, everyone was [saying] 'Hey, how's it going?' [I replied] 'Oh, the children in India are starving.' . . . You know, I just couldn't believe that people were going on with their daily lives. . . . I mean I wasn't like in vain . . . I wasn't trying to push it on people. . . . And it was sort of hard to get back into the swing of things.

## Transformative intellectual and moral development

We asked several questions related to moral and intellectual development and the changes that took place in those domains as a result of the international service experience. In reflecting on their experiences, students commented on situations and events that challenged their belief systems and caused them to reevaluate their own thoughts about morality, peace, justice, fairness, norms of behavior, citizenship, learning, decision-making, and notions of race and sex. One participant noted that she thought she was in one place when she went overseas, "but the experience taught me I was in another." Implied in her statement is the notion that she was not as culturally, intellectually, and morally aware as she originally thought when she set out on her service abroad. Another participant revealed other aspects of moral and intellectual development in the following story:

... I certainly began questioning everything around me when I was there. . . . a lot of issues came up with race . . . dealing with skin tone there in the country—urban versus rural—and there was quite a bit of that [the issue of race] with the family I stayed with. So I was . . . tackling that kind of thing because I was going out to remote areas [where there] were darker color [people], and you know my family [host family] really had their views.

Service experiences also had a transformative effect on students' sense of justice and treatment of others in society:

I would have to say that the experience as a whole made me a more compassionate person. I think part of that is because I feel like I have been given so much over my life. . . . I feel so fortunate in so many ways. I mean everything from my health to my education to my family to my friends, and all the experiences that I've had.

The same student commented on the affirming nature of the experience in relation to his value system:

I don't think many of my values really changed. Things like honesty and integrity and my value of my education, I mean all those have stayed strong and stayed consistent, and if anything I value those more now than I did even back then. . . . Maybe some things that have changed . . . are . . . my value of the material. It's not as important to me as it once was. I don't really feel like my values have changed that much.

Finally, one participant commented on the sheer level of mental activity he experienced when he entered the program, saying that he was amazed at how many levels of mental operation were required to become successfully acclimated to the experience. Students are always processing on an intellectual level when they are living and serving abroad, and they are constantly trying to negotiate things—relationships with people, living with the host family, trying to bridge the language gap.

### Renewed—and not altogether positive—perspective about American values and norms

The impact of the Partnership service experience on the views of students about their home country was well-documented in the various conversations and interviews with alumni. Most prevalent were comments about the wasteful nature of American society, the high regard for material goods and services, and the relative poverty of other nations compared to the United States. Many students returned with a respect and appreciation for their status as American citizens, having learned to appreciate many things that most Americans take for granted—access to public education, freedom of speech, a democratic society, a relatively stable economy, and, of course, electricity and running water. Others returned to the United

States highly critical of American society, their appreciation for the American way of life more cautious. Consider the following:

> It changed my perspective on . . . what a person might need to be happy because both through the Partnership and through my other experiences in Central America and Mexico, I saw people with so little that were perfectly happy and content with what they had. And so that's definitely one lasting effect because it changed my idea of not what it means to be happy, but how little one can have and still be fine . . . Maybe some things that have changed though are just my value of the material. It's not as important to me as it once was.

Another student mirrored these sentiments:

> I think I'm just more understanding, and I think that it's really easy to come from this country. We have so much pride and to think that our way is the way. . . . even though I'm not that familiar with a lot of other countries and their cultures, I'm much more understanding now of trying to figure out why [things are done a particular way], instead of just saying 'That's not right or not good.'

As is evident from these statements, the students with whom I spoke returned home in some ways more critical than ever of American norms, values, and behaviors, yet in other ways they appeared to have a renewed sense of respect and appreciation for American culture. Of course, on several occasions students reported that during the early reentry process their thoughts were focused on the basic amenities they had taken for granted, and in that sense they were grateful to be able to return and have access to such things as hot showers, electricity, varieties of food, sophisticated technology, and the like. It was upon further reflection and after having been significantly "repatriated" into American society—either by virtue of having been back in the United States for some time or by being thrust quickly back into American culture, or both—that they reported feeling guilty at having too much access to creature comforts and being over-stimulated by the fast pace of American society.

## Some Key Questions

Following is a set of key questions to ponder in considering the role of international service in the academy and the nature of student involvement in international programs.

1. What can we do as educators to encourage and support a demeanor and spirit of engagement among our students to prepare them for both national and international service?

2. How can we identify students who have a predisposition towards, or propensity for, service, either at the national or the international level? Further, how can we nurture this will to serve?

3. How do we "seed the pot" in the college environment so that we grow civic-minded, civically aware, and civically engaged students?

4. What are the characteristics of students who gravitate towards international service experience?

5. Going abroad to study is much more than a "cultural experience." Students should be a part of the culture in which they serve and operate when they go abroad, and they should seek a certain degree of prolonged engagement in the environment or setting where they are working and living. What is the best way in which this might be accomplished?

6. What do we know about the nature/nurture question with regard to service? That is, to what extent do service experiences create engaged citizens and already-engaged citizens create ideal service experiences? Are those who gravitate towards international service already engaged citizens who have sought out an affirming service experience?

## Final Thoughts and Conclusions

It is evident the experience of learning and serving abroad was transformative in many ways for the Partnership alumni. Some experienced culture shock upon entering a new and strange environment far away from their homeland, while others experienced what I call "reverse culture shock," whereby they had greater challenges in terms of their re-entry into America than they experienced going to a foreign environment in the first place. Some alumni chose career paths and other future professional opportunities that were directly related to, and in many cases the result of, their international service as a Partnership participant. Other students for whom the Partnership experience perhaps does not feature as prominently in their current professional lives hold the experience to be one of the seminal events in their lives and one from which they discovered a great deal about themselves. Finally, it goes without saying that no two people experienced their service in the same way, and for that reason alone it was important for us as researchers to capture the individual stories of each of the participants. True, many of the students visited the same countries, but they clearly experienced the environment, people, and culture differently. Some nuances of those experiences would not have been adequately documented using a more quantitative approach to data and information gathering.

While the experiences of the four alumni I interviewed and interacted with in focus groups represented just a fraction of the total experiences of seventeen students who were part of the overall study, they provided a rich analysis from which common themes—some more transferable than others—could be drawn. To be sure, the Partnership alumni with whom I spoke and interacted in New York were very adaptable students who were fairly comfortable with ambiguity and who made use of the best available resources to make the strange environment in which they found themselves more familiar. It is unclear whether they were adaptable sorts before they embarked on their service experience or if they became more adaptable because of it, but the notion of adaptability is a very powerful one indeed for many alumni. In addition, my four alumni interviewees not only had a positive attitude towards their experience but also seemed relatively undaunted by the fact that formal programmatic structures at their sites were often very loose, the communication was uneven, and the expectations often unclear. In fact, the students indicated that a lack of formal structure was a good incentive to delve into the culture with curiosity and find some way to create their own structure. As a result, these students learned powerful life lessons about finding ways to be creative in the midst of limited resources and feeling empowered to be the architects of their own experience.

In closing, consider the following reflection by noted ethnographer and anthropologist Bronislaw Malinowski, about landing on foreign soil and trying to make sense of a new and strange world.

> Imagine yourself suddenly set down surrounded by all your gear, alone on a tropical beach close to a native village, while the launch or dinghy which has brought you sails away out of sight. Since you take up your abode in the compound of some neighboring white man, trader or missionary, you have nothing to do but to start at once on your ethnographic work. (Malinowski 1922:4)

His words are remarkably similar to the sentiments shared in the opening of this chapter by Tamara, who felt upon entering her host country that she was thrust onto an unknown stage, standing with her satchel, alone, and had to force herself to come to grips with where she was and tell herself that everything was going to be okay.

While Tamara and the other students with whom we conducted interviews and focus groups in April 2003 were certainly not anthropologists going about ethnographic fieldwork for the purposes of studying a culture, they nonetheless experienced the range of emotions that strangers in a strange land feel: excitement, anxiety, despondency, despair, helplessness, self-sufficiency, and isolation to name just a very few. But like Malinowski, they had nothing to do but set about their work when the protective structures of the familiar world from which they came receded into the background.

As researchers, we were unable to experience the loneliness, physical and mental discomfort, language barriers, and alternating emotions of exhilaration and unrest that the students experienced. In that same vein, the students who gathered for the April 2003 session in New York were in various stages of being removed—emotionally and physically—from their service and study-abroad experience. Some had completed their service more than ten years before and some had only recently returned. So our task was to encourage reflection and contemplation about the particular point in time in which they served—essentially to take them back to that place again—so that we could discover more about the impact of international service-learning on the lives of those who experience it.

# 8 The Partnership Vision

## Study Abroad and Service-Learning

Our fourth researcher, John Whiteley, chose to focus his report on the relationship between the statements of the two founders of the International Partnership for Service-Learning, Howard Berry and Linda Chisholm, about service-learning and study abroad, and the statements of the Partnership alumni who participated in our study. He found some clear connections. In the little book given to each prospective Partnership student, *How to Serve and Learn Abroad Effectively: Students Tell Students* (Berry & Chisholm 1992), the authors utilize the insights of previous students to assist prospective students who are planning to go abroad for service-learning. They emphasize, above all, that a program of service and learning should be based on mutuality: giving and receiving. Whiteley suggested in his report that this concept of mutuality provided a good starting point for our consideration of the effects of the service-learning experience on students.

Berry and Chisholm, Whiteley points out, make an important distinction between an *internship,* devised for the benefit of the learner, and the *service* portion of service-learning, which offers the chance to "be part of an ongoing effort to help make the lives of others better," to be a "contributing and valued member" of a community, to get "into another culture," and to be part of "the application" of "learning, intelligence, energy and kindness to solve—or at least alleviate—human problems." A recurring idea in the writing of Berry and Chisholm about service-learning is that the service-learner will return to America with the recognition that "they gave me more than I gave to them." Mutuality is at the heart of the

Partnership's pedagogy. In this regard it is quite different from most international and intercultural experiences provided by American higher education.

One of the characteristics of the work of Berry particularly, and of Chisholm to a lesser degree, has been a deep skepticism about received opinion concerning the goals and outcomes of American higher education. Like Alec Dickson in the 1950s and 1960s, Berry saw in young people a potential for unbounded intellectual and spiritual energy and in education an opportunity not just to improve the individual but to inculcate in that individual ideals of collective action that could in turn improve the human condition. For Dickson and Berry, education was not just a matter of competition—of pitting individual against individual—but an opportunity to seek out commonalities and to promote cooperation at a time when the still-forming human spirit was capable of it.

In the months before his death, Berry was working with Chisholm on a second book aimed at students and their advisors and concerned not just with service-learning but with study abroad in general. The book, the authors explain in their introduction, is designed "to help students learn about and reflect upon the new culture they will be entering when they go abroad to study," and to do so by "the study of a topic that will be close at hand—higher education." Nothing could be simpler than to take the institution closest to hand and subject it to analysis in order to find a way into the culture that the student has temporarily adopted in his or her stay abroad. It is entirely typical of Berry and Chisholm's thinking that they should advocate the drawing of lessons from the student's immediate surroundings: it is in the simplest of settings that the profoundest truths reside, they seem to say. And it is through an almost nettlesome self-awareness that sympathy for and understanding of the other can arise. That is why the two of them found such potential in international service-learning two decades ago: here was a pedagogy that advocated awareness of the self, through the keeping of journals, through reading, and through group exploration—and awareness of the other, through the self-confidence that derives from self-understanding. Here, too, was a way of discovering the world by doing. So much of study abroad is based on the notion that the rest of the world is simply a kind of theme-parked extension of the classroom, out there for the use of the American student and ready to be discarded (except for the postcards and the photographs) when the credit-bearing semester is over. For Chisholm and Berry the world beyond the

United States is a place where the American is a visitor, and in which the student can learn best by participating and by giving back. International service-learning brings the student into contact with society as it is lived and experienced in the country in question, and with the problems and opportunities of that society. Phrases like "alleviate the suffering" and words like "solve," or "help," or "assist" are juxtaposed with terms like "learn," and "explore," and "study," in an ethic of service and study that is based on reciprocity (giving and receiving) but most particularly on mutuality (not only giving and receiving, but sharing and supporting).

So when Chisholm and Berry produce their primer on study abroad, entitled *Understanding the Education—and Through It the Culture—In Education Abroad* (Chisholm & Berry 2002), it is no surprise that they approach the very idea of higher education with a certain cagey relativism. The American higher education system is based on notions of the transferability of credit—on the fiction that (within certain limits) an educational experience in one setting is comparable to an educational experience in another. Behind such a free-trade concept lies the fiction that all higher education institutions are engaged in doing the same thing, or at least in doing something of equal worth. Transferability of credit tends to erase or reduce institutional difference by creating a free educational market.

Such notions extend beyond our shores into higher education abroad. Faced with the need to give students grades and to complete their transcripts, learned academics spend a great deal of time looking for ways of comparing learning experiences abroad with properly approved and certified learning experiences on their home campuses. If Sociology 123 at American State University is more or less the same as a course taught at the University of Central Asia, then credit can be transferred without difficulty—but if it is different, maybe it cannot be transferred at all. Yet the whole point about studying at the University of Central Asia is that it manifestly is *not* American State University. Over the years, more faculty members and students have found themselves caught on the horns of this particular dilemma than there are stars in the sky.

Similar battles rage over service-learning. If certifiable education is something acquired exclusively in a classroom, how can we square education acquired in other settings with such a definition, and how can we equate what is learned beyond the classroom with equivalent experiences within? Needless to say, international service-learning heaps Pelion on Ossa: it raises all the complexities of certification of study abroad and all those of certification of non-classroom learning.

On the one hand, we wish our study-abroad experience to be different from the educational experiences available on the home campus; on the other, we wish it to be the same. On the one hand, we want to create a different educational experience through service-learning; on the other hand, we wish it to be comparable to what we already have.

But, say Chisholm and Berry, higher education is culture-bound: its goals, assumptions and practices vary widely from country to country and society to society. In the chapter on evaluation in *Understanding the Education*, Chapter 11, they make a number of essential points:

1. Not all in a "society or system" agree on the evaluation system for higher education, and there are "gradations" at each level of evaluation. The authors pose the basic question "How does this system reflect the culture?"

2. In a program such as service-learning, which requires a form of "experiential learning," an open question is how performance fits into the final grade.

3. Institutions that provide higher education may be judged on both qualitative and formal means of evaluation, with both approaches reflecting the culture, and some more highly valued by the society. In this context, praise or criticism reflect the values of the individuals or institutions making the judgments.

This deeply skeptical and relativist approach to the educational process suggests that simple and apparently objective measures of the effectiveness of higher education are likely to fall afoul of cultural differences. Assessing quality is no simple matter. Indeed, education (whatever that may be) may take place in spite of the indications of so-called objective measures. If we are looking for objectivity, perhaps we need to begin by asking some questions about the purpose of higher education and about its outcomes—questions that take into consideration *both* the value of the individual *and* the individual's impact on society.

Given these realities, it is perhaps appropriate that in our student study of international service-learning we took a qualitative approach to evaluation. Qualitative research allows for a deeper and richer understanding of cultural phenomena and human behavior. This is not to say that quantitative measures cannot be developed to assess service-learning (see, for example, Bringle, Phillips & Hudson 2004, and our chapter 15), nor indeed that they are unimportant, only that they need to be rooted in the discoveries of qualitative research, since it is a qualitative approach that is most likely to unearth what matters in service-learning—at least the intensive cross-cultural service-learning of the type practiced by the Partnership. The current study is an attempt to get at some of these essential issues: as Whiteley points out in his report to the research team, in this level of analysis of higher education across the nations and cultures where the requirements combine formal classroom learning *and* acquisition of language and culture *plus* service, a qualitative approach to program evaluation is very appropriate from a methodological perspective.

## John Whiteley's Analysis

In the afterword to *Understanding the Education*, Chisholm and Berry articulate some of the explicit and implicit goals and outcomes of the study-abroad experience. They express the hope that the reader's study-abroad experience has been "wonderful, eye-opening, life-changing" and that the reader is "more confident, more knowledgeable and more sophisticated." This sophistication, Chisholm and Berry suggest, may be reflected on a number of dimensions, including the (increased) use of foreign language, the (greater) understanding of a different system of government, the ability to travel within big cities and on various forms of transportation, the taste for new foods, the ability to analyze and understand a culture (one's own and others), being able to enter the mind-set of another person or group different from one's own (the authors see this as "the mark of the truly educated person"), recognition that a life is made richer when we "extend our own personal experience" and share "in the experience of others," a greater capacity to make sense of "complex and contradictory experiences," and so on.

Some of these characteristics of successful study abroad refer strictly to the self, and to the individual's ability to negotiate another society, while others (particularly the last two or three in our list above) stress reciprocity. Even in study abroad (with no overt element of service), Chisholm and Berry suggest, we leave something behind. Chisholm and Berry's book is about education and how an analysis of one's own educational experience in a foreign culture may serve as a window to understanding that culture, since education in all its aspects "shapes and reflects a culture." Hence they suggest, in addressing the self-aware student, that the student should order and arrange "pieces of your education abroad" into a "complete picture" and use the foreign-study experience as a way of developing insights into how "human beings are the product of our individual life history and the historical moment" and "where and how another person or group of people have formed opinions and developed cultural beliefs and patterns." Their assumption (perhaps a necessary assumption for the educator and the optimist) is that cultures are readable and, at some level, comprehensible: study abroad is a way of acquiring the skills necessary to recognize "a culture's characteristics, how its past shapes its present and its present will shape its future" and it forms "a useful lesson in the multitude of new cultures you will encounter throughout your life." Your study-abroad experience, they say to the student, "will shape you and the role you play in your society in the future."

Clearly, Chisholm and Berry hope that this experience will cause the student to look at the world differently, and hence perhaps slightly at odds with received opinion and received values at home, perhaps with an attitude of critical tolerance toward the world at large. If a leader is a person with fresh insights on received belief, a person able to teach a society to look at the mundane and routine with fresh eyes, there are few better preparations for leadership than study abroad. Thus, the authors assert, family, friends, and colleagues "are likely to see you not only as more sophisticated, but as a leader in a way they have not before."

Such sophistication, they suggest, involves an increased capacity to realize "that another person, group, or nation may see things very differently." It is not that the rest of the world, under the skin, resembles the United States, but that there are many ways of ordering society, and many ways of defining community and institutions: people and societies are profoundly different and we must learn to manage this difference. Study abroad, then, helps in learning "to live cooperatively, happily, and peaceably together" with people from another culture and acquiring the skills to "work out a negotiated settlement so that everyone benefits"—the essence of leadership. For the individual, it implies deciding the extent to which that individual will conform to or challenge a culture's characteristics.

Thus, even as they discuss study abroad, an activity that is conceived purely and simply as an educational experience, Chisholm and Berry stress reciprocity and understanding. How much more, then, these elements are important in the bi-directional, indeed multi-directional economy of international service-learning. By taking Chisholm and Berry's definition of study abroad as his starting point, Whiteley implies that the presumed virtues of study abroad should form a bare minimum for successful international service-learning. He sets about looking for and identifying that minimum in his interviews and discussions.

Whiteley points out that the interviews in New York were "semi-structured" (to cover a variety of topics in less than an hour's time each), but also quite open-ended. They were conceived and conducted, writes Whiteley, in the spirit of what sociologist Herbert J. Gans, in the preface to the book *America At Century's End,* has called an "evaluative portrait." Gans distinguishes between an empirically reasonable portrait and an evaluative portrait. The latter attempts to increase understanding of recurring patterns and their contexts. The method involves "being with and talking to people" and asking them "thoughtful and empathetic questions." Such an approach leads to "analyzing the resulting data without the need to prove prior ideological points." The report, then, is based on "an unstructured and structured series of groups and individuals who had shared an experience they all considered transformative."

The starting point for Whiteley was the series of telephone conversations with the review team as a whole and some members of it leading up to the group teleconference—described in our fourth chapter. While in New York for the interviewing there were further conversations with the review team on a series of questions, which would be a stimulus to "being with and talking to people," but in such a manner as to create an evaluative portrait of the experience.

Whiteley found that "the qualitative interviews provide a rich resource for assessing the impact of the service-learning experience on the explicit and implicit goals and outcomes of the program as articulated . . . by Chisholm and Berry." Of course, in their second book, *Understanding the Education,* the authors were addressing not service-learning but study abroad, and hence "it was not possible to assess the impact of the service-learning experience on some of the articulated goals and outcomes. The reasons for that circumstance relate to the different nature of the goals and outcomes themselves, and the differing nature of some of the experiences abroad reported by the interviewees."

Given that limitation, the interviewees' responses tracked Chisholm and Berry's insights quite closely, as Whiteley's analysis makes clear.

## A life-changing experience

Yes, the experience abroad was "wonderful" (the students, reports Whiteley, "were virtually unanimous" on the point), and, yes, it was "eye-opening" ("it was the people they encountered and the interaction with the culture in which they lived that were compelling"), and above all, it was "life-changing." Whiteley cites one participant as follows:

> I had traveled a lot prior to that anyway, but this was the first time of actually productive travel where you are going and making an impact in a foreign environment. It made a world of difference both for me as an individual, and I can say that we do impact the place and the people that we work with. It is a provident thing for both parties. I can say, and it is not an overstatement to say, and it sounds dramatic but it is the truth, that it definitely shaped who I am today, it shaped the direction that I am going in academically and career-wise.

Participants, Whiteley reported, saw service-learning "as accelerating the evolution of their development as people and as emerging professionals." He attributed this to "the accelerated maturation which resulted from the psychological and physical distance (separation) from family and friends, and the power of self-reliance in promoting growth." "Another source for growth," he added, "was the sense of responsibility they felt for their role in service. For many of them it seemed to be the first time they had experienced themselves as accountable for the welfare of other human beings." They learned about themselves in the process: as one participant observes, "It was just the challenge of learning about myself also, and being thrown into this environment with no instruction, which at first I found really frustrating, but in the end it was really rewarding." Whiteley was struck by the fact that the service-learning experience pushed students out beyond themselves, and he cited other recent research among conventional students that pointed in a different direction: "College students in one of the research samples at the University of California, Irvine, had a different answer to basically the same question: growth was a product of relationships with peers and intimate others." He singled out the following quotation, which, though perhaps tinged with the unanalytical sentimentality of the moment, points to relationships beyond peers and professors and perhaps to life-changing understandings in the most simple of interactions:

> Hopefully I had some kind of an impact on other people. I think I did. I worked at a home for abused and abandoned girls as my service component. And I figured out that my one goal there was just to make them smile, just to give them a moment of happiness when they could be kids. And I hope I did that, and that made it great.

The answer came in response to the question "As you reflect on the meaning of the experience [with the Partnership], what was it that gave the meaning?" Another participant, in response to the follow-up question, "What was it about the program that made this impact?" replied:

> The population that we dealt with, the people that we were dealing with, the portion of the population that need as much intervention as they can possibly get. . . . The opportunity to leave someone a little bit better off for the moment.

## Confidence

Chisholm and Berry cite growth in confidence as an important factor in study abroad, but "This goal could not be addressed as there was no independent information available about the level of confidence of the individuals before their participation." Whiteley did, however, suggest that "Compared to college students with whom I have worked for the last forty years, they are more confident than the usual student."

## Knowledge

Were students "more knowledgeable"? "The open-ended character of the interviews did not require them to demonstrate their knowledge of international affairs or degree of immersion in the role of their host country in the world," wrote Whiteley; "This goal is difficult to assess in broad terms. In specific terms . . . the participants were able to speak at length about the world they had experienced personally outside of the United States [and] about the culture of their host country, more specifically the nature of family life and the role of education in the culture."

### Foreign language

Chisholm and Berry allude to foreign-language learning. Whiteley pointed out that "There were a number of public-school foreign-language . . . teachers in the group for whom, quite obviously, the service-learning experience had become an integral component of preparation for their life's work. It was not a formal element of data collection, but the participants seemed to be more multilingual than American college graduates (beyond the language of their host country) and therefore much more on the model of the highly educated community in Europe." Foreign-language learning is clearly an element in the Partnership experience that merits further investigation, but it is clear that the seventeen alumni invited to New York had an exceptionally high knowledge of other languages—possibly a factor in defining their responses to other questions and their relative ease in moving among cultures. As Whiteley points out elsewhere in his report, "Some participants had sought multiple experiences abroad. This subgroup of individuals appeared to *use* foreign language but not to have the *acquisition* of a foreign language as the centerpiece of their motivation."

### Government

Having knowledge of other systems of government was another of Chisholm and Berry's criteria. "Almost no one spoke about the nature of the government in their host country. Rather, they had a rich commentary about the government of the United States both at home and abroad. The commentaries were more constitutional than partisan and frequently related to differing conceptions of the Bill of Rights. The commentaries were reflective in nature rather than the type of factual comments which might be the product of formal classroom instruction. In a few words, [the participants] seemed to have a nuanced understanding of what is special about being an American." Whiteley cites a response to the question, "You said you saw your own country differently. What did you mean?"

. . . I had a lot more respect for it because I used to think our government was terribly inefficient, but then when I saw other country's governments that were even worse than ours, it made me appreciate what we do have. But on the other hand, I used to see the United States as kind of going out and helping other countries, and then I thought you know, we don't always know what they need. We don't always, you know, we have resources that can help them but we can't just assume that we know what they need, and going in there and sending money and certain resources that really aren't helping the causes of their problems, and really aren't addressing what they really need. So I think I sort of realized, okay, I think a lot of people in the United States assume that we know what's best for other countries whereas then I started to realize we don't always know what's best, and you really need to be there and live there before you can start to learn from their perspective what they need.

## Understanding others

Chisholm and Berry stress the importance of "being able to enter the mind-set of another person or group different from your own" and they see this ability as "the mark of the truly educated person." Whiteley singles this out as "a special contribution of the International Partnership" in which it "is making a vital contribution." "Such a goal is much closer to the understanding of Carl Rogers on the power of empathy and the role of education," Whiteley suggests. "A traditional university usually offers a different version of a 'truly educated person,' focusing instead on the successful completion of a series of courses across different domains of knowledge. The Partnership for Service-Learning articulates a different model. The interviews were not in sufficient depth that it is possible to comment in depth on the capacity of our interviewees to 'enter the mind-set.' As a group, however, they were able to talk very thoughtfully and in depth about the immediate family and different cultures they experienced (in contrast to an academic treatise on culture), and they were particularly insightful about the inner lives of the . . . people with whom they predominantly worked."

*Awareness of complexity*

A problem that Whiteley's report raises on various occasions is the fact that "we don't have real baseline data on [the students'] lives before the experience." For example, assessing whether the participants have "a greater capacity to make sense of 'complex and contradictory experiences'" (as Chisholm and Berry describe it) is hard to do, beyond the dimension of self-report. But, writes Whiteley (including, no doubt, his informal conversations with participants before and after the event), "The participants were able to talk for two days reflecting thoughtfully about their experiences" and "The current capacity is impressive for the group as a whole."

*Context and commitment*

Did the group develop insights into how "human beings are the product of our individual life history and the historical moment"?[1] Whiteley commented: "The 'historical moment' for this group was helping individuals realize their human potential and overcoming threats to dignity. The historical moment was . . . not so much ideology, world events, or culture and much more engagement in the social world and the struggle for opportunity, largely in poorer cultures." And, he added, "This is a self-selected population who as a group seemed to have a greater commitment to solving the problems of societies and being engaged personally in that process. This generalization holds across the different settings. The role of personal self-selection is not diminished by the importance of this experience for the participants." He cites one student (Paula, who spent time with the Partnership, one way or another, in four different locations: India, South Dakota, and, through the MA program, Jamaica and England) at length:

> . . . I think in some ways that I've always had a sense of, you know, compassion for other people, and I think that that's something that in my own family has been just an important part of how I was raised, of sort of looking out for others or just kind of, you know, putting other people ahead of you. But I think in going to India and then going to South Dakota, that it took on a whole new meaning for me to really be compassionate.

---

[1] Chisholm and Berry are apparently drawing here on C. Wright Mills's idea of "the sociological imagination" (Mills 1959).

Paula talks about what she describes as "the most profound change in values" that ensued from this experience. We read in the papers, she suggests, that "there's poverty, there's war, there are all these people who suffer from this and that" but that we "can find ways to shield ourselves from actually engaging in that. And so even though we may on an intellectual level recognize that these problems exist, we blind ourselves from actually engaging or interacting with those people, or with those situations." She came to realize that "you can pull those blinders down and you can actually have some sort of an impact or have some sort of a dialogue or have some means of communicating or working with this other side of life that you may not—that you could otherwise so easily ignore. . . . In doing that that you really have a fuller sense of . . . life or a fuller sense of the human experience in the world. And that you, I mean, and that you have this opportunity sort of available to you wherever you are at all times, but in some ways you have to seek it out because we tend to hide ourselves from that."

### *Difference*

But this sense of engagement goes further. Did the group exhibit increased capacity to realize "that another person, group, or nation may see things very differently"? Whiteley suggests that they did: "One of the most striking features of the group was how differently they had come to see America and Americans as a consequence of learning about how different people and groups from different nations are. Their comments about America were almost never negative but they were reflective and thoughtful at a higher level of insight than is typical for the college students and graduates that I encounter regularly. . . . The service-learning experience and the culture in which it occurred had become important touchstones in the lives of these people." As Paula suggests, in another passage quoted by Whiteley, the Partnership experience creates a certain sense of obligation to engage with others.

### *Independence and individuality*

As a group they also showed high levels of independence: "The issue of individual independence from culture is reflected in their high degree of individuality within American culture. These are people whose individuality is highly distinctive and their conformity hard to observe (because I believe that as a group they are positively individualistic, not eccentric)." Such positive individualism does not negate an observation made by the other researchers, namely that the alumni seemed more comfortable with their places in a group: they were simultaneously independent (with minds of their own) and interdependent (with a sense of their role in the collective). At the same time, Whiteley points out, they are deeply engaged in the here-and-now of their own lives: "As a group these are comparatively young people. Many of them were deeply involved in choosing a path for life's work and establishing family commitments. They spoke almost not at all about where they would fit within America's many cultures. In that sense almost all of them were in a phase of choosing immediate paths and next steps. They were much less engaged in thinking about the encounters that would come later."

What, then, emerges from Whiteley's comments? We can sum them up as follows:

1. The participants demonstrated a sense of responsibility and engagement in their time abroad that went beyond what one might normally expect from foreign study.

2. The service-learning experience set up relationships that allowed students to mature not solely or primarily through interaction with professors and peers but through engagement with the larger society and above all its less fortunate members.

3. The participants showed a high level of self-confidence and seemed knowledgeable and articulate about the world. At the same time these were individuals whose awareness of the world extended to, and was extended by, an exceptional degree of knowledge of foreign languages—more like their cosmopolitan European peers than like the typical American student.

4. The participants were not partisan in their criticisms of America, but based their observations on principled questions derived from the Bill of Rights.

5. They "seemed to have a nuanced understanding of what is special about being an American."

6. They spoke less about other governments, and indeed seemed less interested in current affairs than in people.

7. They "seemed to have a greater commitment to solving the problems of societies and being engaged personally in that process" and "talked very thoughtfully" about the human dimension and the "inner lives" of the people with whom they worked.

8. They showed a high level of individualism and were focused on the here-and-now of social engagement.

Whiteley's observations, of course, are colored by the lack of baseline data—a problem confronted by all four researchers, and a powerful argument for the design and implementation of a longitudinal study that can track Partnership students at least for the future. There is also an obvious methodological limitation in inferring criteria for successful study abroad from one source and applying them to service-learning outcomes in another setting, even if the authors of the criteria are the founders of the organization providing the setting—and yet the exercise is surprisingly revealing, both for what it tells us about Berry and Chisholm's views on international experience and for what we learn about the degree to which international service-learning actually exceeds the conventional expectations of study abroad (a strong argument to colleges that still doubt the educational value of international service-learning).

## A Note on Method

It will be apparent to the reader that this study of student attitudes and of the effect of Partnership programs on students is only a beginning. While a qualitative study may be the place to begin, because it identifies issues and suggests lines of research, it obviously has significant drawbacks. As in all qualitative research, where the sample of individuals involved is typically small, generalizability of analyses and results to other populations is problematic. The study, then, could not establish whether the

Partnership's programs have a profound effect on *all* its students: the seventeen alumni were selected mostly because they were deemed to be particularly articulate about their experiences and because they represented different programs and different ages. The notion of "transferability," however, does apply: some elements of commonality among the unique experiences of a small group of people can be identified and have relevance for other individuals. What we know less about are the unsuccessful experiences of Partnership alumni—the negative experiences and the reasons for these experiences.

But Whiteley's expression of the need for baseline data is clearly to the point. It is crucially important that the Partnership design and put in place a long-term and systematic mechanism for gathering longitudinal data, and also that it begin to apply some of the instruments available for testing attitudes and beliefs (both before and after the experience) and for measuring such factors as language-learning. The meetings in New York, valuable as they were, suffered also from the fact that they were based on self-reporting—and self-reporting under conditions that must inevitably produce distortions.

Perhaps the term "distortion" is the wrong term, since it implies the possibility of an "undistorted" record of the past. All memories are shaped by our desire to make sense of the past: over time, the very framework into which we put them may cause them to take on new forms.[2] Our own unsystematic observations suggest that Americans are particularly given to seeing their lives in terms of conversion experiences—experiences in which the impulse for change comes exclusively from outside, in spite of their own will or desire. Extended stays abroad, because they challenge us to question ourselves and our beliefs, are ideal candidates for such treatment. And so master narratives emerge, in which momentary impulses or temporary realignments of spirit are turned into life-changing events, as though such changes in direction would never have occurred, or been so complete, without the immediate external impulse that generated them. We have all

---

[2] The problem of truth-telling and narrative is well-known to specialists in many fields—anthropology, psychoanalysis, jurisprudence, medicine, to mention just a few. Freud's essay "Constructions in Analysis" (1937) suggested, in the words of Theodore Shapiro (Shapiro 2004:341), "that the uncovered past was about the past, but not from the past, permitting the idea that conviction can be a product of analytic suggestion or transference love, rather than a demonstration of the reality of remembered past events." This process of reconstruction "within the dyad" is, inevitably, culturally and situationally determined and also generically based.

heard these narratives from our students, or our peers, indeed we have probably used them ourselves (and sometimes, as in Linda Chisholm's splendid book *Charting a Hero's Journey* they can be authentically useful). The fact that we recognize narrative as a genre is obviously helpful because it allows us to recognize the forms when they occur.

This is not to say that our students or our researchers spoke untruths or half-truths on that day in New York. Indeed, much of what the students told us, thanks to skilled questioning, was of a kind that did not lend itself to fictionalization or recontextualizing. But the most valuable truths may have come incidentally, and in some instances may still need to be teased out of the transcripts and recordings that remained when the day was over.

So the mere request that a group of Partnership alumni come to New York to talk about their Partnership experience is likely to elevate the experience to new levels, and the mere fact that four researchers are willing to spend the day asking carefully framed questions is likely to produce equally carefully framed responses. So we must look beyond the answers to the questions as we interpret the information before us, reminding ourselves that what alumni *think* happened in India or Ecuador or France years before may be as important as, and merely different from, what actually happened—and that what actually happened can really only be established (if at all) by the careful triangulation of information and by the skilled questioning practiced by our seasoned researchers.

As Pusch points out in her essay, our concerns about master narratives aside, the gathering in New York created an opportunity for alumni to reflect upon the different ways the Partnership experience affected them, to rethink their experiences, narrate their life history, and process their memories in the company of other alumni who shared similar histories. For many, the event presented an opportunity to generate new meanings for events in their past and to discuss an experience that they all agreed was an important turning point in their lives. For the Partnership itself, certain conclusions emerged from the study that can serve both as starting points for further research and important findings in themselves.

# Conclusions: The Student Study

No qualitative study can be reduced to a set of "findings" or "results," and the present study must be absorbed in all its complexity. Yet certain common themes did emerge, and the fact that all four researchers spent time together (increasingly so as the day went on) and the students became noticeably more animated as they shared ideas with one another, meant that the level of agreement on the essential issues was quite high. So certain basic observations emerged and are worth recording as consensus among the researchers. They track the points in Siegel's report (chapter 7) fairly closely, but with some notable additions.

1.  International service-learning, while it shares some characteristics with study abroad, is generally a more radical educational experience likely to have a long-term impact on those who pass through it.

As Tonkin and Quiroga (2004) point out in their *Frontiers* article, "the researchers focused their attention not only on the transformative aspects of service-learning in general (a topic quite widely represented in the research literature) and not only on those aspects of the cross-cultural experience that we associate with study abroad (again, quite well documented), but also, and most particularly, on the double clash of cultures that students confront in a service-learning situation abroad: sharp ethnic and often linguistic differences, but also socio-economic differences and differences in the physical environment." The student "is confronted with social situations, and the need to adjust to them, often wrenchingly different from those experienced at home." Furthermore, "Partnership students are taught and supervised exclusively by in-country personnel, and the Partnership makes special efforts to place them in agencies where they work independently of one another, so the immersion is close to total (much greater than that experienced by most students engaged in conventional study abroad)."

2. **International Partnership for Service-Learning students experience culture shock as they move into the Partnership experience.**

As Pusch suggests, it is often difficult to remember the transition process one experiences after the adaptation to a new culture is complete, and especially after some time has passed. Many students denied that they had suffered from culture shock—until they were asked about when they felt comfortable in their host cultures and if there were any frustrations. Given the characteristics of Partnership programs mentioned above, it would make sense that culture shock symptoms would emerge primarily in the context of the service portion of the Partnership program: it is there that students have the most contact with the local culture and the most difficulty decoding and adapting to it. Often this disorientation manifested itself as frustration at the agencies and a lack of confidence in the students' own contribution: "They were frustrated with the language differences, with what they perceived as the lack of organization within the agency and with the pace at which things moved," Quiroga reports. Students learned to deal with this frustration by turning it into a challenge, and the very lack of structure allowed them to find creative solutions and turn the lack of guidance into a learning situation. But, says Quiroga, "Most students thought . . . that the agencies were making tremendous efforts to maintain the level of support they provided given the limited resources they had. Many students felt that they learned a lot about the ways in which people can be creative and effective, despite their financial limitations."

3. **Partnership students display a high level of adaptability to a new culture.**

Pusch observes that "The interviewees adapted to and learned the culture in various ways, both subtle and practical. Most reached the point of being able to internalize more than one world view and their behavior shifted into different frames of reference without much conscious effort. The recognition of patterns of behavior different from their own and the ability to adjust emerged over and over again, indicating a high level of adaptation and an ability to learn from small everyday occurrences, to gain some level of effectiveness in the culture, and to develop connections with people and institutions." Siegel adds: "The extent to which the majority of students were adaptable prior to entering the program as opposed to developing adaptability as a result of their experience, remains unclear. It is evident, however, that they used or developed a posture of 'adaptability' as a resource for becoming more socialized into their host culture. It was a stance and way of thinking and acting that put them in good stead in confronting any number of situations and scenarios during their service term."

4.   **Partnership students tend to be highly motivated and eager to test theory against practice and practice against theory.**

Although students entered the program for a range of personal reasons, they shared an interest in coupling a focus on service with academic and cultural learning. They wanted to be fully engaged in the life of the community and to have some structure within which to serve, study and live. They also shared a need to experiment, to be involved directly, to connect the experience to theory, and to reflect on everything that was being encountered. "Everyone was an explorer both before entering the Partnership and during the program. This was a group full of curiosity," Pusch suggests. "They sought clarification about what they were seeing, feeling, and experiencing, which required reflection but also drew on academic sources to explain parts of the society and culture that did not otherwise make sense. They all had had enough concrete experience to have developed feelings about what they wanted in an educational experience and how they would go about extracting the learning from whatever situation they found themselves in." Siegel adds: "Students are always processing on an intellectual level when they are living and serving abroad, and they are constantly trying to negotiate things—relationships with people, living with the host family, trying to bridge the language gap."

5.  The pedagogy of reflection is particularly important to Partnership students.

Given the eagerness with which students seized on the combination of learning and service, it is no surprise that they regard the process of reflection as particularly important. As Pusch explains, "They tended to rely on reflection to sort out their own place, their own identity, and their sense of what this meant to them in the long-term. They tended to carry what they had learned in the classroom and from observing people in the culture into the service but also into their everyday lives, using their social interactions and the process of meeting daily needs as a learning resource. Ultimately, this led to an internalization of the learning that was immediately useful but, in some cases, it took years to realize the full richness of what was learned."

6.  Partnership students display optimism and a positive attitude: these are significant factors that help foster success in the international service-learning experience.

"We came to understand," writes Siegel, "that positive self-confidence plays a significant role in the success and work of students on foreign soil, particularly students who are living with native families and faced with the challenge of overcoming daunting language barriers. While some students appear to have been equipped with a certain measure of self-confidence prior to their embarking on the service experience, many discovered a self-confidence in themselves they never knew existed." Some remarked on the courage they felt at having partaken in the service experience in the first place—far from home, often for the first time, for many students.

7.  Partnership students are comfortable with ambiguity and necessarily adaptable to the environment and culture.

Siegel remarks on the students' marked tolerance for ambiguity: "Many students noted the relative lack of structure during their service experience and commented on the way in which they took control of the situation, using ambiguity as a motivator for, rather than a deterrent to, their work and involvement with the local culture. Though the Partnership takes care to provide a structured experience within the context of the service, inevitably there is some degree of ambiguity inherent in the system when working with international programs, disparate language groups and communities, and foreign travel and study." This acceptance of ambiguity was, as we have seen, an important strategy in overcoming culture shock, and a pathway to an understanding of the clash between the values of home culture and host culture that all students experienced.

## 8. Partnership students undergo transformative intellectual and moral development.

"In reflecting on their experiences," Siegel points out, "students commented on situations and events that challenged their belief systems and caused them to reevaluate their own thoughts about morality, peace, justice, fairness, norms of behavior, citizenship, learning, decision making, and notions of race and sex. . . . Service experiences also had a transformative effect on students' sense of justice and treatment of others in society." Students were also faced with what appeared marked inequities. Quiroga comments on the difficulties that students face in confronting abject poverty; and related issues of class and race; students themselves allude to the situation of women and their own sense of being discriminated against or ignored. It is of course not enough to react with anger, but requires understanding, and a consequent shift, or nuancing, of values.

## 9. Student views shift from a task orientation to a people orientation.

Perhaps one reason for students' initial difficulties with their placements was too great a focus on tasks and not enough on people. Pusch refers to "the slow internalization of a new set of values: a greater orientation to being people- rather than task-centered, an increased concern for building and maintaining relationships, a sense of responsibility for the collective and an ability to change one's own goals and objectives because of new ways of perceiving the world and one's place in it. The students had become more mindful, they learned to withhold judgment, and to be flexible— important intercultural skills. The word 'openness' came up again and again: openness to new cultures, ideas, and ways of learning but also openness to what they were learning about themselves."

## 10. Partnership students develop a pluralistic world view.

But the process went further, into what Pusch calls an "ability to move beyond empathy to pluralism." As Pusch points out, the students "had obviously acquired and employed at least a second world view . . . and were able to talk about the shifts they made between them." Some had perhaps reached a level of internal integration in which they could evaluate situations contextually and "analyze situations from more than one cultural perspective."

## 11. The Partnership experience causes students to reconceptualize the nature of service.

Not only did students in most cases adapt to their service situations, but they began to rethink their definition of service. "Many alumni felt that their experience in the agency transformed their conception of service and their understanding of what it truly means to help others," Quiroga reports. "Some of the alumni thought that it was important to make a distinction between service-learning and other types of 'charitable' activities, and that their service helped them understand the difference between help on the one hand and social development on the other. They mentioned that the combination of service and learning allowed them to contextualize good service as related to development and empowerment, and they contrasted that with charity. . . . One of the most valuable aspects of the service experience, emphasized by many, was the fact that service helped the students recognize the limits of their ability to effect change in complex situations."

## 12. Partnership students have a "civic-minded personality."

While, according to Siegel, "Many of the students in the study appear to have a predisposition for service . . . and in many cases they have a long resumé of experiences that suggests service has been either a prominent feature in their upbringing or a choice they have made in their own lives," for others "the service-abroad experience introduced students to civic service and engagement and started them on a path of service on which they continue to this day." For the latter group, the Partnership was a "catalytic" event. Pusch adds: "Partnership students seem exceptional in their commitment to civic responsibility and may come into the program at a higher level than would be expected of most study-abroad students. Thus, the increase in their *level* of sensitivity and intercultural competence may be less dramatic, but the degree of sophistication achieved may be markedly higher." Whiteley echoes this sentiment.

### 13. For some students, the Partnership experience is so powerful that it shapes their subsequent careers.

In several cases, participants traced their present occupations to their time in the Partnership. For these individuals, remarks Siegel, "there appears to be a direct cause-and-effect relationship between the Partnership experience and the work in which they are currently involved." Quiroga noted that "in some cases, the experience was perceived to have had a profound effect on their career choices: they construed it as a 'turning point' and mapped their experiences in terms of after and before."

### 14. Partnership students are deeply engaged with the host society.

Pusch tells us that "Most research on study abroad shows that host-sojourner interactions are limited and the greatest complaint from participants is their disappointment in not getting to know members of the host culture." She adds, "This complaint was never voiced by Partnership alumni. The Partnership program facilitates interaction between sojourners and hosts to a remarkable degree by embedding students in the community through agency service and local living arrangements." Furthermore, whereas in conventional study abroad a student's universe revolves around his or her peers and professors, with perhaps the addition of the bureaucracy of a foreign university to contend with, Partnership students have, in the broad sense, many teachers—most of them unambiguously members of the host culture, and some of them the clients of the agencies where they serve.

### 15. Partnership students gain a sense of interconnectedness with the world.

Quiroga observes, "A much-repeated sentiment was the development of a strong sense of commitment and a certain fellow-feeling with people in a distant country. We are so often encouraged to think globally and act locally that we forget the importance of global action too. Many participants commented on the fact that the service component generates a sense of involvement with a situation that before was foreign and distant, a globalization of their feelings and concerns and of their sense of citizenship. This deterritorialization of social commitments and globalization of sensibilities was often reflected in the way students talked about world issues and current politics."

### 16. Reentry, difficult for all students returning from abroad, is particularly difficult for Partnership students.

"Reentry," says Pusch, "may be the hardest and, for learning, the most productive time: it takes the complete cycle of departure/sojourn/return to solidify the learning. The learning continues long after the return." It is particularly hard for Partnership students, whose level of engagement with the host society has been total, and who, in returning to their own country, leave behind their teachers, their host families, their service agencies, the clients of these agencies, and a pattern of living that they themselves have been largely responsible for constructing. Not only is this wrenching in itself, but it carries with it a measure of guilt. For the seventeen interviewees, reentry was also the most recent memory—still being negotiated by some. As Pusch suggests, "Reentry is still an immediate memory because it is a longer-term process for most people. Unlike culture shock, a recognized phenomenon whose symptoms are widely known although they often go unrecognized by the person in the shock phrase of transition, reentry . . . tends to be a lifetime event: there will always be a "before" and an "after" to the time when they were in another culture." Siegel calls it "repatriation syndrome." Says Pusch, "Such disorientation is in part temporary, but in part close to permanent."

### 17. Partnership students develop a nuanced and complex view of America.

Siegel states that "The impact of the Partnership service experience on the views of students about their home country was well-documented. . . . Most prevalent were comments about the wasteful nature of American society, the high regard for material goods and services, and the relative poverty of other nations compared to the United States." But, as Whiteley points out, views were not particularly partisan and were based on a "nuanced" understanding. As Siegel explains, "Many students returned with a respect and appreciation for their status as American citizens, having learned to appreciate many things that most Americans take for granted— access to public education, freedom of speech, a democratic society, a relatively stable economy, and, of course, electricity and running water."

### 18. Partnership students display qualities of leadership.

Pusch remarks that "Leadership was not specifically explored in the interviews, and I suspect [the participants] would deny being leaders, but they clearly exhibited the potential for leadership roles in professional and community work and organizations. . . . It is clear that service-learning as practiced by the Partnership in a 'foreign' culture context has a significant impact on the lives of its students in terms of personal and professional development and certainly in terms of intercultural competence and learning. While their commitment to service may be what draws them into the program in the beginning, they clearly become more capable of working with a diverse clientele and delivering service under less than ideal conditions during the program. This capability is useful in many situations, both domestic and international, and we have every reason to believe that they have acquired not only intercultural and organizational skills but the ability to be leaders in whatever they choose to do." The Partnership experience develops in the students not only an adaptability and resourcefulness, but also ways of looking at old problems with fresh eyes, and recontextualizing familiar issues in the light of broader experience. Such characteristics are fundamental to leadership.

# PART 3

# How Partnership Programs Affect Agencies and Their Clients

# 9 The Agency Study: Introduction

Service-learning (as we know) has two equal, and equally important, parts—learning on the one hand and service on the other. In this paradigm, we associate service with action, and learning with reflection on that action. Ideally, the service enhances the learning, by providing a place where theories can be tested and knowledge can be applied to particular situations; and the learning enhances the service, by making the service-learner better informed and better able to assemble and evaluate theoretical constructs.

This definition of service-learning, however, is essentially learner-centered: it addresses the experience of the student in the classroom and the field, and it concerns what happens to the student, and only indirectly what happens to the agency. But what if we look at the process from a service-centered perspective? What if we ask how the presence of service-learners in an agency makes a difference to the agency and its work? When service is carried out by a service-learner it is enhanced because ideally the service-learner comes to the community-service agency and its clients having thought hard about how to be effective in the field. Such a student is more than simply a volunteer, more than merely another pair of hands, because the student comes to the agency with an awareness of the context of the agency's work and a responsibility to understand it better. Under such circumstances, the agency has a right to expect a level of thoughtfulness and commitment that an ordinary volunteer might not display.

If learning raises the quality of the service, at the same time the student's learning is enhanced because the student learns to set acquired knowledge in a moral and ethical context: learning becomes not simply so many theories, so many pieces of data, but something that is applied actively and directly in ways that affect people's lives. The result (or so we hope) is that service-learners increase their awareness of social responsibility; and their learning, both within and outside the context of service-learning, comes to be applied, also in later life, in a value-rich way.

So service-learning benefits society because it is concerned on the one hand with the education of the service-learner in justice and social responsibility, and on the other with social betterment through the service-learner's contribution in the field. On the one hand the learner's service is valuable in itself, and, on the other, the indirect benefits derived from educating an informed and ethical citizenry will help society solve the problems that the service agencies exist to relieve. We know that service-learning benefits the individual learner, but it should also (and equally) benefit society as a whole.

As we have noted in an earlier chapter, the theory of service-learning, at least as applied by the founders of the Partnership, posits a certain reciprocity between the learner on the one hand and the service agency (and its clients) on the other. Behind such an assumption of reciprocity is an ethic of service-learning based on the belief that each party has an obligation to the other. Academic leaders may pay rhetorical tribute to the good that their students do for the larger society, but those who do the teaching sometimes take the service agencies for granted, and, if an agency is not perfectly suited to the requirements of the curriculum, they drop it in favor of one that is—without asking any questions about the goals or needs or importance of the agency. As we have stated earlier in this report (in our discussion of the ethics of service-learning), any well-designed service-learning program should have a place for the examination of outcomes not just in learning but also in service, and service-learning that exists for its own sake, without consideration of agency outcomes, contradicts its own terms.

But in reality service-learning should extend beyond reciprocity (university to agency, agency to university; student to client, client to student) to situate itself in a larger context of mutuality, in which an agency is seen as part of a larger effort at solving a problem or alleviating suffering, and the student is learning not just about the particulars of an agency but about a new way of thinking about, and serving, the larger society. Such mutuality implies a willingness of both university and agency to see the other's work as important. If a university is only interested in its own mission of teaching and not the quality of service it provides to the community through its students, the students sense this disparity quite quickly and tend to regard their service not as a part of a larger endeavor but simply as an opportunity to feel good about themselves. Effective service-learning connects the student to an enterprise larger than the self, moving the student beyond self-centeredness to a focus on the needs of others and engagement with the community.

That is why the study that occupies the next chapter is so very important. It is something of a pioneering study: there is very little in the literature about the impact of service-learning on agencies. The goal of the agency study was described in the research plan as follows: "To carry out a study of social service organizations that have worked with the Partnership and its receiving institutions over a number of years, including the development of profiles of these organizations and of the Partnership's impact (a) on the agencies themselves and (b) on the transformation of the communities they serve. The study will also examine the importance of the university/agency connection."

In February and March 2003, we carried out a qualitative study in Glasgow, Scotland, through the University of Glasgow, and in April we conducted a similar round of interviews with service agencies and service-users in Kingston, Jamaica, assisted by staff from the Partnership program at the University of Technology Jamaica. Although these places share common features, there are marked cultural and historical differences between them. Both locations have welfare agencies with a need for volunteer service. Furthermore, both locations have service-learning programs where students take a fully accredited academic course. There are inherent differences, however, because service-learning at Glasgow University is relatively new, not only as part of an academic program, but also as a concept. In addition, the program is presently only available for overseas students. By contrast, service-learning at the University of Technology in Kingston is a well-established program and is compulsory for all undergraduates.

The agencies were selected because they had regularly hosted service-learning students over a number of years. A total of thirteen agencies participated in the study: seven in Glasgow and six in Kingston. Those in Glasgow consisted of two special educational needs schools, an after-school children's resource club, a day center for disabled adults, a day center for the infirm and frail elderly, a drug crisis center, and a museum of social work. In Kingston, the agencies included in the study were a special educational needs school, two primary schools, a medical welfare agency, a national youth training agency, and the YMCA (which has programs for school leavers).

The study makes it apparent that the overriding impact of students on agencies and clients was positive. The study also highlights the need for agencies to have a voice in a program: staff are aware of the needs of the agency and know what type of students would be most suitable for them; their perceptions can influence the effectiveness of the students. Attention to reciprocity is needed to maintain effective communication, and to develop and sustain a collaborative relationship between agencies and universities.

It is sometimes hard for Partnership program participants to see the long-term impact of the program and their part in it, as our student study makes clear. That issue has been eloquently addressed by Victor Mariduena Varela, a Partnership trustee and former director of service agencies in Ecuador, who points to the constant presence of students, year after year, doing small things that mean something to the people with whom they work, making a difference if only by demonstrating that there is a group of people who care. It is the continual presence of Partnership volunteers, not the specific contribution of one individual, that has a lasting and profound impact within the agencies and for the clients.

# 10 The Impact of Experience

## A Comparative Study of the Effects of International Partnership for Service-Learning Students within Welfare Agencies in Scotland and Jamaica

### Susan J. Deeley

Developments in the area of teaching and learning have led to a gradual acceptance of the pedagogy of experiential learning. Much of the literature in this area is focused on the benefits of service-learning for students. Little research has been conducted on the benefits to the community where students gain their experience. This study therefore seeks to redress the balance by investigating the effects of students on welfare agencies that host service-learning programs.

A comparative analysis was made on the impact students have on staff and service-users in two locations that host international service-learning students: Glasgow in Scotland and Kingston in Jamaica. Similar themes and characteristics of the program were present in both locations. Overall, the findings showed that most of the effects of the students were positive. Some of the findings, however, were ambiguous. On the basis of the findings, and taking into consideration the issues raised in the literature, several recommendations are made for the increased efficacy of service-learning programs.

Studies have identified different approaches in the processes of student learning (Entwistle, Hanley & Hounsell 1979; Brown & Atkins 1988; Ramsden 1992). Learning can take place on three levels: deep, surface and strategic, although these levels are not mutually exclusive. Deep learning occurs when concepts are related to experience, and is therefore relevant to service-learning. It is also believed that deep learning produces high levels of achievement (Wisker, Tiley, Watkins, Waller & Thomas 2001). Moreover, the educational value of experiential learning has been validated from various perspectives (Weill & McGill 1989, Kendall et al. 1990, Jacoby et al. 1996). The results of these studies suggest that the nature of service-learning in the educational process is valuable and of benefit to students. Focus has been on the impact of this particular type of experience on students' education (Hein & Conrad 1990, Kinnell 1990, Williams 1990) but "little attention has been focused on the effects of service-learning on the community providers or on development in the community itself" (Jacoby 1996). The dearth of research in this area has been acknowledged by Driscoll, Holland, Gellman & Kerrigan (1996) who state that there are "gaps in our knowledge about the effects of service-learning and the difficulty in measuring those effects." More recent studies have begun to address this issue, in particular Jones (2003), who states, however, that little research has been conducted on the "nature and outcomes . . . from the community agency perspective."

Additionally, there is a growing body of literature concerning the multi-faceted aspects of effective service-learning. Howard (1993), for example, appropriately points out that this type of experiential education cannot be perceived in isolation and that the tripartite relationship between students, academy and community must be considered with regard to the effectiveness of service-learning. The relationship is characterized by three main issues: those of collaboration, reciprocity and diversity. Overriding features in the literature accentuate the importance of partnerships, collaboration and reciprocity in service-learning. These factors are all relevant in varying degrees to the impact that students have on the welfare agencies.

Jacoby (2003) reiterates a commonly held view when she states that the relationship between "campus and community" is of paramount importance. Ideally, it is a partnership. Miller, Watts & Jamieson (1991) describe this partnership as "integrated" to a program, where agencies are "seen as partners in the delivery of the whole program," rather than as "bolt-on" or a medium for the delivery of experience. Much of the literature in this area concerns the features of this partnership: collaboration, communication and reciprocity. For the relationship to be successful, Berry (1988) believes that there must be "parity of esteem and mutuality on the part of all concerned." He explains that respect is essential and that all parties are "both donors as well as recipients" (Berry 1985).

Inherent to the success of this partnership is collaboration: as Jacoby (2003) states, "truly reciprocal partnerships are also termed collaborations." Collaboration may be perceived in various ways, for example in terms of developing effective communication and in creating mutually beneficial goals. Ultimately, it is vital that a positive relationship between the academic institution and the community be nurtured (Caron, Genereux & Huntsberger 1999). Effective communication between these parties is essential for strengthening the relationship (Vernon & Ward 1999), but its content is equally important. Chrislip & Larson (1994) believe that a "shared vision" of the expectations and goals of service-learning is desirable. This is a fundamental prerequisite for the success of any program (Honnet & Poulsen 1989; Giles & Eyler 1994; Jones 2003). Furthermore, Bucco & Busch (1996) claim that "clearly defining expectations and relationships early greatly increases the probability that a high-quality, meaningful, and sustainable service-learning program will develop."

It is therefore vital that welfare agencies involved in any service-learning program have a voice. Indeed, as Jones (2003) believes, agencies have an "integral role," and their needs must be articulated within this context (Kendall 1990; Mintz & Hesser 1996; Chisholm 2003; Jacoby 2003). Berry (1985) states that the agency "should be able to voice its needs and expectations as an equal partner in the design of the experience" and adds that agencies "should be involved in planning and assessing the learning processes and outcomes." Mintz and Hesser (1996) reiterate this, advocating that the "voice and needs of community are included in the development of the community service program," which would involve stipulating selective criteria for students. Vernon and Ward (1999) take this idea further by saying that agencies should be involved in recruiting students. They also advocate evaluations of the effects of programs on agencies. Moreover, Chisholm (2003) recommends that "agencies . . . should be given the opportunity to raise issues about individual students as well as about the program as a whole." What is paramount, however, is that a balance is maintained between meeting agencies' needs and meeting those of the students in terms of their intended learning outcomes (Jones 2003).

Added to the notions of partnership, collaboration and communication is the issue of reciprocity (Howard 1993). Chrislip & Larson (1994) believe that reciprocity is vital because "there is a real risk of exploiting or coercing both the community and the student." Mintz & Hesser (1996) agree that reciprocity is the "most fundamental ingredient for high-quality service-learning programs." Reciprocity is not necessarily a quantitative or a qualitative concept, but flexibility is essential (Torres 2000). Jones (2003) believes that reciprocity implies equality. However, equality is a contested concept (Letwin 1983), and therefore reciprocity might be more suitably described as "an exchange." Giles & Freed (1985) indeed refer to this type of reciprocity as a "social exchange" although Sigmon (1990) goes further, describing it as a "social and educational exchange." Service-learning also involves "reciprocal learning" (Honnet & Poulsen 1989, Stanton 1990). In whatever way this notion is interpreted, it is clear that the reciprocity within the relationship presupposes that the experience is interdependent. In this sense, service-learning implies active participation by all parties involved, rather than passive recipiency. Failure in reciprocity may lead to conflict, but this may be resolved through effective communication (Rue 1996) to restore a "mutually beneficial relationship" (Chrislip & Larson 1994).

Overall, there is an underlying thematic relationship between campus and community common throughout the literature concerning service-learning. Ideal characteristics of this relationship are, then, partnership, collaboration, communication and *reciprocity*. One dimension of the relationship concerns students and agencies, but little research has been conducted on this aspect from the agencies' point of view.

The academic institutions involved in the service-learning programs in this study were the University of Glasgow, Scotland, and the University of Technology Jamaica, Kingston, both of which are host institutions for Partnership programs. The aim of the study was to investigate the effects that service-learning students have on the staff and service-users of voluntary welfare agencies. It was useful to identify these effects for various reasons: first, to improve the experience for agencies and students; second, to discover any negative factors so that appropriate action could be taken to minimize them; and third, to gain insight into the holistic experience of service-learning and therefore contribute to an understanding of the relationship between campus and community.

The study was in two parts, the first based in Glasgow and the second in Kingston. Service-learning is a relatively new course at the University of Glasgow and is open only to overseas students. By contrast, service-learning at the University of Technology in Kingston is a well-established course for overseas students, in addition to the requirement that all students at the University undertake a period of voluntary work during their degree course. It was therefore useful and interesting to investigate the impact of international service-learning students in these two sites in order to identify commonalities and differences. Also useful was the comparison of two culturally different geographical settings that share the common ground of service-learning students working in voluntary welfare agencies while attending a symbiotic and accredited academic course in higher education. Through comparative analysis it was possible to identify characteristics unique to the impact of service-learning students. Some of these findings may be attributed to the cultural heritage of the country and/or the differences that can exist "among agencies and within agencies" (Jones 2003).

## The Study

Two small-scale qualitative studies took place in Glasgow and Kingston between February and April 2003. In Glasgow a total of seven out of twenty welfare agencies that regularly host service-learning students were selected to participate in the research. The agencies were chosen because they were knowledgeable about the nature of service-learning and would be in a position to offer a variety of information on the impact of students. Initially, it was hoped that two members of staff and two service-users chosen at random from each agency would participate. Unfortunately, because of the nature of the welfare provision, service-users from only three agencies actually took part. In some instances, service-users only used the agency on a transitory basis (for example, a center for drug users in crisis), and therefore were not available for interview. Other service-users were unable to participate because of their severe or profound learning disabilities. Consequently, the total number of service-users was eleven, which was almost equal to that of staff, which totalled twelve. In all, twenty-three qualitative interviews were conducted in Glasgow.

All the agencies were located in the Greater Glasgow area and represented a diversity of welfare provision. They included two schools for primary-aged children with a range of special needs, an after school hours children's resource club in a deprived area of Glasgow, a day center for disabled adults, a day center for the infirm and frail elderly, a drug crisis center, which included methadone detoxification and needle exchange for drug users, and a museum of social work.

The second part of the study took place in Kingston. The service-learning program director at the University of Technology arranged interviews with welfare service agencies that host service-learning students. As in Glasgow, agencies that were regularly involved in the program were selected to participate in the research, and, as with the first part of the study, the intention was to interview two members of staff and two service-users from each agency. This was not always possible, for the same reasons as in Glasgow: transitory use and severe disabilities. The total number of service-users was seven, and the total number of staff interviewed was nine. In total, sixteen qualitative interviews were conducted in Kingston.

All the agencies were located in Kingston and, as in Glasgow, represented a diversity of welfare provision. They included two schools for primary-aged children and one school for children and young people with a range of special needs; a medical welfare service agency; a national training agency that provides an educational and vocational program for disaffected young people; and the YMCA, which provides educational and recreational activities for young people some of whom have learning difficulties.

Overall, thirty-nine qualitative interviews were conducted in the study: twenty-one with staff and eighteen with service-users.

## Methods

Ethical approval for the research was granted by the University of Glasgow's Ethics Committee in the Faculty of Social Sciences. Because the study involved research with vulnerable groups, it was also necessary to gain ethical approval from the Local Research Ethics Committee, Greater Glasgow Health Board. Under new legislation in Scotland, a certificate was required from Disclosure Scotland to verify that it was appropriate for the researcher to undertake the research with vulnerable groups.

Following telephone calls to the agencies and their initial agreement to participate, information sheets and two copies of a consent form were given to each member of staff prior to interview. The respondents kept the information sheet and a copy of their consent form. Service-users were given two copies of an information sheet and consent form combined. This was a simplified version to ensure clarity of understanding so that informed consent could be given. Additionally and where appropriate, there was also an information sheet and two copies of a consent form for the parents or carers of the service-users. All respondents were assured of anonymity. The consent of each respondent for tape-recording the interviews was requested. The tapes and all other data were kept securely and the tapes were wiped at the end of the project. The interviews with vulnerable people were held in the presence of members of staff and/or in public areas of the agency.

Semi-structured interviews were conducted with twenty-one members of staff and eighteen service-users. The format of the questions for each group differed slightly. The overarching research question concerned the effects of service-learning students on the welfare agencies, as perceived by staff and service-users. The following areas were also addressed:

- the qualities and skills of service-learning students
- a comparison with other voluntary workers
- the relationship between agency and campus
- the possible changing effects of service-learning students during their time at the agency
- the possible long-term effects of this experience on the agency, staff and service-users.

General information relating to each of the agencies was also collated. Several key areas were covered, for example:

- the nature of the agency
- factors relating to staff (age and gender)
- factors relating to service-users (welfare needs, age and gender)
- the relationship between staff and service-users
- factors relating to students (cultural differences, age and gender)
- duties undertaken by students

All the interviews, except three, were tape-recorded and transcribed verbatim. Two members of staff refused permission for the interview to be tape-recorded (one in Glasgow and one in Kingston). In a third case, the equipment was found to be faulty with the result that the interview was not tape-recorded. In these instances, the researcher took handwritten notes at the consent of the individuals present. The duration of the interviews ranged from fifteen minutes to more than one hour.

Using a grounded theory approach (Glaser & Strauss 1967), an initial analysis of the data gathered in Glasgow was necessary to identify themes, which could be explored further in Kingston. The discovery of these themes arose from the data collection and was later related to characteristics within the campus-community relationship advocated in the literature. The main strategy in identifying the themes was a "general method of comparative analysis" (Glaser & Strauss 1967). From the data there emerged several themes. These were coded under the categories of: needs, time, cultural differences, motivation, age, gender, reciprocity, skills, social interaction, and risks. From the data, properties from each of the categories were then identified. Glaser and Strauss describe a property as "a conceptual aspect or element of a category." In this study, the coding and analysis were performed in close succession to enhance a systematic sequential and comparative analysis. By the end of the study, "saturation" of the categories and properties was reached and replication of the types of responses was noted.

The data from the first part of the study were sequentially and comparatively analyzed. An initial report was drafted that identified themes and characteristics of the nature of the impact of the service-learning students on the agencies in Glasgow. Following this, the data from the Kingston study was also sequentially and comparatively analyzed, together with the findings from the first part of the study.

Clearly, there were limitations to this research, particularly limited time and smallness of scale. The respondents within the agencies were self-selected and therefore their contributions to the data may have been positively biased to some degree. Nevertheless, similar issues were raised by respondents in Scotland and Jamaica, which suggests that these could be attributed to the effects of service-learning students. It is possible that these issues could be further validated if the study were replicated in other sites.

After the interviews, letters of thanks were sent to each of the respondents for their time and help with the study.


## Findings

Although the cultural setting and historical background of the two sites for this study differ in many respects, there are common factors, namely (1) needs of welfare agencies, (2) needs for volunteer service within these agencies, and (3) the fact that both host service-learning programs.

The nature and degree of impact of service-learning students on the welfare agencies varied depending on a number of factors. Some of these were independent of service-learning, but relevant in that they affected staff attitudes, for example the nature of the service provision, the internal structure of the agency, and the agency's expectations of volunteers' work. In other words, the agencies themselves contributed to some extent to the impact of the internship. This confirms the observation by Jones (2003) that there are "differences between agencies and within agencies." Not surprisingly, much also depended on the personality or level of commitment and enthusiasm of the individual students. Some variables were specific to certain individual students, members of staff or service-users; others were generic.

In both Glasgow and Kingston, agencies raised similar issues regarding service-learning students and, similarly, it was found that inter-agency perspectives differed. In one agency, for example, if a student had an outgoing, extrovert personality, this was seen as beneficial to the relationship with service-users. By contrast, a student with an introverted personality might be more suited to working with other types of service-users. In addition, the perspective of the staff influenced their views on particular attributes. In one case, a student was perceived positively as "laid back," calm, almost casual. By contrast, this type of attitude was interpreted by staff in other agencies as a lack of commitment. It is therefore important to be aware of the prevalent attitudes in different agencies and how these can influence perceptions of the students.

Integral to the actual effects of service-learning students on staff and service-users are external factors, which play an essential role. These factors were highlighted by all of the agencies because they shape the perception of students as positive or negative. Such contributory aspects merit examination because they help us gain a clearer insight into the overall impact of service-learning. We will address two such factors: the needs of the service-users and the associated nature of the service provision.

### Needs

Overall, the needs of the service-users were diverse. The agencies in the study represent a range of welfare provision, including the special needs of young children; the social, recreational, vocational and educational needs of materially and, in some cases, emotionally deprived young people; young adults with drug problems; disabled adults; and frail elderly people. Physical care might be needed in one situation, whereas in another, mental stimulation or positive social interaction might be of paramount importance.

In addition to welfare needs, other factors such as age and gender affected the way in which students impacted on service-users.

Students interacted with the service-users in physical tasks such as helping very young or severely disabled children put on their coats or assisting them to eat. Students also helped in activities aimed to mentally stimulate the elderly. Positive social interaction was important to all service-users, for example in Glasgow with drug users in crisis, and with children and young people from a deprived area, and in Kingston with "street boys" who may have been neglected or abandoned by their families.

The needs of the staff in managing the agency were also important. All the agencies in Glasgow stipulated the number of service-learning students they would accept, namely one to five at any one time. One member of staff, however, said she wished there could be more students, in fact "the more the merrier." In Kingston, however, all the staff interviewed at the agencies expressed their preference for more service-learning students, perhaps because of the positive effects of the students or perhaps because of the high ratio of service-users to staff in a number of agencies. In one primary school, for example, "the classes are big, about forty to forty-five children." In such cases, more service-learning students meant that more practical help was available to the agency.

### Time

Relevant to the needs of all agencies and raised by both staff and service-users, was the vital issue of time—a multi-faceted issue with practical implications and qualitative effects. Time mattered to the staff because service-learning students could alleviate the daily demands made on them. Frequently it was claimed that the students were welcomed as "an extra pair of hands" to work with the service-users, thus allowing the staff the time to complete their administrative duties more efficiently. In one of the schools for children with special needs, the teachers found it difficult to acquire the educational and recreational resources appropriate for the children's level of needs. As a consequence, teachers "make up a lot of their own games to supplement whatever we do." One teacher explained, "sometimes we have to adapt what we have to suit the children and that can be quite time-consuming." Having "an extra pair of hands" meant that the teachers' time could be used constructively and effectively.

Many of the agencies in both cities complained that they were short-staffed, either permanently or temporarily because of staff illness. Having a student in the classroom allowed for more flexibility for the teacher, who could organize a small-group activity for the student to supervise while the remainder of the class were involved in another task. Alternatively, the student could work with an individual child. The help that students gave with general tasks for the service-users was seen as an added bonus. As an example, a teacher in Glasgow explained that "some children [with special needs] have to have assisted eating, help with dressing; every time a bell goes somebody's got to put their coats on, somebody's got to give them their lunch and there aren't enough staff." She went on to say that students' help not only meant less stress for the teacher but better service for the children. This view was reiterated in Kingston, where students were "a big help to the services that we offer."

The time spent by students with the service-users was often perceived as "quality time," a feature of additional benefit. In an agency for infirm and elderly adults in Glasgow, the service-users were emphatic about the beneficial effects of having students spend time with them in their daily recreational exercises. One service-user explained that the students "mixed well . . . they helped; they'd say, 'Can I help you with this or that?' And they just sort of blended in. They took part in what was going on." Spending time with the elderly service-users was most appreciated as one elderly service-user said, "They'd sit beside me and we talked about all things." It was not the content of their conversation that was particularly important, but rather that someone new showed interest in them and was prepared to listen to stories that the staff may have heard numerous times before. Despite the difference in age, the students were seen as "one of the crowd." Another elderly service-user described how the students would "really go out of their way" to help the weaker members in team games, such as quizzes that were initiated to stimulate the elderly people. In a center for disabled adults, the students spent more than the required time at the agency. One service-user proudly claimed that the students "got stuck in to what we were doing . . . they mixed in both with the staff and the clients." These views were echoed in the agencies in Kingston, where the students "go out of their way; they really integrate themselves well" and, similarly, "they blend in; they're like one of us." At one agency, a staff member claimed that the students adjusted and assimilated to such an extent that they were regarded as "actually part of the staff . . . they mix very well."

Time spent with service-users resulted in some students building relationships with them. This was an added and welcome bonus to the service-users as well as to the students. For users of the drug crisis center, having a student who was interested in being in their company encouraged them to talk freely, and it gave the service-users the opportunity to socialize with someone outside their usual circle of contacts, most of whom also had a drug problem. It gave them "an awareness of something else . . . outside their small worlds." More importantly perhaps, it increased the service-users' self-esteem and made them feel less "rejected." In one agency, a member of staff found it difficult to encapsulate the particular benefit the student brought to the situation. He said, "They bring something, it's definitely not a loss." Moreover, he claimed that the students did not interfere with his daily tasks, nor did he find their presence time-consuming for him.

A contrasting view, however, was expressed in one agency. Here a more negative view of the students was taken in connection with time. It was believed that students detracted from the staff's time both with the service-users and in their administrative duties. A staff-member said, "The staff don't have the time" to spend supervising students and their tasks. Interestingly, another staff member at the same agency did not agree entirely with this negative view, saying, "I appreciated the help." Nevertheless, she was not in a position to contradict her senior colleague. This is one way in which the internal structure of an agency may be a determining factor in overall perceptions of service-learning students. Regular communication and collaboration between community and campus would alleviate such difficulties. Rue (1996) acknowledges that conflict can arise between the student and the agency and suggests that this could be due to the student's role being unclear. For the success of a program, Rue (1996) recommends that any such conflict be resolved as quickly as possible.

A major issue that concerned most of the staff was the question of how much time the student spent at the agency, that is, in terms of how much time during the day, and for how many weeks. Students' timekeeping was a potentially negative issue. A member of staff explained the problem, saying, "[we] make plans to involve them and then they don't come; things fall apart. If they say they'll come at ten and don't come until eleven, it doesn't really fit in with our routine at all." Another agency reported the absenteeism of a student, although they admitted that the lack of reliable public transport to the agency might have been a contributory factor. They complained that the student had not kept to the agreed timetable and the student's late arrival had "disrupted the kids . . . [it was] a pain in the neck." Clearly, some agencies planned their activities ahead based on the knowledge that they would have "an extra pair of hands." If a student then failed to attend, the plans would go awry.

Most of the staff interviewed in the study expressed a wish to see students' placements at the agencies made longer over a period of time and/or to have them spend more time at the agency per day. A problem relating to time that was apparent in Glasgow did not appear to be significantly troublesome in Kingston. Academic demands, such as lecture timetables, and traveling time from the University to the agencies, frequently proved problematic in Glasgow. Exacerbating the problem were time limits at the agencies. One agency, for example, was closed for two half days during the week and others closed regularly at mid-afternoon. In another agency particular activities that would benefit from the help of a student took place on certain days and at specific times. Academic study hours took precedence over these times should they coincide.

It is apparent, then, that time played significant and multi-faceted roles in the students' stay at the agencies and contributed to both positive and negative views of the experience. This example demonstrates how important it is to maintain a balance between intended learning outcomes for the student and the needs of the agency (Jones 2003). Balance might be better achieved through a sharing of expectations between campus and community—through "partnership" and "collaboration."

## Cultural Differences

Partnership students are typically from universities and colleges in the United States. The fact that the students are usually white American affects staff and service-users in various ways. The students bring their own skills, experiences, ideas and values to the agencies.

In both locations the most striking difference presented by the students was language. Their accents and terminology identified them as foreign and added novelty to their presence in the agencies. A nine-year-old child said, "I liked the way they talked." An elderly service-user said that the students could not always understand his broad Glaswegian accent and vernacular. He stated, "They couldn't understand what we were saying and I had to explain to them two or three times." He found this amusing and took great delight in being able to help them understand. As an elderly service-user, he was accustomed to being dependent on others, but in this instance he was helping someone else who was two generations younger. Although difficult to quantify, it may be that this empowered the service-user and helped to increase his self-esteem. The benefits were clearly reciprocal. Another elderly service-user reiterated the problems of language in a light-hearted way. She was not surprised if the students did not understand her fast speech, because, she said, "sometimes I don't even understand mysel', the way we talk . . . some of it isnae very good [laughter] we were teaching them bad habits [laughter]." She added, "I love their twang." Students in Kingston also experienced difficulties in understanding Jamaican dialect or "patois." One member of staff stated that she was frequently asked by students to explain and clarify what the service-users said.

Inherent in language differences was humor. In one agency, it was regarded as a key element for well-being. A manager explained: "Humor's very important. The people here may be in pain, constant pain . . . humor keeps them positive and it's a great icebreaker. When people come in here they should look on this as a joyful experience." He believed that the students "take a while to tune into the language and humor" but that they quickly appreciate "the banter that goes backwards and forwards . . . there's always a wee bit patter about taking the mick and I think sometimes that's important." In this example, and in both locations in the study, students assimilated easily and were accepted through language and humor.

Differences in language were not always perceived in a positive light. It was argued in both cities that for young children with special needs different accent and terminology was actually a disadvantage. It was confusing for the children who "don't catch on at first" especially where a noun was used with a different meaning. A degree of confusion had arisen among some British service-users, for example, when a student misplaced her "purse." The different accent of the students also caused minor problems in communication with the service-users, especially if they had a learning difficulty or were at a remedial level of education.

One factor that was not apparent in Glasgow but was an obvious difference in Kingston was skin color. Most of the international students were white. Although this factor mostly played little or no role, in two agencies skin color had had negative and positive effects. In one school, a member of staff explained that when students initially arrived for their volunteer placement, there were feelings of unease among some of the parents of the children: "They believed that seeing a white person around they might take away the child. That was their fear." Here a historical and cultural inheritance was evident, but the staff had successfully alleviated parental anxiety by explaining the role of the students to them. The staff member went on to say how much the young children enjoyed seeing the physical differences of the foreign students and would always want "to comb and play with their hair" because of its different color and texture.

A positive aspect of skin color was described by a staff member in another agency in Kingston. He said that service-users in his agency were accustomed to white professionals from abroad working with them and that many service-users assumed that the white international students were also professionals. He said the service-users would therefore welcome them and think "they get a better service . . . which isn't true really. It's a little extra that they're getting." Indeed, in this agency it was noted that the presence of white people increased the number of service-users. A staff member commented, "It brings more people in; it actually increases our activity whenever they're here." Their presence helped to increase the agency's funds because the service-users paid a nominal fee for the service.

Cultural differences were also evident in students' strong social confidence. Although most staff saw such confidence in a positive light, in some agencies in Kingston it was regarded as hazardous and therefore potentially negative. Students had to be discouraged from going "out on public transport alone" and were encouraged "always to go with others, always in a group" because of concerns for their safety in certain areas of the city.

Overall the students "seem to have a confidence that comes from the culture there, an air of confidence about themselves"—a positive characteristic, especially in a Scottish culture of reticence: a staff-member in Glasgow added laughingly that it was "something to live up to for us." Although acknowledging their confidence, one member of staff recognised the demands made on the students: "They're coming from another culture, maybe from a rural background and possibly a first experience in Europe, and into an urban area." His view was tempered by the prevailing belief, however, that "we're all Jock Tamson's bairns" despite our differences. This view was reflected in comments made by young people in another agency who did not perceive the students as different at all, apart from the way they spoke. Nevertheless, cultural differences had an impact in various ways and varying degrees on staff and service-users in a number of agencies.

For several staff, interacting with culturally different students was a social and learning experience. Although when the students "first come [to the agencies] they are strangers, after a day it's like they've known everyone a long time." The students invariably "use the right approach, they are not confrontational." Furthermore, they tend to "go out of their way, they really integrate themselves well." Likewise, the staff are welcoming; indeed, one staff member said that they would "like them to be here all the time." Another stated that the students were "good company . . . [I] learned about the different culture and their type of·life which is different from ours." The benefits of hosting the students were multi-faceted as a senior staff member in Glasgow explained: socially, their presence "livened up the place," especially if the work was heavy and perhaps at times depressing. In this sense, having students from a completely different background "brings a bit of fun into the workplace . . . [because usually] you see each other day after day, year after year." This staff member believed that recognition of cultural differences led to reflection on Scottish life and welfare provision, resulting in a wider vision through an "exchange of ideas, sharing new ways of doing things, discussing problems and seeing other people's solutions . . . a new way of thinking." She encapsulated the positive effects of this experience by claiming that "it's a catalyst, it's something that changes things."

The service-users also benefited from being exposed to the cultural differences of the students. One student was Jewish and, at the behest of the staff, explained the basic tenets of her religion to the service-users, describing what she did at particular religious festivals. In addition to its educational value to the service-users, it was also interesting to the staff. Another agency had adopted songs American students had taught them, which they now sing "year in, year out, so the culture is very much [evident] throughout the [children's] play." Children in both locations demonstrated great interest in the students—from their home country to what they do during their time off at weekends.

Students talking to service-users about their different lifestyles proved enlightening. A member of staff explained that some of the severely disabled children "don't get to go out of the door, never mind go anywhere. They haven't got a clue about America." This was echoed by a staff member in another agency who said, "sixty to seventy percent of the kids haven't been outside Glasgow in their life . . . it's like [the students] have opened this big wide world because they're talking about a different country, different weather, a different way of life and they share that with them." Similarly, in an agency in Kingston, one member of staff explained that because of the level of poverty, "many children haven't been to another country" and have no expectations of doing so.

## Motivation

Although cultural differences affect staff and service-users in various ways, their impact is tempered by factors other than cultural. Many of the staff and service-users were impressed by the students' high degree of motivation and enthusiasm. They admired and were inspired by what they saw as courage in leaving the security of their home country to study and work abroad. In Kingston, a member of staff expressed the belief that motivation was a major asset of service-learning students. He explained that because the students had traveled from overseas they tended to be more enthusiastic than other volunteers. The Partnership was the reason for their being in the host country, so that "when they do this program, they have a little extra incentive anyway." Such incentive is often demonstrated in students' willingness to participate in agency activities and their ability to "pick up things quickly." The fact that students have chosen service-learning is "maybe why it works." The keenness of students was generally much admired; one service-user in Glasgow wondered poignantly whether as many British students volunteered abroad.

The perceived motivations of the students affected the way the agencies regarded them. One member of staff explained that he worked with a vulnerable but potentially volatile group of service-users and usually did not accept volunteers. He had previously been skeptical of the benefits of volunteer work, but after witnessing the quality and beneficial effects of the students' interaction with the service-users he was prepared to host more students in future. Cynically, he explained that he had known of other types of volunteers or students who wished only to use the experience for their curriculum vitae. Staff in other agencies expressed the expectation that the students would use their experience as a base for their future career. In this case, the agency welcomed students as potential future developers of welfare provision and was keen to offer them insight into the politics and workings of the system. Overall, the notion that volunteer work could be instrumental in influencing a student's future career, or nurturing interest in a particular field of welfare provision, was important to the agencies.

All the staff in the study expressed an interest in the students' academic work. Other than the service-learning program, however, the staff admitted that they had scant knowledge of the students' other studies. When asked how they felt about being an integral part of the students' education, the staff expressed delight in being involved. One staff member said, "That would be fantastic," adding that it would be complimentary for the staff and agency to be regarded in this way. Some staff believed that "we could help them in their education" and help to "enhance their studies." It was clear, however, that some staff had not previously perceived themselves in this role. If this aspect were explicit, it could enhance the community role in the relationship with the campus.

Not all the agencies, however, viewed the underlying motivation of students as altruistic or humanitarian. The opportunity for foreign travel is a bonus with this type of program. It could prove problematic, as one staff member in Glasgow explained: "This may be their only visit to Scotland and, where the opportunities to experience other parts of the country emerge, they will take them." He went on to say, "I have no objection to that, but occasionally it's conflicted and [the student] has said to me, 'I can't come tomorrow because I'm going here or going there' . . . Sometimes that experience [of travel] was the most important part." Students have varying levels of commitment to their volunteer work, which may affect the agencies. Similarly, as we have already noted, poor time-keeping or absenteeism can reflect a low level of commitment and be disheartening for staff. Conversely, a high level of commitment, when there is a high quality of volunteer work and students might attend extra hours, reaps rewards for the agencies. This example demonstrates the role of expectations and attitudes (Howard 1993). Difficulties can ensue if such expectations and attitudes are not shared between staff and students. However, as Enos and Morton (2003) recommend, providing prior appropriate orientation and support can ameliorate the situation. Effective communication among the university, students and agencies is therefore essential.

## Age

Age and gender were two factors that staff believed to have an effect on the service-users. The elderly service-users in an agency in Glasgow regaled the young students with old stories and personal histories. The students formed an eager audience for tales oft-repeated to the staff. The students benefited from this experience as they learned of the hardships of everyday life during World War II and how Clydebank, in the West of Scotland, had suffered during the blitz. Some staff in another agency were of an older generation and for them it was a "learning curve" to have young students discuss their views on a variety of topics, from fashion to politics. Young service-users in Kingston identified with the youthful students and were impressed when they learned from them about pop culture in America. The learning experience was, however, a two-way process, with students also learning from the host country. In Jamaica, students learned to rap with the service-users. The students' age was an asset in that, as one staff member remarked, "It's somebody to relate to on a less structured basis." Although the service-users were of different age groups, the students' youthfulness mattered to them.

### Gender

A few agencies admitted that it was difficult to attract male staff. In both cities, primary school teaching traditionally and predominantly attracts female staff. It was of additional benefit therefore if students, who worked in these schools, were male. The staff explained that male students represented a role model for the young boys growing up in the deprived areas of both cities. The staff found that the young service-users quickly became attached to the male students and were keen to learn from them. In a school for children with special needs in Glasgow, the staff expressed the view that male volunteers were usually a "very good influence on the class . . . [especially] on the noisy little boys." In another school in Kingston, a staff member was explicit. She said, "These children need a father figure. They don't all have one in the home, and with a male student, they can relate to them. It's very good." She explained that all the teachers in the school were female and "so," she added, "if we get male students, we gladly take them."

For other agencies, if there was a mix of male and female staff, the gender of the student was of no consequence.

*Reciprocity*

An overriding feature of the service-learning programs in both locations was reciprocity. For the program to be successful in any setting, such reciprocity is essential. We have already noted that there is a triadic and reciprocal relationship among the student, the agency and the educational institution; but there is a further triadic and reciprocal relationship among student, staff and service-users. It is the reciprocity of the latter relationship that is a particular focus in this study. Although there is mutual benefit to all the parties involved, equality is not implied. In other words, reciprocity does not necessarily specify qualitative or quantitative benefits to any particular party in the relationship, but each member of the tripartite relationship benefits in some way and also contributes to the benefits of the others. Fundamentally, it is an exchange: it involves giving and receiving. This reciprocity is linked to interdependence. Morris-Brown (1993) sums up both interdependence and reciprocity when she explains the Jamaican patois proverb, "bud cyan fly pan wan wing" as "people must cooperate with each other in order to ensure the successful implementation of projects and activities."

It was evident that students' volunteer work was a learning experience for everyone involved. One staff member said, "We learn, they learn." Ideas were also shared, as the staff said that the program "helps their studies and it benefits us." Furthermore, the program was a "cross-cultural exchange," and social interaction was rewarding for all concerned. The students' help to the service-users and the staff was reciprocated. One member of staff explained that a student "learned a lot from the [service-users], it's a two-way thing: he shared his skills and we shared what we have."

In Glasgow, a member of staff said that she wanted to look after the students at the agency because the area "isn't the safest place in the world . . . there is this tendency to look out for them, to check they're all right." She explained that the staff extended care and warmth to the students as they did to the service-users. In return, the students responded with enthusiasm for their service work and by participating in social outings with staff. In Kingston, this type of reciprocity was clearly evident. In one agency, staff expressed their desire to protect and care for the students: "We keep them safe like mothers; we make sure they're taken care of." In another Kingston agency, staff actively ensured the safety of their students by introducing them to members of the community so that "if they're walking alone, nobody would interfere with them, everybody knows that they are working with us."

## Skills

Students brought many skills to their volunteer work, from which both staff and service-users benefited, ranging from interpersonal communication skills to specialized technical and practical skills. On a practical level, students helped service-users develop their arts and crafts or their computing skills. Others helped "to train a few children in basketball" or with swimming coaching, while in another agency students took a counseling or mentoring role with the service-users. Some students had good academic skills, for example in mathematics, and would work with small groups under the supervision of the teacher. Others had musical talents: one student "had his guitar and would sit with them," helping with a music class. A service-user was pleased that this student had "taught us notes on the guitar."

The students' skills were useful to staff too: as one member of staff explained, creatively they had become "stale . . . doing the same thing year in, year out." The students offered fresh ideas, and their enthusiasm, as one member of staff described it, "shines the second you meet them." Staff also benefited from other skills that the students brought with them, such as ideas of alternative organization or different methodology. One student was invited to attend a staff meeting as a participant observer. As an outsider she was more objective and consequently was able to suggest ways of making the system within the agency more efficient. The agency manager had sought her views as he needed "more opinions . . . from someone outside the organization." In a primary school, a teacher admitted that the student had ideas about classroom management that the staff could learn. To illustrate this, she said, "to get the children quiet she will just sit there and she wouldn't say a word and then they learn they must be quiet." She added that the student then used a reward system for the children's good behavior.

An agency may bring out skills in a student that they were previously unaware of and which have long-term benefits for that agency. At one agency, a student was asked to create an archive during her time there. The staff member was delighted with the outcome of this activity, saying, "that was by far . . . most successful and she did it extremely well and it is something that *remains* . . . and has been useful thereafter."

The students' desire to volunteer was clearly apparent in many cases and this promoted goodwill within the agencies in addition to developing positive social interactions.

## *Social Interaction*

Students who were equipped with particular skills for the type of work they were doing were a bonus for the agencies, but in many instances it was the quality of their social interaction with the service-users that held major benefits. Some service-users bonded well with the students, attracted by the interest shown to them. One staff member recalled, "The kids just love them: they form lovely relationships. . . . The excitement the students generated was unbelievable. It was a lovely experience."

It was not surprising then that the students had a long-term effect on the agencies. In addition to their ideas and their creative talents, students left behind fond memories of positive relationships. For some service-users, with perhaps limited opportunities for social contacts, this was very important. An elderly service-user described how his peers asked about the students after they had completed their placement, wishing they would return to "cheer them up." For other service-users, interacting with the students was a window of opportunity, either to see beyond their own world, which might be one of drugs and of other drug users, or to see alternative lifestyles in a foreign country. Many students remained in contact after their return home. Some of them, "when they go back will send books, toys and things for us, which will help. Most of the students who come to our school leave something for us: one left a tape recorder." This staff member added, "we'll always remember them." In one case, a friendship between a student and a member of staff had been maintained for several years. As Tonkin (1993) states, "When all of this has gone on, there is something left behind, and that something is good."

Unfortunately there is a negative side to departure: the sense of loss that follows. As one staff member quipped, "Parting is such sweet sorrow." A staff member in another agency explained how they felt after the students had left. She said, "It was as though they'd been here forever and it's a terrible loss when they go. It's like a death in the family. It's amazing how you miss them. The kids are really quite saddened as well; you hear their wee voices, 'Where have they gone?'"

The students' departure was perceived as having negative effects on the service-users in one agency. It was described as "awful," with the service-users very upset and unable to understand why students leave. In some instances, counseling had to be given to overcome their distress. A member of staff was stoical, saying that the effects of departure are "negative, but at the same time nothing goes on forever and ever. You do find, when you develop a relationship with an individual over a period of time, to be suddenly [bereft] . . . it sometimes throws them back." This can be problematic, as Rue (1996) acknowledges: "At the end of term, the students' participation may end but the community realities remain [which can be] a source of profound disappointment."

Clearly, the students had an impact on both social and emotional levels. Overall, their presence had positive effects on staff and service-users. Although there were no significant changes to the overall atmosphere within the agencies, the days were brightened by the students' "new and fresh faces."

### Risks

None of the staff in the study perceived the students to pose a threat or a risk to the service-users. They were aware that students were vetted prior to their undertaking service. Nevertheless, they were careful to prevent undue responsibilities being placed on students. Moreover, a member of staff was always present during the activities of the service-users. Staff professionalism was clearly evident, and one of their concerns was "not to create a situation where potential danger could arise." Similarly, for the students' protection against possible accusations, risks or threats, they were not placed in any potentially vulnerable situation. Although the staff were provided with information regarding the students prior to their placement at the agencies, none of them wished they could choose whom they hosted, which is contrary to Vernon and Ward's recommendation (1999).

## Conclusion

Overall, service-learning students have numerous and diverse effects on the staff and service-users. These effects are multi-faceted because there are other contributory but indirect factors. Such factors include the nature of the welfare agency; the needs of the service-users; and the internal structure and politics of each organization. Staff perspectives can influence their views on the efficacy of students' voluntary work. Consequently, what may be considered to be an asset in one agency may be a distinct disadvantage in another. Other issues however are less ambiguous and, overall, there appear to be more positive effects than negative ones. All of the service-users in the study expressed positive views of the students. One member of staff summed up her experience by saying, "I've not got any negative experience with any student we've ever had. I can honestly say that." Conversely, a member of staff holding generally more negative views said that she "would hesitate to take more students back."

The findings in this study may be biased to some extent by possible weaknesses in the research design and methods. Unfortunately, with the time limitations, the study is small-scale. In addition, the respondents were self-selected. These factors could suggest, first, that the sample is unrepresentative of agencies in general, and, second, that the respondents were biased in favour of the service-learning program. It is possible that some staff might have been reticent in articulating negative comments if they believed that the students' volunteer work might be withdrawn in the future or that the individual students who had already worked with them might suffer adverse consequences in their studies as a result. The aims of the study, however, were clearly presented to the respondents and anonymity was assured.

The study has identified particular characteristics of the service-learning experience that, admittedly, may be idiosyncratic to the agency, or to its location. The findings are valuable in that they highlight problematic issues that could constitute negative effects of the students on staff and service-users. Interestingly, the staff did not always regard these issues as negative, but rather as opportunities for improvement. What might be a problematic issue therefore could lead to a positive outcome.

The findings from this study reflect the relevance of issues raised in the literature, for example the nature of the relationship among the parties concerned, namely university, students and agencies. Effective and regular communication among all three is essential and can promote harmonious collaboration around such issues as meeting expectations, addressing diverse needs, and achieving individual goals. This suggests a partnership built on reciprocity, or a mutually positive exchange.

Many staff were emphatic that they wanted more students, with one encapsulating the general sentiment of staff and service-users with the directive, *"Keep them coming!"*

## Recommendations

### *Nurturing reciprocity*

It would be useful for students to be aware of potential positive and negative effects their work might have on the staff and service-users within the agencies. This would encourage a more reflective approach and could reinforce their levels of responsibility, commitment and motivation.

It is also important that the needs of both the campus and the community are expressed and that expectations and goals are shared. This approach would help to avoid misunderstanding between the parties and alleviate any risk of exploitation or coercion. As a result a "mutually beneficial relationship" (Chrislip & Larson 1994) may develop fully.

### *Maintaining effective communication*

It is imperative that there are "clear service and learning goals for everyone involved" (Kendall 1990). It is equally important that the channels of communication between campus and community remain open and continuous, especially in times of potential difficulties or misunderstandings. This could help to sustain positive relations as well as to "generate a more porous and interactive flow of knowledge between campus and community" (Caron, Genereux & Huntsberger 1999).

### *Developing and sustaining a collaborative partnership*

As agencies play a vital role in service-learning, it is essential that their voices be heard. In this respect, critical reflection on the type of students that are sent to particular agencies is important. At present the major concern is matching the students' interests with their service assignments, but it is imperative that the needs of the staff and service-users are also fully taken into consideration. It would therefore be useful if agencies stipulated the type of qualities or skills best suited to the needs of the service-users. This "allows for those with needs to define those needs . . . [and] . . . what service tasks are needed" (Kendall 1990). Agency involvement in the planning and implementation of service-learning is a progressive step towards developing and sustaining a collaborative partnership. This, for agencies, could be empowering.

# Appendix 1

## Partnership Program in Jamaica

Students spend a semester, summer or year studying Jamaican and Caribbean history, literature and social issues; serving fifteen to twenty hours per week meeting human needs in a local service agency.

The academic base of the program is in the University of Technology. The University is also host to the Partnership's Master's Degree in International Service.

1. **Jamaican and Caribbean History.** Analysis of Jamaican and Caribbean history, political systems, economics, culture and society from pre-Columbian times to modern independence. A major research paper is required.

2. **Literature of the Caribbean and Literary Journal Writing.** The course is conducted in two concurrent parts. In the first part, the study of novels, poetry, biography and historical journals examines the culture, values and society of past and present Jamaica and the Caribbean. Field trips to cultural events (plays, concerts and art exhibitions) are scheduled. In the second part, students use *Charting a Hero's Journey* (Chisholm, 2000) to write a literary, reflective journal documenting inner and outer journeys of service-learning in Jamaica.

3. **Institutions in Jamaican Society.** This course is conducted in two related parts. One is a course that uses material from sociology, psychology, history, religion, human services, government and administration to examine the ways social institutions relate to and reflect the larger society. The second involves an exercise, Profile of an Agency, for which a major paper is required using the community agency—its mission, history, governance, socio-economic background of those served—as the basis for examining the political, social, cultural and demographic conditions of the larger society.

## Partnership Program in Scotland

The Service-Learning Program combines academic study with volunteer service and is designed specifically for overseas students. The program gives the opportunity to gain insight into the theoretical, ideological and historical framework of welfare in Britain. It begins with an introduction to the origins and historical development of State provision of welfare from the nineteenth century. The British Welfare State is critically analyzed from an anti-collectivist perspective. This is followed by an evaluation of New Right ideology and its influence on social policy, drawing comparisons with US welfare policy where appropriate. In addition, the issue of citizenship is examined, with reference to communitarian values. To conclude, there is an analysis of the concepts of equality, social justice and liberty as perceived from different perspectives. This series of lectures and seminars will provide an opportunity for reflection on the principles of a 'good society.'

1. **Welfare Ideology.** *Aim:* to provide a theoretical, ideological and historical framework for understanding welfare provision in Britain. *Intended Learning Outcomes:* having attended the course, and having undertaken the complementary reading, students should be able to: give a historical account of the development of welfare in Britain; offer a critique of the British Welfare State; outline and evaluate New Right ideology and its influence on welfare policies; critically analyse communitarian values; critically analyse the concepts of equality, social justice and freedom from different perspectives. Students are required to submit a paper of 3,000 words based on this part of the course.

2. **Experiential Study** (10–15 hours per week). *Aims:* to provide insight into the needs of service users and how effectively these needs are met; to provide the opportunity for increased personal development. *Intended Learning Outcomes:* having participated in voluntary service, having attended the course and having undertaken the complementary reading, students should be able to: outline the development of the service agency; evaluate the contribution made by the service agency to welfare provision; understand the needs of service users and assess how effectively their needs are met; make a reflective assessment of their experiential learning. Students are required to submit a journal of 3,000 words based on this part of the course.

# Appendix 2

## Profile of Welfare Agencies in Glasgow

### School 1
The school provides primary education for eighty-seven children with special educational needs and physical disabilities aged between five and twelve years. Disabilities include cerebral palsy and communication difficulties. Ratio of eight pupils to one teacher and five pupils to one adult (includes support workers). A medical department is within the school; physiotherapy and speech therapy are also available. State-funded.

### School 2
The school provides primary education for seventy children with special educational needs aged between five and twelve years. There are fourteen members of staff. The school also provides 'enhanced care' for children with greater needs. State-funded.

### After school hours children's resource club
The club is described as a 'play station base,' where children's activities include cooking, games and sports, art and crafts, computer use, trips to the local swimming pool and other places of interest. Approximately 500 children and young people attend at different times. They are aged between five and fourteen years, but are divided into groups according to their age: 5–8 years; 9–12 years; 13–14 years. Attendance is between 3–5 p.m., 4–6 p.m., and 7–9 p.m. (teenagers only). There are twenty-one staff and several volunteers. Grant-maintained but also dependent on charitable donations.

### Day center for disabled adults
The center provides activities for seventy adults with physical disabilities. Activities include art and crafts, cooking, computing and group outings to places of local interest. Personal hygiene facilities designed for disabled people are also available. There are six care staff and several volunteers. Grant-maintained but also dependent on charitable donations.

## Day center for the infirm and frail elderly

The center provides day care for thirty-four elderly people. At present, their ages range from late fifties to ninety-six years. Daily activities involve physical stimulation through gentle physical exercises and soft ball games; mental stimulation through group quizzes and games of bingo. The center is a forum for social contact. Lunch is provided in addition to tea breaks. There are eleven staff. Grant-maintained but also dependent on charitable donations.

## Drugs crisis center

There is open access to the center for those in need. The center provides a residential unit for a maximum stay of twenty-one days. A detoxification unit and a methadone stabilizing unit are also available.

## Museum

This is a museum of social work located in a higher education establishment within Glasgow. It developed and grew from a private collection.

## Profile of Welfare Agencies in Kingston

## School 1

The school provides primary education for children aged between six and twelve years. There are 1,530 children on the school roll with forty-four staff. The school day is in two shifts: 7 a.m. to 12 noon, and 12 noon to 5 p.m.

## School 2

The school provides infant education for young children aged between three and six years. There are 108 children on the school roll, with six teachers.

## School 3

The school provides education for children with special needs, most of whom have mild to moderate learning difficulties. There are 136 children on the school roll, with fourteen teachers. It is connected with a children's home and is an outreach of the Methodist Church in Jamaica.

## Medical welfare agency

The clinic offers health care provided by doctors, dentists and optometrists/ophthalmologists. Between eighty and one hundred people use the service daily. Maintained by patients' fees and charitable donations.

## National training agency

The center provides education and vocational training for one hundred disaffected young people. Eighty percent of the young people are male and most are fifteen years old. Some of them receive special education. Music is also taught; counseling and crisis accommodations are available. There are twenty staff members. State-funded, with tax donations from major businesses.

## YMCA

The YMCA provides educational and recreational activities for boys aged twelve to fifteen. At present there are 128 young people who spend two years in the program. There are two YMCAs in Kingston, and thirty staff are divided between the two locations.

# Appendix 3

### Interview Schedule: Staff

I'd like to start by asking you some general questions about this service provision and then move on to talk about service-learning students and what effects they have.

1.  Could you tell me, first of all, what kind of service you provide?
    *Probes:* Type of client group / number of clients / age / gender / needs / number of staff, enough? / gender / age

2.  Would you like to see any changes made to the service?
    *Probe:* In what ways?

I'd like to ask you what it's like to work here.

3.  How would you describe the relations between the service-users themselves?

4.  How would you describe the relationship between the staff and service-users?

5.  How would you describe the relations within the staff group?

6.  What would you say it's like for a new voluntary worker coming in?
    *Probe:* In mixing with staff? / in mixing, helping with client group?

7.  What affects the way service-learning students are seen by the staff and client group?
    *Probe:* Being from the US / age / gender / socio-economic group (class) / attitude (related to their doing voluntary work?) / anything else?

I'd like to talk a little bit now about the service-learning students, their voluntary work and the service-learning program.

8.  What kind of tasks do you ask the service-learning students to do? *Probe:* Do you feel prepared in working with service-learning students?

9.  How would you rate their work? *Probe:* Abilities, willingness to carry out tasks, willingness to learn new tasks, attitude to staff, clients, work ethic.

10. What would you say were the qualities you found in these students? *Probes:* Enthusiasm / interest / care / different perspective (US) / 'typical Americans'? describe / vitality / maturity / patronizing / arrogance / what else?

11. Have service-learning students had any positive effects on staff? *Probe:* What are these? / Learning? What? / are they different from other students / voluntary workers? How? Why do you think this is?

12. Have service-learning students had any negative effects on staff? *Probe:* What are these? / are they different from other students/ voluntary workers? How? Why do you think this is?

13. Do you think the clients are happy with these service-learning students? *Probe:* Why? why not? in what ways?

14. Do you think service-learning students could cause any harm or pose a risk to the service-users?
    *Probe:* In what ways? How could this be prevented?

15. Might the service-users pose a threat to service-learning students? *Probe:* (Physical or accusation of physical/sexual abuse) prevented?

16. Have service-learning students had any positive effects on the service-users?
    *Probe:* What are these? How? Why do you think this is?

17. Have service-learning students had any negative effects on the service-users?
    *Probe:* What are these? How? Why do you think this is?

18. Do the effects the service-learning students have *change* during (over) the time they are with you?
    *Probe:* In what ways?

19. Do you think there are any lasting effects of having service-learning students here?
    *Probe:* (after they have left) / On staff / on the service-users / any mutual benefits, e.g., learning, teaching, awareness.

20. Do you think service-learning students are different from other voluntary workers / students?
    *Probe:* In what ways?

21. How do service-learning students compare overall with other voluntary workers / students?
    *Probe:* Why do you think this is?

22. How might the service-learning students' voluntary work be improved?

23. What kind of improvements could be made to the arrangements that we have?
    *Probe:* does agency need more information about program/student / should there be more communication/collaboration between agency and Program Director / time-keeping and attendance of student / do students have enough time in service? / is preparation for students adequate (e.g., clients sharing confidences; expectations of work load / monitoring / Should agency 'interview' student before final acceptance for internship and should clients consent to service-learning students working with them? / What are the agency's, staff's and clients' needs in terms of service-learning voluntary work?

Is there anything else you'd like to add?
Are there any questions you'd like to ask me?
Thank you for your time and help with this.

## Interview Schedule: Service-Users

I'd like to start by asking you some general questions about what it's like coming here and then move on to talk about service-learning students and what it's like having them here.

1. Could you tell me, first of all, what you do here every day?
   *Probes:* Is it the same / different / varying each day?

2. What do you like best about coming here? *Probe:* Why?

3. Is there anything you'd like to change about it?
   *Probe:* What do you like least about it? Why?

4. How do you get on with the others here? (other service-users)
   *Probe:* Why do you say that? (Example)

5. How do you get on with the staff?
   *Probe:* Why do you say that? (Example)

6. How do you think the staff get on together?
   *Probe:* Why do you say that? (Example)

7. What do you think it's like for a service-learning student coming in to help? *Probe:* In mixing with staff? / in mixing / helping with service users?

8. What kind of jobs do the service-learning students do?

9. Do they help you? *Probe:* How? Practical tasks / Attitude: willing, friendly, helpful, enthusiastic, forward, embarrassed. If not, how could they help you?

10. How do you feel about them being here? *Probe:* Why? (Example)

11. What do you like best about these students? *Probes:* Being from the US / age / gender / socio-economic group (class) / attitude (related to their doing voluntary work?) / enthusiasm / interest / care / different perspective (US) / 'typical Americans'? describe / vitality / maturity / anything else?

12. What do you like least about them? *Probe:* Why?

13. Do you think it's good having them here?
    *Probe:* Why? How? Why do you think this is?

14. Do you think it's not so good sometimes?
    *Probe:* Why not? How? Why do you think this is?

15. Do you think the staff like having them here?
    *Probe:* Why? How? Why do you think this is?

16. Do you think the staff sometimes don't like having them here?
    *Probe:* Why not? How? Why do you think this is?

17. Does it change things having them here?
    *Probe:* In what ways? Do you get to know them?

18. What's it like when they've gone?
    *Probe:* How do you think the staff / service-users feel?

19. Do you think they are different from other voluntary workers / students?
    *Probe:* In what ways? Why do you think that?

20. So, if you had the choice, would you rather have service-learning students here or other students / voluntary workers?
    *Probe:* Why?

21. What would make it better when service-learning students are here?
    *Probe:* Why? How? Would you like to choose whether they work with you or not?

Is there anything else you'd like to say?
Are there any questions you'd like to ask me?
Thank you for your time and help with this.

# Conclusions: The Agency Study

The following conclusions have been culled from the findings and recommendations of Susan Deeley's study (the quotations are from her text). They represent our best attempt at summarizing a complex and detailed document.

1.  **Partnership students tend to be particularly useful to agencies because of their high degree of commitment.**

    "Many of the staff and service-users were impressed by the students' high degree of motivation and enthusiasm. They admired and were inspired by what they saw as courage in leaving the security of their home country to study and work abroad."

2.  **Partnership students tend to be particularly useful to agencies because they bring special skills and experiences.**

    "Students brought many skills to their volunteer work, from which both staff and service-users benefited, ranging from interpersonal communication skills to specialized technical and practical skills." "Partnership students are typically from universities and colleges in the United States. The fact that the students are usually white American affects staff and service-users in various ways. The students bring their own skills, experiences, ideas and values to the agencies."

3.   **Partnership students display self-assurance and optimism.**

According to one service-agency representative, the students "seem to have a confidence that comes from the culture there, an air of confidence about themselves." This is "something to live up to for us," and this optimism and self-assurance has a positive effect on both staff and service-users.

4.   **Partnership students build close relationships with service-users.**

"Students who were equipped with particular skills for the type of work they were doing were a bonus for the agencies, but in many instances it was the quality of their social interaction with the service-users that held major benefits." "The time spent by students with the service-users was often perceived as 'quality time,'" and it resulted in some students building close relationships with the service-users. "This was an added and welcome bonus to the service-users as well as to the students."

5.   **Time management and dependability is extremely important to agencies.**

"A major issue that concerned most of the staff was the question of how much time the student spent at the agency, that is, in terms of how much time during the day, and for how many weeks. Students' timekeeping was a potentially negative issue."

6.   **Regular attendance over an extended period is advantageous.**

Most of the staff interviewed in the study expressed a wish to see students' placements at the agencies made longer over a period of time and/or to have them spend more time at the agency per day.

7. **Partnership students bring a challenging cultural diversity to the agencies.**

"For several staff, interacting with culturally different students was a social and learning experience. . . . The service-users also benefited from being exposed to the cultural differences of the students." "Students talking to service-users about their different lifestyles proved enlightening."

8. **Partnership students, because of their commitment and reliability, tend to overcome skepticism about the value of volunteers.**

"The perceived motivations of the students affected the way the agencies regarded them. One member of staff explained that he worked with a vulnerable but potentially volatile group of service-users and usually did not accept volunteers. He had previously been skeptical of the benefits of volunteer work, but after witnessing the quality and beneficial effects of the students' interaction with the service-users, he was prepared to host more students in future."

9. **Agencies are interested in students' academic work and eager to help, but they need to know more about it.**

"All the staff in the study expressed an interest in the students' academic work. Other than the service-learning program, however, the staff admitted that they had scant knowledge of the students' other studies. When asked how they felt about being an integral part of the students' education, the staff expressed delight in being involved."

10. **Some agencies are particularly interested in having male students as volunteers.**

"A few agencies admitted that it was difficult to attract male staff," and, therefore, male service-learning students were particularly useful as role-models, both for staff and for service-users.

11. **International service-learning programs bring a valuable sense of reciprocity.**

"An overriding feature of the service-learning programs in both locations was reciprocity. . . . We have already noted that there is a triadic and reciprocal relationship among the student, the agency and the educational institution; but there is a further triadic and reciprocal relationship among student, staff and service-users."

12. **Such reciprocity benefits all parties.**

"It was evident that students' volunteer work was a learning experience for everyone involved. One staff member said, 'We learn, they learn.' Ideas were also shared, as the staff said that the program 'helps their studies and it benefits us.' Furthermore, the program was a 'cross-cultural exchange,' and social interaction was rewarding for all concerned. The students' help to the service-users and the staff was reciprocated."

13. **Partnership students have a long-term effect on agencies and create close ties that are hard to break.**

"It was not surprising then that the students had a long-term effect on the agencies. In addition to their ideas and their creative talents, students left behind fond memories of positive relationships. For some service-users, with perhaps limited opportunities for social contacts, this was very important. . . . Unfortunately there is a negative side to departure: the sense of loss that follows. . . . 'It was as though they'd been here forever and it's a terrible loss when they go. It's like a death in the family.'"

14. **Students are well looked-after and protected by their agencies.**

"None of the staff in the study perceived the students to pose a threat or a risk to the service-users. They were aware that students were vetted prior to their undertaking service. Nevertheless, they were careful to prevent undue responsibilities being placed on students. Moreover, a member of staff was always present during the activities of the service-users."

## 15. Students must develop a good understanding of the needs of the agencies.

"It would be useful for students to be aware of potential positive and negative effects their work might have on the staff and service-users within the agencies. This would encourage a more reflective approach and could reinforce their levels of responsibility, commitment and motivation."

## 16. There should be clear goals for all concerned, in a context in which communication is valued.

"It is also important that the needs of both the campus and the community are expressed and that expectations and goals are shared. This approach would help to avoid misunderstanding between the parties and alleviate any risk of exploitation or coercion. . . .

It is equally important that the channels of communication between campus and community remain open and continuous, especially in times of potential difficulties or misunderstandings."

## 17. The voices of the agencies should be heard, and the agencies should be fully involved in planning as equal partners.

"As agencies play a vital role in service-learning, it is essential that their voices be heard. In this respect, critical reflection on the type of students that are sent to particular agencies is important. At present the major concern is matching the students' interests with their service assignment, but it is imperative that the needs of the staff and service-users are also fully taken into consideration."

# PART 4

# How the Partnership Influences Institutions

# 11 The Institution Study: Introduction

Unlike many colleges and universities that run their own programs overseas, complete with salaried staff, real estate, and all the trappings of a small-scale educational establishment, the International Partnership for Service-Learning and Leadership works through existing institutions in the locations where it operates programs, for the most part using the physical facilities and the staff of the institutions in question. Hence, a Partnership student arriving at a Partnership location is immediately integrated, at least in some measure, into a local academic environment. Partnership students are generally housed with host families—a second form of integration—and soon they begin work at their service placements—a third.

The institutions with which the Partnership works have been selected because of some initial connection, serendipitous or providential, not only because the Partnership seeks institutions out. These institutions are often leading academic establishments in their respective countries. The setting up of a Partnership program on a campus is likely to have some impact on that campus—perhaps the introduction and diffusion of the service-learning pedagogy that is central to the Partnership's activities. We were interested in exploring these connections and hence decided to examine the influence of the Partnership, as innovator and problem-solver, on those institutions where it has programs.

The research plan enumerated the following questions as particularly worthy of attention:

1. **Change agents.** Who have been the principal agents of change?

2. **Changes in mission.** How have the stated priorities and missions of the institutions changed?

3. **Changes in institutional philosophy and practice.** What impact have the philosophy and practices of service-learning had on the faculty, staff, students, service agencies?

4. **Role of the Partnership.** To what extent has the Partnership's involvement been the determining factor, or one in a number of factors, influencing changes in policy and practice?

5. **Applicability to US institutions.** How applicable are the experiences of these institutions to US institutions?

The research plan went on to state that "The study will draw on any research or data within the institutions themselves, might be linked to funding for follow-up projects, and might include recommendations on institutional integration of service-learning. Most, or all, of the institutions involved will be in countries outside the United States. One of the purposes of the study will be to explore the applicability of their experiences to US institutions."

The institutional study began in April 2003 at the regular meeting of Partnership program directors from across the world. On March 6 the directors were sent a letter asking them to do "a little reflection and perhaps research or conversation in advance of [their] arrival in New York," in preparation for a meeting on the morning of April 4, at which time "we plan an exercise linked to the Partnership's Ford Foundation-funded research program." The letter continued as follows:

Among the objectives of this program is an assessment of the impact of the Partnership's programs on the institutions in which they operate—so on your various home institutions. In some cases, the Partnership's activities were the institution's first exposure to the principles of service-learning, and from this small beginning institution-wide [service-learning] programs have now developed. In this way, the seed planted by the Partnership years ago has now touched hundreds, maybe thousands, of additional people, and the very direction of the institution has changed in certain respects. In other cases, the Partnership's activities have had less impact on the institution as a whole.

The letter explained that "We want to learn what factors have encouraged or retarded the growth of service-learning at your university or college, and the role of the Partnership in this process . . ."

So we are planning to ask each of you to reflect on the history of the Partnership's association with your institution and the extent of its impact. When you come to New York, we will ask you (a) to interview one of your fellow directors about the history of the association between the Partnership and his/her institution, and its impact, and (b) to be interviewed by one of your colleagues. We will ask a member of our staff or a volunteer to sit in on the conversation and take notes, which will then be written up as a report. We will share the text of the report with you, so that you can make changes or corrections. Then we will select two or three institutions where the Partnership has been particularly influential and arrange for two-day site visits to those institutions for further interviews and conversations.

The result of this process, the letter explained, "will be a final report that will highlight our successes and failures, that will identify the factors that have been most effective in disseminating Partnership ideals, and that will serve as a guide for other institutions planning to introduce or strengthen [service-learning] programs."

The directors were asked to "reflect on these ideas and come prepared to talk about them at the meeting. If you would like to put pen to paper (or fingers to keyboard) and write some things up in advance of the meeting, that would be good too, but not essential."

Attached to the letter were "a few preliminary thoughts on the kinds of questions we might ask at the meeting," to which directors were encouraged to make changes or additions. These "Questions on Institutional

Impact of Service-Learning" were designed to feed into the five questions mentioned above and were as follows:

1. **Early History.** When and under what circumstances did service-learning begin at your institution? In what areas of the institution did it begin? Who were the principal people involved? Are they still at the institution and available for interviews?

2. **Partnership Involvement.** Was the Partnership involved in these initial efforts, or did the Partnership come later? Did these early leaders attend Partnership functions or have other forms of contact with the Partnership?

3. **Reasons for Adoption.** What aspects of the institutional goals of your institution did service-learning support? Did it fit with the mission of the institution easily or with difficulty? Was the principal factor behind the adoption of service-learning for certain students and programs the improvement of student learning, the institution's commitment to the community, or some other factor?

4. **Causes of Expansion.** Has service-learning expanded at all extensively since it first began at your institution? Into what areas of the institution? What caused it to expand: personal interest of the people involved, student demand, changes in institutional mission, other factors? Have other institutions in your country or region started service-learning programs because of your experience or advocacy?

5. **Forms of Service-Learning.** Are there distinctive features to the type of service-learning practiced at your institution? How is it organized: through a central coordinating office, at the department level, by individual faculty members? How are placements secured for your students? How are Action and Reflection linked and coordinated?

6. **Rewards.** Are faculty members who use service-learning as a pedagogy rewarded for doing so, financially, through recognition of their achievements, through promotion, or in other ways?

7. **Support.** Would you describe the attitude of your institution as highly supportive of service-learning, somewhat supportive, or essentially neutral (or hostile)?

8. **The Future.** What do you predict for the future of service-learning at your institution and in your country or region?

9. **Partnership Support.** How can the Partnership assist you in promoting and supporting service-learning at your institution? How can the Partnership gain greater visibility among your colleagues and students?

10. Any other questions, suggestions on people we might talk to, ideas about things we might read?

## Institutional Profiles

On April 4, the directors duly interviewed one another on the history and organization of their programs and their relationships with their host institutions. They were supplied in advance with a list of suggested questions, and the interviews were observed and summarized by rapporteurs. As might be expected, the resulting reports varied in quality and detail. Some were based on many years of experience, and on a thorough knowledge of the institution in question; others were less thorough, either because the director was relatively new to the Partnership or because the program itself was a recent addition. One program, the Russia program, did not report because of the absence of the director.

The following summaries are based on the reports, with additional observations submitted later by directors or supplied from other data collected as part of the project. They are therefore a mixture of the views of the individuals interviewed and additional facts supplied outside the interview process. Given that our purpose was not to assess the perceptions of the interviewees but to learn about the programs, we are comfortable presenting the summaries in this form, but the reader should be sensitive to the fact that these are both assessments of strengths and weaknesses from the point of views of the interviewees and compilations of contextual information.

## 1. Universidad San Francisco de Quito.

The San Francisco University of Quito is a private liberal arts university. Diego Quiroga, dean of academic affairs, directs the Partnership program and has been associated with the service-learning program at USFQ from the beginning. He worked on setting it up, along with his wife, Tania Ledergerber, who went on to obtain the Partnership's degree in International Service at Roehampton. He was dean of social sciences at the time (1994), and he took the initiative with the strong support of the president. The university is in many respects a middle-class and upper-class university, whose students may have relatively little contact with less privileged people. Quiroga and his colleagues "wanted to get students to areas where they don't usually go." Their president, a strong advocate of such community involvement, was driven by the Buddhist idea that everyone should at some stage in life become humble. So at USFQ the conditions were right for service-learning. University leaders were sensitive to the fact that the university was seen by many as elitist, and they were eager to inculcate in their students a sense of social awareness and social responsibility. Cultural diversity in Quito was becoming more of an issue, and the university wished to respond. The president met several times with Howard Berry, president of the Partnership, who also no doubt helped shape his thinking.

Service-learning started as a university-wide liberal arts program, which in due course became a requirement, in one of two forms: professional internships and service internships. Early on, the university hired a Partnership student to vet agencies and establish relationships with them. She stayed for a year and made a significant contribution.

Some 600 students a year now pass through the program. Such large numbers have their positive and negative sides: the sheer numbers have a significant effect on the university's community impact and on many students; but inevitably there are students who slip through the cracks. Three full-time people work on the administration of the service-learning program, arranging placements and the like, and there is a faculty committee of some four or five professors to oversee operations, approve agencies, and so on. The university has more than enough contacts with service agencies and cannot fill all the needs. On the academic side, students take a seminar in which they are introduced to the principles of service and they are presented with the different options open to them. However, one of the major problems is recruiting good professors. In principle, there is no great resistance among the faculty to the idea of service-learning; in fact, several departments have quite aggressive social service programs. But faculty members have heavy teaching loads (nine courses a year), and this pressure limits participation.

The program involves weekly reflective sessions, but this aspect of the operation still needs attention. Currently, these sessions can have as many as 200 students in them, so there is not much room for direct interaction.

The Partnership program was set up in 1992, and two years later the university-wide effort was launched. Hosting the Partnership conference made a big difference, creating visibility for service-learning and demonstrating the seriousness of the endeavor. The goal at USFQ is to build a community development capability and to narrow the distance between the campus on the one hand and the larger community on the other.

Resistance to service-learning at USFQ was minimal. As Quiroga started his work, he had to convince the provost and president to go along with the changes, but that was easy since they were highly supportive. And the faculty was also accepting of the new emphasis. The University also hosted the Partnership conference, which generated interest in the program and in the service and learning philosophy.

While there are Ecuadorian universities that have service-learning programs, Quiroga feels that USFQ's university-wide approach is unique. At USFQ professors in the humanities and social sciences (literature, anthropology, and other fields), in education, and in the medical sciences, have taken the lead. Often they themselves have been involved in community development activities. Recently, some professors at the university also created a foundation, which raises funds to intervene in the disenfranchised neighborhoods around the university in medical, educational and development programs.

## 2. University of Surrey Roehampton (now Roehampton University)

Roehampton began as a federation of church-related teachers' colleges in suburban southwest London. It gained university status as an affiliate of the University of Surrey and was recently (2004) elevated to independence as Roehampton University. The service-learning program at Roehampton began because David Peacock, who at the time was pro-rector, met with people from the Partnership and was inspired to launch it. Initially, in 1992, Chris Walsh, the deputy principal of Whitelands, one of the constituent colleges of USR, ran the program. At first, the program was open only to overseas students, through the Partnership, and was not integrated into the curriculum. Then in 1993 service-learning became an option for British students under certain circumstances. In 1997 it became an optional offering within the standard curriculum.

Most of the students who participated in service-learning initially came from the social sciences, particularly psychology. About thirty enrolled in the undergraduate program. Then, in 1997, a reorganization took place, and a new position (now occupied by Dr. Jenny Iles) was set up in the Department of Sociology and Social Policy. Also in 1997, the master's program was established.

Changes in the philosophy and practice of British higher education favored the expansion of service-learning: the government encouraged universities to become more active in the communities around them, and it also sought to make academic work more relevant to preparing students for work (see the Dearing Report particularly). Inevitably there was a degree of passive resistance to such emphases on the part of some professors, but the annual external review of the department was consistent in commenting highly favorably on the service-learning program.

The master's degree in service-learning (offered through Roehampton, with the cooperation of Universidad Autonoma de Guadalajara and University of Technology Jamaica) is highly regarded, fitting more and more with the academic culture in the social sciences (e.g., in its analysis of the processes of globalization). There are plenty of connections to be found between this degree program and other initiatives in the social sciences and trends in the larger society—for example the decentralization of policy through NGOs and the consequent elevation of their importance.

The master's program really came into being through the Partnership —particularly conversations involving Chris Walsh and Howard Berry and curriculum design by Linda Chisholm. Mora Dickson was on the original validation committee. The program was approved in 1997 and actually launched in 1998, though without much institutional support (there were 4 students in the first group, 4 in the second, 8 in the third, 19 in the fourth). More mature students were allowed to enter the program in the second semester if they had had international experience—an arrangement that came about because of contacts with agencies.

The international intake through the master's program has been impressive (including students from Canada, Nepal, Togo, Somalia, Ecuador, Japan, Liberia, Greece, the Dominican Republic and Guatemala), and Roehampton faculty associated with the program would like to expand the connections with institutions in other countries, perhaps through the Partnership's network (Ecuador and South Africa are both possibilities) and to look for fruitful connections not just with Jamaica and Mexico but with the Partnership as a whole. Also needed are research and publication on aspects of service-learning.

### 3. Université de Montpellier

The service-learning program at Montpellier (a large research university divided into parts at the time of the French reform of higher education in the 1970s) started in 1988 though a connection with Brookdale Community College (the Partnership had started at Rockland Community College, which had close connections with Brookdale). Twenty students arrived to participate in the program in the first year, but Chantal Thery, the director, was unprepared. At that time she was responsible for IUT's (Institut universitaire de technologie) international relations. She set up a non-profit agency, IML (Institut méditerranéen de langues) to handle the program. Then she became director of international relations at the university's management school. She is now retired from the university but still active as president of the IML, acting as resident director for service-learning programs and with time to work on new connections.

Initially she set up placements for students with state agencies, but there was resistance to the possibility of taking jobs away from paid employees. Later, she turned her attention to NGOs, which are always short of help. The academic side was still more difficult: Service-learning does not exist in France, although professional internships do, so that academics should have no problem with the concept of combining the theoretical with the practical—though in practice they sometimes do.

Most Partnership students come to Montpellier because they want to study French. They receive instruction through the Institute for French as a Foreign Language and also tutor in English in the University's management school. The academic credits are given by the Institut d'études françaises pour étrangers (IEFE) of the Université Paul-Valéry—Montpellier III. But their activities are not recognized by the institution as a whole: the School of Management has an internship program, but it is not accredited as service-learning.

Since her retirement Chantal Thery is trying to expand her connections with Université de Montpellier I & III, both of which house the social sciences, by establishing an advisory committee there for the service-learning program.

The fact remains, however, that conditions in French higher education are unfavorable to the concept and practice of service-learning: the great unsolved issue remains that of institutionalization. Indeed, voluntarism is not a part of French culture in the way in which it is in the United States, because of emphasis on the idea of the welfare state. While numbers of faculty members approve of service-learning, for the most part they do not involve themselves in it and there are no particular incentives for them to do so (indeed there are disincentives). One reason for their approval of and support for the Partnership students is these students' seriousness: they are emphatically not "academic tourists" (like so many other foreign students, particularly American students, at Montpellier), but show greater maturity and greater enthusiasm for what they are doing. Through their placements they are immersed in the French language and so tend to speak it better than their counterparts in other programs.

Chantal Thery felt strongly that the Partnership should continue to work at changing the attitudes in much of Europe to the idea of service-learning, perhaps by making contacts in Brussels and by seeking a European advocate.

There are encouraging signs that some French business schools are beginning to adopt the idea of service-learning. Business schools are not part of the French Ministry of Education and are quicker to react to new ideas. While the field of management is part of the university, the field of business is not (business schools are "homologues," i.e. accredited independent institutions). Chantal Thery is working on strengthening both connections: the University of Montpellier and a business school in Montpellier.

## 4. South Dakota State University

SDSU is a land grant institution.[1] Although some eight to ten percent of the population of South Dakota is Native American, less than one percent of SDSU students are Native American. There has been a push at SDSU to reach out to the tribal colleges.

At the time of the interview, Valerian Three Irons, the director of the program, was working with two colleges within SDSU: the College of General Studies and College of Nursing. Partnership students are enrolled at SDSU, but are on campus only for the first and last week of the program: during the rest of the time they are placed on the reservations and are in touch with their mentors at a distance (though with some local arrangements as well). Hence they are not well integrated into the life of the university nor likely to have much visibility there.

The program consists of both formal and informal instruction, on-site and at a distance. For Partnership students, there are required readings prior to the beginning of the program that set the foundations of Native Cultures/Issues (Indian Studies); other courses the students take are geography, literature, sociology, anthropology, and Lakota language.

During the final week of the Partnership program, students return to the SDSU campus, where they make formal presentations that members of the campus and the local community attend as invited guests. This program has been very successful and instills in the students a sense of pride at their accomplishments in the field.

Valerian Three Irons came to service-learning through contact with the Partnership. When SDSU was approached by the Partnership in the late 1980s, through the good offices of the episcopal bishop, university leaders, seeing an opportunity both for the design of a new educational experience for students and for the provision of various kinds of support to the Lakota nation, negotiated the hosting of a Partnership program at the University, which began in 1990. Service-learning at SDSU was originally limited solely to the Partnership. Four years ago, however, a University initiative called "Lead Forward," designed to develop campus/community

---

[1] Land grant universities were established under the provisions of the Morrill Acts of 1862 and 1890 through grants of government land, with the intention of serving the higher education needs of the states, providing low-cost, high-quality education to their citizens, and accordingly benefiting their economies.

engagements, was launched. Valerian Three Irons joined the Lead Forward Committee a year after its initiation and has been called on to present service-learning orientations for SDSU classes. Currently, service-learning at SDSU is found in small pockets of specific courses, but discussions about mandatory service (with service-learning as an option for this) and institutionalizing service-learning have begun. While the Partnership's program at SDSU is clearly having an influence on the university's thinking, and while it pre-dated other initiatives, the connection between the Partnership's pioneering efforts and the current expansion of service-learning at SDSU is unclear.

### 5. University of Glasgow

The University of Glasgow is one of the most distinguished Scottish research universities, known throughout the world for the quality of its programs. Dr. Susan Deeley, now the director of the Partnership program at Glasgow, became convinced of the efficacy of service-learning through her observation of the Partnership. In the early 1990s, as a junior faculty member, she was asked to serve as the University's liaison with the Partnership and, with the collaboration of others, began the long and arduous effort to have service-learning accepted by her colleagues and the university administration. A plan for a service-learning program was presented to the Board of Studies so that service-learning courses were formally recognized and it became possible to award credit for them. Her office is now recognized as coordinator of service-learning placements at the university, and there are some limited opportunities for regular University of Glasgow students to link community service with their academic work in a service-learning context. The Glasgow program, despite its connection with a prestigious British institution, draws relatively small numbers of Partnership students, whose impact on the institution is accordingly relatively small. While service-learning itself, as a pedagogy, is gaining some acceptance in the university, progress is slow.

## 6. Payap University

Payap is a church-related comprehensive university in Chiang Mai in northern Thailand. The Partnership program at Payap is still in its early stages: at the time of the interview with Dr. Yuthachai Damrongmanee, the program director, the first students had still not arrived (the first class was to enter in January 2004). Service-learning itself is a relatively new pedagogy at Payap, and the institution itself is a good example of the way in which the Partnership has served as a catalyst for service-learning at institutions in numbers of countries across the world.

In 1999, Damrongmanee attended a Partnership-sponsored service-learning seminar at Trinity College of Quezon City in the Philippines, sent there by his university (primarily at the initiative of vice-president Martha Butt). With help from Florence McCarthy, vice-president of the Partnership and director of the program operated by the Partnership and funded by the United Board for Christian Higher Education in Asia to stimulate service-learning in Asia, he learned about the different methods of developing and using service-learning. A grant from the United Board enabled Payap to establish a service-learning center.

Payap is the only institution in Thailand that is incorporating service-learning into its curriculum, and Damrongmanee is the principal person at Payap who is actively developing it, with support from a limited number of faculty members and administrators. Thus, in his judgment (though perhaps not that of outsiders unaware of the difficulties) it has been a slow process.

Currently, Payap is administering two types of service activities. The first links academic coursework and service (for credit), while the second consists of straight service activities, without credit.

Five academic departments are currently incorporating credit-bearing service-learning into their programs:

- Law (students volunteer at a law counseling and legal rights center),
- Nursing (students teach health education in the villages),
- Macroeconomics, finance and banking (students teach villagers how to utilize micro-lending schemes, how to budget, and how to use money most efficiently),
- Theology (students teach Sunday school),

- Sociology (Yuthachai Damrongmanee teaches a course in Contemporary Social Problems to fifty-eight students, who volunteer at one of nineteen agencies).

Non-credit service is also taking place at Payap and gaining in popularity. Exchanges with International Christian University (a Distinguished Partner) are taking place with the help of Partnership board-member Kano Yamamoto.

Service-learning at Payap was given a significant boost when the university hosted the Partnership's biennial conference in January 2004, with participation from many countries across Southeast Asia and the world. But Payap, like many other institutions new to service-learning, needs more guidance from the Partnership on the essentials of service-learning and on the difference between service-learning and service activities, especially since students learn from both.

## 7. Ben-Gurion University

Most BGU students go to the University after completing military service, so service is part of the cultural ethos of Israel and on campus. BGU is one of the newer institutions in Israel, founded specifically to help develop the Negev region of Israel and hence perhaps more oriented toward the practical and hands-on than some of the other Israeli universities. The Partnership's association with BGU dates to the mid-1990s (the first students arrived in 1994) as a result of contact between Partnership leaders and senior members of the university's staff. Dr. Mark Gelber is currently director of the Partnership's program.

Although BGU has always had a commitment to service (and this commitment is growing in the form of more diverse and expansive service activities), it has resisted adopting service-learning as a model of instruction. This is in part due to BGU's efforts to develop its graduate programs and emphasize its research accomplishments and opportunities: while it has offered a service-learning course or project here and there, it has not yet been ready for service-learning on an institutional level. The Partnership's Prague Conference (2002) opened a window of opportunity for service-learning at BGU, but results never really materialized, in part because of the war and security issues (such advocacy on the part of the Partnership should continue). Furthermore, the number of students from the Partnership at BGU has really been too small to have had much institutional impact or influence on the faculty.

## 8. Charles University

Charles University is the flagship research university in the Czech Republic, an ancient foundation of great prestige, with a wide and sprawling range of programs and jurisdictions.

Service-learning began at Charles in 1995 through a visit by Dr. Marie Cerna to the University of Surrey Roehampton, where she met with Dr. David Peacock, pro-rector of the University and leader of Roehampton's efforts to introduce service-learning through its association with the Partnership. Service-learning was new to Dr. Cerna: there were volunteer activities and practical experiences in special education, but they were not incorporated into service-learning until later. In some ways the environment in the Czech Republic was right: students are required to do 400 hours of volunteer work before applying for university study.

The visit to England led to an agreement to send Roehampton students to Prague. The Partnership program grew out of this initial contact and was focused in the area of care for handicapped people, Marie Cerna's area of specialty. Howard Berry, president of the Partnership, visited Prague to explore the establishment of a Partnership program, and Dr. Cerna attended the Partnership's Mexico conference. An agreement was drawn up and she was appointed program director.

Support for service-learning has grown at Charles University in part because of the Partnership's involvement, and in part because political shifts in the 1990s raised the acceptability of volunteering and self-help. Furthermore, US students came with experience in integrating special education students into mainstream education, a priority for Czech special education.

However, service-learning has yet to expand at all extensively at Charles University. The Socrates/Erasmus program in the European Union sends about twenty students of special education each semester who follow a similar program to that of Partnership students, but the influence has not expanded into the mainstream. On the other hand, various community activities at the University are integrated in some measure into the curriculum but the result is not called service-learning. The situation is the same at other universities in the Czech Republic.

Service-learning for the Partnership and other students from abroad is organized by individual faculty members who have contact with service agencies. The Partnership students serve people—children and adults—with mental disabilities, giving them support in living skills, and also students with visual impairments (most of them blind), with whom they work on English conversation. Agencies give faculty an evaluation of each student. Faculty and students review the evaluation and discuss changes for the student and agency. Students write a final paper (Profile of an Agency), which provides an analysis and critique of the work of the agency from student's point of view. Marie Cerna translates the papers and gives them to the service agencies, who find them helpful to make improvements.

The Institute of Special Education and the Faculty of Education are highly supportive of service-learning, but Charles University overall, decentralized as it is, is neutral. There are no specific rewards for faculty members who engage in service-learning, beyond personal enrichment of an intangible kind. The faculty who teach in the program like service-learning because it gives them a new experience with new students and enriches their own teaching. They learn about differences in language, philosophy, background, practices, and so on.

For the future, it seems likely that service-learning at Charles University will grow but will need more students in its existing service-learning program if it is to become more visible and make a difference. A highly desirable way to make the Partnership better known would be to have Czech Republic students participate in Partnership programs in other countries.

## 9. Universidad Autónoma de Guadalajara

The Autonomous University of Guadalajara is an independent comprehensive university founded in the 1930s (Berry & Chisholm 1999:20) and located in Mexico's second largest city, with expanding social-service challenges.

Early on in the university's history, leaders of UAG understood the importance of service in the teaching-learning process of young people, and the institution continues to emphasize the need for students to become highly developed and committed human beings in addition to obtaining work skills.

Service-learning began at Guadalajara in the early 1960s as a learning strategy in the area of medical/health sciences education. The long-time president (rector) of the university, Dr. Luis Garibay Guttiérrez, who died a few years ago, was the major promoter. President Garibay wanted professionals not only with international skills but also committed to the community. Service-learning expanded into the Schools of Education, Psychology, Architecture & Design, and the University Students Association. It expanded because people saw how medical students were learning more and doing good work and because the president promoted the idea. Service and service-learning is accordingly a core element of UAG's educational philosophy and fits its mission closely.[2]

The Partnership became directly involved in 1988. Alfredo de los Santos (Partnership board member), Howard Berry, Linda Chisholm, and Bill Berry (from Maricopa Community College) came to UAG in about 1988 to learn about UAG's programs. Later they invited the Dean of Health Sciences and the president to the Partnership's annual conference to speak about these programs, and this soon led to a formal agreement to establish a Partnership program in Guadalajara. The program was helped by Dr. Garibay's assistant, Alvaro Romo de la Rosa (a former Partnership board member who is now with the Hispanic Association of Colleges and Universities), Guadalupe Delgadillo (who became the first director of the Partnership program and has recently retired), and the Dean of Health Sciences Nestor Velasco (now rector of the University).

UAG has different types of service-learning strategies according to academic area. There is no central office; each school has its own program/office. UAG has its own agencies run and owned by UAG. They also send students to other agencies if there are special opportunities or if students request a type of service that UAG does not have. Students report on what they do at the agency and discuss it in groups under a professor's guidance.

Service-learning is highly supported at all levels but not all disciplines. There is no special reward for service-learning because those who do it do so as part of their basic responsibilities. They find it personally enriching.

---

[2] "La Universidad Autónoma de Guadalajara es una institución de cultura, ciencia, educación, arte y tecnología al servicio de la humanidad, que educa al más alto nivel y forma íntegramente a la persona en lo intelectual, moral, social y profesional, así como en lo físico. La UAG ha sido, es y seguirá siendo, formadora de hombres y mujeres de bien, de profesionales inspirados en altos valores, generadores de bienestar y progreso a las comunidades a las que sirven" (www.uag.mx, April 19, 2004).

There is a social service requirement in Mexico for all students to do 500 hours of unpaid work to get their degrees and provisional licenses to work. This has led to a number of experiments at a number of institutions with variants of service-learning (Berry & Chisholm 1999:82).

As for the future, service-learning needs to grow and become more effective if it is to be consistent with the philosophy and mission of UAG. Service-learning is growing nationally, but with a wide variety of visions. There is a need for guidelines for service-learning and UAG wants the Partnership to take ownership of this process. Service-learning results in leadership, cultural competence, and personal growth and the development of commitment.

UAG would like to see the Partnership support lectures, conferences, and workshops at UAG and institutions around the world, at which the principles and pedagogical techniques of service-learning could be examined and taught. Syllabi and other information about service-learning courses should be made available to institutions around the world, and faculty development programs are badly needed.

## 10. Trinity College of Quezon City

Trinity College is an Episcopalian foundation in a heavily Roman Catholic country. Modeled after the United States liberal arts college, it was originally established in a suburb of Manila, but the city has long since expanded, often in unplanned fashion, to surround it—complete with all the difficulties associated with urban Filipino life. The college forms part of a complex that includes the Episcopal cathedral and a major teaching hospital. From the beginning, the college regarded service and involvement in the larger society as an important part of its mission.

The college became involved with the Partnership through the Association of Episcopal Colleges (AEC), of which Linda Chisholm was then the president, and later the Colleges and Universities of the Anglican Communion (CUAC), which Dr. Chisholm established. Erlinda Rosales (dean of the College of Arts and Sciences), Linda Chisholm and Howard Berry worked to develop the Partnership program (which took its first students in 1985), but, as they did so, President Rafael Rodriguez was looking for ways of introducing service-learning to the college as a whole, building on the college's already well-established community service activities. Service-learning was formally incorporated into the Trinity curriculum in 1990 by Dr. Kate Botengan, then vice-president for academic affairs and later commissioner for higher education of the Philippines.

Service-learning started in the Colleges of Education, Arts & Science, and Nursing and then expanded to other levels of the educational system from elementary to graduate programs (the college runs elementary and high schools as well). Each division of the college now has its own community outreach program, but there is a central coordinating mechanism known as CAUSE: Community Alliance Union for Service and Education. Service-learning operates within this framework but operates largely at the division level, and each program has a faculty coordinator. The coordinators partner with an adopted community near the college, including seven barangays or neighborhoods in the villages, and they coordinate with NGOs.

Students write journals, and there are newsletters and publications. The agency also evaluates the student. Faculty are recognized by a certificate on "recognition day," and service-learning is considered during evaluation of faculty for promotion.

The administration is highly supportive of service-learning. There are still only minimal numbers of faculty involved in service-learning, and the administration wants to cultivate the involvement of more faculty and staff both in service-learning and in community outreach programs in general.

Most universities in the Philippines have community outreach programs but do not call them service-learning. Many NGOs work closely with the private and public sectors, including universities. Recently a major governmental initiative was launched as a partial replacement for military training. Known as the NSTP (National Service Training Program), it focuses on advocacy and such problems as drug addiction and prostitution. Students are expected to give time to the NSTP in their freshman year.

If faculty resources are to be used effectively, faculty members need training in the techniques of service-learning, and particularly the connection between service and learning. The Partnership could help by supplying visiting fellows, giving lectures, sponsoring research and publications, and running faculty development programs. The college would like to hold a service-learning conference locally for Trinity and other local institutions. The college would like to be able to send students on Partnership programs but cannot afford to do so. They would like the Partnership's summer program, which is hosted by Trinity College, to be longer, perhaps up to a semester or year, and they are eager to create an alumni association of service-learning students: there is an e-group of the Partnership's 2002 service-learning program still in contact with each other.

## 11. University of Technology Jamaica

Geraldene Hodelin and Carmen Pencle both contributed to the following comments. The University of Technology Jamaica was founded in Kingston as CAST, the College of Arts, Science and Technology, a higher-education alternative to the country's only university, the University of the West Indies. Early on, under the leadership of its dynamic long-time president, Dr. Alfred Sangster, it began to emphasize the importance of service—a trend that accelerated with the meeting of Dr. Sangster and Partnership founders Howard Berry and Linda Chisholm in the early years of the Partnership. This connection led to the establishment of a Partnership program at CAST. Today, the university has compulsory community service as one of its degree requirements, and every lecturer must have some component of service-learning in his/her program of instruction. There is a special convocation in the first week for first-year students, where students learn about the importance of service. A central coordinator signs off on the student's service hours and placement. The service agency submits a report to the university.

Fully integrated into the curriculum, service-learning, which was once a function of the university administration, is now a part of the faculty's charge. An internal steering committee is responsible for operating the program, assisted by an external advisory committee representing the larger community. Staff and faculty must have a service project and are rewarded through scholarships and promotions. The university has adopted a high school and has been involved in urban planning in the community.

The government is also involved and supportive, providing resources and expertise. For example, government representatives sit on the advisory committee.

The idea of service is not new to university students. Many Jamaican high schools have community outreach programs. Students are also involved in the National Youth Service program (http://www.nysjamaica.org), a government-sponsored volunteer program. Other higher education institutions in Jamaica are now adopting community service plans in their academic and administration planning.

As for the Partnership, not only does it operate its undergraduate program at the university, but the university also serves, along with the Autonomous University of Guadalajara, as a base for the first half of the Partnership's MA program in International Service.

The biggest issue identified by the Jamaican representatives of the Partnership was the need to promote the pedagogy of service-learning. Much of the activity described above is community service rather than service-learning, and even credit-bearing activities do not always involve an adequate reflective component. There is a major need for faculty development. In the future, the program directors would like to integrate the Partnership students more closely with the general student population—which would be good both for the Partnership students and also for the visibility of a strong service-learning experience. The representatives also see the need for further research and are interested in expanding the reach of Partnership programs to Jamaican students.

## 12. India

Dr. Kalyan Ray, who divides his time between a faculty position at Morris College in New Jersey and his home in Calcutta, became acquainted with the work of the Partnership in its early days in New Jersey. In 1990, along with Martha Merrill, he took the first group of Partnership students to India. He now directs the program, with additional in-country assistance. The program in India is unique in that it works largely outside the formal structures of Indian higher education. It draws its faculty from five institutions in and around Calcutta, including Calcutta University and Rabindra Bharati University, and credit is awarded by Loreto College, an affiliated college of Calcutta University.

Recently, Ray and a group of Indian educators involved in service-learning have established a new institution, the Tagore-Gandhi Institute, based on service-learning pedagogy. The institution will begin with nine faculty members and sixty-four students and offer a bachelor's degree in cultural studies. The hope is that this new institute will eventually become a full-fledged college and later a university. The Partnership program uses the institute as an administrative and academic base, and its faculty are affiliated with it. It also draws on the resources of Loreto College. An initiative as ambitious as the creation of a new institute for service-learning is made possible in the Indian setting in part by the existence of a mandatory retirement age of sixty for faculty members: a great deal of experienced faculty talent (and faculty dedication to a worthy enterprise) is available, and it in turn can be combined with that of part-time faculty drawn from Kolkata colleges and universities.

One of the long-term goals of the new institute is to serve as a location for advocacy and training in service-learning in South Asia, in effect as a South Asian base for the Partnership and its work. In January 2004, the institute, along with Indian Institute for Social Welfare and Business Management, sponsored a two-day conference on service-learning in Calcutta, primarily for educators and with the participation of Partnership leaders. Several other institutions in India are already practicing service-learning and are affiliated with the Partnership as Distinguished Partners.

### 13. Universidad Espiritu Santo, Guayaquil

The Partnership has been operating in Guayaquil since 1984, with connections with various institutions. Its program began at Espiritu Santo when Albert Eyde, who had become acquainted with the Partnership and with service-learning while in the community college system in New Jersey in the 1980s, moved to the University, where he is now executive vice-president. The Partnership program now operates through the University's highly active office of international education.

At Espiritu Santo, service placements or internships are required of all students to graduate: eighty hours of community service and additional hours of work in line with degree concentration. There is no connection between community service and academics for these students. Partnership students do have this connection. The agencies also understand and appreciate the connection between service and academics (see Brown 2004).

Service-learning as such has not really expanded beyond the Partnership program, even though community service is a required component of the degree. In contrast to the Partnership students, the students engaged in community service have little opportunity for reflection or for the application of their service to their studies.

Partnership students are housed with host families and serve in carefully chosen agencies identified before the students arrive (students have a two-week trial period). The students are given a language placement test, and orientation takes place one week before classes start. Agencies are involved in the assessment of students' performance.

The Partnership program seems to be "another college within the college." The faculty integrates the service and the classroom primarily through homework assignments, discussion, and journals with the agency work as the subject, but for the most part it has no special training. Students need more reflection time, and the faculty needs additional training in service-learning teaching techniques. The Partnership could support these efforts through special training of faculty, perhaps in an intensive program in Guayaquil. The Partnership might consider a system of medical rotation —a summer immersion program specific to more male-dominated programs for health-care professionals.

## Analysis

An analysis of the thirteen reports reveals some common threads and some significant distinctions among the institutions concerned. We have already noted that the origins of the Partnership lay in two successive developments: first, the interest in service-learning at New York's Rockland Community College in the early 1980s—stimulated by the support of a strong president, Seymour Eskow, and by the desire of Partnership founders Howard Berry and Linda Chisholm to enlist the cooperation of other colleges in the area; and, second, the appointment of Linda Chisholm as president of the Association of Episcopal Colleges and the location of the Partnership office in New York at the headquarters of the AEC. Several of the contacts leading to the establishment of Partnership programs came from one of these two sources. The New York State and New Jersey connections brought Guayaquil, Jamaica, and India. Church-related connections brought the Philippines, Roehampton, and South Dakota.

In most instances where the Partnership had a marked impact on the institutions in question, the arrival of the idea of service-learning at those institutions, promoted by the Partnership, coincided with the admin-istration of a strong leader. The Philippines, Mexico, Quito, and Jamaica are all examples—and in each case the president in question made service-learning one of the principal distinguishing features of his administration and of the institution in question. Many of the institutions had service as a part of their mission (notably Quito, Guadalajara, the Philippines, and, as the latest addition, Payap).

In institutions where service was an accepted part of the institution's mission, the challenge was to link the service mission to the academic mission. While it was relatively easy to persuade faculty of the importance of performing service, the expansion of community service programs threatened to outrun the capability of the institution to turn this service to academic account (Jamaica and Guayaquil are notable examples, and Quito and Payap to a lesser extent). Such linkage of service and learning required more than mere throwing of the two together: faculty had to be trained in the techniques of service-learning pedagogy, and the labor-intensive nature of such pedagogy was a major limiting factor. In several of these countries (e.g., Mexico, Jamaica, the Philippines), government-sponsored programs of national service increased the pressure on institutions to engage their students in service, but did not necessarily help them in the creation of authentic service-learning experiences.

On the other hand, in institutions where service was not so firmly established as a goal, or was not part of the prevailing culture (Montpellier, Roehampton, Glasgow), the opposite problem arose: faculty resisted the notion that service outside the classroom might contribute in a direct and credit-bearing way to education within the classroom (see Plantan 2002 and our discussion of this issue in chapter 13). These institutions, either long-established prestigious universities (Glasgow, Montpellier) or establishments aspiring to such status (South Dakota State University, Roehampton, Ben-Gurion), no doubt also felt substantial outside pressures not to compromise their conventional academic focus. Mitigating this tendency, at least in the case of Roehampton and Ben-Gurion, was a commitment to community involvement, derived either from their founding mission (Ben-Gurion, South Dakota State) or their historical origins (Roehampton), resulting nonetheless in a certain schizophrenia as elements within these institutions sought to escape the institution's origins while others sought to reassert them. In several cases, the Partnership established a niche for itself precisely because it was marginalized (Glasgow, Montpellier, perhaps Charles, perhaps Roehampton), and in numbers of instances the service-learning offered for Partnership students was quite specifically unavailable to students within the institutions in question (Ben-Gurion, Glasgow, Guayaquil, Charles, Jamaica), until, in some instances (Jamaica, Charles to a lesser extent, perhaps South Dakota State), its presence on the campus led to its broader expansion.

In a few cases, notably Quito, a balance seems to have been struck between the expansion of service-learning on the one hand and the twin demands of the service and academic missions on the other, but such balance is rare.

Almost all the interviews pointed to a role for the Partnership in promoting service-learning. Numbers of interviewees (Guadalajara, Philippines, Jamaica, India) called on the Partnership to provide training and faculty development; several (Payap, Philippines, Guadalajara) urged the Partnership to help clarify what is meant by service-learning and how its pedagogy is distinctive, others (Guayaquil, India) asked that the Partnership run programs for their own institutions and perhaps others in the area. Some (Roehampton, Jamaica) urged the importance of research and publication on service-learning. Others (Charles, Philippines) asked that ways be found to include their students in the Partnership's programs in other countries. Still others (Montpellier, India, Ben-Gurion) stressed the importance of advocacy. One (Philippines) urged the need for a strong alumni network, and another (Guayaquil) suggested the launching of a new health-related program. In some cases interviewees pointed out that they were themselves involved in advocacy or in training (India, South Dakota State). Notably lacking in these appeals (though this is hardly a surprise) was any indication by the interviewees as to how such activities might be funded, but the fact that the Partnership was so influential in getting service-learning established in their institutions suggested that its continuing role as advocate and trainer was as important as it would be welcome.

On the basis of these reports, and on the profiles of the institutions, the researchers selected Trinity College Quezon City, in the Philippines, the University of Technology Jamaica, and the University of Surrey Roehampton (UK) as the three institutions to be studied in greater detail. All three are institutions with which the Partnership has enjoyed a long and productive relationship. Jamaica and Roehampton also host the Partnership's master's degree program, and Trinity is host to a summer program in service-learning that the Partnership runs for students from Southeast Asia. Tonkin conducted site visits to the Philippines and Roehampton, and his colleagues Brad Blitz (UK), Linda Chisholm (USA), and Nevin Brown (USA) carried out interviews and fact-finding in Jamaica.

As we have already noted, the March 2003 letter to the program directors explained that "we will select two or three institutions where the Partnership has been particularly influential and arrange for two-day site visits to those institutions for further interviews and conversations." In fact the selection of sites came about as much for reasons of contrast as because of the Partnership's influence on the institutions in question. Roehampton is a comprehensive institution in an industrialized country, aspiring to a stronger position among universities in Britain—but originating in a federation of suburban, church-related teacher-training institutions; the University of Technology Jamaica is a secular foundation in a developing country, originally with a strong vocational bent; and Trinity College originated as a US-style suburban church-related liberal arts college but has become an urban, partially vocational institution. In the chapter that follows, we will focus most particularly on Trinity College, comparing its history and experience with the other two institutions that we selected.

# 12 Service-Learning and Institutional Priorities: The Philippines

Humphrey Tonkin

## The Philippines: A College in a City

Trinity College of Quezon City was founded in 1963 by the Joint Council of Philippine Episcopal and Independent Churches. The college shares its urban campus (Quezon City is now part of Greater Manila) with St. Luke's Hospital (a leading Filipino medical center and teaching hospital), St. Andrew's Theological Seminary, and the Cathedral of St. Mary and St. John. The goal of the college, according to the website of CUAC (Colleges and Universities of the Anglican Communion), "is to provide low-cost, quality Christian education." Of its 3,000 students, says the website, "more than half are economically disadvantaged."

Traditionally the college has had close links with the United States. It owes its beginnings to a gift of 160 shares of Procter and Gamble stock, valued at $25,000, presented to the Diocese of the Philippines in the 1920s and held in a trust fund for many years. In 1961, Lyman C. Ogilby, the then bishop, decided that the money, now grown to almost $500,000, should be used to establish a Christian college. At the time, plans were afoot to transfer the capital of the Philippines from war-torn Manila to Quezon City, and the University of the Philippines had already made the move, along with numbers of other institutions and government entities. When the premises of the defunct Capitol City College in Quezon City became available in 1963, the diocese acquired them and launched the college. A few years later, in 1968, after construction of a science building (a gift of the Netherlands government), the college moved to its present site on Cathedral Heights close by. A year later, fire destroyed the college's elementary and high schools, but donors and well-wishers rallied round to build a new building, and two years later a gift from the United Thank Offering of the Episcopal Churchwomen permitted the construction of a gymnasium for the college.

Trinity College was named after Trinity College, Hartford, Connecticut, whose president at the time was Bishop Ogilby's father. Dr. Arthur L. Carson was named as its first president, and he was succeeded in 1967 by Dr. Arturo M. Guerrero, who served until his death in 1983. After a year in which the executive vice-president Ester A. Santos served as acting president, Dr. Rafael B. Rodriguez was appointed in 1984, serving until 1998. Dr. Orlando B. Molina succeeded him, and in 2001 Dr. Josefina S. Sumaya assumed the presidency.

Despite the dreams of the 1960s, Quezon City did not become the Philippines' new capital city. While today it still has its wealthy neighborhoods, it is in most respects indistinguishable from the remainder of Metro Manila—overrun by galloping population density, mushrooming slums and squatter settlements, and all of the urban problems that accompany unplanned growth and a constricted economy.

The college, which, as its website explains, "started as a one-building campus," continued to expand. After completion of the early premises, further buildings followed: Trinity College Learning Center for Children (TLCC), built with funds from a bequest; the library building, constructed and equipped with a grant from the US Agency for International Development and additional gifts; the elementary school, funded by donors led by the United Board for Christian Higher Education in Asia (UBCHEA) and St. Margaret's School, Tokyo; the Trinitian Center for Community Development, funded by the government of Japan and other benefactors; a swimming pool and sports arena, and, most recently, a building for the College of Medical Technology and the College of Nursing, and a building for the Colleges of Education and of Business Administration. Because of the encroachment of the city, however, there is now little room left on the site for expansion without displacement of adjacent neighborhoods.

Trinity College offers four-year undergraduate degrees in liberal arts, business administration, education, nursing, and medical technology, and graduate degrees in education. It also operates an elementary school and a large high school.

An early publication of the college, dating from the 1960s, describes the philosophy of the college in the following terms: "The purpose of Trinity College is to nurture the development of her students towards a meaningful, compensating and constructive life, imbued with the Christian ideals of freedom and responsibility and enriched with varied interests and abilities, so that through the lives and service of her graduates society may be continually strengthened by sound learning, technical skills and the abiding values of culture and faith." The college, we are told, "encourages her students in every way to search for the truth," and each student "should learn as much as possible about himself as a person, about the society and civilization in which he lives, about the physical universe and the spiritual realities around him." Knowledge should be linked with understanding and faith, which in turn "will ripen and bear the good fruit of service to our nation and to the whole state of Christ's Church." While the Christian mission of the institution is emphatically stated, much of the philosophy of the college as stated here could apply equally well to an American liberal arts college of the day. Indeed, Trinity was clearly modeled on American collegiate education, and engagement with the community did not appear as part of its mission in the earliest mission statements, though it very soon became incorporated in the practices of the college as the city grew and as the college's vocational programs expanded.

The statement from the 1960s stresses the importance of the faculty. The same point is made on the website today: "The faculty has been one of the strong points of Trinity College. Over the years, a great number have pursued graduate degrees either on their own or subsidized by the college through its Faculty Development Program. While attending to their academic responsibilities, they have shown commitment to religious and civic service." Trinity is, in fact, very much a teaching institution, and a firm tradition, clearly initiated soon after the college began, has imbued it with a strong sense not only of academic commitment but also of commitment to the larger community. The website states: "Trinity College is committed to service. Educational opportunities for children and residents of the outlying depressed areas, programs in manpower skills training, health, and entrepreneurial livelihood—such offerings are a Christian response to felt needs." As the site visit revealed, these are no idle words: Trinity is firmly committed to engagement with the community.

A section of the website gives further information on Trinity's outreach programs:

> To enable students and faculty to assist those in need, the College has sixteen outreach programs. Among them, STEP (Skills Training and Enablement Program) helps train out-of-school youth and adults in such fields as carpentry, tailoring, electronics, and cooking. These six-month courses meet once a week, and upon completion the participant is given a certificate of attendance. HEALS (Health Education and Life Services) allows students in nursing and medical technology to help squatter families with nutrition, family planning, and sanitation. The program also includes an infant care clinic. BEST (Business Education for Self-Reliance and Trade) is an entrepreneurial program for itinerant vendors, teaching them practical methods for marketing their products. They learn how to keep accounting ledgers and to apply for loans. . . . A student/faculty/staff group also attends to the livelihood, education, and welfare of a tribe displaced by the eruption of Mt. Pinatubo.

As is usual in higher education in the Philippines, instruction at the college is in English. While faculty and staff members tend to speak and use the language fluently, levels of comprehension and articulation vary among the students. Limitations of language are in some cases probably a barrier to learning. While most community work is carried out in Tagalog, the local language and the language of a majority of Filipinos, the formal, classroom side of service-learning is conducted in English.

## The Visit

The site visit took place over four days, August 11–14, 2003. It was timed to coincide with the Partnership's summer program at Trinity, which brought together thirty-or-so students from institutions across eastern and southern Asia, and whom I would therefore have the opportunity to meet. Dr. Cesar Orsal, dean of the College of Arts and Sciences and also director of the Partnership program (a felicitous combination of roles), was responsible for the on-site arrangements. While he and his colleagues set up several meetings in advance, in response to my requests or on the basis of their own judgment, several meetings were arranged at my request as the visit proceeded, allowing me to check information, gain new perspectives, and follow up on suggestions provided by people I interviewed. In all, I spent time in formal meetings with upwards of a hundred people, visited several agencies, and engaged in numerous casual conversations. I was impressed throughout by the openness of the staff and faculty and by their dedication to the institution.

Before leaving, in addition to reading materials sent to me by Dr. Orsal, I reviewed the notes compiled by Maureen McHale from the interview with Dr. Orsal in April (summarized in chapter 11) and prepared a set of questions to serve as prompts for my meetings. The questions were expansions of those already asked in the program directors' meetings in April, and the list was neither comprehensive nor intended for use in all sessions, but it did assist me in focusing my inquiry. In many instances the questions remained unanswered, perhaps because there was no occasion to raise them, or because of my sense that the culture (institutional or national) precluded my raising them. The questions were as follows. First I list those already asked in April (not all were answered in April, and in other cases I repeated them in my on-site interviews); second I list the questions that I added.

## 1. Early History

*Questions to directors*:
When and under what circumstances did service-learning begin at Trinity? In what areas of the institution did it begin? Who were the principal people involved? Are they still at the institution and available for interviews?

*Additional questions*:
a. Did service-learning have precursors at Trinity? Were there ways in which students got involved in communities before service-learning came along?
b. How many people were involved in these early activities?
c. How did you get faculty involved?
d. How did you recruit students?

## 2. Partnership Involvement

*Questions to directors*:

Was the Partnership involved in these initial efforts, or did the Partnership come later? Did these early leaders attend Partnership functions or have other forms of contact with the Partnership?

*Additional questions:*
a. What expertise did Linda Chisholm and Howard Berry bring to the table? How did they help?
b. How important was the visit to the Partnership conference?
c. How important does the Partnership continue to be?

## 3. Reasons for Adoption

*Questions to directors:*
What aspects of the institutional goals of your institution did service-learning support? Did it fit with the mission of the institution easily or with difficulty? Was the principal factor behind the adoption of service-learning for certain students and programs the improvement of student learning, the institution's commitment to the community, or some other factor?

*Additional questions:*
a. How seriously do people take the vision statement of the college? Are they aware of it and of how service-learning fits with it?
b. Do you report to your various constituencies on the fulfillment of the vision? Does service-learning play a part in that reporting?

## 4. Causes of Expansion

*Questions to directors:*
Has service-learning expanded at all extensively since it first began at your institution? Into what areas of the institution? What caused it to expand: personal interest of the people involved, student demand, changes in institutional mission, other factors? Have other institutions in your country or region started service-learning programs because of your experience or advocacy?

*Additional questions:*

a. We did not record an answer to the question about what caused service-learning to expand: personal interest of the people involved, student demand, changes in institutional mission, other factors. Can you rank them in order of importance?
b. Have you experienced pressure from outside (the church, the civil authorities, the ministry of education) to expand your service-learning programming?
c. Have you found the existence of such programming to be advantageous when dealing with these outside agencies? How?

## 5. Forms of Service-Learning

*Questions to directors:*
Are there distinctive features to the type of service-learning practiced at your institution? How is it organized: through a central coordinating office, at the department level, by individual faculty members? How are placements secured for your students?

*Additional questions:*

a. How is the above brought together at the student level? What is the typical experience of a typical student?
b. How are Action and Reflection linked and coordinated?
c. How long does a student serve?
d. Do students stay with the same agency or move from agency to agency?
e. How many agencies are involved and what do students typically do for them?
f. Is the service tailored to the needs and specialties of students?
g. How close or distant from the average student's experience is the kind of thing the student confronts in his or her service?
h. Have you formally evaluated the program?
i. What do you know about outcomes—lasting impact on students, on agencies?

## 6. Rewards

*Questions to directors:*
Are faculty members who use service-learning as a pedagogy rewarded for doing so, financially, through recognition of their achievements, through promotion, or in other ways?

*Additional questions:*
a. Do faculty members appreciate this recognition? Is it enough? How does it fit with other rewards and recognition?
b. Are there any similar activities going on at the college that are not formally under the umbrella of service-learning?
c. Might there be a role for the Partnership in recognizing meritorious service?

## 7. Support

*Questions to directors:*
Would you describe the attitude of your institution as highly supportive of service-learning, somewhat supportive, or essentially neutral (or hostile)?

*Additional questions:*
a. What do you know about faculty attitudes to service-learning?
b. What about student attitudes?

## 8. The Future

*Questions to directors:*
What do you predict for the future of service-learning at your institution, and in your country or region?

*Additional questions:*
a. How can the Partnership be helpful in having people understand the relationship between service and learning?
b. Are there ways of joining with other institutions in the Philippines in this effort?

### 9. Partnership Support

*Questions to directors:*
How can the Partnership assist you in promoting and supporting service-learning at your institution? How can the Partnership gain greater visibility among your colleagues and students?

*Additional questions:*
a. What can the Partnership do, on its own and in partnership with the college, to persuade more paying students (from the US and elsewhere, e.g. Australia, Japan) to participate in the Partnership program at the college?
b. Are there philanthropists, in the Philippines or the US, who might be interested in assisting with scholarship support (for Filipino students doing service-learning abroad or students from all countries coming to the Philippines) or faculty exchanges?
c. What about support from Filipino firms doing business in the US, or US firms doing business in the Philippines?
d. Are there ways of expanding the program to other interests, e.g. environmental issues?
e. Are there other forms of cooperation that might be possible between the Partnership and the college?

### 10. Any other questions, suggestions about people we might talk to, ideas about things we might read?

## Interviews: Day One

The visit began with a meeting with the president of Trinity College, Dr. Josefina Sumaya, and members of her staff: Leonora Yngente, vice-president for administration and finance; Deana Aquino, dean of education; Cesar Orsal, dean of arts and sciences; Esperanza San Diego, coordinator of community outreach; and Cindy Dollente-Ang, dean of students, former coordinator of community outreach.

The purpose of the meeting, in addition to providing a welcome to the college, was to offer an overview of the college's involvement with service-learning and community service. The meeting was focused, businesslike and extraordinarily productive. The following summary represents contributions from all of those present at the meeting, partly spontaneous and partly generated by my questions.

We began with the big picture: the national emphasis on community service. The National Service Training Program (NSTP), newly mandated by the government, requires that all students do a certain amount of community service, but institutions are free to design their own programs. At Trinity (TCQC), students do service-learning under the NSTP in the second semester of their freshman year, and they take courses in the first semester to prepare them for the experience. Trinity has an advantage over most other institutions in that it has long experience over four decades in the running of community programs and hence felt no negative pressure when NSTP was introduced.

After the first year, students go their own way, but most parts of the institution provide opportunities for further community experience. For example the course in Ethics and Values of Civil Society gives such opportunities. The concepts of "each one reach one" and "each one teach one" are built into this course. Likewise, Nursing and Medical Technology (MT) do community care, Business has a course in entrepreneurship with a community service component, Arts and Sciences runs literacy programs, and so on. In the graduate school a project is now moving forward to evaluate TCQC's community outreach programs, with heavy student involvement. There are various opportunities for students to continue relationships with agencies established in the first year.

Are students reluctant to engage in community service and service-learning? While there is of course some resistance, service-learning (and community service in general) is well received by students and faculty. Occasionally students say, "I'm poor. Why should I go to the poor?" but this is not a common response. A recent study at the University of the Philippines has shown that, among socio-economic classes, categories A and D are more ready to share than categories B and C, but in general volunteerism and teamwork are important values in Filipino society, reinforced by Christianity. "Concern for others" is an important value among Filipinos and people have a strong social conscience.

But, as several participants stressed in this meeting and in later meetings, Trinity College is eager to avoid "dole-out" situations. The service-learning program (and community service in general) stresses reciprocity: all parties should benefit, and all parties should give back and be willing to contribute. The goal of the college's outreach is increased self-sufficiency, not dependency.

All in all, there is quite strong support among students for the college's activities in the community. Students often do not come into the college with a strong sense of values—not even in fields like nursing, where an interest in getting a good job abroad may be of paramount importance. But the college works at making sure that they graduate with a sense of values and the kind of awareness that comes from community work. The programs of the College are also designed to help students make connections between micro-problems in the lives of individuals and macro-solutions through public policy.

The college has built up a close relationship with neighboring barangays (local government units), and relations with each barangay are looked after by a representative from the college. Student feedback takes place primarily at the community level. Establishing good relations with barangays takes time and patience. Sometimes low-level government officials will throw up roadblocks, perhaps out of a desire to control, perhaps because they are afraid that the students will uncover things they would prefer not to have uncovered.

Such problems are seldom apparent in the agencies themselves, which are hungry for volunteers. While it is true that all the first-year students are out in the field at the same time, the agencies are able to find replacements for them from other institutions and from individuals during the rest of the year, and so the issue of continuity is not much of a problem. Other occasional (but infrequent) problems include the preservation of confidentiality by students—but in general, relations with the agencies are good.

Student service is well documented. Students are expected to keep journals, and these journals are evaluated by supervisors, and the level of commitment is recorded for each student. In general, a real effort is made to document programs and to give them occasional evaluation.

While service-learning began with TCQC leadership, the support of faculty was solicited early in the process, and faculty in general continue to be supportive. The Community Center works with faculty to prepare them to participate in service-learning. It runs seminars for them and involves them in other ways. Involvement in community leadership programs is a factor in the evaluation of faculty members, and the Community Center works with faculty in finding connections between their area of expertise and community needs.

In all this, community work is seen as a means of testing and re-orienting values. "When you are faced with poverty," asked Cindy Dollente-Ang, "how will you handle values?"—how, in other words, will your values shift, and how will that process be managed, by yourself and others? "The question, 'Who am I?' is a different question in a slum," added Deana Aquino.

From top to bottom, Trinity is community-oriented, I was told. The college's vision and mission statements reflect this commitment. The small ten-member board consists almost entirely of church members, who readily accept and support this priority.

Most students who come to Trinity as regular Partnership participants are heritage students. We can perhaps recruit more of them by emphasizing the differences in family values between the Philippines and the US. Other special features of the TCQC location that are worth bearing in mind include:

- The importance of homestays, especially for heritage students.

- The problem of the academic calendar (June–March), which does not fit easily with the US calendar.

- The need to emphasize Filipino history as a kind of encapsulation of American history over the past 150 years.

- The fact that students can study in English in a multilingual environment.

In sum, this was an extremely informative and useful conversation. It seemed to confirm that service-learning and community involvement are widely accepted as fundamentals in people's sense of the college—a point reinforced, by the way, by the fact that all through the college there are photographs and other reminders illustrating that involvement. But the question, of course, needed further testing.

After this initial gathering I sat with Dean Cesar Orsal, my host and Partnership colleague, in one of several conversations that I was to have with him over the next several days. On this occasion, we talked initially about the Partnership's summer service-learning program and the arrangements that he had made for it. The emphasis in the program was on youth leadership and on getting an idea of the nature of community service in the Philippines context. After a period of initial coursework, the students were assigned to placements in several social-service agencies in the Metro Manila area. They were asked to address two questions:

1. What can they do to correct weaknesses in the agency they are assigned to? The goal, then, is to do an assessment of the agency and make suggestions for improvement.

2. What can they do for the Partnership in the future?

We turned to the substance of the earlier meeting with the president and other key staff members. I asked about the mission and vision of the college and the extent to which they were translated into commitment to service-learning and community outreach. In essence, Dr. Orsal explained, there are three types of service-learning at Trinity:

- the compulsory, nationally required first-year program in which all students must participate (and which the college has turned into a service-learning experience, thus reinforcing its educational value and tying it to the curriculum),

- programs offered for credit as a normal part of the curriculum in individual colleges or programs,

- volunteer not-for-credit programs (i.e. programs that are not, strictly speaking, service-learning, but may well contain elements of service-learning, if only because students are used to the pedagogy and approach).

Dr. Orsal was quite emphatic: the mission and vision of the college are crucially important. However, it is also important that the government requires community service, since this lends credibility to the mission and vision and also causes students to perceive it as a normal part of higher education. Furthermore, higher education accrediting agencies include social orientation and community development among the criteria for evaluation.

While there is no general institution-wide accrediting procedure, individual colleges are accredited on a rating scale of one to three; if it can achieve three on all programs, the college is entitled to make curricular changes without going through ministry approval, so it is important to achieve level three in the future.

My next meeting was with Mrs. Norma G. Du, of the College of Education. Mrs. Du has been associated with Trinity College since the beginning. She was dean of education from 1980 until she retired at age sixty in the late 1990s. She then went off to head a school of the Philippines Independent Church for five years. One of the provisions that she set up was that the school not be headed by the same person for more then five years. When her five years were up, she came back to teach at the college. In the 1960s, soon after her arrival at the new Trinity College, she became interested in giving the students experience in the community: it is not enough for education students to see their charges as pupils, since they also need to understand their pupils' way of life if they are going to teach them effectively. And if community outreach was a part of the mission of Trinity College, "the College of Education should go first."

She started with the local barangay. "At the back [of the college's high school] there were so many children just wandering around." So she began Community Outreach for Preschool Education (COPE) and established a nursery and a kindergarten. She also sought to involve parents, because they needed access to education too. Her efforts started when Dr. Arturo Guerrero was president. Then she worked with Dr. Rodriguez.

Our conversation was cut short by my need to keep an appointment with Dr. Rafael Rodriguez, who had been president of Trinity College from 1984 to 1998, the period in which service-learning as a formal pedagogy was introduced to the college and took root. This was clearly an important conversation. Dr. Rodriguez studied at the University of Montana at Bozeman, the University of North Carolina, and the University of Connecticut, where he earned a Ph.D. in microbiology. He served on the faculty at Trinity for twelve years, from 1967 to 1979, moved to the College of Medicine at the University of the East for five years and then returned to Trinity as president. As I reflected on the matter, he had several natural advantages in returning to the college in 1984 as president: he knew the college well, he had impeccable academic credentials, he was familiar with US higher education and the role of the president as fundraiser, and, as his conversation made clear, he had all the characteristics of the determined and optimistic reformer.

One of his wishes as president, he said, was to engage the students more actively in the community. There were several community outreach programs in place already, including activities in health and education embracing the colleges of nursing, education, medical technology, and arts and sciences. But he was looking for something more comprehensive. "I wanted my students to talk to people other than their own," he explained. Such contact, he felt, would benefit both sides.

Linda Chisholm, in her new capacity as president of the Association of Episcopal Colleges, came to his inauguration early in 1985. They began talking about service-learning. It seemed an ideal model for what Dr. Rodriguez was trying to achieve. He set up a committee on service-learning and began looking for funds to support an initiative. Linda Chisholm gave him suggestions on what to do. "We did it because we had to do it," he remarked, with all the enthusiasm of the true convert. Vice-President Linda Rosales, at his urging, went to the Partnership conference in New York in 1985.

The development of service-learning, Dr. Rodriguez explained, was made easier by the vision and mission of the college, with which service-learning fitted extremely well. It was not difficult to convince people to become involved. While it is true that the president's wishes count for a lot in such matters, there was no resistance and indeed active cooperation on the basis of the vision and mission.

The college became affiliated with the newly established Partnership and received the first batch of students from the US. "We agreed to take PSL [Partnership for Service-Learning] students," said Rodriguez, "and *then* figured out what to do with them."

A service-learning program was established for TCQC students with a small number of participants—some twelve or fifteen carefully selected students who in due course became leaders. The students met together as a group; they got to know one another and also learned how to work in the community. The first batch of newly arrived PSL students worked with these Filipino students. PSL students also worked in the high school. A program to work with itinerant farm workers was developed, along with other programs.

Limited funding was obtained for the program from the US and Rodriguez continued to work with the Partnership and with Linda Chisholm. As he explained it, she told him what to do each step of the way. He kept close to the Episcopal Church, drawing resources from the

Bishop's Fund and speaking in churches in the US to raise money for community outreach. In due course, service-learning grew as each of the individual programs got bigger. It became firmly institutionalized, which was a positive development—but at the same time it became more difficult to change.

The faculty liked working with the foreign students, who opened their minds and horizons. After initial skepticism, the barangays got interested when they found PSL students were sincere. The barangays tend to be turned in on themselves as closed communities because they fear outside interference: the foreign students accordingly became a device for overcoming this fear, thereby opening the way for TCQC students as well.

By this time the dean of arts and sciences was running the program because it grew too big for the president's office. When a crisis arose in the program, it became essential to modify it. While this was achieved, it was difficult.

Among the new initiatives was a mushroom farm, started in 1995 in sheds close to campus (known, whimsically, as Project MUSH). The idea was to train community members in mushroom cultivation. The project was quite successful, but the lead faculty member left for the US and the project faded—a good example of what happens when a program is dependent on a single individual.

In the 1990s President Rodriguez was able to interest the Japanese government and private donors from Japan in building a community outreach center on campus—so outreach programs had their own physical location. In addition to the convenience of such an arrangement, the design and building of the center, and its continued presence on campus, served as an important symbol of the high priority placed by the college on community involvement. The center became the locus for the coordination of all the various outreach programs of Trinity College, though it is important that these programs remained housed in the individual colleges and only their coordination was done centrally: the colleges continued to have responsibility.

But programs of this kind depend on more than ideas, or even willing participants: ideally they arise from conviction. Where did Rafael Rodriguez's conviction come from? His response was revealing. He grew up in the hard days of World War II, moved around a lot and always had difficulties coming into new communities and making friends all over again. These difficulties helped inculcate in him skills of coping and negotiation.

He accordingly developed a strong sense of the importance of community and sought to apply it through the development of service-learning and community outreach. His goal? To create self-sufficient and self-motivated students and future citizens, and to help build self-sufficient and self-sustaining communities. Service-learning was designed to do both, and it was his good fortune to take over the helm of the college at precisely the same moment as the Partnership for Service-Learning was establishing itself as the advocate for this new pedagogy.

Thus far, my day had been well spent. Not only had I learned a good deal about the history of service-learning at the college, but I had already met several of its most determined proponents, and particularly Dr. Rodriguez, one of the key players. While I wished to continue to test the assertions of those I had met, I was struck by what appeared to be a remarkable combination of administrative determination and personal conviction among those whom I had met.

Late in the day, I met with Dr. Remedios Rosal, a faculty member in the Graduate School, who was conducting a study of certain of Trinity's outreach projects in medical technology, nursing, and the chaplain's office. She was interested in assessing the impact of these programs on the recipients (i.e. agency clients). In cooperation with her students, she designed a survey instrument and prepared the students to conduct interviews, which were carried out in part through Trinity's Lawin Project in the country north of Manila. The instrument, in Tagalog, asks a series of questions on the basis of indicators drawn from the goals of community outreach at Trinity. There are eight of them, as follows:

- Spiritual nurturance
- Educational upliftment
- Economic sufficiency
- Physical health
- Sociocultural consciousness
- Self-reliance
- Empowerment
- Respect for the environment

The instrument was administered to the recipients through student interviewers, and the results are now being analyzed. The interviews were conducted over two days in one outlying area and more extensively locally.

I asked her to let me have a translation of the instrument and to send me results when they were ready.

Following an evening of performances by students in the English department, I met with faculty members in the department, mostly simply to get acquainted. Those at the meeting included linguist Teresita Capacete and creative writer Alona Guevarra. Our conversation was mostly about the work of the English department.

## Day Two: Community Outreach

My second day, August 12, began with a meeting of the coordinators of outreach programs in the various colleges, at the Community Outreach Center, organized by Esperanza San Diego, coordinator of the center. In attendance, in addition to Ms. San Diego, were Ellen Catalo (Education), Cory Marqueda (Business), Fely Medino (Arts and Sciences), Bernard Ebuen (Medical Technology), Mila Gutierrez (Center for Human Kinetics), Rhea Mallari (Nursing), Alice Balaoing (high school), Father Ferdie (Fernando) B. Boyagan (chaplain), and Virginia E. Varilla (high school principal).

The Community Outreach Center (CAUSE Resource Center) was opened in 1995, a gift of the Japanese government. It has three main goals (according to its website): (1) to "expand service-learning programs to the community through volunteerism," (2) to "share unselfishly the skills and expertise in nurturing others for self-empowerment" and (3) to "establish [a] harmonious working relationship and linkage with the community, government and private institutions for socio-economic development." It carries these goals out through a variety of activities, including the encouragement of student volunteerism, the coordination of outreach programs, the coordination of programs that "enhance international linkages for global awareness," such as the Partnership for Service-Learning, the establishment of community networks, the facilitation of training skills for the community, and the conduct of research and program evaluation (www.tcqc.edu.ph, August 2004). In 1999 the CAUSE Center was renamed the Trinity Center for Community Development (TCCD).

The first of these goals raises some issues of terminology and practice, since it seems to elide service-learning (a rather specific pedagogy) and volunteerism (an exclusively service activity)—a tendency increasingly prevalent also in American parlance. We will return to this question.

The center has kept a good record of its activities, including numerous photo albums. According to one of the notebooks I saw, service-learning "aims to ensure change in the lives of the people involved: the helpers and the helped: the teachers and the taught: the givers and the receivers." It "aims to promote respect for the dignity of each person regardless of one's situation in life." Of course, the center is responsible above all for the maintenance and development of a wide range of programs, in close cooperation with the divisions of Trinity College, and only some of these programs involve credit and should be described as service-learning: the Center is a support mechanism, not a credit-granting mechanism.

CAUSE: Community Allied Urban Service and Education started offering basic health services in 1977 (before it acquired its present name), then developed numerous other programs, in health, education, literacy, scholarship assistance, skills training, social assistance, and research. One program run out of the center is an income-generating activity, known as Living Initiatives for Enablement (LIFE). Under this program, women from the community learn sewing by making school uniforms for Trinity. In due course they are given sewing machines and sent out into the community as small entrepreneurs. Currently the programs coordinated by, or run out of, the center include the following (with the years in which they began; again my source is the college's website):

CHANGE Community Health and Nursing
  Geared toward Empowerment (1977)
HEALS Health Education and Life Services (1990)
COPE Community Outreach Pre-School Education (1982)
REAPED Review Assistance Program for the
  Empowerment of Dropouts (1984)
ASPIRE Arts and Sciences Programs for Inspired
  and Responsive Education (1990)
PET Primary Education for Tomorrow (1988)
SET Secondary Education for Tomorrow (1994)
STEP Skills Training and Enablement Program
BEST Business Education for Self-Reliance and Trade (1987)
LEAD Leadership Education and Development (1990)
LIFE Living Initiatives for Enablement (1990)
CORE Community Outreach Research (2002)
SAGIP Social Assistance Geared for Indigenous People (1991)

(The acronyms might seem daunting, but there is a certain charm to acronyms that also carry meaning as descriptors: early in our conversation I lost any sense that I was using acronyms, and the letters turned into solid names.)

After an introduction to CAUSE by Ms. San Diego, there followed a series of reports (with interpolated questions from me) by each of the participants. These reports proved very informative. They were followed by general discussion.

**Ellen Catalo (Education)** explained that the position of coordinator in Education rotates among the faculty, with each person serving for a year and with a reduction of six units for looking after it (Education is the only college that provides a course reduction of this kind to its coordinator). She described COPE, which puts sixty-three students in the field in kindergarten programs where the children are taught reading, writing and numeracy in preparation for entering elementary school at the age of six or seven. Since its inception it has served 1000 families. The program works though barangays close to campus. The barangay provides space right in the heart of the community. The coordinator appoints a student as assistant coordinator, who manages each of the spaces, and this individual is assisted by parents who clean the space each day and help in other ways. The program is largely student-run, with the coordinator providing back-up, counseling, advice and support. Students are also responsible for administering a questionnaire to parents to establish whether their children are eligible for the program (in effect, a means test is applied). Approximately eight students look after the program for one month, to be followed by another group of students. These students do this work in addition to their normal practice teaching and receive credit for it. Echoing a sentiment that I had heard the previous day in my meeting with the former dean of education, Norma Du, Espie San Diego referred to the concept of "the teacher in the community" as basic to the approach in Education: a good teacher must be a part of the community he/she serves and understand the situation of his/her charges.

**Cory Marqueda (Business)** described a somewhat less satisfactory situation in Business. The goals of the outreach programs in business are creating new jobs and generating income for the clients. The college has adopted a barangay, where its students work as volunteers. Three faculty members are helping out. No credit is given. Efforts are currently underway to get a for-credit course put in place, but I did not get the impression that this is a matter of any urgency. In short, there are no service-learning opportunities in Business after the first year.

**Fely Medina**, head of the Filipino Department, described the situation in **Arts and Sciences**. From her description, and from what I had already learned from Dean Orsal, I gathered that there were three types of community service:

1. NSTP, a compulsory, nation-wide program of community service to be carried out in the student's first year, at Trinity reconceptualized as service-learning;
2. RLE (Related Learning Experience) for credit, normally linked to a student's major or degree program;
3. community outreach on a volunteer basis.

RLE courses are integrated into the curriculum. This is the case in the departments of sociology, biology, and hotel and restaurant management. Sociology stresses social organization and community development, Biology runs an environmental campaign, HRM is concerned with entrepreneurship. Mass Communication, English, Filipino and Psychology do voluntary work (community outreach). Mass Communication runs seminar-lectures on drug addiction and pornography. While Mass Communication does have a for-credit practicum, it does not involve community service. English, Filipino and Psychology do tutoring in reading, writing and arithmetic. Psychology has recently introduced a 100-hour community service requirement, to be fulfilled through the tutorial program, but it does not offer credit for it, nor is it tied in with the curriculum. This is an experiment. If it works, the hope is that a similar not-for-credit requirement can be added in other fields. The ASPIRE program (tutorial) involves thirty-three students in the morning and twenty-five in the afternoon, doing two or three hours each day and largely confined to grades 1–4. Dr. Orsal added that Arts and Sciences is working on the possibility of launching a theater program around theatrical performances dealing with community or family problems.

The NSTP (National Service Training Program) is run through Arts and Sciences, since students start out taking most of their courses in Arts and Sciences and this program must be fulfilled in the first year. The program is only two years old. Institutions have a good deal of flexibility as to how they design their programs. At Trinity, in the first semester of their freshman year, students take courses in topics that will prepare them for their community service, which they carry out in the second semester. The program is huge: there are forty-seven sections with forty-five students in each. Students have six areas to choose from, so they can link their NSTP service to their interests. They go out into the field in groups, both because of the sheer numbers involved and also because of their relative lack of experience.

**Bernard Ebuen (Medical Technology)** described the highly original program in that college. HEALS started in 1990, bringing together some voluntary work in existence before that. The program was described in the CAUSE brochure of the mid-nineties as follows: "blood typing, sputum testing, urine and stool examination, de-worming of children, dialogues on health practices and procedures, demonstrations on desirable health habits, home visitations for follow-ups and other allied activities." The curriculum in medical technology introduced in the year 2000, includes a community service requirement for credit, supplemented by a voluntary part that also involves alumni and others. The college works in seven barangays, but on a selective basis, depending on conditions in the barangays. The major innovation is that the ingredient in the old program, "dialogues on health practices and procedures," has been significantly expanded. About one hundred students go into the field in the second year under the for-credit program. They are assigned two families to work with, whom they visit twice a week. They are concerned with family management—helping the families understand the importance of preventive measures, like personal hygiene, clean water, washing hands, child care. The students are provided with assistance in how to deal with families, and the families, after occasional initial resistance, seem mostly willing to work with the students. The students also refer the families for other kinds of help as needed. Over the four years of the program the students have shown themselves remarkably responsible and also persistent. The coordinator serves as back-up person for the program, assisting students in learning how to hone their interpersonal skills and to deal with tricky issues with the families, and each student is evaluated on the basis of self-reporting of progress. Other faculty members assist the coordinator. The faculty also does additional volunteer work for adopted agencies and is very supportive of the program. Occasionally students wonder why they are being asked to embark on such activities given that their work after graduation will be largely hospital-based, but they soon come round to an understanding that they should know their clients (compare this observation with those of Norma Du and Espie San Diego about education). An additional feature of the program is that Bernard Ebuen has arranged for the growing of medicinal plants in small gardens in the areas where the students work. Plants are available from these gardens for individual families.

Mila Gutierrez, of the Center for Human Kinetics (physical education), described Project LEAD, a volunteer program that started in 1990, in response to the need for ways to persuade the community to spend its time wisely. LEAD organizes sports competitions in volleyball, basketball, etc. Inter-barangay competitions are organized in the college gym. LEAD also runs first-aid training, seminars on leadership, etc. Unfortunately, in recent years lack of money has led to a cutback in activities, and efforts are now underway to revive the program. Planned are basketball clinics run by the college's varsity athletes, seminars on values and leadership, and training in coaching and officiating.

Rhea Mallari described programs in Nursing, which has both an RLE program and a volunteer community outreach program. Students work in a community close to the college. There are several different programs, in women's health, for youth, for the handicapped, for children, in herbal medicines, etc. Nursing works in a given area of the city for six years or so, until it becomes self-reliant. They then move on to another area. Students work for two weeks over three years (2nd–4th years). In the second year they concentrate on the healthy individual, in the third on the sick and the elderly, and in the fourth on community research.

Alice Balaoing, of the High School, spoke about the STEP program (Skills Training and Enablement), which has been in existence since the 1970s. High school faculty train members of the community in new skills, associated with the work of these teachers in the high school (home economics, etc.). The people working in the LIFE program get to LIFE by way of STEP. There are plans to make the LIFE program income-generating in the future. The program is not, of course, service-learning, but is a means whereby high school teachers can become involved in community projects.

Fr. Ferdie Boyagan, the Chaplain, described a program now known as Community of Excellence Among Indigenous Peoples, which started in 1991, although its present name is recent. It was begun following the eruption of Mount Pinatubo in 1991. Trinity College adopted Lawin, an indigenous community in the vicinity of the eruption, and provided it with relief. Over time the program was recast as a program that provides medical and other assistance to tribal people. Students go out to the community (which is three and a half hours from Manila) and stay overnight. There is also a scholarship program involved, made possible through gifts from private individuals and organizations, e.g. Kobe International University in Japan. Project READ is also a part of the project, providing informal training in literacy for tribal people. The goal is to find ways of developing resources of all kinds for the community and to assist the people in becoming self-sustaining.

After the presentations, positive in tenor and presentation, I praised the work of the participants, but asked them a question about resistance to their efforts—from faculty, students, or the communities themselves. Fr. Boyagan, the chaplain, observed that in his case he had not encountered resistance from the community—though sometimes politicians are suspicious of volunteers coming in from the outside. In his project, however, relations with the local mayor are good. Cory Marqueda (Business) said that there was no resistance in the barangay where her students worked, but that it was hard to attract students and faculty to participate (students, I inferred, because no credit is involved and they are under a lot of pressure, faculty because they do not see it as a priority).

Ellen Catalo, in Education, felt that the faculty and students are willing—and coordination is not a problem because the coordinator is compensated by course relief. The community is very supportive. The college has been working in the field for twenty years, so some of the children helped by the program are now in positions of influence in the barangays. The fact is that in Education, service-learning and community outreach are thoroughly institutionalized.

A somewhat similar response came from Fely Medina, of Arts and Sciences. Working with the community is easy, she said: the college works through the barangays and briefs residents ahead of time on its activities. "They love our performance." Bernard Ebuen (Medical Technology) gave a thoughtful reply: students sometimes have difficulty seeing the connection between the RLE and their careers, but there tends to be "a personal transformation" along the way. Clients need to be convinced that college students have something to tell them and that they can gain by working with them, but the college is getting better at that.

Mila Gutierrez (Kinetics), working with a volunteer program, explained that it is difficult for students to find time for volunteer work. In the Philippines, "sport is not a priority," so it is often difficult to raise funds or get attention. As for the high school (Alice Balaoing), there is a regular supply of clients. For example, students in the high school often refer their house helpers to the STEP program, with a view to improving their skills. And the program can point to a track record: numbers of successful small entrepreneurs who went through the STEP program. In Nursing, explained Rhea Mallari, students and faculty are committed. Different communities have different cultures (migrants from out of the city tend to stay together in different neighborhoods), and so the college must adjust accordingly. In one barangay, Nursing has four units, each with a different culture. Clients are required to define their needs, their objectives, and possible solutions. Nursing responds, then, to the community's definition of its needs.

Clearly credit serves as an incentive to students, and there are plenty of opportunities for the delivery of programs—far more than can be met by the resources of the institution. But Trinity's various divisions clearly have different internal cultures—ranging from the mild resistance of Business to the long established dedication of Education. Some programs seem relatively conventional, but there are also some strikingly original cases, for example the program in medical technology.

We turned to other subjects. Virginia Varilla, principal of the high school, described the two scholarship programs under her direction. Primary Education for Tomorrow offers scholarships that provide full tuition (something over $200 a year) in grades 1–6. For the most part, the students come from Education's COPE program. The SET program (Secondary Education for Tomorrow) picks the students up when they leave elementary school and enter high school. It works in the same way. Support for both programs comes, or has come, from the United Board and now from the Japanese business foundation. There are currently ten students in SET and twelve in PET. The scholarships are competitive, and students must pass an exam. For the most part, they stay in the program once they have started. Students sometimes come into PET after the first grade, but all SET students begin at the beginning in SET. There are 980 students in the high school, with 37 full-time teachers, and 650 students in the elementary school.

In response to my question about organization, Ms. San Diego explained that the coordinators (so-called project-holders) meet with her as a group once a month. She also has a network of local resident volunteers who serve as contact people in the various communities. She goes out to meet with them from time to time. She repeated an observation that I had heard the previous day: Trinity College tries to avoid "dole-out" programs. The goal is to make people self-reliant and to provide them with education and teach them skills.

Why does community service come easily to people in the Philippines? Perhaps because it is so embedded in Filipino culture. *Pakiki pag kapua tao*, "concern for others," is a basic concept of Filipino society.

Not only had this extended meeting given me a good sense of the community outreach at Trinity—pervasive, comprehensive, and firmly established—but it made clear to me that service-learning was firmly embedded among the strategies for engaging the community. Less clear, though growing clearer, was the question of whether service-learning was equally firmly embedded across the institution among the strategies for the delivery of academic programs. Here, there was perhaps work still to be done, particularly in certain parts of the institution.

## Day Two: The Summer Service-Learning Program

My meeting at the Community Outreach Center had consumed most of the morning. In the afternoon I went on to a meeting with all 31 of the students participating in the Partnership's summer program, which had been operating at the Trinity for the past couple of years. Strictly speaking, this meeting was little concerned with the main purpose of my visit to Trinity College—to assess the extent to which the Partnership and its philosophy was influencing the institution as a whole—and hence it should receive little attention in this report. On the other hand, this highly international service-learning program is a good example of the commitment of Trinity's Partnership program under Dean Cesar Orsal to the mission of promoting service-learning across the region and identifying Trinity with that initiative.

With the support of the Henry Luce Foundation, the program ran in 2003 for six weeks, from July 21 to August 29.[1] Students from Asian institutions were encouraged to apply, through the Partnership office in New York, and most were subsidized by the Partnership and in some cases by their home institutions or governments. Selection was competitive, though such factors as geographic spread were also taken into consideration, the Partnership viewing this program not only as educational in itself but

---

[1] Unfortunately this was the final year of the Luce grant. The program could not be held in 2004: despite its evident merits, and despite the Partnership's energetic efforts to secure funding, no other source of funding for this heavily subsidized activity could be identified.

also as a means of spreading the word about service-learning and lending support to institutions experimenting with it.

The program consisted of two courses, taken by all participants, followed by three weeks of service activities in the city. Students took two three-credit intensive courses: "Major Asian Religions: Visions of Service" and "Contemporary Social Issues." The first explored Christian, Buddhist, Hindu and Muslim approaches to community responsibility for those in need and featured visiting speakers from each of the religions. Its purpose was to assess how the various religions approached the notions of service, the provision of what westerners would call "help" or "assistance," and the responsibility of the individual to the community. The second took a comparative, primarily sociological approach to the major issues facing the Philippines and the countries from which the students themselves came.

Under the direction of Dr. Cesar Orsal, who provided continuity in the two courses and was primarily responsible for assessment, the faculty consisted of nine lecturers:

Dr. Rene Romero, national coordinator of the UNESCO Associated Schools Project and professor of education and political science at Philippine Normal University, who lectured on youth leadership.

Dr. Eufracio C. Abaya, associate professor of anthropology and director of the Office for Initiatives in Culture and Arts at the University of the Philippines, who lectured on contemporary social issues.

Fr. Dixie Taclobao, bishop coadjutor of the Central Diocese of the Episcopal Church in the Philippines and former chaplain (1988–2000) of Trinity College, who lectured on Christianity and service.

Dr. Magdalena Villaba, former dean of the College of Arts and Letters and of the Graduate School at the University of Santo Tomas, who lectured on Buddhism.

Dr. Grace Aguiling-Dalisay, visiting scholar at the Bank Street College of Education in New York, who lectured on community service-learning and the academic connection.

Dr. Cindy Dollente-Ang, dean of student affairs at Trinity College, who lectured on nongovernmental organizations.

Prof. Yuthachai Damrongmanee, of Payap University, director of the Partnership's new program in Thailand, who came to get acquainted with activities of the Partnership and also lectured on Buddhism.

Dr. Kalyan Ray, director of the Partnership's India program, who came as visiting professor to lecture on Hinduism.

Mr. Ustaz Mokhtar Haron, a member of the Office of Muslim Affairs under the Office of the President of the Republic of the Philippines, who lectured on Islam.

For the service component of the program, each student was assigned to a project and a team, with each team of four to six students serving approximately twenty hours a week in projects that involved working with children, the elderly, or the disabled, or providing other community services. Students were housed at the college.

Students were drawn from a total of seven Asian countries and a wide range of higher education institutions: two came from East Timor, nine from India, two from Indonesia, two from Japan, seven from the Philippines, one from Korea, and two from Thailand (students from Taiwan and mainland China were accepted for the program, but could not attend because of the outbreak of SARS). The program was also open to selected US students, six of whom attended. Among the institutions represented were Lady Doak College and the American College of Madurai, India, institutions in which service-learning is already established; International Christian University, Japan, with which the Partnership enjoys a close working relationship; and Payap University, Thailand, where the Partnership's Thailand program is located and which is newly committed to service-learning. Five of the Filipino students were from Trinity College. By the time of my visit, the courses were completed and the students were now heavily engaged in community service—supported of course by reflective exercises. They therefore were capable of a good formative sense of the program, though their views would undoubtedly change with the benefit of reflection after their return.[2]

---

[2] A 48-page booklet, *Passing Through the Gates*, was assembled by Cesar Orsal and Angelita Bugnalen after completion of the program, consisting mostly of material written by the students themselves and reflecting on their experience. Similar compilations of often eloquent testimonials have been produced in earlier years: see for example Aquino 1999 (on the 1999 program), Ang 2002 (on the 2001 program).

The meeting with the students was, for the most part, upbeat and positive. For many, the visit to the Philippines was their first time abroad and their first experience of organized service-learning or even community service. I was struck, however, both in the meeting and in informal contacts with the students, by the sheer range of backgrounds and nationalities represented in the program. Some students were sophisticated, well-traveled and relatively prosperous; others appeared to come from sociocultural backgrounds far less cosmopolitan. This appeared to lead to a certain stratification in the group—a stratification exacerbated in the meeting by the fact that the common language of the group was English (it came as no surprise that the first students to talk were American and Indian—and that I had to go out of my way to move past them to the other students, some of whom had relatively limited English) and that this linguistic advantage was compounded by the demonstrative cultural context from which these students appeared to derive. Among the students who spoke up, several suggested that the balance in the two courses between social issues and religion was too biased toward religion and gave too little attention to contemporary social issues. Perhaps attention needs to be given to additional techniques to meld the two, since part of the purpose of the instruction appeared to be an attempt to show how contemporary issues and cultural and religious context are intertwined.

A few students also suggested that some lecturers seemed not to grasp fully what the students were about. Perhaps there could be a written briefing sheet provided to them in advance? The American students felt that there was too much attention given to theory and not enough to its applicability, but this criticism was not much echoed by other students. However, several expressed regret that there was not enough time left for community service after the coursework was done, and they suggested that, despite the logistical complications involved, there should be more overlap between coursework and work in the agencies. Several indicated that they enjoyed the youth leadership component of the program—something that spoke to them rather directly.

I must confess that, at a distance, I shared some of the frustration evident among both students and lecturers about the shortness of time available for the program. The Partnership prides itself on the immersion of students in a new culture, but a six-week course is barely long enough for such immersion. Furthermore, most Partnership programs are engaged above all in a kind of bilateral mediation between cultures—between

American culture on the one hand and the host culture on the other. Here, the hosts were grappling with numerous cultures, varied expectations, and a kind of multilateral negotiation of cultural space in which meaningful dialogue could take place. The fact that they were living with one another, rather than with host families, and that they were also together both in their studies and (in small groups) in their placements, only served to reinforce the rather tentative nature of the common culture that they created for themselves. The students stressed that they benefited greatly from one another, sharing experiences and learning about one another's cultures, and also disagreeing, productively, on many issues of principle. When one student suggested, with the support of others, that perhaps some briefing on intercultural communication at the beginning of the session might help them make the most of their time with the other students, I was unsure, however, whether this was a suggestion about maximizing the benefit to be derived from the students' six weeks together or a plea for minimizing tensions. Perhaps it was both.

Many students expressed their appreciation for the work of Trinity College and the Partnership in general, pledging to continue to work for service-learning back at their home institutions and asking for the help and support of the Partnership in their efforts. It goes without saying that this stress on the need for moral and practical support from the Partnership echoed the sentiments of the program directors at the New York meeting the previous April.

### Day Three: Agency Visits

August 13 was largely taken up with visits to agencies, accompanied by Cindy Dollente-Ang (dean of Students, former director of community outreach) and her assistant. We made three visits, to the Asociacion de Damas de Filipinas, the Manila YWCA, and the Serras Center for Girls. These are good examples of the kinds of agencies in which Partnership students serve, not only in the Philippines but in numbers of other program locations (I was struck by similarities with agencies I had visited in Jamaica and Mexico).

The **Asociacion** is a very old organization, founded in 1913. It operates a home for young children, primarily children whose families cannot cope with them, abandoned children, etc. They are referred to the home largely by social workers, though sometimes the families themselves will bring the children in. The Asociacion includes some of the leading women in Manila, including society women. It has a foundation of its own, and the foundation is the primary supporter of the home, though some additional funding has come from Japan. We met some of the four- and five-year-olds downstairs in the courtyard and then went upstairs to meet younger children, some as young as two or so. Then we went to the classroom of the four- and five-year-olds and listened to them sing (mostly religious songs: the Asociacion is church-related, with a chapel downstairs).

A few of the children stay at the home simply overnight, but most are there for weeks or months, sometimes even longer, while the situation of their families is sorted out. Afterwards, they either return to their families or are moved on for longer-term care, sometimes through adoption or with foster families and occasionally in other institutions. The children we met were generally bright, alert and energetic, though there were others that were emphatically not—indeed more silent staring than one would like to see in small children.

We met with the director of the program, Maribeth Florido, a highly competent woman, who described some of the difficulties of running the operation and explained how she handled such problems as the sudden arrival of parents (especially fathers, sometimes drug addicts or alcoholics) insistent on seeing their children. The program suffered a major tragedy in 1998, when a fire destroyed the old building and took the lives of twenty-three children and five adults. The new building was built within a matter of weeks with the help of Philippine President Estrada and his high school classmates.

The home makes a lot of use of volunteer help. Maribeth Florido said that volunteers are extremely helpful, and she was particularly full of praise for the Partnership students in the summer program, who, although their stay is short, bring their own customs and songs and quickly build rapport with the children. They are good for the staff too. We met several other students who were completing their Caregiver Certificates, a government-recognized program designed to qualify people for various child-rearing, etc. jobs overseas.

We went on to the **YWCA**, where we met with a group of street children of various ages who live at the Y and were preparing to go off to the second shift at school (which starts at 11:30; the first shift runs from 6:00 a.m.). Four of them performed a dance for us. We also met with a class of day-care children, mostly children of street vendors, who are there during the day. Cindy Dollente-Ang chairs the board of the Y and so knows the programs well. She described some of the other programs run there, such as the program for the elderly. We met with two young workers at the Y, who are responsible for running several of the volunteer committees and also have heavy programmatic responsibilities. They stressed how much they liked working there.

The **Serra's Center for Girls** is in a secluded house off a main street close to the red light district. Most of the girls who live there are sexually abused, generally in a family setting, generally victims of incest. They attend school (when we arrived there was much coming and going, because some are morning shift school goers, and some afternoon shift). At the center we met with Sister Alma, a young woman of strong and convincing views, who is a trained psychologist, and with a (young) psychologist and a (young) social worker. The center is run by the Redemptionist order (Oblate Sisters of the Most Holy Redeemer). In addition to the residential program for the sexually abused, the center works with therapy groups of young women outside the center and it actively works with prostitutes, trying to get them into education (rather than attacking their prostitution directly). The situation of prostitutes varies. Some are members of families in which prostitution has a long history. Others are essentially white slaves, often brought in from the countryside with false promises and under the control of unsavory characters whom one cannot address directly. The center is supported by the congregation of the order. The position of the government on prostitution is somewhat ambivalent: sex tourism is big business in Manila.

In the afternoon I paid visits to kindergartens in two barangays and to the White Cross Home for orphans, accompanied by Esperanza San Diego (director, community outreach) and Ellen Catalo (coordinator for Education). The two kindergartens were projects associated with the College of Education and so were good examples of the way in which service-learning for regular Trinity College students is practiced—with strong emphasis on self-help and the creation of self-sustaining communities.

Our first stop was a barangay close to the college, where a little shelter was provided by the barangay to house the kindergarten. Right next to it was an even smaller room also set up as a classroom, so the two could be used at the same time. We met there with three women associated with the kindergarten. Two were mothers, and the third, a somewhat older woman, had helped out in getting the place established and now looked out for the students when they were there, since this was an area of undesirables, particularly drug addicts.

According to the mothers, the school had made a big difference to their lives. Both mothers were extremely articulate and perhaps not entirely typical of the parents in the neighborhood. Both, for example, read regularly to their children and helped them with their school work. They also helped the school by cleaning it as part of the daily cleaning schedule. In both cases the mothers did not work, but their husbands did. One operated a machine in a printing works and the other had a similar job. One of the mothers—the younger one—informed us, to my great surprise, that she had dropped out of the last year in college, where she was studying psychology. She had only three courses to complete. She dropped out because of her first pregnancy. She now has two additional children and is pregnant with a fourth. She is probably in her mid-twenties.

The home situation of the two mothers was quite significantly different. The college-educated one lived with her husband in rented space—a room in one of the nearby "houses" (shacks really). They came from outside the city and had no extended family in the area, so she had to look after the children. The other lived in a "house" with her family, her elderly mother, and her sister-in-law and family. We went and visited this house. We were taken up a back alley, past curious children and bystanders, assorted dogs and cats and roosters. We turned into a dank passageway and then into a tiny space consisting of a kitchen (there was a gas stove and a faucet) and a room off it where the sister-in-law and family lived (six of them in all). We went up a narrow, tight staircase and into an upstairs room that covered the space of the two rooms downstairs (but was still only about 14 ft. by 14 ft.). The father was there, looking sick, the grandmother (who seemed to be blind), and assorted children and the sister-in-law. Ten people live in this upstairs room, so there were sixteen in all in this tiny space. Off the kitchen was a toilet, though I did not discover if it had running water, but I suspect not.

The grandmother has lived in the place for ten years. While the family is trying to acquire the rights to the space, the land is in fact owned by someone else and they can be evicted at any time. Such evictions do take place on a wholesale basis when land is redeveloped, but that did not seem to be happening in this area.

The older woman whom we had met earlier now took us to her place, which was a single room with a little kitchen off it—even smaller than the place we had just seen. It was extremely neat and tidy, but again full of people. Most were children from the neighborhood who had come over to play. Her children were somewhat older, though some of them still at home.

There was a lot to be learned here—about pregnancy and family size, about extended families, about bright and intelligent people caught in a trap, and about people doing a remarkable job of coping. And it was clear that there was an important and productive role to be played by the young people of the College, not only in providing early education to the children, but also in delivering other forms of support.

From here we went to a second barangay, where the school was a one-room hut but was better laid out (mostly with the assistance of Trinity), with a little library, a couple of elderly computers given by a local firm, and even an air-conditioning unit. Several student volunteers from another university in town were there, and they were joined by three of our Partnership students who were assigned to the school—and also by a local councilor, a businessman from the area. We were late for our next appointment, so we did not stay long.

The White Cross center was different again. It had been built as a tuberculosis hospital in the 1930s and was spacious, airy and bright, if a little frayed at the edges. The clientele here was a little different from the Asociacion. Many of the children had been deposited there by mothers who wanted to take time to earn money and then reclaim their children. Many of them came to visit their children each Sunday. Other children were there until they could be adopted, either in the Philippines or by families in other countries—principally, according to the director, the US, Australia, and various countries in Europe. We met up with four Partnership students, who went with us on a tour of the building, showing us the wards where they were helping out—for four-year-olds, for toddlers, and for babies. We spent quite a time in the babies' wards holding the babies and talking with the students. Some of the babies were only a week or two old and a few of the older ones were clearly quite traumatized. Here, of course, volunteers were particularly useful, because they could spend time with the children, who were clearly starving for such attention—with the tentative desire of the often rejected.

## Day Four: Trinity Students

The morning began with a visit, accompanied by Cesar Orsal, to the high school, where I met with Virginia E. Varilla, principal, and La Paz Brito, principal of the elementary school).

The schools were set up in their present form in 1985, in a building built in the 1960s and previously occupied by Trinity College. There are 980 students in the high school, with 37 full-time teachers, and 650 students in the elementary school. English is the main medium of instruction (content-based instruction in English). Filipino (Tagalog), however, is used for social studies, home economics, and technology. There is an accreditation system for religious schools (Association of Christian Schools and Colleges Accrediting Agency), and the high school is fully accredited. Both the high school and the elementary school provide numerous opportunities for students in education not only to do their practice teaching but also to assist in other ways. Ms. Varilla said that contact with Trinty College is very close—and some college classes are held in the building.

The main meeting of the morning was with a group of eighteen Trinity College students, from various parts of the College, to talk about community service and service-learning. The group consisted of the following individuals:

Richard J. Ragunton, Dionisio R. Homol, Anna Liza David, Joy Tricia
    Mata, Marsha M. Deniega – Education
Anette Santos, Jeffrey Mira, Cherry Lou Haluag – Business
Argel Basti Sebastian, Johnielyn D. Hung – Medical Technology
Gail Therese T. Gustilo, Stefan John Cajivat – Arts and Sciences
Richard Dayrit, Jasper Diaz, Tristan Jordan C. dela Cruz, Juanita C.
    Garcia, Karla Mila S. Flores, Frances D. Fontanilla – Nursing

The group was selected in part because the students were known to the deans, but in large part because of their availability on a weekday morning. They varied in their articulateness and level of engagement, but in general struck me as a thoughtful group. I specifically asked that I meet with the students alone—an advantage in that they were more likely to be free in their responses, but a limitation in that I took my own notes (the session was not recorded).

I explained that I was conducting a research project about institutional exchange and community service, laid out some of the details, and asked the students to introduce themselves. I discovered that some had gone through the NSTP program and some had not, since the program is only two years old. (There was not time to ask them how much difference the NSTP program has made.)

**Richard Ragunton** began community service when he was still in high school, doing a feeding program for his church. The College of Education has adopted a rural barangay and he did a literacy program there initially for a month, and then kept going for a semester.

**Dionisio Homol** and **Anna Liza David** also worked in this barangay in the same program.

**Joy Tricia Mata** and **Marsha Deniega** looked after the kindergarten in the Tatalon barangay (one of the ones I had visited the previous day).

**Anette Santos, Jeffrey Mira** and **Cherry Lou Haluag** (Business) worked with a barangay adopted by the College of Business, where they and their fellow students devised a project to assist the inhabitants in preserving and marketing fruit (there was an effort here to link their work with their academic activities, but no credit was awarded).

**Argel Basti Sebastian** (Medical Technology), explained how the Med Tech program works: he spent the first semester of his second year (Health Care 1) working with two families. The students have to go door-to-door collecting information about families and then, on the basis of this, they select two to work with. In the following semester (Health Care 2) they engage in a community-based activity, whose form is determined by a planning process at the end of the first semester, which brings the families together to talk about needs for the future.

**Johnielyn D. Hung** followed the same program as Argel Basti Sebastian. He explained that the students do some distribution of food—but they do so only *after* the health checks, which are their main reason for being in the community. The students also work with plants: the communities grow plants in their small gardens, and the families can then buy them at a very low price and use them as herbal remedies.

**Gail Therese Gustilo**, in Arts and Sciences, participated in a volunteer program in a community elementary school as part of her psychology program. She said that the work that she did was useful preparation for her other courses, where knowledge of the community is expected and where students are expected to have real-life experience. It is also valuable preparation for the psychology practicum.

**Stefan John Cajivat** (Arts and Sciences) worked in an adopted barangay, going there every day to provide tutorial services and arranging special events, e.g. at Christmas.

**Richard Dayrit** (Nursing) found that his freshman volunteer program was mostly recruitment for a church, under the auspices of a faculty member—not a total success. Later, he took Health Care 1 (which is different from the Medical Technology Health Care 1), gathering family data in a community known as the Planters and Green Revolutionists Association (though really much like any other community). The demographic data were designed to identify potential problems (e.g. dirty streets). In Health Care 2, in a different community, he and other students called a meeting of residents, discussed their problems, and then worked at implementing projects to alleviate them. They also organized a Christmas program.

**Jasper Diaz** (Nursing) was previously a student at the University of the Philippines, where he took a BS in Family Life. He volunteered to work with the elderly, bringing them to the college for programming.

**Tristan dela Cruz** (Nursing) volunteered for a community organization before entering college, working in sports programs for young people designed to deal with drug abuse. He participated in the freshman volunteer program, mostly involving community facilitation.

**Juanita C. Garcia** (Nursing), after taking Health Care 1 and 2, continued work as a community organizer, and **Karla Flores** and **Frances Fontanilla** (Nursing) had similar experiences.

The meeting now shifted to general discussion, in which I posed questions of the group in general, in some cases asking particular individuals to reply on the basis of their own experience. I began by raising with the group a variant of the question I had asked the coordinators of outreach programs (my questions are in italics; individual student responses, paraphrased unless contained in quotation marks, are numbered).

*What can you tell me about student attitudes to community work?*

1. Many students just see the first-year program as an obligation—as something mandated by the government (the first-year program).

2. Many students see community service as a burden at first, but then become convinced.

3. It's a challenge for us. We gain experience from it that we can then use in our various fields.

4. For those of us in business studies, it provides a sense of fulfillment and achievement because we can actually help people earn income.

The general consensus appeared to be that student attitudes tend to change: students become more accepting of community service when they are actually engaged in it and understand what it is.

*What about faculty attitudes to community work?*

As for faculty, several students remarked that for the most part they are fully convinced of the importance of community service and convey that attitude in their teaching.

1. Everybody in nursing wants us to give back to the community and wants us to create change and make communities self-reliant.

2. But there are teaching-load constraints on faculty. It is hard for them to find time.

3. Furthermore, faculty want us to graduate, so they may urge us to concentrate on our studies. Such attitudes are entirely understandable and do not represent a lack of respect for the ideal of community service.

4. In Business, we do community service on Saturday and Sunday so that it doesn't get in the way of our studies.

5. The education faculty gives its full support.

Students were unanimous in their view that the faculty is supportive of community outreach and that faculty members are available when there is a need to consult with them or their help is needed. But students also emphasized that community outreach is dependent on their own initiative and is in most cases very much in their hands. I pressed the business students on their situation. They seemed to feel that, while faculty were often short of time, they supported outreach efforts.

*Did you run into any resistance from the community?*

As for the community, the local barangay officials sometimes feel that student volunteers are a nuisance: they get in the way of the orderly running of things, and they are of course not under their control. For the most part, however, this is a relatively minor problem. I might have found out more about this if there had been more time and a smaller group. I asked the medical technology students about the families assigned to them and how they got on with them. They stressed the fact that the families were selected after they had responded to questionnaires, so a measure of cooperation was already there. Furthermore, these students were not the first on this project: a feeling of trust had been built up by earlier groups of students, and the families saw that there were benefits to their participation.

*Had you done community work before you went to college?*

About half of them had already done such work.

*Has your participation in community service changed your attitude toward the community?*

While it is hard to live in the Philippines without being reminded of poverty, I suggested that perhaps some of the students had not come face to face with it in quite the way they do through community outreach. They agreed. Among their comments:

1. I watched TV and saw plenty of poverty. Indeed I became desensitized to it. It's different when you actually see it up close.

2. "Our minds were opened by the experience [of community service], and we learned to mingle with the people we were working with. We've learned that these are people; we need to help them."

3. "In Business, nothing is enough. It's frustrating yet rewarding."

4. "In Education, we're exposed to the traditional way of teaching. But I want to be a change agent. I want to focus on literacy, but I've got to deal with values too. The learning process is more than traditional teaching." In other words, one has to understand the context and the process of learning in order to match that learning with effective teaching.

This last point was repeated by students in many ways: that you can do your work best if you know the people on whose behalf you are working—in health care, in medical technology, in business, in teaching, indeed in all the fields represented. The point had been made by Mrs. Du and by others with whom I talked: clearly it was one of the main principles on which the College's commitment to the larger community was based— and it was well suited to treatment in the context of service-learning.

I came away from this meeting convinced that students at Trinity College, like students anywhere else, come in many philosophical and political shapes and sizes. Many of them, children of the middle class, are no more aware of the implications of poverty and inequality, indeed of the principles of social justice, than students anywhere else. But the integration of service with learning at Trinity helps them address such questions in their studies and in their lives beyond the classroom.

### Day Four: Final Meetings

At my request, a meeting was arranged with Victorina V. David, college librarian, along with a visit to the library. I wanted to follow up on early statements of the Trinity's mission and to take a look at the library holdings. The college wrestles with the problem of supplying its students with the library materials they need. Though the Internet has helped, bringing to the students a wealth of information previously inaccessible, the library budget remains painfully small.

I had also asked for a second meeting with Norma G. Du, of the College of Education, because our earlier meeting had been cut short and because I wanted to go back and reexamine the early history of the college, especially the early years of the Rafael Rodriguez administration (Mrs. Du, we recall, took office as dean of education in 1980, under President Guerrero). I asked Mrs. Du about Dr. Guerrero. He was, she said, very open: he used to hold public meetings with the students in the early 1980s and answered their questions very directly.

My visit to the library had established quite clearly that, despite the assertions of various members of staff, the earliest mission statement made no mention of service or community involvement as such. Mrs. Du explained that, although service may not have been mentioned in early mission statements, it "was internalized to the mission." She quoted Dr. Guerrero's frequent statement, "We have a mission to serve."

When Kate Botengan was vice-president for academic affairs, she put together the idea of CAUSE, the central mechanism for community outreach—with the assistance of the deans. Its purpose was not so much expansion as coordination. The deans were already doing community outreach, and Dr. Botengan wanted to give it greater prominence and coordination. President Rodriguez was very supportive.

By this time, in the early 1980s, Nursing , Education and Medical Technology all had their outreach programs, but Linda Rosales started hers in Arts and Sciences in 1991. She put outreach in the hands of the students. Mrs. Du repeated her earlier observation that with the education students the college tried to stress that teaching is a mission: students have to be trained in the workings of the community. "It's like a movie: you see beautiful things, but behind it is poverty," she observed. "You have ten children; the rich have only two," the students say to their clients in a moment of illumination, perhaps for both parties.

My meeting with Mrs. Du was followed by a meeting with Leonora Yngente, vice-president for administration and finance. I had asked to talk to her again to ask some questions about the budgetary situation regarding community outreach. Kate Botengan created CAUSE, she said, and donations came in to support it. But then the donations began to dry up. The deans asked for help and help was supplied. Each dean now receives a separate budget for community outreach—an arrangement in place probably as of the mid-1990s. Ms. Yngente insisted, in the face of my rather insistent questioning, that this money was regarded as a fixture—as a line-item that might be subject to budgetary constraints, like any other line-item, but could not be removed. Indeed, such an eventuality was unthinkable: community outreach was a part of the mission of the college, and had the firmness of an academic program. It was an important moment in the visit, and a fitting ending to the interviews. I had heard from many people that service and service-learning were integral to the college, but, as every college administrator knows, rhetoric without budgetary support is of little value. Here there was every indication that words were backed with resources.

Of course these resources were limited. I had heard from a number of individuals that budgets were severely limited across the board. But there was no possibility that the resources would disappear altogether.

## A Follow-up Meeting with Kate Botengan

I was unable to meet with Dr. Kate C. Botengan, former vice-president for academic affairs, during my visit to the Philippines, but we were able to talk a few months later, on January 9, 2004, in Chiang Mai, Thailand. Dr. Botengan started at Trinity in 1971 as a classroom teacher of psychology and anthropology. Shortly after, she took a leave to complete her Ph.D., returning in 1974.

From her first arrival on the campus, she had started submitting ideas to President Guerrero about community work—now clearly established as the third goal of the institution (after teaching and research). He liked her ideas and gave her a mandate to begin discussions with Education, Nursing, and Arts and Sciences about expansion of their community commitment. As Dr. Botengan remembers it, only Nursing had an organized program (Ester A. Santos was dean of nursing and executive vice-president at the time; later she became acting president after the death of Dr. Guerrero; Dr. Botengan had been appointed dean of education). In 1980–81 an institutional structure was created to coordinate community programs. "I called it CAUSE," Dr. Botengan explained. From the start, the idea was that all units of the college would contribute to CAUSE and the programs associated with it on a voluntary basis, but Business paid its faculty volunteers, which was something of a problem.

Rather than worry about the less committed members of the college community, however, Dr. Botengan worked with people who were receptive and shared her vision. Her assistant, and later her successor as dean of education, Norma Du, was such a colleague: she was a live wire and "didn't count the hours." In her efforts to persuade more faculty members to participate, she stressed the potential link between community outreach and research, and she made it clear that involvement in service-learning would help bring merit increases and promotions. President Guerrero was very supportive of these efforts. Indeed, in Dr. Botengan's estimation, "without President Guerrero it would have been very difficult."

When a graduate school was added to the College, Dr. Botengan was named vice-president for academic affairs and dean of the graduate school, but continued to work on voluntary community service—over and above conventional academic work. When Linda Chisholm came to attend the inauguration of Dr. Rodriguez as president, volunteerism took on an international dimension. Soon the first courses in service-learning began in Education and gradually the pedagogy of service-learning took hold across the institution.

By the time Dr. Botengan left Trinity in 1994 to go into government service, she had established budget lines in each of the divisions of the College to support community outreach initiatives. When I asked her how she managed to achieve such a level of acceptance for outreach activities, she stressed the quality of the programs rather than her powers of persuasion: "The outreach programs sold themselves."

In her new government position, Dr. Botengan was one of the architects of the NSTP, the National Service Training Program. Today, she observed, all Filipino institutions are doing some community service. Trinity is different because it started with volunteer help and then added service-learning, so that it was ready for the NSTP when it came.

After Dr. Botengan left, Linda Rosales, assistant dean of education, became involved in the community service program (Ms. Fe Alcantara, former dean of nursing, assumed the coordinatorship; Dr. Rosales handled the ASPIRE project in the College of Arts and Sciences). Like Norma Du, Linda Rosales was "a real live wire," but, in Dr. Botengan's estimation, she and President Molina, who succeeded Dr. Rodriguez in 1998, did not always see eye to eye. Since the appointment of President Sumaya in 2001, Dr. Botengan added, community outreach is back on track.[3]

Asked about her principal difficulty in promoting community outreach and service-learning, she emphasized lack of time, but she stressed that if one can link outreach with faculty expertise, the task is easier. And how might the Partnership assist at this stage, I asked? We need more direction, she replied—more clarity on the philosophy of the Partnership and more support for preparing faculty to develop service-learning options. The Partnership's support has been strong, she added, but there is still much to do.

## Some Conclusions

We should perhaps begin by stressing the limitations of my several days of conversation at Trinity. Through no fault of the people I met, I did not have the time to cross-check many of the observations made by individuals I met in the course of the visit—though the subsequent conversation with Dr. Botengan was particularly valuable. As we have learned in other contexts in this study, we shape our recollections into coherent narratives—or, rather, pre-existing narrative structures become devices for assembling those recollections. The narratives shift and change depending on their context, on the questions asked, and on assumptions made by interviewees about the interviewer's goals. Since I was in fairly regular contact with him during my visit, I was able to draw on the accumulated knowledge and judgment of Dr. Cesar Orsal, who helped inject a certain objectivity into my judgments, even if he was also a player in the drama. I was also crossing a cultural divide, likely to refract in various ways both the import of the questions asked and the meaning of the responses delivered.

I felt throughout the visit that our shared assumptions about the nature of service-learning needed examination. Was what my Trinity friends described as service-learning the same thing that I, from my Partnership perspective, believed it to be? Were the Trinity faculty allowing to pass as

---

[3] Cesar Orsal suggests, however, that Dr. Molina made significant contributions to community outreach by establishing extension classes in the work place, allowing professional employees to finish their academic work and gain promotion. Community outreach moved forward during this period thanks also to the successors of Fe Alcantara, namely Dr. Cindy Dollente Ang and subsequently Dr. Lea Paquiz, Dean of Nursing, who provided leadership and continuity.

credit-bearing service-learning, activities that would not be awarded credit at a US institution? Did their service-learning provide adequate opportunity for reflection and clarification of values? I came away from my informal conversations with students and faculty members, and from questions about how they spent their time, with a sense that, yes, the academic quality of the service-learning would pass muster in the United States, but that, no, the opportunity for reflection was perhaps not as extensive as we might expect of the best service-learning experiences (though I fully understand that much of what goes on in the United States is lacking in this regard). Faculty members were certainly available to talk with students and address their problems, but, if the problems did not surface, they may not have sought them out—and indeed, if the simple processing of student experiences (in the absence of "problems") was part of the goal of service-learning pedagogy, it probably was not receiving all the attention from this harried and hardworking faculty that it might have received under more leisured (and affluent) circumstances. The problem, in my view, extends to many service-learning programs in third-world settings—though we should add that the American preoccupation with the self is in any case inherently suspect in much of the rest of the world.

But, in an institution as vibrant and as connected to the community as Trinity College, it is unwise to generalize: undoubtedly the service-learning experience varies from part of the institution to another, depending on curriculum, the purpose of the degree, and the skill and imagination of the faculty. Indeed, one of the most impressive characteristics of the college is the fact that it employs multiple strategies in its relationship with the community. It has a clear central structure to coordinate its efforts and a clear philosophy of service, but at the unit level it engages with the community in differing ways, working with different barangays, shifting its ground as local conditions dictate. This diversity is one of the program's greatest strengths: deans and faculty members are free to work directly with the barangays of their choice, and they are free (subject, of course, to approval) to design their own service-learning activities in ways that make sense to them. The college resists the temptation to over-centralize, and this is wise, because it keeps people involved at all levels, and free to claim ownership of their programs.

Despite my reservations about communication and narrative, and my rather systematic effort to compensate for them, we can none the less draw some very general conclusions as we turn to look at our other two institutions. At Trinity a number of factors came together to help with the institutionalization of service-learning:

- **Mission.** A mission that was early perceived as extending the outreach of the college to the community.

- **Coordination.** A consequent creation of centralized coordinating structures for community outreach.

- **Outreach.** A location of responsibility for community outreach (despite the centralized coordination) firmly in the academic units of the college, thereby forcing these units to address the connection between community outreach and curriculum and allowing them to design programs to fit their needs and expertise.

- **Leadership.** Strong leadership from the president and the president's senior administration.

- **Confluence.** A new president, Dr. Rodriguez, firmly committed to community involvement, meeting a fledgling movement for service-learning, the Partnership, and having the vision to see the connection between the two.

- **Environment.** A city expanding into the physical and intellectual space of the college, causing it to expand its offerings in vocational and professional fields, and to deal with increasingly intrusive urban issues.

- **Stability.** Continuity of leadership, both in the presidency (from the early 1980s to the late 1990s) and in the academic vice-presidency (until 1994).

- **National Policy.** Increasing national interest, and ultimately a national mandate, in volunteer service.

Several of these factors are perhaps observable at other Partnership institutions, notably Payap University and the University of Technology Jamaica—and there were other factors that were decisive at Trinity, less tangible and more elective, but we will return to these after examining our other two institutions.

# 13 Service-Learning and Institutional Priorities: Comparisons and Conclusions

Humphrey Tonkin

## England: A New University

Like many of the newer universities in Britain created out of federations of older institutions, Roehampton University (so titled as of August 2004) has a complex history, involving four separate colleges. Whitelands College was founded by the Church of England in 1841 as a teacher training college for women. Quite early on, it attracted the interest of John Ruskin, who not only became a benefactor of the college himself but also brought it to the attention of the poet and artist William Morris and the pre-Raphaelite painter Sir Edward Burne-Jones, who contributed some of their work to the college. The college moved to a new location in Putney in the 1930s and is now in the process of moving to a site closer to the other three colleges. Southlands College was set up by the Methodist Church in 1872, as a teacher training college. Digby Stuart College was a foundation of the Roman Catholic Society of the Sacred Heart, established in Roehampton as a teacher training college for girls in 1874. Froebel College, the most recent of the four colleges, dates from 1892 and was founded by a group of radical educational reformers, followers of Friedrich Froebel (1782–1852), who, according to the college's website, "taught . . . that education should be a creative and interactive process, developing the whole personality in all its aspects—social, moral, aesthetic, linguistic, spiritual and scientific."

Each of these institutions began somewhat out of the mainstream—because they were focused on the higher education of women at a time when women were not accepted at the major universities, because they were founded by Nonconformists or Catholics, or because they espoused progressive theories of education. While the colleges prospered, to varying degrees and in various ways, until after World War II, supplying teachers to the schools when education degrees were customarily awarded by non-university institutions, the 1950s and 1960s put them under increasing pressure, as more and more teachers were drawn from the ranks of university degree-holders and the government called for reforms. Higher education reforms in the 1960s and 1970s marginalized them still more, with the result that they banded together in the mid-1970s to form a higher education federation known, as of 1978, as the Roehampton Institute of Higher Education, offering a range of degrees (through the University of Surrey) in the humanities, social sciences, and sciences. While each college retained a separate identity, they divided up the responsibilities for academic programs and student services. In the year 2000, the Institute became the University of Surrey Roehampton, restructuring its relationship with the University of Surrey in Guildford. While cooperation between the two will continue, the newly named Roehampton University will award its own degrees and will be administered, as are other English universities, by a vice-chancellor.

The university consists of eight academic schools offering a wide range of undergraduate and graduate degree programs, established in this configuration in 2002: (1) Arts, (2) Business, Social Sciences & Computing, (3) Education Studies, (4) English & Modern Languages, (5) Humanities & Cultural Studies, (6) Initial Teacher Education, (7) Life & Sport Sciences, and (8) Psychology & Therapeutic Studies. Total student population is approximately 7,500, of whom almost 5,000 are undergraduates. The university is located on the edge of Greater London, in a leafy suburban setting close to Richmond Park and the River Thames.

The university's Undergraduate Prospectus features service-learning prominently, along with study abroad and language learning:

> Service-learning is a unique and exciting course which enables you to undertake voluntary or paid work in the community and gain academic credits . . . which count towards your degree. The course links practical experience with academic learning and personal growth, and is normally available in either your second or final year of study. On the service-learning course you'll work in various social, community, educational or charitable agencies for 12–15 hours per week. Recent examples of service placements

for Roehampton students include tutoring children at a school for the blind; working for an anti-slavery organisation; assisting in a hospital; and working with disabled adults and children. You'll be expected to produce a service placement file which contains five core elements: a journal of reflection; an initial orientation paper; a set of critical incident papers analysing your social interaction with the agency; a structural analysis of your agency and its relationship to the wider society; and a concluding paper which draws links between the experience, academic learning and broader social issues.

## The Visit

My visit to Roehampton took place on March 18 and 19, 2004, and was arranged by Brad Blitz, director of the Partnership's graduate program at Roehampton. I came with questions similar to those for Trinity, and I attempted to look at the institution both on its own terms and also through the prism of the Trinity experience. The two institutions presented a marked contrast.

I began my interviews in advance of the visit itself through an extended telephone conversation on March 13 with Dr. David Peacock, who, as principal of Whitelands College at the time, was the person most responsible for bringing the Partnership to Roehampton and establishing Roehampton not only as a site for the Partnership's undergraduate program but also as the anchor institution for the Partnership's master's degree in International Service. I had indicated in advance the kinds of questions I wished to ask him, and he was well prepared for our conversation.

The first link between Whitelands College and the Partnership, he said, came through the Anglican Church: Linda Chisholm was in touch with Church House, the administrative center of the Church of England, concerning the establishment of CUAC, Colleges and Universities of the Anglican Communion. This led in October 1990 (as a result of conversation with Tony Evans, who at the time was directing a small Partnership program in England through Westminster College, a Methodist college of higher education in Oxford) to a meeting with representatives of the Anglican Colleges of Higher Education, still the main training ground for teachers in Church of England schools. David Peacock attended this meeting, at which there was some talk about service-learning and the Partnership. He was particularly interested in the Partnership's international reach, since he had been asked to assist in recruiting international students and making international contacts for the Roehampton Institute. Later, he and others visited several AEC (Association of Episcopal Colleges) colleges in the US (Sewanee, Kenyon, Bard, Saint Augustine's, and others) and also attended the Partnership conference in St. Louis, at which Lee Knefelkamp and Parker Palmer were speakers. By the time he left, as Dr. Peacock puts it, he was sold on the pedagogy of service-learning.

Upon his return, he asked his deputy, Chris Walsh, to meet with Howard Berry and Linda Chisholm to explore ways of cooperation. As a result of these discussions, an agreement was signed and Whitelands and Roehampton accepted the first Partnership students in the fall of 1991. A summer program was also established in the following year.

In January 1993 David Peacock, retaining the principalship of Whitelands, also became pro-rector of the Roehampton Institute. He championed service-learning. Inspired by the success of the arrangement with the Partnership, Chris Walsh worked with the Department of Sociology and Social Administration, which began to offer service-learning for UK students—from about 1993 on—for twenty credits (one semester) and forty credits (two semesters). This attracted six or eight students at a time. Chris Walsh was also instrumental, under David Peacock's direction, in designing and setting up the Partnership master's degree in the mid-1990s, after agreement was reached with the Partnership on its basic structure. This program, as we have noted, sends students to the Autonomous University of Guadalajara or the University of Technology Jamaica for the fall, and then students move to Roehampton, where they complete their course work and write their master's dissertations over the following six months or so. In both places, they spend part of their time in service placements, generally with community service agencies in Jamaica and Mexico, and with NGOs in London.

In 1997 Chris Walsh withdrew for reasons of health. David Peacock turned a crisis into an opportunity to move service-learning into the Institute's mainstream. Kevin Bales took charge of the MA program, and Jenny Iles was put in charge of the institute's service-learning programs, including the Partnership's undergraduate program. When Bernadette Porter became rector and chief executive in 1999, she grew increasingly interested in service-learning and more and more convinced of the efficacy of its pedagogy, meeting with Howard Berry and Linda Chisholm and attending Partnership conferences. Although David Peacock tried to get other departments to consider service-learning, there was a feeling (as he explained it) that the program should be kept to manageable size and limited to the social sciences. The relationship with the Partnership has not always been smooth, Dr. Peacock pointed out—in part because of the rough bureaucratic edges between the UK university bureaucracy and the US headquarters of the Partnership, and in part because of occasional philosophical differences and some disagreements over admissions policies. As he saw it, the Partnership did not always understand that Roehampton had its own requirements and needs that had to be met.

In due course David Woodman replaced Kevin Bales as director of the graduate program (he has in turn been replaced by Brad Blitz: see below), and David Peacock himself retired in the year 2000. Asked why service-learning had found a foothold at Roehampton, in a national academic environment largely hostile to unconventional pedagogies, Dr. Peacock suggested that the history and tradition of Roehampton, as a federation of church-related colleges, helped. Service-learning, he emphasized, is "an educational approach among many," and therefore worthy of a place in a diverse and open institution of the kind that Roehampton aspires to be. Roehampton continues to encourage service-learning: the prospectus and website allude to it prominently.

## Day One: The Leadership

My first meeting was with Brad Blitz, director of the MA program in International Service. He is a relatively recent addition to the School of Business, Social Sciences and Computing, having been recruited from Middlesex University to oversee this program and to teach in his field of political science (international and development studies). He came to Middlesex from the United States and holds a US doctorate (Stanford 1998) and undergraduate degrees from Belgium and Britain.

We began our discussion where my conversation with David Peacock left off—on the question of why service-learning seemed to have gained a degree of academic credibility at Roehampton. Like Dr. Peacock, Dr. Blitz pointed to the church-based connection of the university and the fact that many people at the university took civic engagement seriously, seeing it as a part of the mission of higher education. Service-learning fits with the community mission of the university.

He stressed, however, that it was important, on an ongoing basis, to asses the benefits accruing to the university from its association with the Partnership. Service-learning tends to be labor-intensive and capital-intensive. The university's RAE submission (the Research Assessment Exercise, the basis on which research funds are distributed by the government among English universities) includes the Partnership, and a strong RAE submission is essential for university funding.

The benefits to the curriculum are easier to identify. They include cross-fertilization between the School's BA in Human Rights (and perhaps other programs) and students in the Partnership, and the other benefits that come from such international involvement by the university, especially the networking abilities that it produces. Strong international programs such as those associated with the Partnership are important to the university and essential in raising its profile (it hardly hurts that the Partnership office is located in New York two blocks from the United Nations).

The university offers two programs in service-learning—one through the Partnership, for Partnership students, and the other partially integrated with the first and focused on a course in service-learning offered by Jenny Iles. At the graduate level, the MA in International Service is accessible either through the Partnership or through direct application to Roehampton. While service-learning as such may be relatively little known and understood at Roehampton, at least beyond the School of Business, Social Sciences and Computing, the concept of internships is well understood. Thus the BA in Human Rights has a system of internship placements, but not really service-learning. The university also has a Voluntary Action Management MA, run by Colin Rochester in the business program (with internships). Bill Rushbrooke (Business) co-teaches with Brad Blitz. Bill Rushbrooke's course requires each student to do a management audit of an organization.

Dr. Blitz indicated that getting more students and more colleagues involved in the kind of outreach represented by the International Service degree is high on his agenda. After a year at Roehampton—a year in which his unit has been under enormous pressure because of the process of periodic review (so-called validation)—he feels that he understands the program better, and that the validation process has made it more secure. He can now turn his attention to building it up, through intensified recruitment, the development of course materials, and (his long-term vision) the creation of a center for international cooperation and social research. The past year proved more work than he had expected: it was difficult to divide time between outreach and work on campus, but the campus side of the operation, he feels, is now more firmly established.

As I left the meeting with Brad Blitz, I reflected on the contrast between the comments of David Peacock, who, working with a relatively loose structure, was able to introduce service-learning to Roehampton through a combination of advocacy and opportunity, and the observations of Brad Blitz, new to an institution in transition, in which the cold calculus of external prestige and government funding had replaced the idealism of an earlier era. Blitz was working with structures already in place, in which the judgment of outsiders had in essence replaced his own and that of his colleagues. The need to move Roehampton up in the comparative rankings in British higher education (a system that at the best of times labors under the often deadening hand of quantitative assessment and "validation") had put the institution into a defensive mode, quite at odds with the history of its component parts.

I moved on to lunch with Dr. Bernadette Porter, university rector and chief executive, herself very much a representative of an institution in transition. Dr. Porter had recently indicated to her governing council that she had decided against a further tour of duty as rector, after five years in the post. She is a member of the Order of the Sacred Heart and came to Roehampton to join the faculty of education at Digby Stuart College (by this time Roehampton Institute) twenty-one years ago, teaching the Postgraduate Certificate. She had been head of department at a big London comprehensive school. During the first five years she completed her doctorate, then became principal of Digby Stuart for five years, then deputy rector of the Roehampton Institute for five years, then (in 1999) rector of what soon became the University of Surrey Roehampton. During the coming year (2004–2005) she will take a year off and then return to the faculty.

It was, she said, David Peacock who convinced his colleagues to accept service-learning when he was principal of Whitelands College and pro-rector of the institute. His initiative fit well with her own vision of Roehampton as an institution interested in giving service, in the promotion of human rights, and in involvement with the larger community. In UK universities, she suggested, "we don't always know how to make best use of faculty talents." If service-learning is to be fully institutionalized at Roehampton, it must be built into the faculty's contractual understanding, and the faculty must be both competent and motivated to carry it out. This process of institutionalization might take place also through allied fields, for example the program in human rights, which is only a step away from service-learning.

Asked about obstacles to (as opposed to incentives for) the expansion of service-learning at Roehampton, she stressed that at the undergraduate level there are no barriers that can be described as specifically institutional. Although the service-learning program is prominently featured in the university's program announcements, it has not expanded beyond the school in which it is now housed, nor have student numbers increased significantly, perhaps because students find it too demanding. At the graduate level there is something of a danger that the program will go its own way, i.e. that it will become more like, say, the program in human rights, rather than that human rights will become more like service-learning. It is important that the Partnership remain active and involved, also in promoting the uniqueness of the pedagogy of service-learning and maintaining focus.

I should add that the imminent departure of Dr. Porter from the rectorship raised an additional uncertainty: she repeated several times in the course of our meeting her conviction that the pedagogy of service-learning has much to offer an institution like Roehampton, and it is clear that her leadership has helped the program to retain and strengthen its position.

## Day One: Continuity

My next conversation was with David Woodman, who until recently was the program convener for the MA in International Service (and director of the program for the Partnership). David Woodman is a sociologist, a former dean, and now the leader of the social sciences division of the School of Business, Social Sciences and Computing. His senior status at the university helps lend credibility to service-learning and the association with the Partnership. He was instrumental in bringing Brad Blitz to the university and has worked with him to bring about a smooth transition for the program.

As he explained in our conversation, he started at Southlands in 1971 as lecturer in sociology—before Roehampton Institute was founded and when Southlands was a teacher training college. He gradually moved out of education and, as the field developed at Roehampton, into sociology itself (initially with an emphasis on the sociology of medicine, and then on globalization and new technologies). In 1989 he became dean of the faculty of social sciences, occupying that position until 1996 and overseeing Chris Walsh's launch of the MA in International Service (along with members of the social sciences and business faculty, including Bill Rushbrooke, mentioned already by Brad Blitz). His successor as dean had a less smooth working relationship with Chris Walsh, who in any case left the university in 1997, leaving management of the program in the hands of Kevin Bales. David Woodman took on the headship of social sciences for a year on an interim basis. Yvonne Guerrier (Business) was then appointed as head with Woodman as deputy head of school (the other deputy head, Cindy Ferguson, covers business and computing). Continuing responsibility for the MA fell to him, until the arrival of Brad Blitz.

When David Woodman took on responsibility for the MA in 1999 (the same year, we note, as Bernadette Porter was appointed to the rectorship), the service-learning course for undergraduates was operating somewhat outside faculty oversight, and the master's program also needed to be pulled into the mainstream. There was, as he saw it, a relative lack of faculty buy-in. Eager to overcome the low prestige of practice-based education, Woodman set about integrating it into the school's offerings. He stressed that the prestige that the MA in International Service now enjoys was established by insistence on academic quality. At the same time he had had little experience in the field and wanted to recruit someone who had—a process that culminated several years later in the appointment of Brad Blitz.

Recently, Woodman said, he has been at work on a proposal for a Center for Excellence in Teaching and Learning, which would include attention to service-learning and specifically the Partnership. This proposal, he explained, builds on Roehampton's recent institution-wide quality audit, which proved positive, but did criticize the university for lack of cooperation with employers and external agencies. Service-learning is a powerful way of countering such criticism.

I returned to a question I had asked of Dr. Porter: How do students come to service-learning at Roehampton, and why are there not more of them? Students come to service-learning, David Woodman explained, as part of their academic work, or career preparation, or social responsibility.

It adds employability skills as well. While the numbers enrolling in the course on service-learning may be quite small, the human rights program involves a process akin to service-learning (i.e. work placement) on a compulsory basis. Such placements are also an option in criminology, anthropology, social policy, and childhood and society. Discussion is currently underway about developing a program at the MA level in intercultural communication (diversity management) that might well include service-learning, and there is a proposal for a program in visual anthropology (to replace the current anthropology program in travel and tourism)—with service-learning as a component.

In response to my objection that internships and service-learning are not entirely the same thing, he suggested that the definition of service-learning inevitably gets stretched beyond NGOs. Service-learning essentially addresses disadvantage and social exclusion linked to personal transformation.

What can be done to expand service-learning at Roehampton? Expansion of service-learning into other parts of the institution is at a standstill and cannot be advanced without a solution to two problems: resources (the principal difficulty) and placements (good and productive placements at accessible locations are hard to come by). Service-learning at Roehampton is limited less by the resistance of colleagues than by resources: they can't proselytize without more to work with.

Jenny Iles, with whom I met next and who is in charge of the undergraduate course in service-learning and of student placement, was head of the Principal's Office at Whitelands, as of 1991, under David Peacock. It was there that she first heard of service-learning. After completing her master's degree, she began to work with service-learning students and in due course became a part-time lecturer to coordinate the service-learning program under Chris Walsh. At the time she was enrolled in the Ph.D. program (which she has now completed). When Chris Walsh left in 1997, "there was no handover," and so she had to make new contacts with agencies and find placements for students. She enlisted the services of the Wandsworth Volunteer Bureau. From there, she developed her own links—through word of mouth, the Internet, telephone calls and so on.

Her course in service-learning has some twenty students this semester. Students can do community service all year with lectures in one of two semesters (I found the materials for the course, contained in two Module Handbooks, impressive, both in focus and breadth). Students have access to her during the off-semester. When the Partnership sends students, they are integrated into this course. Currently, she has students from health and social care, psychology, and social sciences. Service-learning is compulsory in health and social care, and brings about five students a year. There is some talk about setting up a separate service-learning course for these students, a matter of some concern for Dr. Iles, who is apprehensive about enrollment and somewhat disinclined to promote such a development.

The students who come to her arrange their own service-agency placements, or she assists them in finding placements. Some are already doing volunteer work and remain with their agencies. Others need some guidance but follow up themselves. Yet others need more help: she finds contacts for them and arranges an interview. Agencies are generally pleased with the students. She does some placement visits.

I asked her about the academic standing of service-learning within the institution. It used to be that faculty wouldn't touch service-learning, she replied: it was a Whitelands activity and therefore, suspect. Now, most people accept it and realize that it is a serious endeavor with strong academic content. David Woodman's support made a big difference in gaining this status for service-learning. People realized that Roehampton was a leader in the field, and that service-learning tied in with the Dearing Report's emphasis on work experience and civic engagement.

She is, however, concerned for the future, with a new vice-chancellor coming in ("Bernie talks about service-learning all the time," she said, referring to the current vice-chancellor). At the same time, more institutions in Britain are becoming interested in service-learning. Liverpool Hope University College and Napier University (Edinburgh) are doing something like service-learning—and also Glasgow and Middlesex (Middlesex organized a conference on community-based learning). None of this would have happened without the Partnership's planting of the seed.

A chance meeting with Neil Taylor, director of research at Roehampton and former dean of arts, offered me a good opportunity to test some of the statements made in my earlier meetings. He said that he knew relatively little about service-learning. He knows that it can be labor-intensive and time-consuming, as is demonstrated in the arduous search for placements in education, counseling, clinical psychology, and so on. At the same time, there might be fields where service-learning would be readily applicable, especially education, and perhaps even his own field, drama. Little can be achieved, however, without two ingredients: practical leadership and resources. Without resources, it is hard to have much impact.

Knowledge of service-learning is relatively low on campus, he explained: he is by no means unique in this regard. At the same time he was quite emphatic when asked whether it was regarded as an academically respectable activity. "Absolutely," he replied. He expressed a strong interest in my research, suggesting that it would be interesting to expand the research dimension to focus on pedagogy, student development, and community development.

The meeting was useful because it confirmed David Woodman's observations about the status of service-learning at Roehampton—and also the fact that idealism without resources may be in a weaker position than resources without idealism.

### Day Two: Students

Brad Blitz and David Woodman were summoned to an extended meeting on the proposed Center for Excellence in Teaching and Learning, and so I did not have an opportunity to follow up with them on some of the questions raised by my intensive day of interviews. My main activity for the day was to meet with the students in the Partnerships MA program in International Service. Seven of them (Audrey, Sarah, Kali, Dawn, Mary Beth, Darla, Romelle) were in attendance, all of them from the Jamaica program. The students from the Mexico program were at their agencies or otherwise occupied (during the day it is hard to find a time when everyone is available). I asked the students to tell me about their placements. Mary Beth and Audrey (who is a lecturer in family studies at the University of Technology Jamaica) are working at the Guildford Institute, doing research on social empowerment. Romelle will soon start at STAR (Student Action for Refugees). Darla is working with attorneys at the European Human Rights Advocacy Centre, primarily in Chechnya, and including also work with the European Human Rights Court. Kali is working at Voluntary Service Overseas (the organization founded by Alec Dickson). Dawn is at a new organization, PLAN International. Sarah is at World Jewish Aid.

Our discussion ranged over technical and practical aspects of the MA program that need not detain us here. In general, the students seemed pleased with their experience, and particularly pleased that efforts are underway to integrate the experience in Jamaica or Mexico more effectively into the degree program as a whole. They were pleased that Brad Blitz came to Jamaica at the opening of the program in August and they found the New York stay in January, between their time in Kingston and their arrival in London, particularly useful: it gave everyone a chance to see the New York scene (aided by the Partnership's ability to open doors with foundations, NGOs and international organizations), and it also helped create a sense of cohesion in the group.

Service-learning in general, and the MA program in particular, need more visibility, said the students. They spontaneously expressed a willingness to work for such an objective when they returned home. I came away from the meeting with a sense that the program was growing steadily stronger, and also that it was fully integrated into Roehampton's degree offerings.

At the conclusion of my comments on Trinity College, I listed those features that seemed to me to have allowed for the expansion and acceptance of service-learning at the institution. At Roehampton the situation was very different, expressing, first, the nature of higher education in a very different country, under a very different set of academic and governmental priorities, and, second, the condition of an institution at a different stage in its development.

- **Mission.** As at Trinity, the mission of the institution, at least as it is conceived historically, is supportive of service-learning—but Roehampton is an institution conflicted about its past, eschewing its old status as an agglomeration of teacher-training institutions and seeking a new status as co-equal with other British universities.

- **Coordination.** Roehampton is more decentralized than Trinity, with no evident centralized coordinating structure for community outreach, and with somewhat ambivalent views on the relation between community outreach and academic rigor.

- **Outreach.** The individual units of the institution are not held responsible for this outreach, unless it is linked to academic endeavors.

- **Leadership.** As at Trinity, service-learning at Roehampton has made progress in large part through the exercise of leadership—by David

Peacock in the early years, and by David Woodman's principled defense of David Peacock's achievements.

- **Confluence.** There was a happy coincidence of the Partnership's philosophy with David Peacock's leadership, and a series of events that strengthened the connection.

- **Environment.** The university itself maintains the appearance— and the reality—of a suburban campus, somewhat remote from the urban environment.

- **Stability.** The program itself has been plagued by discontinuities of program leadership—at a time of significant institutional change.

- **National Policy.** Recent national initiatives, such as the Dearing Report, have reinforced the importance of UK universities' community involvement and civic engagement—but in the face of a long and distinguished, and essentially conservative, academic tradition.

## Jamaica: A National University

### The Partnership and UTech

The third institution that we resolved to look at more closely was the University of Technology Jamaica. Linda Chisholm and Nevin Brown, of the Partnership, and Brad Blitz, director of the Partnership's master's program in the United Kingdom, visited the university in August 2003 and conducted a number of interviews. The present account is based on their reports, and on my own observations from two visits to the university in the 1990s and contacts with its personnel since then.

The University of Technology Jamaica, as we have already noted, was founded in Kingston as CAST, the College of Arts, Science and Technology, intended originally as a non-research-based higher-education alternative to the country's only university, the University of the West Indies. In 1984, Howard Berry and Linda Chisholm visited Jamaica with the intention of setting up a service-learning program for American students under the auspices of Rockland Community College. Rockland had had a service-learning program in Ghana, a "roots" program sponsored by the Presbyterian Church USA, but Ghana was experiencing political troubles and the program had to be abandoned after two or three years. They selected Jamaica as a black nation, independent, at the center of the Caribbean, home of Caricom and the Caribbean Conference of Churches (CCC), with many institutions of higher education. They had located in New York, through the Episcopal Church, a Jamaican who had been educated in Jamaica, worked for the Caribbean Conference of Churches and was active in such organizations as Rotary. He knew people who could help, and arranged appointments and accompanied them to Jamaica. They visited eight colleges and universities throughout the island and many service agencies, and they met with the minister of education, sports and culture. They selected the College of Arts, Science, and Technology rather than the University of the West Indies because CAST was more community-focused and connected than the University of the West Indies, which was more research-oriented. CAST was better located for service and housing than were the other colleges they visited, and much better academically. In the initial plan, CAST delivered the academic work, and the CCC arranged and supervised the placements. CCC was in a unique position to do this because most grant money for agencies came through the CCC. Their program officer was responsible for visiting agencies to evaluate their worthiness to receive support, and thus was familiar with virtually all the service work on the island.

CAST had a program of required community service from its early days, but the program was only partially fulfilled. Service also included work experience in business and other places. This made sense and could be legitimately called service since any development in the newly independent Jamaica (1962) was indeed service to the nation.

This was the period in which the Partnership was just coming into being, and Linda Chisholm was moving to the Association of Episcopal Colleges. Soon after, Howard Berry made the move from Rockland to the Partnership. Hence it is a little difficult to establish whether the prime mover was Rockland or the Partnership, and the program ultimately became the Partnership program.

The president of CAST, Dr. Alfred Sangster, recognized the experimental nature of the program and all parties were honest that it might not succeed. He was willing to become a partner in the endeavor, declaring service-learning to be "a beautiful idea." Indeed, it fitted his own sense of CAST as an academic institution linked with the local community and national priorities. His support for the initiative was decisive: holder of a Ph.D. in chemistry and a senior lecturer at the University of the West Indies, he had come to CAST as president in 1971, when the college had some 1500 students. By the time he left, twenty-six years later, it had 6,000. He himself was firmly identified with the institution that he served, and little happened at UTech that he did not know about or that he did not support. The mid-1980s were a particularly important period in the development of the college, since it was granted independent degree-granting status as of 1986.

Dr. Sangster made his vice-president, Dr. Gloria Hamilton, program manager for service-learning and treated the activity as an extra-departmental program. CAST issued a transcript to the students but otherwise the college was not directly involved. In January 1985, Berry and Chisholm took fourteen faculty members (three from Rockland, others from around the United States) to Jamaica for a ten-day program introducing them to service-learning, agencies in Jamaica, and CAST. In the summer of 1985, the student program was initiated with seven students, three of them from Pacific Lutheran University.

When, by about 1989, the program proved to have staying power, Dr. Sangster moved it, as a way of institutionalizing it, into the technical education department, headed by Dr. Veta Lewis, who taught the literature course in the Partnership program. Regular faculty members taught, the department chair managed the program, it was listed in the college catalogue, and the financial arrangements were assumed by the finance department. In the meantime, efforts were moving forward to integrate the studies more closely with the service. The program officer from CCC was finding his role in the program more difficult, and it was mutually decided to assign a member of the sociology department to the role of service placement and supervision. Carmen Pencle took on the role and has been fulfilling it ever since.

In the meantime, CAST was moving towards university status. As of 1986, as we have noted, it had been entitled to award its own degrees, but the plan was now to turn it into a full-fledged university with a research component. Faculty were told that they must secure doctorates and many did, including Veronica Salter, who taught in the program and who had been involved at every stage. University status was achieved in 1996. Howard

Berry had been asked to advise on various plans needed for university status, including how to design the course requirements so as to satisfy graduate schools in both the US and the UK where many Jamaicans seek advanced degrees. He did so willingly. In 1996, the university presented the Distinguished Service award to Berry and Chisholm for "their long involvement with and support for UTech" in a university-wide ceremony which several hundred people attended, thereby increasing the number of people who knew about service-learning and the Partnership. Also in 1996, the Partnership held its biennial conference in Jamaica.

In 1997, Dr. Sangster retired and was succeeded by Dr. Rae Davis. Dr. Davis attended the Wingspread conference and became even more deeply committed to service-learning, community service and the IPSL. Upon the retirement of Dr. Veta Lewis, Dr. Davis appointed his dean, Dr. Geraldene Hodelin, to oversee the newly inaugurated MA in International Service. Carmen Sanguinetti was appointed to breathe new life into the old university-wide community service program and moved quickly to reconstitute it as a service-learning requirement. In 2001, the University of Technology became a Distinguished Partner of the International Partnership for Service-Learning.

### An Interview with a Participant

On September 3, 2003, Brad Blitz interviewed Veronica Salter and tested on her some of the above observations.

*When and under what circumstances did service-learning begin at UTech? In what areas of the university? Who were the principal people involved?*

It was part of the whole idea of work experience which went towards the diploma (rather than degree). It started off in the liberal arts faculty and spread to others very quickly. But there has always been a tradition of volunteerism which grew out of the extended family system—in part due to the fact that the state was unable to provide and therefore people needed to find support from individuals. I think this happens in every rural or peasant society. The principal people at the time were Dr. Sangster who came up with the idea of providing service for the community. At the time, we supported the National Children's

Home (quasi-governmental), the School for the Deaf and the Mona Rehab Unit (both government supported). It was not like nowadays. It wasn't about providing deep skills but reading to children, helping them to bathe and nurture them. Now it is about developing skills.

*Was the Partnership involved in these efforts, or did the Partnership come later?*

No, this was before IPSL. But many of the organizations used in service-learning were our service organizations, which had benefits and disadvantages. Some people in certain organizations saw this as an extra pair of hands, as baby-minding and as a result [the students] did some very menial jobs.

*What aspects of UTech's institutional goals did service-learning support? Did it fit with the mission of the institution easily or with difficulty? Was the principal factor behind the adoption of service-learning for certain students and programs the improvement of student learning, the institution's commitment to the community, or some other factor?*

All really in terms of the philosophy of what it is about. It fitted in perfectly. Probably [that was] why it was accepted. It was driven by community needs. I don't think students originally thought they would benefit from this.

*Has service-learning expanded ... since it first began at UTech? What caused it to expand: personal interest of the people involved, student demand, changes in institutional mission, other factors? Have other institutions in your country or region started service-learning programs because of your experience or advocacy?*

Yes, and it has expanded to other places. I see more and more programs offering service-learning—other foreign programs at UWI [University of the West Indies]. I think education has seen the relevance and benefit to students and the community, especially with the idea not only in a city community but e.g. squatters at the community hospital who are offered self-help and job-creation possibilities. People no longer see the college as external. They see it more as enriching programs. . . .

*Are there distinctive features to the type of service-learning practiced at UTech?*

The distinctive features are that it was primarily focused on the disadvantaged—not necessarily on the exchange of skills. It is authentic service-learning. . . . Regarding staff understanding, it is a two-way process, articulated with material from academic programs and constant feedback e.g. with the case study and further research by means of the dissertation.

*Would you describe the attitude of your institution as highly supportive of service-learning, somewhat supportive, or essentially neutral (or hostile)?*

Very positive. I never noticed any students balking at the idea. Sometimes they are more receptive than the agencies because they don't use the skills as they should but see it as an opportunity for baby-minding.

*What do you predict for the future of service-learning at UTech, and in your country or region?*

I think people do pay attention to the reports we circulate and some of the implementation. I would like to see continuity with students e.g. if they have gone to the same agency before, and always involvement with the NGOs.

## Some Conclusions on Jamaica

The interview with Ronnie Salter offers several insights. First, it is evident that the distinction between community service and service-learning is not entirely clear, perhaps because our questions make certain assumptions about terminology that may not be apparent to an outsider. Community service, as we have noted, has a long history at UTech, stretching back to the early years of Alfred Sangster's leadership, but credit-bearing service-learning does not put in an appearance until the 1980s, at the time of the contact between Dr. Sangster and the Partnership. Unfortunately the new credit-bearing program used many of the same agencies as had been used before for the community service program, and they were slow to perceive the distinction between the two.

Second, it is clear that service-learning, when it began at UTech, fit the mission of the institution and the philosophy of its leader; and, once established in Jamaica, it has now surfaced at other institutions and in other contexts (the relationship between these later developments and the Partnership remains unclear, but, if not directly causal, it may well have been influential). Equally clear is the fact that presidential leadership was crucial in its adoption at UTech.

Conversations with Carmen Sanguinetti and Geraldene Hodelin have convinced me that the principal problem facing service-learning at UTech is not the acceptability of the idea or general support for it, but the fact that the desire for its inclusion in the curriculum has outrun its implementability. Carmen Sanguinetti's success in reconstituting the community service requirement as a service-learning requirement has not in itself produced faculty members capable of handling the pedagogy of service-learning (even though all of them are expected to participate in the teaching), particularly the crucial ingredient of reflection, without which the pedagogy is powerless. Furthermore, as with the situation at Trinity, faculty members carry heavy teaching loads and are stretched to the limit, with little time to take on new assignments or learn new techniques. Although the university has adopted a neighboring high school as its partner (as we learned in chapter 11), it is difficult for the agencies to make the commitment to authentic service-learning as well, given their limited resources and the growing needs (as Susan Deeley points out in her chapter). Furthermore, the university is dealing with daunting numbers of students needing placements and course assignments. Needed at this stage at UTech is a thorough assessment of the effectiveness of the service-learning requirement and the introduction of a systematic effort at faculty development.

As we assess the observations that we made about Trinity, and the comparison with Roehampton, we can perhaps draw the following conclusions about the University of Technology, based on the recent observations of Chisholm and Blitz, on the interview conducted in New York, and on the Partnership's long and close acquaintance with the institution:

**Mission.** From the beginning, the institution has been committed to engagement with Jamaican society and with national development. This mission is supportive of service-learning. While, as at

Roehampton, UTech embarked on a move to university status, it did so under less externally competitive circumstances and hence less traumatically and with less philosophical conflict.

**Coordination.** The reinvigoration of the community service requirement and the management of the Partnership and related programs were assigned to different offices and individuals at UTech, making for less coordination than at Trinity, but were at least university-wide, unlike the situation at Roehampton, which is fully decentralized.

**Outreach.** It is unclear to what extent the individual units of UTech see outreach as a part of their mission. It is clearly not as integrated into their thinking as it is at Trinity.

**Leadership.** Leadership at UTech, as at Trinity, has been crucially important in the adoption of service-learning. At an institution such as Roehampton, with a growing tradition of faculty self-governance, there has perhaps been less scope for the exercise of leadership, but clearly leadership has been important at Roehampton too.

**Confluence.** As with Trinity and as with Roehampton, there was a happy confluence of Alfred Sangster's desire to breathe new life into the commitment to the community and the arrival of the Partnership. And as with Trinity, but not Roehampton, community service was already going on, so that the introduction of service-learning was a process of adaptation rather than total innovation.

**Environment.** As at Trinity (and unlike Roehampton), the problems of the city, and the problems of national development, have increasingly engulfed UTech, lending urgency to its community mission.

**Stability.** The years of Dr. Sangster's leadership and the relative stability of staffing have brought continuity to UTech's efforts, though this has been hampered by a less than ideal configuration of the individual units.

**National Policy.** The establishment of the National Youth Service program and its National Volunteerism Project as a national priority has put pressure on UTech to move in the direction of systematic community service, much as Trinity has been encouraged to move in a similar direction, and even Roehampton has been prodded by the Dearing Report.

## The Institutional Study: Some Findings

The pedagogy of service-learning involves much more than simple community service and much more than mere teaching about community: It puts practical experience and theoretical thinking together. In this process, reflection on experience, and the testing of theory through practice, are crucial elements in the learning that takes place. It follows, then, that any institution desirous of adopting service-learning as a pedagogy must be able to cope with the notion that through this pedagogy student learning takes place not in the classroom alone but at the point of intersection of experience and theory—and that both experience and theory are part of the learning. This is a difficult philosophy to embrace, at least for American academics, used to linking credit to classroom attendance and seat time, and tending to favor theoretical analysis over the acquisition of sensory data. While European academics are perhaps less concerned with time served in the classroom (though increasingly they are surrendering to the blandishments of credit systems that facilitate the transferability of course work and degrees), they are perhaps more focused on the theoretical even than their American colleagues. Furthermore, their cultures look less favorably on the philanthropy that we associate with service-learning. A project launched a few years ago by the International Consortium on Higher Education, Civic Responsibility and Democracy (housed at the University of Pennsylvania) examined the degree of commitment within universities in Europe and North America both to participatory democracy within their boundaries and to involvement with the community beyond. On the European side, fifteen universities across the continent participated. The project's report states, "Many sites reported that university faculty and administrators had no expectations to advocate democracy or civic responsibility. Many thought that civic responsibility cannot be taught and there is a general lack of encouragement by the university to do so" (Plantan 2002). This is a heavy burden to overcome.

American institutions have already seen some of the sharp division between experience and data-gathering on the one hand and analysis on the other. Language-learning entered the curriculum as an allegedly liberal-arts endeavor, focused on literature and culture, even though its primary goal was something close to rote-learning (a development that has sown lasting confusion in the field); credit was given for laboratory work; then some institutions began giving credit for experiential learning of various kinds, and this was followed in turn by the giving of limited credit for internships and similar activities (for example cooperative education) whose purpose was clearly linked with, and clearly instrumental to, a degree program.[1] So the wall between theory and practice has been breached—though it seems that sometimes that only makes the resistance in some quarters greater. Counterbalancing such resistance are organizations like Campus Compact, which, as we have noted, began as an organization of US university presidents and accordingly carries with it a certain persuasive weight. And, while the report mentioned above was quite negative concerning the situation in Europe, the corresponding US report (Teune & Plantan 2001) was rather less so. Interestingly, in the European context, American students are often able to engage in, and even receive credit for, activities sponsored by their institutional hosts for which their own resident students are ineligible (Charles University, as we saw in chapter 11, is, or was, a case in point).

This conservatism (or some might call it the maintenance of standards . . .) is perhaps the biggest institutional hurdle that service-learning must overcome. Unfortunately it leads, as foreign-language study led, many years ago, to a certain fudging of definitions and practices— the downplaying of the service component in service-learning when faced with investigative faculty committees, or a reluctance to include service-providers as equal partners in the process.

At the other end of the scale, among the already converted, who may have established a credit-bearing beachhead in an institution, a counter-balancing progressivism can lead to the inclusion in service-learning of simple acts of community service that should by rights not be included, or the desire to give community service greater dignity or prestige by

---

[1] Such options, quite early on, became a device for creditworthy overseas experience outside the academic environment. See Tonkin & Edwards 1981:123. On innovation in US liberal arts institutions, see Bennett 1997.

mislabeling it service-learning. The latter is common in the United States, where offices of service-learning have sprung up on campuses all across the country, largely to handle volunteer placements and to coordinate agency contacts, and even such respected organizations as Campus Compact are apt to elide the distinction. These abuses in turn reinforce the resolve of the conservatives to exclude service-learning from the curriculum altogether.

Roehampton has been largely successful in establishing service-learning within the institution as a respectable academic endeavor. It has done so, however, at considerable cost, perhaps losing in the process some of the excitement and innovation potentially associated with this form of study and apparently giving relatively little attention to the community impact of the work of its students—matters outside the purview of academic committees. By making service-learning look like everything else, we preserve it but it loses its edge. On the other hand, this adoption of protective coloring may have been necessary in an institution whose academic aspirations, and willingness as a consequence to subject itself to outside scrutiny disinclined to take institutional uniqueness into consideration, outweighed all other considerations. Service-learning at Roehampton has emerged much strengthened as a result, but much of the altruism that animates such institutions as Trinity College or Payap University has been drained out of the system by the demands placed upon it from outside.

Meanwhile, the University of Technology, and to a lesser extent Trinity College, have perhaps been led to regard as service-learning, activities that hardly qualify. Reflection, which many consider the key element in service-learning, is expensive in time and requires great pedagogical skill. In institutions under simultaneous pressure to deliver community service (for the benefit of nation and community) on the one hand, and generate academic credit (for the purposes of national development) on the other, the *appearance* of service-learning may be an inexpensive way of dealing with both pressures at the same time, a kind of double-whammy—but the *reality* of service-learning is a different matter altogether. Service-learning is not cheap—though perhaps, with the right research, of the kind that we are seeking to initiate here, we can establish that the results of service-learning properly conducted exceed that of conventional pedagogies, while at the same time addressing needs beyond the university.

In both instances—the potential conservatism of established institutions and the potential opportunism of the less established—the key is faculty development: without faculty members competent to design and conduct service-learning effectively, little can be achieved, and indeed much damage may be done. Faculty development means resources—and the Partnership, if it can find the resources to put such a program into operation, could and should be a key player in the delivery of knowledge and expertise for institutions across the world.

But behind faculty development issues, as a prior issue, is the question of advocacy. Many of the institutions in our study have called on the Partnership to provide help in convincing their faculty and administrators to adopt service-learning as a strategy (on the process of institutionalization see Bucco & Busch 1996, Jacoby 1996, Rubin 1996, Holland 1999, Bringle & Hatcher 2000, Holland 2000, Ramaley 2000). Only by internalizing and incentivizing service-learning, as Dr. Porter of Roehampton rightly points out, can it become accepted: administrators can remove barriers, but they cannot easily inspire. We might retort that it is precisely inspiration that has led to the successes documented here: leadership (including that of Dr. Porter, and emphatically that of Dr. Rodriguez at Trinity and Dr. Sangster at UTech) has been a fundamental ingredient of success. Yet arguably the most effective leaders are those who lead through structural change: one cannot stop the ocean, but one can engage in a little strategic dredging of the beach.

What, then, are the ingredients of success? Our observation of the Partnership institutions leads us to the following tentative conclusions about success in the introduction of service-learning.

**The institution in question has a longstanding interest in civic engagement, derived either from its original mission or from the influence of powerful leaders who have reshaped mission and direction.** In Jamaica, the arrival and continuance of a strong leader, Dr. Alfred Sangster, caused a number of existing connections with social service agencies to blossom into a more comprehensive service-learning program, and this led, shortly after his departure, to a decision to make service-learning part of the general undergraduate curriculum. In the Philippines, a largely unstated commitment (there is no mention of it in the original mission statement), deriving from the fact that the college is a Christian foundation, quickly led to the engagement of the college in the community, and a succession of dedicated leaders created a commitment to service-learning. Compared to this energy, the recently discovered European and American commitment to civic engagement (represented for example in the consortium mentioned above) is pale indeed, but may represent the tentative emergence of conditions favorable to service-learning in places like Roehampton, for example. And US universities are at something of an advantage over their European counterparts: there is at least an enduring undercurrent of responsibility to the community in public higher education and in what might be described as the moral aspect of liberal arts education, to say nothing of the strong and longstanding involvement of American churches in the delivery of higher education.

**Responsibility for service-learning is both supported by strong and well-established central coordinating mechanisms (and budgetary commitment) and diffused among faculty and students.**
At Trinity College, the most successful of the three institutions in this regard, each of the constituent schools receives a budgetary allocation for community service and service-learning—an allocation that is as firmly identified with such activities as the funding for, say, the physics department. The individual schools make their contacts with the larger community, and have the flexibility to do so, but they are assisted by a centralized office that runs some programs of its own and collaborates with the academic units by providing support services for their initiatives. In the United States, the models vary: some institutions lack central coordinating mechanisms; some have such mechanisms, but they are limited to non-credit-bearing activities; some, like the Center for Community Partnerships at the University of Pennsylvania, do both. "When transformation of the work of colleges and universities on the scholarship of engagement occurs that is integral, enduring, and meaningful to all stakeholders, then service-learning will be institutionalized" (Bringle & Hatcher 2000:274).

**The idea of community service is supported by public policy at the national level, and institutions are expected to engage with the community, and it is also a part of the larger culture.**
In the Philippines the establishment of the National Service Training Program means that all institutions must prepare their students for community service through programs for first-year students. The launching of the program was possible because of the example set by such institutions as Trinity and by a strong culture of mutual support and caring in the larger society (see Aquino 2000). In Jamaica a long

tradition of community commitment wedded to a national volunteerism movement presents similar opportunities.[2] In the United States this role is played in part by such organizations as Campus Compact.

The Partnership has had a decisive influence when its perhaps deeper and more comprehensive philosophy has given shape and direction to activities already in place, giving them a sense of purpose and coherence. The contacts between the founders of the Partnership and Dr. Sangster in Jamaica in the 1980s came at precisely the point when Dr. Sangster was consolidating his academic leadership and looking for ways of engaging the community. The Partnership's philosophy of action in the community on the one hand and reflection in an academic setting on the other coincided precisely with Dr. Sangster's thinking, and his college soon began hosting Partnership students from the United States. However, engaging the faculty in establishing opportunities for student reflection on experiences in the field was more difficult, and this remains the weakest link in what is now an institution-wide activity involving well over a thousand students.

A similar process took place in the Philippines. Linda Chisholm, now president of the Partnership, attended the inauguration of President Rodriguez, and out of their conversations came his decision to take the already existing community-service programs at the college and integrate them into the curriculum through service-learning. Thus, community service shifted from an essentially extracurricular (even if, for some students, preprofessional) activity, to a credit-bearing academic pursuit. The college has, over the years, pushed more and more of the responsibility for operating programs on to the students themselves, encouraging self-reliance while providing good back-up support. A heavily committed faculty (Trinity has limited resources and is dependent on tuition income) is unable to provide the degree or depth of reflection that we might expect of service-learning programs in the United States, but this may be due in part to the very different educational, cultural and social expectations of Filipino students and faculty.

In both of these instances—Jamaica and the Philippines—we are looking at many years of Partnership engagement with the institutions in question. The program run by Trinity for students from Southeast Asia is

---

[2] Berry & Chisholm 1999 offer an overview of national service programs.

now beginning to spawn a new range of contacts and a new round of service-learning initiatives. With the assistance of funding from the Luce Foundation, a number of institutions in the region have been working together on the design of service-learning programs, under the direction of Partnership vice-president Florence McCarthy. The new Partnership program at Payap University, in Chiang Mai, Thailand, is built on a burgeoning set of service-learning activities now coming into being at that institution, and we may well see a similar round of activities in which the Partnership helps shape the culture and direction of that institution.

There are of course institutions that have been far less responsive to the presence of the Partnership, indeed where the Partnership operates successfully with very little engagement by the central administration. These tend to be the larger institutions with which the Partnership works and they tend to be situated in industrialized countries with a less firm tradition of community involvement by institutions or individuals but with a stronger received sense of traditional academic procedures and modes of pedagogy. Examining success and discovering its authors is always easier than exploring indifference, but the successes, where they have occurred, have been notable, if imperfect. It may be that the Partnership will serve its mission best by lending support to already existing momentum, and introducing a sense of quality and sound educational and social philosophy where the will to succeed is already present.

We should also observe, in keeping with the assertions of Chisholm and Berry (2002), that educational customs vary from culture to culture, and that strictly American approaches to service-learning, or even to the process of reflection at its heart, may be culturally biased.[3] One of the hardest tasks facing the Partnership is maintaining a balance between insistence on quality (both the integrity of the pedagogy and the competence of its execution) and a willingness to entertain differing approaches to service-learning in different cultures.

---

[3] There are many issues here—and issues that service-learning is well equipped to address, e.g. the relationship between (a) epistemologies of knowledge that students have received and internalized and (b) culturally embedded interpretations of experience demonstrated by the clients of the agencies where they work; or the tension between these epistemological systems that is evident in agencies mediating between western ideas of development and in-country interpretations of service; or western senses of self and personality and self-actualization. See Reagan 2005, Chisholm 2004, Chisholm & Berry 2002.

At the beginning of chapter 11, I suggested that the Research Plan gave us five questions to address. The first related to change agents and the process whereby change came about. Change always implies an element of discontinuity: leaders, recognizing the potential for innovation to solve a problem or to afford an advantage that others may not have perceived, enlist the help of others in introducing an innovation.[4] The rapidity of its acceptance will depend, in the first instance, on prior conditions. To what extent is the innovation a response to felt needs or perceived problems? How different from previous practice is it? To what extent is it at odds with the prevailing institutional culture?[5] Is that culture likely to be supportive of the innovator, i.e. does it encourage risk-taking or is it risk-averse? The process whereby the innovation of service-learning arrived on the three campuses that we have looked at can be readily analyzed in these terms. At Trinity and UTech there was a *felt need* and an identifiable *problem*: moral pressure (at the very least) to address community problems, awareness of the importance of inculcating into young people a sense of community responsibility, but also the need to provide them with an academically and theoretically strong education with very limited resources. *Previous practice* had addressed these external problems primarily by way of community service programs, and service-learning was a logical extension of these efforts. The *prevailing culture* in the academic communities in question made the addressing of community problems a matter of valid concern. Finally, courageous and forthright leadership at both institutions apparently included an openness to *risk-taking*.

In his classic theory on the diffusion of innovations, Rogers (1995; first edition 1962) invokes research on the notion of *homophily*—"the degree to which two or more individuals who interact are similar in certain attributes, such as beliefs, education, social status, and the like" (Lazarsfeld & Merton 1964), suggesting that such individuals are more likely to accept innovations than those who are heterophilous. Another way of expressing the same idea might be to suggest that in such contexts it is easier to build

---

[4] Theories of leadership often focus on this characteristic. See, for example, Kanter 1983, Bennis 1989. Green 1988:17 cites Mayhew 1979, who, discussing leadership in higher education, emphasizes the well-known distinction between management, on the one hand, and leadership, on the other (and see Bennis 1989:44–47). But see our earlier observation about structural change, e.g. at Trinity. On college presidents as leaders, see Fisher, Tack & Wheeler 1988.

[5] On the importance of institutional culture, see, for example, Chaffee & Tierney 1988, Teune and Plantan 2001.

a critical mass of support. My observation of Trinity College suggests a strong degree of homophily—one perhaps encouraged by repeated reference to, and reinforcement of, the mission of the college toward the larger community.

Adoption (or rejection) of an innovation, according to Rogers (1995:20,163), involves a five-stage process, beginning with *knowledge* of the innovation, moving to the forming of an attitude towards it (the process of *persuasion*), followed by a *decision* to adopt or reject it, followed by *implementation* of this decision, followed by *confirmation* of this decision. In all three cases—at Trinity, UTech and Roehampton, *knowledge* came almost accidentally, but at the right moment in each case. By all accounts, Rodriguez, at Trinity, meeting Chisholm and Berry under the right conditions (Chisholm was there, after all, as representative of a prestigious outside organization, the AEC), rapidly formed a positive attitude, leading to *persuasion*; Peacock, at Roehampton, was convinced over a period of months, again under conditions in which the plausibility of the proposition was high (a meeting at Church House, a trip to the United States, attendance at a Partnership conference); Sangster, in Jamaica, was a little more careful, perhaps less swayed by a delegation from a New York community college, perhaps aware of the sheer complexity of implementation. Convinced that he should move ahead, he set things up in such a fashion as to minimize the impact of failure, but to maximize the long-term possibility of success.

No doubt many other factors played into the *decision* of these three leaders to move ahead (the topic might be worthy of study in itself), among them an attempt to position their institutions in a particular way (UTech was moving to degree-granting status, Whitelands was determining its role within the federal structure of the Roehampton Institute, Trinity was shifting from a liberal-arts model to a greater level of community engagement), to challenge and nurture their faculty, and to put their own individual stamp on their institutions (and this list could be much extended).

*Implementation* took place on the three campuses in different ways and to different degrees, perhaps determined by the extent of the felt need for innovation. Rodriguez, having set up the conditions for success by putting structures in place to facilitate the innovation and by giving his senior staff a mandate to support it, pushed the decision down to his college's academic units; Peacock appointed members of his staff to implement the innovation more or less directly, and lobbied the central administration for support. In Sangster's case, the process was less clear: he gave help and validation to the Partnership, but the full implementation of service-learning at UTech is still in the process of emerging. (Peacock, of course, never saw service-learning as a predominant pedagogical strategy at Roehampton, stressing that it is but one form of teaching and learning among many.[6]) As for Rogers's final stage, that of *confirmation* (reinforcement based on positive outcomes), we can see it as an ongoing process at all three institutions: at Trinity service-learning is firmly established, at UTech slightly less so, and at Roehampton those involved are working hard to win confirmation of their innovation through outside validation and administrative support.

The principal agents of change in all three cases were, above all, the leaders; but their proposals resonated to a greater or lesser extent with the people around them.[7] When someone was needed to pick up the pieces in the undergraduate program at Roehampton, Jenny Iles, who had worked with David Peacock and saw in this assignment an opportunity, was available; Geraldene Hodelin and Carmen Sanguinetti were available to move Alfred Sangster's innovation forward with the necessary conviction; Kate Botengan and numerous others were in place at Trinity (we might note the shift from male innovators to female implementers—a commentary on the gender stratification of institutions in the 1980s and 1990s, shifting now as a result of pioneers like Bernadette Porter at Roehampton, and Josefina Sumaya and Kate Botengan in the Philippines).

The most interesting shift in mission (my second question at the beginning of chapter 11) took place at Trinity, where there was complete unanimity among the people I spoke to that service to the community had been part of Trinity's explicit mission *from the start*. The earliest mission statement does not bear this assertion out. Clearly the original vision of Bishop Ogilby and President Arthur Carson, American expatriates both, to create an American-style liberal arts college in Quezon City, while it was never repudiated, and while in many respects it informs the institution today, was rapidly reshaped after 1967 by its dynamic second president, and first Filipino, Arturo Guerrero (the linguistic shift from Arthur to Arturo encapsulates the distinction . . .). This reshaping was so emphatic that it reshaped the sense of institutional history as well.

---

[6] For a far more radical view, see Harkavy & Benson 1999.

[7] Teune and Plantan 2001 remark, "Leadership is critical to engagement. The President's role is especially important both in education for civic engagement and in actual university outreach efforts and community relations."

At Roehampton, of course, institutional mission ran counter to Peacock's innovation, to the extent that the institution sought status as a university among universities, moving away from its vocational mission as a teacher training college (and, in the case of Froebel, educational innovator) towards a more conventional academic status. At the same time, a lesser current flowed in the opposite direction—towards civic engagement and the university's assumption of responsibility to the community.

My third question related to changes in institutional philosophy and practice. What impact have the philosophy and practices of service-learning had on the faculty, staff, students, service agencies, I asked? This is less easily answered. At UTech, service-learning may have actually worked in recent years to reinvigorate community service; at Trinity the impact has been profound, above all in what appears to be a sense that service to the community and the provision of vocational and academic training are not necessarily in conflict at all—in part because community service addresses people, and Trinity education is strongly people-centered, even in fields like medical technology, where students are taught that they are serving real people whose lives they need to understand. At Roehampton the impact has been limited, perhaps because of lack of resources, perhaps because of a conscious decision on the part of those involved not to rouse or provoke opposition.

The fourth question addressed the role of the Partnership as determining factor, or one in a number of factors, influencing changes in policy and practice. Despite Ronnie Salter's recollections, I remain convinced, on the basis of the evidence, that the arrival of the Partnership, with its ideas about service-learning, had a significant impact at UTech—indeed that without this connection service-learning would not have found a foothold in the institution—though it is worth remarking that the philosophy of service-learning is least clear among its practitioners at UTech: there is a clearer sense of direction at the other two institutions among those engaged in service-learning. At Trinity, as Rafael Rodriguez and others make clear, the Partnership had a decisive influence on policy. At Roehampton, while service-learning remains at the educational periphery, its presence is directly attributable to the initial contact between David Peacock and Linda Chisholm. In short, the Partnership was a major catalyst in all three instances.

Finally, what can US institutions learn from these three case studies? Some lessons about leadership, perhaps (though US institutions may be more like Roehampton, with strong faculty prerogatives, than like Trinity or UTech, where dominant personalities, at a particular moment in history and in rapidly growing institutions, held sway), but also some lessons about the need for careful planning, for the creation of accommodating administrative structures, for the engagement and buy-in of administrators and faculty at many levels, and for the linkage of institutional mission and its implementation through service-learning. Some years ago, Campus Compact worked with a group of forty-four institutions across the United States to develop campus plans for the introduction of service-learning. They found that the institutionalization of service-learning was most likely to occur when six factors were present: "(a) congruence exists between institutional mission and strategic planning, (b) there is broad acceptance of the need for long-range planning and allocation of resources to support service-learning, (c) faculty are central to planning, (d) incentives are provided to faculty . . . (e) faculty work is widely publicized, and (f) campus plans for integrating service into academic study evolve over time and across personnel" (Bringle & Hatcher 2000, quoting Morton & Troppe 1996; see also Hollander, Saltmarsh & Zlotkowski 2002). Many of these factors exist at some of the institutions connected with the Partnership; at others, institutionalization is a long way off. For its part, the Partnership is faced with a daunting task: to bring about, on a worldwide scale, both a receptiveness to the new pedagogy and also the means for putting it into effect.

# Conclusions: The Institution Study

1. The Partnership has had a profound effect on the adoption of service-learning at many of the institutions where it operates programs. The presence of these programs has served as a device for the introduction of service-learning into the regular curriculum of these institutions.

2. The adoption of service-learning by a given institution works best when certain key ingredients are in place:

   · The institution has a long-standing interest in civic engagement.
   · Service-learning is supported by well-established central coordinating mechanisms (and budgetary commitment) and also diffused among faculty and students.
   · The idea of community service is supported by public policy at the national level, and institutions are expected to engage with the community.
   · Community service is part of the larger national culture.
   · The institution has strong leadership.
   · The philosophy of service-learning is presented coherently and well understood.

3. An institution desirous of adopting service-learning as a pedagogy must be able to cope with the notion that through this pedagogy student learning takes place not in the classroom alone but at the point of intersection of experience and theory—and that both experience and theory are part of the learning.

4. When faced with opposition to this belief, the supporters of service-learning are apt to compromise, downplaying the service component in service-learning when faced with investigative faculty committees, or displaying a reluctance to include service-providers as equal partners.

5. On the other hand, where support already exists, such support can lead to the inclusion in service-learning of simple acts of community service that should by rights not be included, or the desire to give community service greater dignity or prestige by mislabeling it service-learning.

6. In institutions under simultaneous pressure to deliver community service on the one hand, and generate academic credit on the other, service-learning may seem an inexpensive way of dealing with both pressures at the same time, but in reality it is expensive and time-consuming when done well.

7. Strong faculty development programs are essential to develop skills and also an understanding of how quality is established and maintained in service-learning.

8. The Partnership, if it can find the resources to put such a program into operation, could and should be a key player in the delivery of knowledge and expertise on service-learning for institutions across the world.

9.  Only by internalizing and incentivizing service-learning can it become accepted: administrators can remove barriers, but they cannot easily inspire.

10. However, strong leadership has been a fundamental ingredient of success in maintaining and expanding service-learning at the institutions studied. The most effective leaders are those who lead through structural change—by putting the right administrative structures in place.

11. The Partnership has had a decisive influence when its perhaps deeper and more comprehensive philosophy has given shape and direction to activities already in place, giving them a sense of purpose and coherence.

12. Colleges and universities less responsive to the presence of the Partnership tend to be larger institutions in industrialized countries with a less firm tradition of community involvement by institutions or individuals but with a stronger received sense of traditional academic procedures and modes of pedagogy.

13. Educational customs vary from culture to culture, and strictly American approaches to service-learning, or even to the process of reflection at its heart, may be culturally biased. There is a need to be adaptable to local mores and customs.

14. The Partnership has been most successful where its philosophy and pedagogy have addressed a specific problem or institutional opportunity, and where institutional leaders have been seeking new approaches to old problems. Where the arrival of the Partnership has coincided with new leadership, the results have in some cases proved remarkably impressive.

15. The study of these institutions suggests to US colleges and universities (a) the importance of leadership, (b) the need for careful planning, (c) the need for the creation of accommodating administrative structures, (d) the need for the engagement and buy-in of administrators and faculty at many levels, and (e) the need for linkage of institutional mission and its implementation through service-learning.

**PART 5** Evaluation

# 14  Evaluating Partnership Programs

## Humphrey Tonkin

### Program evaluation

While the research project undertaken by the Partnership was intended to open avenues to the investigation of the effects of international service-learning on students, agencies and institutions *in general*, at the other end of the spectrum we identified a need for better means of monitoring quality in Partnership programs *in particular*—in such a way that the evaluation of programs might also generate data to be used to assess the effectiveness of the Partnership's programs over time. So we made the development of better criteria for evaluating the success of individual in-country programs a high priority of our efforts. "The Partnership," we declared in our Research Plan, "hopes to establish a systematic program of assessment and self-improvement, designed to help programs and their directors serve the needs of the students and the community-service agencies more effectively, and to assure the sending institutions that the work the students are doing is fully credit-worthy and intellectually fully engaging. Such assessment might include regular peer evaluation of programs, with the active involvement of sending institutions."

"Such evaluation," we decided, "must be a collective undertaking, in which the directors and faculty in individual programs are fully engaged, both in the assessment of their own in-country programs and in an ongoing professional dialogue with their peers in other programs, aimed at strengthening consensus in the Partnership and fully exploiting new developments in the field. . . ." Our goal was to make our programs as responsive as possible to our various constituencies and to ensure the highest possible standards of academic work, service, and the relation between the two. We also felt that the development of common criteria would create a greater sense of common goals and would cause weaker programs or less experienced directors to learn from their stronger counterparts.

We began with a review of other organizations' efforts at assessing study-abroad programs,[1] gathering whatever materials were accessible to us, and consulting with study-abroad administrators and accrediting agencies. We also assembled existing Partnership documents on program evaluation. We then prepared a draft document, which we shared, in separate sessions, with program directors (who would ultimately have to work with it) and, after revisions to take the directors' views into account, with board members. At these sessions, we discussed particular provisions of this draft protocol in some detail, making changes and adjustments as the process went along, and checking back at every stage to make sure the directors were comfortable with changes. We then submitted the text to the board for their final blessing. Our goal, in accordance with the Research Plan, was to develop a document that could be used by individual programs as the basis for a self-study, and then by a visiting team of two or three Partnership representatives who might spend two or three days at the program site and subsequently submit a report to the Partnership. We stressed above all that the purpose of the process was to offer opportunities for the strengthening and improvement of programs, and we explained that, once established, the process would move forward on a rotating basis, with each program visited every few years (in addition, of course to the visits by Partnership staff that occur with considerable frequency, and the annual meetings of all program directors with the headquarters staff and often the board of trustees).

Once the draft was thoroughly reviewed and adapted in this way, we invited three program directors (those in Montpellier, Guadalajara, and

---

[1] The MAP (Model Assessment Practice), developed by the Institute for the International Education of Students (IES), is perhaps the most extensive such instrument. The IES is now conducting further research using the MAP as a basis. Well-established programs, such as those at Butler University or those operated by the Council on International Educational Exchange (CIEE), have regular program review built into their procedures, using a combination of site visits and written criteria for evaluation. The Middle States Association of Colleges and Schools publishes a Manual for Study Abroad Evaluations, and as early as 1961 its Commission on Higher Education developed guidelines on study-abroad programs. However, no standard instrument, available to, and designed by, all organizations exists for study-abroad programs, though there is considerable interest among some program administrators in producing one.

Guayaquil) to conduct a self-assessment of their programs using the new document. They carried out this assignment with varying degrees of thoroughness, in some instances involving students on site; and a few suggestions for improvement came back.

The "Evaluation Criteria for Partnership Programs" that we reproduce below, the final product of this process, are based on a simple Framing Principle: "Regular monitoring and evaluation of all phases of the Partnership's activities are essential to ensure quality education, effective service to the community, and adequate support services for students away from home." The Evaluation Criteria attempt to address two questions: (1) "What can students, parents and sending institutions expect of Partnership programs?" and (2) "What do we as Partnership professionals regard as good practices, and what do we aspire to achieve through our programs?" The criteria address such issues as the quality of predeparture programs, the arrival process, quality of instruction, service placements, learning, staffing, and on-site resources. The first two site visits using the new criteria will take place, somewhat later than originally planned, in October–November 2004 in Guadalajara, Mexico, and Guayaquil, Ecuador. The document follows.

## EVALUATION CRITERIA FOR PARTNERSHIP PROGRAMS

### Framing Principle

Regular monitoring and evaluation of all phases of the Partnership's activities are essential to ensure quality education, effective service to the community, and adequate support services for students away from home.

### Framing Questions

1. What can students, parents and sending institutions expect of Partnership programs?

2. What do we as Partnership professionals regard as good practices, and what do we aspire to achieve through our programs?

## Predeparture

1. Students receive information on the program, in timely fashion, that includes practical details about academic program requirements and expectations (including language requirements, where appropriate), community service placements, living and travel arrangements, and expenses.

2. Students are introduced to the issues and strategies involved in dealing with a new culture, including the particular issues associated with the host program, and the pedagogical practices of the host culture.

3. Students have adequate health insurance and other forms of insurance as appropriate.

4. Students have a clear understanding of the Partnership's expectations of them, and of what they can expect of the Partnership, before they depart. These expectations are reinforced by on-site directors after their arrival and in the course of their stay.

5. Parents and sending institutions are also provided with appropriate predeparture information, and sending institutions are encouraged to communicate to the program any special academic requirements that they may have of their students.

6. When academic requirements of the sending institutions (e.g. concerning special projects or papers) are communicated to the host program in a timely fashion, any necessary arrangements are put in place in advance (or the students are informed that they cannot be met).

## Arrival

1. An orientation program upon arrival provides students with information on the host country, on the host institution, and on local conditions. It includes attention to local expectations about

interpersonal relations, especially gender and racial relations, and it includes information on work ethic and expectations, and on issues of health and safety. The program is planned and conducted by responsible members of the local Partnership staff.

2. Students are assisted in making their initial contacts with the host country, host institution, and host family.

3. Students are given a clear sense of the program's expectations about their academic work and their community service and the relationship between the two.

4. Student programs are designed to provide a balance between academics and service and adequate ways of integrating the two.

5. Included in the orientation is a one-on-one meeting with the director or other responsible staff member in which the particular needs and expectations of the student are discussed, his/her academic needs (particularly in relation to his/her sending institution) are reviewed, his/her visa status is verified, and the student is provided with an opportunity to raise any questions or issues. A written record of this meeting is preserved.

## Instruction

1. Students are provided with syllabi and other appropriate material at the beginning of the semester, and expectations about grading, exams, due dates, etc. are conveyed to the students.

2. While teaching is conducted in the manner consistent with the practices of the host culture, class sessions are adequate to the credit assigned to them, and scheduled regularly, in suitable accommodation.

3. Faculty members are fully qualified to conduct the courses to which they are assigned, and qualified to meet both home-country criteria and the expectations of the sending institutions. They are also

effective teachers, able to respond to and deal with the expectations of students from other countries with different educational systems.

4. Faculty members are familiar with the goals and purposes of the Partnership, including the principles of service-learning.

5. Faculty members are available to students for informal consultation outside class sessions.

6. Faculty are evaluated by student surveys for each course operated by the Partnership, and the results of this evaluation are taken into consideration by program directors.

7. Faculty are available to work with students on projects assigned to them by their sending institutions.

8. There is adequate opportunity in the academic setting to process experiences undergone in the community-service setting.

9. Appropriate levels of academic rigor are maintained; written work is assigned and is adequately assessed, with appropriate feedback; students are held to standards that maintain the reputation and effectiveness of the Partnership and satisfy the requirements of both host institutions and sending institutions.

## Service Placements

1. Placements make effective use of location, local talent, and local resources.

2. Placements provide students with opportunities to learn about the agency in question.

3. Agencies offer students work activities that are meaningful and productive in themselves and sufficiently structured to use student talent and energies effectively.

4. Mechanisms are in place for the reassignment of students if the program staff deem it appropriate.

5. Agencies and supervisors are familiar with the Partnership and with the principles of service-learning.

6. There is a formal procedure in place for student evaluation of their placements at the end of the semester, and this feedback is taken into consideration by the program director.

7. Agencies are within reasonable distance, and public transportation is available (or transportation is provided by the program).

8. Programs and agencies are in regular contact and provide information to one another on student progress. Agencies are encouraged to provide evaluative feedback on students.

## Learning

1. Students learn to do (practical experience), to learn (lifelong improvement), to be (increasing self-awareness), and to live harmoniously (as members of a community).

2. Students learn to adapt to the host culture and its institutions and customs while developing a capacity for critical thinking.

3. Students learn the benefits, to themselves and to others, of effective community service.

4. Students develop their interpersonal skills and, where appropriate, their language skills.

5. Students acquire a greater appreciation of and respect for persons with differing cultural values.

6. Students develop increased self-reliance and an increased ability both to listen to others and to take initiatives.

7. Students acquire general adaptive skills that prepare them to live in a variety of foreign cultures.

8. By encountering new experiences in a new environment, students increase their ability to examine, evaluate and critique their own value system and the culture that supports it.

9. Students keep journals, and are encouraged to use them both to record events and experiences and to examine their own growth and adaptation. They are provided with guidelines and examples in carrying this process out.

10. Appropriate assessment tools are in place to assess student knowledge and awareness on arrival and on departure.

## Staff

1. Administrative staff are adequately qualified to perform their function and available and responsive to students.

2. Administrative staff are familiar with the principles of service-learning, supportive of the Partnership's goals and objectives, and familiar with the needs and expectations of students from other countries with different educational systems.

3. The program director's performance is evaluated annually by the president of the Partnership, and adequate opportunity for feedback is provided.

4. A similar system of annual performance evaluations is in place for the program staff, conducted by the program director.

5. The program director enjoys credibility with the academic host and with the agencies, has appropriate administrative qualifications, and is familiar with Partnership procedures, protocols, financial arrangements, and contractual terms.

6. The program director is proactive in putting in place procedures for dealing with emergencies and other eventualities, particularly emergencies related to health and safety.

7. The program director has adequate command of the English language.

8. The program director is supportive of the Partnership and its programs.

9. The program director is responsive to legitimate student concerns and the concerns of their parents.

10. The on-site administrative staff is adequate to the needs and requirements of the program.

11. There is ongoing communication between administrative staff and the faculty teaching in the program.

## On-site Resources and Procedures

1. Students have access to adequate medical facilities at all times.

2. Students have access to adequate library facilities, preferably including the library facilities of the host university.

3. Students have access to computers, including Internet access.

4. Students have a safe and accessible place to live.

5. Host families are carefully chosen, in accordance with appropriate local criteria. Student feedback on host families is sought and taken into consideration in planning for future years.

6. A clear understanding of the relationship between each host family and the Partnership is in place, and no host family assumes that it will receive Partnership students in perpetuity.

7. Students have adequate opportunities to get to know one another and to integrate themselves into the local community.

## Assessment

1. Students complete a questionnaire before return to the US. This questionnaire covers all important aspects of their stay and may include questions specific to individual programs.

2. Procedures are in place for additional and varied long-term evaluation and student feedback on the impact of Partnership programs.

3. Procedures are in place so that the results of this assessment are adequately reviewed and are used in planning both by the Partnership staff in New York and by host-country staff.

This document, while it addresses the question of quality, omits two other very important questions. First, what can be done to address weaknesses? The Partnership must be willing to invest resources to deal with material shortcomings of various kinds, or to renegotiate with host institutions, or both. It must also put in place programs for addressing shortcomings in instruction, by providing faculty development or in other ways. It is not enough to have a system of evaluation: the organization must be prepared for the eventuality that aspects of its programs are found in need of correction. If this awareness can be inculcated into the central administration of the Partnership, administrators are more likely to become proactive, not waiting for faults to be revealed, but addressing them before the occasion arises.[2]

The second unaddressed question is at the level of the individual student. While these criteria assess the program overall, they do not assess or measure the progress of the individual student, nor of students in the aggregate. As we observe in our next chapter, on future research, this question should receive high priority in a new research plan.

---

[2] Josef Lazarus, of the Joint Education Trust (South Africa), reported at the October 2004 International Conference on Service-Learning Research in Greenville, South Carolina, on criteria that the Trust is developing for the assessment of service-learning outcomes. These criteria may offer guidance in broadening and refining the Partnership document.

PART **6** Next Steps

# 15 International Service-Learning: A Research Agenda

Robert G. Bringle and Humphrey Tonkin

As a form of experiential education, service-learning shares similarities with internships, field education, practica, and voluntary service. However, there are two features of service-learning that differentiate it from these other activities: first, civic education (or whatever term we use to describe the type of education acquired by the student through service-learning) is a deliberate educational goal through which students develop an understanding of their current and future roles in their communities; and the process whereby such civic education is conveyed to the student also incorporates a second, co-equal beneficiary of the process, namely the agency or other setting in which the service is performed, and its members or clients.

Study abroad is also a form of experiential education—and one that is increasingly receiving the attention of researchers, who are examining both study-abroad programs (in an effort to establish their educational effectiveness and their academic quality) and the students who participate in them (see Michael Vande Berg, forthcoming; on research on study abroad in general, see our note on the subject in chapter 1). Although study abroad is a powerful pedagogy (Carlson, Burn & others 1990), it sometimes has its shortcomings. Research on study abroad shows that student interactions with resident populations are often limited and students are often disappointed that they did not get to know members of the host culture (Ward, Bochner, & Furham 2001). There is concern in some circles that so-called island programs, in which groups of American students study together in a foreign location, are exploitative of local culture and give very little back to their communities. Of equal concern is the fact that the duration of study-abroad experiences appears to be getting shorter on average, with students often going abroad for no more than a few weeks. Do such short sojourns abroad have effects comparable to more extended stays?

International service-learning presents additional ways of interacting with a host culture and developing civic skills in ways that are not possible or are quite limited in domestic service-learning. We have noted elsewhere (Tonkin & Bringle 2004) that international service-learning is unique because (a) it adds a significant educational component to traditional study abroad; (b) unlike domestic service-learning, it is done in another country; (c) it may use a foreign language; and (d) it immerses students in cross-cultural community-based experiences that place them in situations that may not occur in their customary roles as students or tourists. These generalizations, of course, apply to greater or lesser degrees depending on the design of the program in question:

- the precise relationship between agency and classroom and the role of reflection in this relationship,

- the nature of the agency work (there is a world of difference between project-based service-learning, in which the purpose might be to build a school or vaccinate a local population, and process-based service-learning, in which the student works directly with an agency's clients),

- the degree of embeddedness (in some service-learning programs students may work with their peers, whereas in others they may work exclusively or almost exclusively with in-country co-workers),

- the intensity of the service (e.g., the number of hours per week),

- the duration of the service (short-term versus semester-long or year-long experiences),

- the nature of the population served,

- the setting (urban environment, rural environment, industrialized country, developing country, etc.).

As noted on various occasions in the present volume, there is very limited research on international service-learning. The present volume offers preliminary findings in three areas: students (alumni), institutions, and agencies. It also presents a protocol for the evaluation of service-learning programs and provides demographic data on the Partnership. Each element of this research opens further avenues and raises further questions. Would a second group of Partnership alumni express similar sentiments to those expressed by the first? Might the design of the study (perhaps with an initial quantitative instrument in advance of the interviews and focus-groups) produce differing results? Could the findings of this qualitative study be tested by a broader quantitative approach? The study was designed and carried out largely without a context of quantitative data. What might be done to design a process for the formative evaluation of students' experiences in Partnership programs, and how could data be collected for this purpose? One of the outcomes of such formative evaluation might be a better understanding of what students actually *acquire* in the process of service-learning, as opposed to what they carry into the process, i.e. what relates to preparation and what to experience. A good framework for addressing this question is knowing who the students are before they leave, what they do and feel while there, and how they have changed when they return (cf. the I.E.O. model in education: Inputs, Environment, Outcomes). And, as we suggest in chapter 2, it would be helpful to triangulate our findings by drawing other parties into the study: parents, professors, advisors. We might also gain some insight into the reentry process, which the study in this volume highlights as the most difficult part, and perhaps the most fruitful part, in the entire experience.

Finally, what do we know about how students tell their stories? Are there master narratives, or generic tropes, particular to foreign travel, cross-cultural experience, and, above all, moving into adulthood through such experiences? Are we victims of our own occupational *Bildungsgeschichte* (Tonkin & Quiroga forthcoming—and see the conclusion of our chapter 8), or can these narratives be turned to good account in the preparation of students, as Chisholm (2000) has done so well? As is noted elsewhere in this volume, the Partnership itself has a considerable body of written material—student testimonials, exit questionnaires, journals, term papers, agency profiles, etc., that form excellent data for addressing these and related questions.

Related to this set of issues is another, equally thorny question. International service-learning mediates between a largely western, often American, view of education and its purposes (a view tied to accreditation, notions of academic quality, and the award of credit), and an often non-western cultural view, in which epistemological assumptions may be quite different, and ideas about the nature of service, or the purpose of the alleviation of poverty, or even of poverty and education themselves, may differ from ours (see Chisholm 2004b, Porter & Monard 2001, Monard 2002, Reagan 2005). The literature of international development and capacity-building addresses this complex issue quite frequently (most recently, for example, in the UNDP's 2004 Human Development Report: Fukuda-Parr 2004). Bringle has written extensively on reflection, the key ingredient in successful service-learning, particularly in a cross-cultural setting (see, for example, Bringle & Hatcher 1999; Hatcher, Bringle & Muthiah, forthcoming). What do these major cross-cultural considerations have to say for the purpose and design of the reflection component in international service-learning?

Relatively underexamined in the student study in this volume (because, interestingly, it seldom came up, and, when it did, it was accompanied simply by expressions of satisfaction), is the major question of academic content, an issue to which we allude in chapter 2. What do international service-learning students learn that is immediately applicable in the classroom upon their return? What is the content of their learning? And do they develop problem-solving skills that they can apply in their subsequent studies? In chapter 2 we asked, "To what extent do students acquire academic knowledge (however that is defined) in service-learning situations? Do they do so at a speed or with a thoroughness comparable to the speed and thoroughness of conventional study abroad (again, however that is defined) and comparable to the process of knowledge acquisition if they were to remain on their home campuses engaged in conventional study?" Further research on international service-learning will need to address components of learning and their cognitive outcomes (see Eyler 2000)—along with their affect and behavioral outcomes.

Our study of agencies addresses a topic seldom confronted in service-learning research, as we have seen (Sigmon 1998, Cruz & Giles 2000, Clarke 2003). The study, meticulously carried out by Deeley, was limited by the small size of its sample, the logistics of working in two locations in a restricted amount of time, and the difficulty of defining outcomes. What constitutes agency success, and how do service-learning students contribute to it? Furthermore, can and should we make a distinction between agencies on the one hand and clients on the other? It is not obvious that a positive contribution to the one necessarily translates into a positive contribution to the other. Related to this issue is the larger question of the ethics of service-learning, a topic that came up with increasing frequency as our study progressed (see Langseth 2000, Aquino 2001, Rich 2002, Schaffer, Paris & Williams 2003, and our comments in chapter 2).

The study of academic institutions points in a number of potentially fruitful directions: the nature of leadership in complex organizations, the diffusion of innovation, the potential of service-learning as a means of reconciling conflicting demands on institutions (academic quality and credentialing on the one hand, and responsibility to the community or to nation-building on the other), the nature of academic change, the institutionalization of alternative pedagogies. Particularly intriguing is the question of how an external agent (in this case, the Partnership) can bring about internal change in an institution—in its organizational structure, its practices, its sense of mission, its pedagogy. And of course a perennial issue is how to address faculty concerns about service-learning, the acceptability of its methods, and its outcomes (Driscoll 2000, and see our chapter 13), to say nothing of the relationship of all of this to study abroad.

Research agendas exist for domestic service-learning. Wingspread conferences were conducted in 1991 and 1993 to develop such agendas. In addition, Giles and Eyler (1998), the Research Advisory Council convened by Campus Compact during 1997–1998, and the Campus Compact's *Presidents' Declaration on the Civic Responsibility of Higher Education* (Boyte & Hollander 1999) each provide agendas to stimulate research about important questions related to service-learning. In the year 2000, a special issue of the *Michigan Journal of Community Service Learning* addressed the question of "Strategic Directions for Service-Learning Research" (see, for example, Ramaley's helpful list of priorities under the heading "What is the Evidence for the Value of Service-Learning"—Ramaley 2000). Although the Wingspread Conference of 1998, convened by the Partnership, called for "the encouragement of service-learning research projects" (Berry & Chisholm 1999:112), no corresponding research agenda exists to guide research on international service-learning.

Research tools have either been developed for service-learning or are easily adapted to service-learning research (Bringle, Phillips, & Hudson

2004). However, there are few good examples of procedures, scales, or data gathering techniques developed specifically for international service-learning. The Model Assessment Practice (MAP) of the Institute for the International Education of Students (IES) is perhaps the most extensive model designed for study abroad and was one of the principal inspirations for the assessment protocol described in chapter 14, but more work is needed in this area, including careful tracking of the program evaluation process now being launched by the Partnership as a result of the development of the protocol.

We should perhaps add that there may well be existing research in neighboring fields with applicability to international service-learning. No small part of a research agenda is the establishment of what we already know. Furthermore, our own research in international service-learning may have applicability outside the immediate field: comparative research could be especially valuable.

The research agendas that currently exist for service-learning revolve around several foci (e.g., students, courses, institutions, community, faculty—and also efforts to bridge these categories, e.g. Harkavy, Puckett and Romer 2000, Moore 2000). These frameworks are largely descriptive, but provide important guidance for framing subsequent, more detailed research questions that are embedded in appropriate theories. Tonkin and Bringle (2004) conducted a workshop on research on international service-learning at the 2004 Conference of the International Partnership for Service-Learning (Chiang Mai) that resulted in a set of topics that constitute a preliminary research agenda. With some additions derived from the present volume, the list is as follows:

## 1. Student Recruitment, Applications, and Acceptances

A. Student motives for international service-learning, including religion and other personal convictions, and prior experience with service and service-learning
B. Students' financial resources as a selection factor
C. Criteria and procedures for student selection to ensure that students have a successful international experience
D. Student readiness and preparedness
E. Characteristics of likely successful candidates for international service-learning

## 2. Student Characteristics and Outcomes

A. The role of language proficiency (and its acquisition) in service settings

B. Comparisons of language proficiency gains among study abroad, international service-learning, and other ways of learning a foreign language

C. Changes in students' political, social, cultural, and personal views on international issues (e.g., foreign aid, peace initiatives, monetary policies)

D. Changes in students' knowledge, values, and behavior that encompass a global perspective on civic issues (and compared to domestic service-learning)

E. Changes in students' behavior as a result of international service-learning (voting, public service, volunteer service, etc.)

F. Growth in students' academic preparedness and knowledge

G. International service-learning compared to other forms of international experience

H. Life-long learning outcomes

I. Reentry and reverse culture shock issues

J. Effect of international service-learning on career choice

## 3. Community Service

A. Characteristics of successful agency placements

B. The impact of community service on communities

C. The impact of community service on agencies and their clients

D. Diverse views of service that might be shaped by local social, cultural, religious, and political characteristics and beliefs

E. The importance of indigenous resources (e.g., NGO infrastructure, support personnel) to service and service experiences

F. Role of students and others in responding to and shaping community issues

G. Ethical issues in international service-learning

H. Views of agency leaders and their clients on service-learning

### 4. The Design of International Service-Learning

A. Structuring effective preparation for cross-cultural service-learning
B. Structuring reflection for international service-learning
C. Designing effective faculty development for US faculty who accompany students and for local faculty who teach US students
D. Curriculum development for international service-learning

### 5. The Practice of International Service-Learning

A. Differences between short-term and long-term international service-learning and between project-based and process-based activities
B. The impact of international service-learning on faculty members who practice it
C. Faculty and student attitudes toward service agencies and their clients
D. Faculty attitudes to service-learning and its institutionalization
E. Reciprocity and mutuality between programs and host countries

### 6. Theoretical Issues and Research Design

A. How can service, learning, and service-learning be defined and re-defined from multiple (non-US) perspectives?
B. Developing appropriate language for "service," "community service," "civic engagement"
C. Leadership education and its relationship to international service-learning
D. The interaction of theories of development, theories of culture, and practical experience in service-learning settings
E. Narratives of service-learning and approaches to journal-keeping
F. Special issues associated with conducting research (distant sites, collaboration, language, community impact, comparison groups)

This preliminary agenda provides guidance for conducting future research on international service-learning. In addition, there are several aspects of research that are unique in role and scale, including preparation of students for immersion experiences, cultural sensitivity and issues of diversity, and global (vs. domestic) civic responsibility (we alluded at the opening of the chapter to civic education; what is the nature of the civic education conveyed by non-local, cross-cultural, transnational experience?). When research on international service-learning addresses these issues, there will be important lessons learned that can also improve domestic service-learning, study abroad, and knowledge acquisition generally.

Approaches to the topics that we have singled out as worthy of further research might take numbers of different directions—qualitative and quantitative, narrowly focused or comparative. Such comparison might merely involve pre- and post-testing, looking at the changes that take place as a result of the experience of international service-learning. It might compare international service-learning with traditional study abroad (e.g., attitudes, language proficiency, civic understanding), or with domestic service-learning (diversity issues, learning, civic understanding), or with traditional, classroom-based study (international knowledge, problem-solving, language proficiency).

Just as useful comparisons could be made among different learning structures, the pedagogy and experience of international service-learning could be used to evaluate theories of experiential learning, teaching and learning, student persistence, intergroup contact, collaborative learning, the formation of learning communities, and any of a number of other teaching and learning theories. Research on international service-learning has the potential to extend our understanding of general areas of interest to higher education, such as the design and delivery of instruction, student motivation, and credentialing.

There are also some important research priorities for the Partnership itself. We have already remarked on the fact that we now have a protocol for the evaluation of *programs*, but program evaluation must be accompanied by measures, specific to the Partnership, for assessing student outcomes. Also needed are better instruments for formative assessment of students. The Partnership must also continue to address the question of the impact of its programs on agencies and their clients and refine the mechanisms for identifying agencies and drawing them into active participation as partners in the service-learning enterprise. Ideally, such activities might be carried on in cooperation with host institutions, by researchers from those institutions, and the results of such studies might be published by the Partnership. The Partnership could also take on responsibility for developing instruments and research models to assist partner colleges and universities in conducting their own assessments. In short, the climate of active research created by the Ford study should be maintained as a permanent part of the Partnership's mission both to improve its own programs and to assist others in launching and sustaining service-learning.

# 16 The Future of the Partnership: Leadership, Quality, Service

What conclusions can we draw from the study outlined in this volume, and how will they have an effect on the future work of the Partnership? Our study has confirmed many of the assumptions outlined in our first chapter: the profound effect of our programs on students, their impact on agencies, and their influence on institutions. The Partnership is poised for a new chapter in its history.

In 2003, the International Partnership for Service-Learning became the International Partnership for Service-Learning and Leadership. The change in title, approved by an enthusiastic board, came about only after a good deal of soul-searching. Americans, belonging to a nation which, some would say, has more answers looking for questions than it has questions looking for answers, and which, under the guise of leadership of the free world has contributed in about equal parts to its progress and its confusion, may be the worst people to lay claim to the truth about how to lead.

But it is precisely because of the American preoccupation with leadership that the Partnership should be concerned with it, by offering an alternative to the go-it-alone, culturally disengaged style of the moment. Many of the courses in leadership that pepper American business schools, and many of the admiring books about leadership written before the recent *chute de l'homme d'affaires* in Enron, Worldcom and a dozen other businesses, pay remarkably little attention to the ethics of leadership, nor do they attend adequately to its collaborative qualities.[1] Leadership for what, we

---

[1] This is particularly so of the hagiography of business leaders and of the popular conception of strong leadership. Certainly the serious leadership studies of the 1980s and 1990s (popularized in the work of Kanter 1983, for example, and in such concepts as TQM, Total Quality

may ask? And leadership of whom? Partnership board member Adel Safty, in his recent book on leadership and democracy (Safty 2004), explains that leadership is essential to the building of democratic and participatory institutions:

> Democratic governance manages better than other alternatives to guarantee individual liberties and humanitarian equality . . . there is a positive correlation between democratic governance and human development . . . democratic governance within nations helps produce a democratic culture *between* nations that promotes peace and development . . . [Therefore] to advance and promote the principles underlying these propositions, there is a need for leadership in the public and private sectors, in governmental and nongovernmental organizations, in national and international institutions, in the academy, and in citizen movements.

But while "leadership is a crucial factor of change and empowerment necessary to bring about the emergence and consolidation of democracy . . . leadership must, or at least ought to be, positively related to the higher achievements of the human spirit for the benefit of humanity. Leadership ought to be normatively apprehended as a set of values that promote human development. . . . Value leadership . . . necessarily promotes democracy."

Safty's vision of "value leadership" is not a vision of the lonely figure moving among the sleeping soldiers on the night before Agincourt, nor of the free agent working his will among his followers by sheer charisma. In the world of the twenty-first century—a world in which, in the memorable words of Harlan Cleveland, "nobody is in charge"—leadership implies the building of consensus, compromise, tolerance. As Safty remarks, "The strong consensus on the need for leadership at all levels in the society, the paucity of any coherent approach to leadership in public affairs, and the increased need for multilateral cooperation, especially among the countries of the South, have converged to present unique opportunities for leadership." It is this form of leadership that the Partnership seeks to embrace.

Such a recognition caused Linda Chisholm to raise many questions about leadership as the team set about its work in the Partnership's student

---

Management) stressed participatory management—but such strategies work best in static or expanding economies and give little guidance in the handling of conflict. They are especially unhelpful in dealing with the ethics of competition.

study (see chapter 4, and Chisholm 2004a). Her vision of leadership included observation of leaders and how they "recognized a problem, conceived of ways of addressing it, were able to communicate a vision to others, built community support, and developed organizational structures to sustain their efforts." Margaret Pusch suggested, in chapter 5, that many of the students who participated in the April 2003 exercise "exhibited the ability to take charge of their own experience, find ways to fit into the agencies they served, and develop patterns of service that demonstrated leadership qualities," and Diego Quiroga, in chapter 6, pointed out that the process of coming to understand how agencies operated developed "leadership and initiative" in the students and "forced them to be more organized." Some tried to introduce changes and reforms in their agencies, and discovered that the process required "not just good ideas but also negotiating skills in a different culture." In short, leadership is an ingredient in the Partnership experience whether or not we recognize its presence.

Leadership manifests itself in the Partnership context above all in the capability of working across cultures. Implied in such leadership is an ability to mediate between cultures, finding values or ideas in one culture that are transferable to another, and working with others to apply them effectively— but doing so in a spirit of reciprocity and tolerance.[2] Chisholm and Berry (2002), in their book on study abroad, write of acquiring the skills to "work out a negotiated settlement so that everyone benefits." In chapter 8, we suggest that "The Partnership experience develops in the students not only an adaptability and resourcefulness, but also ways of looking at old problems with fresh eyes, and recontextualizing familiar issues in the light of broader experience." The goal in adding leadership education to the

---

[2] As we noted in chapter 13, the problem of leadership across cultures is particularly acute. Are all cultural values coequal, are there many different approaches to human development, or should we learn about difference primarily in order to overcome it? Samuel P. Huntington, in a memorable and deeply problematic question, leans toward this last possibility: "To what extent do cultural factors shape economic and political development? If they do, how can cultural obstacles to economic and political development be removed or changed so as to facilitate progress?" (Harrison & Huntington 2000). But perhaps the successful management of difference is the key to effective leadership— in a context in which some consensus on human values is achievable. Such an approach is closely allied with prevailing ideas of human development (see, for example, the 2004 UNDP Human Development Report: Fukuda-Parr 2004). See also Schweder 2004, who responds in part to Huntington's question, though his contrarian view is roundly and somewhat crudely criticized by other participants in Harrison and Huntington's symposium.

Partnership's mission is to make explicit certain implicit characteristics of the Partnership experience. As we conclude in chapter 8, and as the April meetings made abundantly clear, "Partnership students display qualities of leadership."

Recently we asked fourteen members of the Partnership board and administration to write a brief and spontaneous answer to the question, "What do we mean by leadership in the context of service-learning?" While a couple of responses failed to address the question directly, discussing instead the Partnership's role as a leader in service-learning, the others were about evenly divided between what might be described as conventional ideas of leadership and efforts to find in the Partnership experience something uniquely suited to the practice of leadership.

One respondent, a member of the staff, referred to the notion of "servant-leadership," "the concept that a leader who has experienced service-learning will know how to *empower* others to engage in efforts to improve the world and fully discover and use their own talents in doing so." Leadership, in other words, implies the discovery of talents in others and empowering them to apply them. The point goes back to an observation that Quiroga makes in chapter 6, about the distinction between service-learning and other types of "charitable" activities. His interviewees, he explained, told him that "their service helped them understand the difference between help on the one hand and social development on the other. . . . The combination of service and learning allowed them to contextualize good service as related to development and empowerment." Help, charity, the dispensing of largesse, is essentially static: self-help is dynamic and stimulates positive change. This distinction animates the service work at Trinity College, which quite systematically pulls back from "dole-outs," from programs that simply sustain communities by outside support unrelated to social change. Recently Trinity decided to discontinue one of its programs, the DEEP program for the disabled, not because it was failing, but because it was creating dependency. While on special occasions, like Christmas, the medical technology students at Trinity may give away food or clothing, their reason for doing so is to create goodwill in the community so that they can achieve their other goals of self-help and sustainability.

An Asian board member expressed similar sentiments about empowerment when he suggested that leadership is a "process of facilitating, not indoctrination" that involves "understanding the context and approach," and a European board member added that the Partnership should seek "to encourage and promote a style of leadership which is collaborative and which empowers individuals and communities to envision and realize new futures." To this an American board member added the encouragement of "the development of values or value systems needed to expand active learning through service," leading to an expansion of the knowledge base, presumably both in the future actions of the student and in the work that the student performs through service.

What this implies, an American board member remarked, is "understanding the cultural dimensions of leadership: that direct confrontation, individual recognition, etc. may be seen as elements of leadership in one context, whereas triangulation, face-giving, etc. show a mature awareness of *context* that defines leadership in other cultures." This view goes beyond those already recorded because it suggests that styles of leadership, while they should all demonstrate a sensitivity to cultural difference and a spirit of empowerment, vary from culture to culture: leadership is not just an awareness of cultural difference and a sensitivity to it, but also a willingness to work differently in different contexts, where the cultural norms are different. "In Russia," this board member added, "people say, 'The stalk of grain which stands above the rest is empty.' This is literally true: it's put all its energy into growth and contains no grain. Metaphorically, it means the person who sticks out from the crowd is shallow and empty-headed. So leadership should not always mean recognition/uniqueness/individual action."

This flexibility of approach, remarked another board member, is facilitated by international service of the kind offered by the Partnership. Certain qualities of effective leadership are developed particularly well in an international, cross-cultural setting: "(1) understanding contexts, (2) identifying problems/opportunities, (3) conveying a view of reality to others, (4) developing group decisions, reaching consensus and shared goals, (5) envisioning change, (6) developing action plans, (7) recognizing resources, (8) mobilizing resources." Another board member added to this list by stressing "self-confidence as a result of [a] wider cultural world view" that comes with living in another country, coupled with the "task orientation" and "goal orientation" that comes with service. An additional quality of such service, according to another board member, is "teaching by doing," and thus serving as an example to others.

In the practical terms of the Partnership experience, another board member suggested, "Leadership occurs on several levels—directing agencies and taking personal responsibility for one's contributions. In both, leadership is about accountability, commitment, service to clients, and the ability to comprehend the context for the service and the flexibility and capability to direct its delivery in an appropriate manner." She added "three important phrases:" "cognitive flexibility, compassion, behavioral capability." A staff member suggested that the Partnership experience helps build leaders because they are able to recognize "problems in community, nation or world," "have a vision or goal for a better society," and "know how to work with a community to develop and realize the mission." These qualities create "a cascade effect, so more and more people share the vision and will work towards the goal."

Other views of leadership were more conventional, and less connected to the specificities of the Partnership experience. One board member defined leadership as "the creative investment of one's time, energy and spirit in the life of the community." He referred to "accountability, creativity, risk-taking, caring, commitment, energy, patience, compassion." Another stressed honesty and vision, and "ownership of the process," and a third echoed these other two, referring also to the need to set an example.

What is striking about most of these definitions is that they stress cooperation, self-effacement, negotiating skills—and empowerment. While a few members of the group present a vision of the leader as somehow fundamentally different and apart from the community (the Henry V model), most stress the way in which the leader is a part of the community, and often not a particularly visible part. Furthermore, nobody suggests that leadership is *simply* self-sacrifice, or indeed self-sacrifice at all. Words like "help" or "charity" are entirely absent from the definitions.

At about the same time as we polled the Partnership board on definitions of leadership, a working group composed of members of the board, adapting a definition of leadership used by the Global Leadership Forum, the extension of the UN Leadership Conference of the 1990s, singled out the following qualities as defining the Partnership's idea of leadership:

- ethical and humane governance
- social responsibility
- multilateral and multicultural cooperation for capacity building and human development.

"Leadership is the shared vision for a better society," the working group declared. It is also a process "that is genuinely democratic, relational, and interactive, that serves the people and promotes responsible citizenship and engagement in a globally interdependent world."

While such concepts might underpin the Partnership's approach to leadership, the major question confronting the organization is operationalizing grand concepts in the context of an approach to service that has always stressed reciprocity and self-effacement. All too often, discussions of leadership seek to impose external values on the internal workings of the human psyche: the Partnership has a history of avoiding such impositions in favor of a process of self-discovery, in which values are teased out of practice. Can these grand concepts be made to emerge from the process of service itself? One reality favoring such an emergence is the Partnership's interest in the utility and effectiveness of the service it delivers: the Partnership's pedagogy does indeed see agencies as extensions of classrooms, but it also sees classrooms as extensions of agencies and seeks to blend the two in a reciprocity whose outcomes should be both student learning and social utility.

It is clear that the Partnership is embarked on a course of action that will emphasize leadership and its development, with a view to embedding it both in the instruction that students receive and in the action/reflection process that accompanies such instruction. What else might arise from the Partnership's present situation and from the research that it has been engaged in? The following imperatives come to mind.

First we should note the bifurcated nature of the Partnership's activities, between the offering of academic programs on the one hand and advocacy of service-learning on the other. The first activity, as well as performing a valuable function in itself, supplies the resources for the second and hence should receive priority attention.

This attention must inevitably begin with effective administration. After the major blow, in 2002, of the death of President Howard Berry, the administrative staff has been greatly strengthened, primarily through the appointment of an academic dean, Nevin Brown, and the augmentation of the support staff. A completely redesigned website is now up and running, and the response time in dealing with applications has been shortened.

The academic programs come in three forms: undergraduate programs, primarily for American students and involving single locations; the master's program in international service (possibly soon to be joined by a second master's program in leadership and service), essentially international in scope, involving three sites; and special programs, such as the summer program in the Philippines for Southeast Asian students. Each requires attention to recruitment, particularly the undergraduate programs. The Partnership has improved its liaison with sending institutions and is in the process of developing new publications. Enrollment in the master's program is growing both in numbers and in quality, and coordination among the three campuses and the New York office is more harmonious and more responsive. The master's program has been enhanced by the addition of a midyear one-week program in New York. Resources for the Philippines program were not available in 2004, but several other special arrangements were worked out with sending institutions for income-generating special programs or special arrangements within programs.

The research made possible by the Ford Foundation will be of great value in increasing the planning capability, the visibility, and the status of the Partnership. As a result of this research, the Partnership knows more about its students—their external characteristics as well as their thinking—and can plan its programs accordingly. At the same time it has been stimulated to improve its data-collection still further, and to build individual and programmatic evaluation into its ongoing activities. Program evaluation (newly in place) will help enhance and maintain quality, and individual evaluation (still to come) will show students and sending institutions what they can expect of the Partnership. The research has also highlighted the importance of the agencies in the service-learning matrix and will encourage the Partnership and its programs to give them more sustained attention and to ask questions about the efficacy of its service placements. Furthermore, this research delivers a clear message that the Partnership is interested in maintaining and enhancing the quality of its programs in terms of both academics and service.

The Partnership is addressing internal communication among its various partners. Plans are proceeding for a communication network among Distinguished Partner institutions, the Partnership has developed its own faculty directory for all its programs, it has revived and revitalized its alumni program, and there are serious discussions going on among those interested in research about the launch of a journal in international service-learning research.

The journal is just one aspect of the second part of the Partnership's mission, advocacy. The institution study has helped define the circumstances and conditions under which the Partnership philosophy can be expected to take root, and it has also demonstrated quite convincingly that the Partnership must identify funds to increase its faculty development efforts and to provide other services to its partner institutions. These other services should include attention to the philosophy of service-learning, which is still insufficiently understood across the world, and which must be intelligently adapted to local circumstances while staying true to its overall purpose and goals. A common refrain among partners is that the Partnership should establish itself as the international voice of service-learning, setting standards, promoting dialogue, identifying best practices, and recognizing excellence.

Such an advocacy role might well extend beyond institutions of higher education, to governments and to intergovernmental organizations. A natural corollary of the Partnership's increased attention to agencies through the present study might be its involvement also in NGO work internationally: the Partnership is, after all, both a higher education organization and an NGO, with an interest in leadership for development, capacity-building, and civic engagement—as the current discussion of leadership makes emphatically clear.

If the Partnership is truly mindful of its role in addressing major world priorities while preparing its students for active citizenship, it should, as we have seen, also seek to address the nature of the service that it provides. Fundamental to the work of the Partnership is a strong belief in the value of service, in and of itself, but such service should be linked to desired outcomes, not only for the students but for the communities they serve. At the Millennium Summit convened by the United Nations in September 2000, the world leaders who gathered in New York agreed on an agenda for collective action in the future, which they called Millennium Development Goals. There are eight such goals, several of which coincide with the work of the Partnership in various parts of the world. These goals include the eradication of extreme poverty and hunger, the reduction of child mortality, ensuring environmental sustainability, and, as goal number eight, "developing a global partnership for development." The word "partnership" in this context is striking. For too long, development has been a top-down, unequal enterprise. In line with Adel Safty's comments on leadership and democracy, development must be seen as a common enterprise in which everyone has ownership and all people are partners—including those who are served. Not everything that the International

Partnership does is directed at the goals identified by the world leaders, nor should it be (indeed we should be mindful of my observation in chapter 1 about the need for questions as well as answers, and for ideological objectivity), but the spirit of partnership, newly discovered by leaders increasingly frustrated by the difficulties they encounter in creating a better life for their peoples, but well known to the International Partnership for Service-Learning and Leadership, is a spirit to which the moral force of the Partnership's philosophy might be actively applied. "Peace, justice, sustainable development, and participatory governance are linked inextricably to the quality of leadership in our communities," writes Linda Chisholm (2004a), "and . . . service-learning is the most and indeed only effective pedagogy for leadership education."

Thus the Partnership might advance its principal agenda of promoting the philosophy and pedagogy of service-learning by promoting it as an international experience above all, but also as something of value within institutions and communities across the world. There is a point where the cold mechanics of operating and administering programs give way to the inspiring vision of a new pedagogy revitalizing higher education and connecting it with the issues of the day. The Partnership requires the first in order to achieve the second, but the second, the vision, is what vitalizes and animates the entire enterprise. We are deeply grateful to the Ford Foundation for bringing this vision closer to reality, but we are equally conscious of the fact that there is so much more for us to do.

We began with a quotation and we will end with one, this time from Kirsten Jo Eby, a service-learning student in Jamaica:

> When I arrived I was told that I was to work at Carberry Court Special School for children with mild to severe mental and physical disabilities. To say that I was unnerved would be a vast understatement. This was the one placement I did not want. My first reaction was to say, "This isn't what I asked for. I want to be moved." . . . But I refused to ask. . . . There had to be some reason for my placement. If nothing else, it would be a learning experience. And that it certainly has been. I have learned about Jamaican schools, society, working with disabled children, and the limits of my own patience. The most important lesson ... has been about the essence of service. I had to be flexible and accept a placement I wasn't comfortable with. . . . I came to realize that

real service is not about working where you would like to, or even where you are most qualified to be. Service is, instead, about working where you are most needed. The challenge is accepting that people do not always need or want what you come ready to offer. If you are truly there to serve, you have to adapt and try to contribute whatever is asked for, whether or not you think you have it in you to give. . . .

So as I go back to the US, my return trip seems bitter-sweet. I have accomplished much, but I don't feel that I have finished my journey. I am going back to where I come from, but I feel I have much farther to go, much more to see and learn and do before I will be able to sit down, relax, and be comfortable saying, "I have finished my journey. I have returned, and now I am home."

# Appendix

## Declaration of Principles of the International Partnership for Service-Learning and Leadership

Service-learning is the pedagogy that links academic study with the practical experience of community service. It has become an international movement that offers new approaches to teaching and learning and to the civic engagement of institutions of higher education. It provides students with an education that meets the highest academic standards *and* delivers meaningful service that makes a difference to the well-being of society.

Service-learning aims to develop in students a lifelong commitment to service and leadership. It promotes understanding of local issues as well as recognition of the inter-relatedness of communities and societies across the world.

### What is service-learning?

Service-learning unites academic study and volunteer community service in mutually reinforcing ways. The service makes the study immediate, applicable and relevant; the study, through knowledge, analysis, and reflection, informs the service.

The service may involve teaching, health care, community development, environmental projects, construction, and a host of other activities that contribute to the well-being of individuals, communities, nations, or the world as a whole.

The academic study may be related to one or more of many disciplines, especially the liberal arts, the humanities, the social sciences, and the physical sciences such as biology, chemistry, and environmental studies, *and* to professional fields, including medicine, law, social work, engineering, education, and business.

In service-learning programs, students and teachers use the experience of service as one source of information and ideas, along with the classroom, laboratory, library, and Internet. They are asked to analyze critically what they learn from the service, just as they analyze the information and ideas garnered from the sources of traditional academic study. When academic credit is awarded, it is not for the service performed, but for the learning, which the student demonstrates through written papers, classroom discussion, examinations and/or other means of formal evaluation. In service-learning programs that are not offered for credit, the learning should be intentional, structured and evaluated.

Service-learning is different from community service unconnected to formal study in two important ways. First, it demands that the student understand the service agency—its mission, philosophy, assumptions, structures, activities and governance—and the conditions of the lives of those who are served. Second, it is characterized by a relationship of partnership: the student learns from the service agency and from the community and, in return, gives energy, intelligence, commitment, time, and skills to address human and community needs. In addition, the service agency learns from the students. College and university faculty and service agency personnel both teach and learn from one another.

Service-learning is different from field study, internships, and practica, although it may have elements of all of these. Unlike field study, service-learning makes the student not only an observer but an active participant. While the student may gain from service-learning many of the benefits of an internship or practicum, service-learning has two goals: student learning *and* service to the community. The success of a program is measured not only by what the student learns but also by the usefulness of the student's work to those served.

## Why is service-learning important, valuable and necessary?

Service-learning addresses simultaneously two important needs of our societies: the education and development of people *and* the provision of increased resources to serve individuals and communities. Service-learning:

- enriches students' learning of academic subjects. Theory is field-tested in practice and is seen and measured within a cultural context. Because the learning is put to immediate use, it tends to be deeper and to last longer.

- develops in students leadership skills as they learn to work collaboratively with the community. They learn that the most effective leadership is that which encourages the active participation—and indeed leadership—of others.

- promotes intercultural and international understanding. The service, whether local, domestic, or international, almost always occurs with people whose lives are very different from that of the student. By working with them, the student comes to understand and appreciate their different experiences, ideas and values, and to work cooperatively with them. Service-learning thus nurtures global awareness and socially responsible citizenship.

- fosters in students personal growth, maturity, the examination of values and beliefs, and civic responsibility, all within the context of a community and its needs. Students explore how they may use their education for the benefit of the community and the well-being of others, especially those in need.

- provides help to service agencies and to communities, addressing needs that would otherwise remain unmet. Service-learning does not replace paid work. Rather, it supplements and extends such work, offering service that would otherwise not be available.

- sets academic institutions in a reciprocal relationship with the community that supports them and in which they are located. In today's world, with pressing issues in every community and nation, academic institutions are called to apply their knowledge and resources to these problems and needs.

- advances our understanding of societies, cultures, and world issues by testing scholarship against immediate practical experience and theory within a cultural context.

## Where and how is service-learning practiced?

Recognizing the many needs of communities, nations and the world, wishing to respond to these needs, and wanting to provide the most stimulating and valuable education to their students, educators around the world are discovering the richness of service-learning. They are applying the pedagogy of service-learning in a wide variety of situations and through various models. In developing service-learning, they are not following the lead of any one nation or system. Instead, they are creating their own versions, compatible with their national systems of education, the prevailing educational philosophies, the mission, curricula, and structures of their own institution, and identifying the needs that they may most effectively assist in addressing.

Institutions of higher education initiating and developing service-learning include old and prestigious universities and colleges, as well as young and less-established ones. They may be public or private; open-enrollment or highly selective. Their curricula may focus on the liberal arts or on career-related training. They may specialize in a particular field or offer a comprehensive program of studies.

The most common setting for service-learning is the local community near the campus, so that the studies occur on campus and the service is performed nearby. But many programs also exist that take students into a new setting, sometimes to another country. International service-learning can be especially rich, as it exposes students to many conditions, ideas, assumptions, and people that are substantially different from those with which they are familiar.

Service-learning may be designed to link one course or subject to service or it may join several disciplines. It may be offered to a group of students or for an individual through independent study. The students may serve together in a single agency or village, or they may be individually placed in a variety of service positions.

The pattern may be that of study, followed by a period of service and concluding with reflection and examination, or the service and study may be intertwined throughout the period of service-learning.

Increasing numbers of universities and colleges throughout the world are requiring that students have a service-learning experience to receive a degree. But the more common pattern is to offer service-learning in a variety of departments and courses of study so that students may themselves elect service-learning. In most institutions offering service-learning, there are opportunities throughout the degree-program to participate; in others it is year-specific, such as for first- or final-year students.

## Principles of good practice

The best-designed and executed service-learning programs ensure that:

- there is reciprocity between the community served and the university or college, and their relationship is built on mutual respect and esteem.

- the learning is rigorous, sound, and appropriate to the academic level of the students. The studies do not offer foregone conclusions but rather, in the spirit of academic inquiry, expose students to a wide range of points of view, theories and ideas, asking that they critically examine these ideas and their experience in service, thereby reaching their own thoughtfully considered insights.

- the service is truly useful to the community or agency. Experience has shown that the agency or community is best qualified to define what is useful. The time and quality of the service must be sufficient to offset the agency time spent in planning supervising and evaluating the program; otherwise the institution and student are exploiting the very people they intend to assist.

- there is a clear connection between the studies and the service. The studies may focus on the general culture of those served or be more specific in relating subject matter and the service experience. Either pattern is effective.

- students are allowed and indeed encouraged to develop and demonstrate leadership skills, using their own initiative when appropriate, bearing in mind that they should first listen to the community and be responsive to its values and needs.

- opportunity for personal reflection on the meaning of the experience in relation to the student's values and life decisions is built into the program in a structured way. The keeping of a journal is a common means of providing this opportunity for the students to connect what they are learning and experiencing with their own lives.

- support services are provided. Students are prepared for their service and the community in which they will serve. Provision is made for their health care should it be needed, and students are advised on issues of safety. Ongoing advising services are available.

### What is The International Partnership for Service-Learning and Leadership?

The International Partnership for Service-Learning and Leadership (IPSL) is a worldwide association of universities, colleges, non-governmental and related organizations united to foster service-learning. It was founded in 1982 as The Partnership for Service-Learning and incorporated in the state of New York, USA, as a not-for-profit educational organization. In 1996, the Board of Trustees incorporated the word "international" in the name to reflect the international nature and focus and, in 2003, incorporated the concept of leadership development into its mission and the title.

The International Partnership is governed by a Board of Trustees that consists of outstanding leaders in education and the service sector from around the world. With headquarters in New York City, it is managed and led by a full-time professional staff. For its work in developing service-learning, the International Partnership has been awarded grants from major foundations and trusts, as well as individual donors.

The mission of the International Partnership is two-fold: to promote service-learning through publications, conferences, research, and training opportunities for faculty and service agency staff *and* to offer international programs for undergraduate and graduate students from institutions of higher education around the world.

Each year the International Partnership publishes and distributes books and newsletters related to service-learning, leadership and/or international education. The biannual conference, which has been held in Europe, Asia, and the Americas, draws participants from around the world. Ongoing research evaluates the impact of service-learning on students, institutions of higher education, and on the agencies and communities in which the students serve.

Today the International Partnership offers undergraduate service-learning programs in thirteen nations—programs in which almost 4,000 students from 400 universities or colleges in the US and twenty-five other nations have participated. The International Partnership-coordinated Master's Degree in International Service, developed in cooperation with partner universities in Jamaica, Mexico and the United Kingdom, prepares graduates for careers in international nongovernmental relief and development agencies. Other special programs are designed and managed to fit the needs of particular institutions and organizations.

## How can universities, colleges, nongovernmental and related organizations participate?

There are a variety of ways in which to affiliate with The International Partnership for Service-Learning and Leadership:

- **Become a supporter** by signing the Declaration of Principles, thereby indicating your institution's willingness and commitment to strive for the goals stated herein. All such institutions will be considered supporters of the International Partnership, listed in publications and on the website, sent information about programs and activities, and invited at the biennial conference to participate in the General Assembly of the International Partnership, advising the Board of Trustees on future directions. In these ways, supporters will be acknowledged as among those institutions that are striving to provide high-quality and responsible service-learning programs.

- **Become a Distinguished Partner**. Member institutions that have instituted service-learning programs and are committed to extending and deepening these programs form a local chapter of the International Partnership, enabling them to fulfill their goals for the development of service-learning. Each Distinguished Partner is entitled each year to award to two students, one faculty member, and one local service agency the Certificate for Distinguished

Leadership in Service-Learning, issued in the name of the International Partnership and all of the Distinguished Partners.

- **Send students on International Partnership-sponsored programs.** Institutions around the world use the programs of the International Partnership to make available to their students programs in a wide variety of locations. A special category called **Affiliate** enables universities and colleges sending more than five students a year on the regular undergraduate semester-long programs to receive financial incentives and to work especially closely with the central office.

- **Commission special programs.** Institutions and organizations often ask the International Partnership to design and administer programs especially designed for their students, teachers, or members.

- **Participate in activities.** The International Partnership holds conferences biennially and conducts faculty seminars.

- Use—and possibly write for—**International Partnership publications** such as the newsletters, textbooks and training materials.

# References

Allport, Gordon W. 1954. *The Nature of Prejudice*. Reading, MA: Addison-Wesley.

Ang, Cindy Dollente, ed. 2002. *Bound with a Bond Which Had No Boundaries*. Quezon City: Trinity College.

Annette, John. 2002. Service learning in an international context. *Frontiers*. Winter: 83-93.

Aquino, Deana R. 2001. Ethics and values in civil society: The service-learning paradigm. *Anthropos* (Trinity College of Quezon City) 1/2:109–117.

Aquino, Deana R., ed. 1999. *Reflections '99*. Quezon City: Trinity College.

Battistoni, Richard M. 2002. *Civic Engagement Across the Curriculum: A Resource Book for Service-Learning Faculty in All Disciplines*. Providence, RI: Campus Compact.

Bennett, Douglas C. 1997. Innovation in the liberal arts and sciences. Orrill 1997: 131–149.

Bennett, Janet M. 1993. Cultural marginality: Identity issues in intercultural training. Paige 1993.

Bennett, Milton J. 1993. Towards a developmental model of intercultural sensitivity. Paige 1993.

Bennis, Warren G. 1989. *On Becoming a Leader*. Reading, MA: Addison-Wesley.

Benson, Lee & Ira Harkavy. 2000. Academically-based community service and university-assisted community schools as complementary approaches for advancing learning, teaching, research, and service: The University of Pennsylvania as a case study in progress. Kenny & others 2002:361-378.

Berry, Howard A. 1985. Experiential education: The neglected dimension of international/intercultural studies. *International Programs Quarterly*. Spring–Summer:1, 3–4, 23–27.

Berry, Howard A. 1988. Service-learning in international and intercultural settings. *Experiential Education*. May–June:13, 3.

Berry, Howard A. 1990. Service learning in international and intercultural settings. Kendall 1990:311–314.

Berry, Howard A. & Linda A. Chisholm. 1992. *How to Serve & Learn Abroad Effectiveley: Students Tell Students*. New York: Partnership for Service-Learning.

Berry, Howard A. & Linda A. Chisholm. 1999. *Service-Learning in Higher Education Around the World: An Initial Look.* New York: International Partnership for Service-Learning.

Billig, Shelley H. & Andrew Furco, ed. 2002. *Service-Learning Through a Multidisciplinary Lens.* Greenwich, CT: Information Age Publishing.

Billig, Shelley H. & Janet Eyler, ed. 2003. *Deconstructing Service-Learning: Research Exploring Context, Participation, and Impacts.* Greenwich, CT: Information Age Publishing.

Boyer, Ernest L. 1996. The scholarship of engagement. *Journal of Public Service & Outreach* 1/1:11–20.

Boyte, Harry, & Elizabeth Hollander. 1999. *Wingspread Declaration on the Civic Responsibility of Research Universities.* Providence, RI: Campus Compact.

Bringle, Robert G. & Julie A. Hatcher. 1995. A service-learning curriculum for faculty. *Michigan Journal of Community Service Learning* 2:112–122.

Bringle, Robert G. & Julie A.Hatcher. 1999. Reflection in service learning: Making meaning of experience. *Educational Horizons* 77/4:179–185.

Bringle, Robert G. & Julie A. Hatcher. 2000. Institutionalization of service-learning in higher education. *Journal of Higher Education,* 71/3:273–290.

Bringle, Robert G., Mindy A. Phillips & Michael Hudson. 2004. *The Measure of Service Learning: Research Scales to Assess Student Experiences.* Washington: American Psychological Association.

Brown, George & Madeleine Atkins. 1988. *Effective Teaching in Higher Education.* London: Methuen.

Brown, Nevin. 2004. Service agencies in Guayaquil, Ecuador: Essential partners in the work of IPSL. *Action/Reflection.* Summer:6–7.

Bucco, D.A. & J.A. Busch. 1996. Starting a service-learning program. Jacoby & Associates 1996.

Burn, Barbara, Jerry Carlson, and others. *Research on U.S. Students Abroad to 1987: A Bibliography with Abstracts,* at www.usc.edu/dept/education/index2.html.

Carlson, Jerry S., Barbara B. Burn, and others. 1990. *Study Abroad: The Experience of American Undergraduates.* Westport, CT: Greenwood Press.

Caron, Barbara, Diane P. Genereux & Briana Huntsberger. 1999. *Service Matters: The Engaged Campus.* Providence, RI: Campus Compact.

Chaffee, Ellen E. & William G. Tierney. 1988. *Collegiate Culture and Leadership Strategies.* New York: American Council on Education & Macmillan.

Chao, Maureen. *Research on U.S. Students Study Abroad: An Update 1988–2000,* at www.usc.edu/dept/education/index2.html.

Chisholm, Linda A. 2000. *Charting a Hero's Journey.* New York: International Partnership for Service-Learning.

Chisholm, Linda A. 2003. Partnerships for international service-learning. Jacoby & Associates 2003:259–288.

Chisholm, Linda A. 2004a. Action/Reflection ... and leadership. *Action/Reflection.* Summer:1–3.

Chisholm, Linda A., ed. 2004b. *Visions of Service*. New York: International Partnership for Service-Learning and Leadership.

Chisholm, Linda A. & Howard A. Berry. 2002. *Understanding the Education—and Through It the Culture —in Education Abroad*. New York: International Partnership for Service-Learning.

Chrislip, David D. & Carl E. Larson. 1994. *Collaborative Leadership: How Citizens and Civic Leaders Can Make a Difference*. San Francisco: Jossey Bass.

Clarke, Melinda. 2003. Finding the community in service-learning research: The 3–"1" model. Billig & Eyler 2003:125–146.

Cruz, Nadinne I. & Dwight E. Giles, Jr. 2000. Where's the community in service-learning research? *Michigan Journal of Community Service Learning*. Special Issue. Fall:28–34.

Dearing, Ron, ed. 1997. *Report of the National Committee of Inquiry into Higher Education* [The Dearing Report], at http://www.leeds.ac.uk/educol/ncihe/sumrep.htm.

Dickson, Alec G. 1958. Technical assistance and idealism: misgivings and mistakings. *Year Book of World Affairs* 12:199–225.

Dickson, Alec. 1976. *A Chance to Serve*. London: Dennis Dobson.

Dickson, Alec. 1980. *Study Service: Problems and Opportunities*. Unesco Document ED-80/WS/130. Paris: UNESCO.

Dickson, Mora. 2004. *Portrait of a Partnership*. New York: International Partnership for Service-Learning and Leadership.

Driscoll, Amy. 2000. Studying faculty and service-learning: Directions for inquiry and development. *Michigan Journal of Community Service Learning*. Special Issue. Fall:35–41.

Driscoll, Amy and others. 1998. *Assessing the Impact of Service Learning*. 2nd ed. Portland, OR: Center for Academic Excellence, Portland State University.

Driscoll, Amy, Barbara Holland, S. Gelmon & S. Kerrigan. 1996. An assessment model for service-learning: Comprehensive case studies of impact on faculty, students, community, and institutions. *Michigan Journal of Community Service Learning*, 3:66–71.

Eberly, Donald & Michael Sherraden, ed. 1990. *The Moral Equivalent of War? A Study of Non-Military Service in Nine Nations*. New York: Greenwood.

Ehrlich, Thomas. 1997. Dewey versus Hutchins: The next round. Orrill 1997: 225–262.

Ehrlich, Thomas, ed. 2000. *Civic Responsibility and Higher Education*. Washington: American Council on Education & Oryx Press.

Elkind, Perrin. 1998. *Tonderai:Studying Abroad in Zimbabwe*. Fort Bragg, CA: Lost Coast Press.

Enos, S. & K. Morton. 2003. Developing a theory and practice of campus-community partnerships. Jacoby & Associates 2003.

Entwistle, N., M. Hanley & D. Hounsell. 1979. Identifying distinctive approaches to studying. *Higher Education* 8:365–380.

Eyler, Janet S. 2000. What do we most need to know about the impact of service-learning on student learning? *Michigan Journal of Community Service Learning.* Special Issue. Fall:11–17.

Eyler, Janet S. & Dwight E. Giles, Jr. 1999. *Where's the Learning in Service-Learning?* San Francisco: Jossey-Bass.

Eyler, Janet S., Dwight E. Giles, Jr., Christine M. Stenson, & Charlene J. Gray. *At a Glance: What We Know About the Effects of Service-Learning on College Students, Faculty, Institutions and Communities, 1993–2000,* at http://www.compact.org/resource/aag.pdf.

Fisher, James L., Martha W. Tack & Karen J. Wheeler. 1988. *The Effective College President.* New York: American Council on Education & Macmillan.

Fukuda-Parr, Sakiko, ed. 2004. *Human Development Report 2004: Cultural Liberty in Today's World.* New York: United Nations Development Program (UNDP).

Gardner, John N., Michael J. Siegel, & M. Cutright. 2001. Focusing on the first-year student. *AGB Priorities* 17.

Giles, Dwight E., Jr. & J.B. Freed. 1985. *The Service-Learning Dimensions of Field Study: The Cornell Human Ecology Field Study Program.* Washington, DC: National Conference on Service-Learning.

Giles, Dwight E., Jr., & Janet Eyler. 1994. The theoretical roots of service-learning in John Dewey: Toward a theory of service-learning. *Michigan Journal of Community Service Learning* 1:77–85.

Giles, Dwight E., Jr., & Janet Eyler. 1998. A service-learning research agenda for the next five years. R. Rhoads & J. Howard, ed. *Academic Service-Learning: A Pedagogy of Action and Reflection.* San Francisco: Jossey-Bass. 65–72.

Gillespie, Joan, Larry A. Braskamp & David C. Braskamp. 1999. Evaluation and study abroad: Developing assessment criteria and practices to promote excellence. *Frontiers.* Fall:101–127.

Glaser, Barney G. & Anselm L. Strauss. 1967. *The Discovery of Grounded Theory.* London: Weidenfeld & Nicolson.

Glesne, Corrine. 1998. *Becoming Qualitative Researchers.* 2nd ed. New York: Longman.

Goodlad, Sinclair, 1982. *Study Service: An Examination of Community Service as a Method of Study in Higher Education.* Windsor, UK: NFER-Nelson.

Green, Madeleine F., ed. 1989. *Leaders for a New Era: Strategies for Higher Education.* New York: American Council on Education & Macmillan.

Hall, Edward T. 1994. *West of the Thirties: Discoveries Among the Navajo and Hopi.* New York: Doubleday.

Harkavy, Ira & Lee Benson. 1999. De-Platonizing and democratizing education as the bases of service learning. Rhoads & Howard 1999:11–20.

Harkavy, Ira, John Puckett & Dan Romer. 2000. Action research: Bridging service and research. *Michigan Journal of Community Service Learning.* Special Issue. Fall:113–118.

Harrison, Lawrence E. & Samuel P. Huntington, ed. 2000. *Culture Matters: How Values Shape Human Progress.* New York: Basic Books.

Hatcher, Julie A. 1997. The moral dimensions of John Dewey's philosophy: Implications for undergraduate education. *Michigan Journal of Community Service Learning* 4:22–29.

Hatcher, Julie A., Robert G. Bringle, & R. Muthiah. Forthcoming. Designing effective reflection: What matters to service-learning? *Michigan Journal of Community Service Learning*.

Hedin, D. & D. Conrad. 1990. The impact of experiential education on youth development. Kendall & Associates 1990.

Higher Education Research Institute. 2002. *Findings from the 2002 Administration of Your First College Year (YFCY): National Aggregates*. Los Angeles: UCLA, Higher Education Research Institute.

Holland, Barbara A. 1999. Factors and strategies that influence faculty involvement in public service. *Journal of Public Service & Outreach* 4/1:37–43.

Holland, Barbara A. 2000. Institutional impacts and organizational issues related to service-learning. *Michigan Journal of Community Service Learning*. Special Issue. Fall:52–60.

Hollander, Elizabeth L., John Saltmarsh & Edward Zlotkowski. 2002. Indicators of engagement: Campus Compact. Kenny & others 2002:31–49.

Honnet, Ellen Porter & Susan J. Poulsen. 1989. *Principles of Good Practice for Combining Service and Learning (Wingspread Special Report)*. Racine, WI: Johnson Foundation.

Howard, Jeffrey, ed. 1993. *Praxis 1: A Faculty Casebook on Community Service Learning*. Ann Arbor: OSCL Press.

Iles, Jennifer. 2004. *Service Learning: Module Handbooks*. Roehampton: School of Business, Social Sciences and Computing, University of Surrey Roehampton.

Institute of International Education. *Open Doors*.

International Partnership for Service-Learning and Leadership, website, www.ipsl.org.

Jacoby, Barbara. 1996. Securing the future of service-learning in higher education. Jacoby & Associates 1996.

Jacoby, Barbara. 2003. Fundamentals of service-learning partnerships. Jacoby & Associates 2003:1–19.

Jacoby, Barbara & Associates, ed. 1996. *Service-Learning in Higher Education*. San Francisco: Jossey-Bass.

Jacoby, Barbara & Associates, ed. 2003. *Building Partnerships for Service-Learning*. San Francisco: Jossey-Bass.

Jones, S.R. 2003. Principles and profiles of exemplary partnerships with community agencies. Jacoby & Associates 2003:151–173.

Kanter, Rosabeth Moss. 1983. *The Change Masters: Innovation and Entrepreneurship in the American Corporation*. New York: Simon & Schuster.

Kendall, Jane C. & Associates, ed. 1990. *Combining Service and Learning*. Raleigh, NC: National Association for Internships and Experiential Education.

Kenny, Maureen E., Lou Anna K. Simon, Karen Kiley-Brabeck & Richard M. Lerner, ed. 2002. *Learning to Serve: Promoting Civil Society through Service-Learning*. Boston: Kluwer.

Kenny, Maureen E., Lou Anna K. Simon, Karen Kiley-Brabeck & Richard M. Lerner. 2002. Promoting civil society through service learning: A view of the issues. Kenny & others 2002:1–14.

Kinnell, Margaret, ed. 1990. *The Learning Experiences of Overseas Students*. Buckingham: Society for Research into Higher Education (SRHE) & Open University Press.

Kolb, David A. 1984. *Experiential Learning*. Englewood Cliffs, NJ: Prentice Hall.

Kraft, Richard J. 2002. International service learning. Kenny and others 2002:297–313.

Langseth, M. 2000. Maximizing impact, minimizing harm: Why service-learning must more fully integrate multicultural education. C.R. O'Grady, ed. *Integrating Service-Learning and Multicultural Education in Colleges and Universities*. Mahwah, NJ: Erlbaum. 247–262.

Lawson, Hal A. 2002. Beyond community involvement and service learning to engaged universities. *Universities and Community Schools* 7/1–2:79–94.

Lazarsfeld, Paul F., & Robert K. Merton. 1964. Friendship as social process: A substantive and methodological analysis. Monroe Berger and others, ed. *Freedom and Control in Modern Society.* New York: Octagon.

Lazarus, Josef. 2004. Guidelines for good practice of service-learning: Results of a multi-campus study. Paper presented at the 4th Annual International Conference on Service Learning, Greenville, SC, October 10–12.

Letwin, William, ed. 1983. *Against Equality.* London: Macmillan.

Lisman, C. David. 1998. *Toward a Civil Society: Civic Literacy and Service Learning.* Westport, CT: Bergin & Garvey.

Lockyer, Andrew, Bernard Crick & John Annette, ed. 2003. *Education for Democratic Citizenship*. Aldershot, UK: Ashgate.

Malinowski, Bronislaw. 1922. *Argonauts of the Western Pacific*. Prospect Heights, IL: Waveland.

Mayhew, Lewis B. 1979. *Surviving the Eighties: Strategies and Procedures for Solving Fiscal and Enrollment Problems.* San Francisco: Jossey-Bass.

McCarthy, Florence E. 2002. Service learning and the construction of networks and curriculum. Yamamoto 2002:23–37.

Miller, Andrew, Anthony G. Watts & Ian Jamieson. 1991. *Rethinking Work Experience*. London: Falmer Press.

Mills, C. Wright. 1959. *The Sociological Imagination*. New York: Oxford University Press.

Mintz, S.D., and G.W. Hesser. 1996. Principles of good practice in service-learning. Jacoby & Associates 1996.

Monard, Kathia. 2002. *Nurturing Senses of Care, Justice and Reciprocity through International Service-Learning*. Ph.D. dissertation, University of Pittsburgh.

Montrose, Lynne. 2002. International study and experiential learning: The academic context. *Frontiers.* Winter:1–15.

Moon, Jenny. 2001. *Reflection in Higher Education Learning*. PDP Working Paper (University of Exeter) 4.

Moore, David Thornton. 2000. The relationship between experiential learning research and service-learning research. *Michigan Journal of Community Service Learning.* Special Issue. Fall:124–128.

Morris-Brown, V. 1993. *The Jamaica Handbook of Proverbs.* Mandeville, Jamaica: Island Heart.

Morton, K. & M. Troppe. 1996. From the margin to the mainstream: Campus Compact's project on Integrating Service with Academic Study. *Journal of Business Ethics* 15:21–32.

Orrill, Robert, ed. 1997. *Education and Democracy: Reimagining Liberal Learning in America.* New York: College Entrance Examination Board.

Orsal, Cesar D., & Angelita Bugnalen, ed. 2003. *Passing Through the Gates.* Quezon City: Trinity College.

Paige, R. Michael. 1993. On the nature of intercultural experience and intercultural education. R. Michael Paige, ed. *Education for the Intercultural Experience.* Yarmouth, ME: Intercultural Press.

Patton, Michael Quinn. 1990. *Qualitative Evaluation and Research Methods.* 2nd ed. Newbury Park, CA: Sage.

Pettigrew, Thomas F., & Linda R. Tropp. 2000. Does intergroup contact reduce prejudice? Recent meta-analytic findings. Stuart Oskamp, ed. *Reducing Prejudice and Discrimination.* The Claremont Symposium on Applied Social Psychology. Mahwah, NJ: Erlbaum. 93–114.

Plantan, Frank, Jr. 2002. *Final Report of the Universities as Sites of Citizenship Project,* at http://iche.sas.upenn.edu.

Porter, Maureen & Kathia Monard. 2001. *Ayni* in the global village: Building relationships of reciprocity through international service-learning. *Michigan Journal of Community Service Learning* 8/1:5–17.

Pusch, Margaret D. 1994. The chameleon capability. Richard D. Lambert, ed. *Educational Exchange and Global Competence.* New York: Council for International Educational Exchange (CIEE).

Pusch, Margaret D. 1998. Going home: Styles of reentry. Donal Lynch, Adrian Pilbeam & Philip O'Connor, ed. *Heritage and Progress.* Bath, England: SIETAR Europa.

Pusch, Margaret D. 2001. Research on reentry and reintegration into the home community. Yellow Springs, OH: Antioch University. Unpublished paper.

Pusch, Margaret D. 2003. International service-learning and intercultural competence development. Paper presented at the 3rd Annual International Conference on Service-Learning, Salt Lake City, November 6–8.

Ramaley, Judith A. 2000. Strategic directions for service-learning research: A presidential perspective. *Michigan Journal of Community Service Learning.* Special Issue. Fall:91–97.

Ramsden, Paul. 1992. *Learning to Teach in Higher Education.* London: Routledge.

Reagan, Timothy. 2005. *Non-Western Educational Traditions: Indigenous Approaches to Educational Thought and Practice.* 3rd ed. Mahwah, NJ: Erlbaum.

Rhoads, Robert A. & Jeffrey Howard, ed. 1999. *Service Learning: Pedagogy and Research.* San Francisco: Jossey-Bass.

Rich, Barbara L. (University of Southern Maine). 2002. Ethical issues and questions for service-learning practitioners and researchers. Paper presented at the Second Annual Conference on Service-Learning Research, Nashville, October.

Roehampton University 2004. *Roehampton the Greater London University.* Undergraduate Prospectus 2004. Roehampton: University of Surrey Roehampton.

Rogers, Everett M. 1995. *Diffusion of Innovations.* 4th ed. New York: Free Press.

Rubin, S. 1996. Institutionalizing service learning. Jacoby & Associates 1996:297–316.

Rue, P. 1996. Administering successful service-learning programs. Jacoby & Associates 1996.

Safty, Adel. 2004. *Leadership and Democracy.* New York: International Partnership for Service-Learning & Leadership.

Schaffer, Marjorie A., Jenell Williams Paris & Kristin Vogel. 2003. Ethical relationships in service-learning partnerships. Billig & Eyler 2003:147–168.

Schweder, Richard A. 2000. Moral maps, "First World" conceits, and the new evangelists. Harrison & Huntington 2000:158-176.

Shapiro, Theodore. 2004. Use your words! *Journal of the American Psychoanalytic Association.* 52/2:331–353.

Showalter, Stuart W., ed. 1989. *The Role of Service-Learning in International Education: Proceedings of a Wingspread Conference.* Goshen, IN: Goshen College.

Siegel, Michael J. 2003a. The intersection of service-learning and the first year of college: A primer. Paper presented at the 55th Annual Conference of NAFSA: Association of International Educators, Salt Lake City, May 29, 2003.

Siegel, Michael J. 2003b. The impress of international service-learning on the lives of students. Paper presented at the 3rd Annual International Conference on Service-Learning, Salt Lake City, November 6–8.

Sigmon, Robert L. 1990. Service learning: Three principles. Kendall & Associates 1990.

Sigmon, Robert L. 1996. The problem of definition in service-learning. Robert L. Sigmon and others, ed. *The Journey to Service-Learning.* Washington: Council of Independent Colleges. 9–11.

Sigmon, Robert L. 1998. *Building Sustainable Partnerships: Linking Communities and Educational Institutions.* Washington: National Society for Experiential Education.

Stanton, T. 1990. Service learning. Groping toward a definition. Kendall & Associates 1990.

Stanton, Timothy K., Dwight E. Giles, Jr. & Nadinne I. Cruz. 1999. *Service-Learning: A Movement's Pioneers Reflect on Its Origins, Practice, and Future.* San Francisco: Jossey-Bass.

Teune, Henry & Frank Plantan, Jr. 2001. *General Report: United States Study, Universities as Sites of Citizenship and Civic Responsibility,* at http://iche.sas.upenn.edu.

Tonkin, Humphrey. 1993. Service, values, and a liberal education. *Action/Reflection* Winter:1–3.

Tonkin, Humphrey. 1994. Learning through service, service through learning. *Universities and Community Schools* 4/1-2:22–25.

Tonkin, Humphrey. 1999. Service learning: Making education more meaningful. *International Educator,* 8/1:35–37.

Tonkin, Humphrey. 2001. Study, service, and the self transformed. Martin Tillman, ed. *Study Abroad: A 21ˢᵗ Century Perspective, Volume II—The Changing Landscape.* Stamford, CT: American Institute for Foreign Study. 21–25.

Tonkin, Humphrey. 2002. *The International Partnership for Service-Learning: A Review of the Demographics of the Undergraduate Programs.* New York: International Partnership for Service-Learning. Available also at www.ipsl.org.

Tonkin, Humphrey. 2003. International service-learning: A framework for research. Paper presented at the 3ʳᵈ Annual International Conference on Service-Learning, Salt Lake City, November 6–8.

Tonkin, Humphrey, & Diego Quiroga. 2004. A qualitative approach to the assessment of international service-learning. *Frontiers.* 10 Fall:163–182.

Tonkin, Humphrey, & Robert G. Bringle. 2004. Research design and findings of service-learning on students, institutions of higher education, and communities. Workshop presented at the Conference of the International Partnership for Service-Learning and Leadership, Chiang Mai, Thailand, January.

Tonkin, Humphrey & Jane Edwards. 1981. *The World in the Curriculum: Curricular Strategies for the 21ˢᵗ Century.* New Rochelle, NY: Change Magazine Press.

Torres, Jan. 2000. *Benchmarks for Campus/Community Partnerships.* Providence, RI: Campus Compact.

Turner, Victor. 1974. *Dramas, Fields and Metaphors: Symbolic Action in Human Society.* Ithaca: Cornell University Press.

Vande Berg, Michael, Al Balkcum, Mark Scheid & Brian Whalen. 2004. The Georgetown Consortium study: A report at the half-way mark. *Frontiers* 10, Fall.

Vernon, A. and K. Ward. 1999. Campus and community partnerships: Assessing impacts and strengthening connections. *Michigan Journal of Community Service* 6:30-37

Vogelgesang, Lori J., Elaine K. Ikeda, Shannon K. Gilmartin & Jennifer R. Keup. 2002. Service-learning and the first-year experience: Outcomes related to learning and persistence. Zlotkowski 2002:15–26.

Ward, Colleen, Stephen Bochner & Adrian Furnham. 2001. *The Psychology of Culture Shock.* 2ⁿᵈ ed. Philadelphia: Taylor & Francis.

Ward, K. 1996. Service-learning and student volunteerism: Reflections on institutional commitment. *Michigan Journal of Community Service Learning* 3:55–65.

Weill, S.W. & I. McGill, ed. 1989. *Making Sense of Experiential Learning: Diversity in Theory and Practice.* Buckingham: Society for Research into Higher Education (SRHE) & Open University Press.

Williams, R. 1990. The impact of field education on student development: Research findings. Kendall & Associates 1990.

Winter, Greg. 2004. Colleges tell students the overseas party's over. New York Times, August 23.

Wisker, G., J. Tiley, M. Watkins, S. Waller & J. Thomas. 2001. Discipline-based research into student learning in English, law, social work, computer skills for linguists, women's studies, creative writing: How can it inform our teaching? *Innovations in Education and Teaching International* 38/2:183–202

Yamamoto, Kano, ed. 2002. *Service Learning in Asia: Creating Networks and Curricula in Higher Education.* Tokyo: International Christian University.

Yoshikawa, Muneo J. 1987. Cross-cultural adaptation and aperceptual development. Young Yun Kim & William B. Gudykunst, ed. *Cross-Cultural Adaptation: Current Approaches.* International and Intercultural Communication Annual 9. Newbury Park, CA: Sage.

Zlotkowski, Edward, ed. 2002. *Service-Learning and the First-Year Experience: Preparing Students for Personal Success and Civic Responsibility.* Columbia, SC: National Resource Center for the First-Year Experience.

# Contributors

ROBERT G. BRINGLE holds a doctorate in social psychology from the University of Massachusetts and serves as Chancellor's Professor of Psychology and Philanthropic Studies and director of the Center for Service and Learning at Indiana University–Purdue University Indianapolis. In addition to his research and teaching in social psychology, he has been involved in the implementation and evaluation of educational programs and has a strong interest in service-learning and civic engagement. A recipient of Campus Compact's Ehrlich Award for Service Learning, he serves as a consultant on the Community–Higher Education–Service Partnership project in South Africa.

SUSAN J. DEELEY is Lecturer in Public Policy, Adviser of Studies, and Director of Service-Learning Programs in the Department of Urban Studies at the University of Glasgow and directs the Glasgow program of the International Partnership for Service-Learning and Leadership. She holds a Ph.D. in social policy from the University of Glasgow, a research degree in education from the University of Paisley, Scotland, and degrees in English literature, comparative religion and education from the University of Manchester. Her research interests include sexuality and learning disability; the effects of disability within the family, children and young people as carers, and experiential learning in higher education.

MARGARET D. PUSCH is associate director of the Intercultural Communication Institute, Portland, Oregon. Among other activities, in her capacity as associate director, she conducts two or three intensive workshops each year for professionals in the field of intercultural communication. She holds an MA in Intercultural Relations from Antioch University. She has also served as leader/trainer for the European Association of International Education and was for many years president of Intercultural Press. In 1995–96 she served as president of NAFSA: Association of International Educators, and she currently chairs the board of the IPSL.

DIEGO QUIROGA has been successively dean of social sciences, dean of academic affairs, and dean of the graduate school, at Universidad San Francisco de Quito. He holds a Ph.D. in anthropology from the University of Illinois and teaches courses in such fields as ethnography, Andean anthropology, and medical anthropology. He is co-director of the Galápagos Academic Institute for the Arts and Sciences (GAIAS) and has conducted extensive research on community health in the Upper Amazon Basin and the Ecuadorian Highlands. He directs the IPSL programs in Quito and the Galápagos Islands.

MICHAEL J. SIEGEL is an associate consultant with Noel-Levitz and a research fellow at the Policy Center on the First Year of College, Brevard, North Carolina. He holds a Ph.D. in higher education from Indiana University, and degrees also in psychology and in counseling. He has done extensive work in survey instrument design, assessment, and related activities, and has coordinated inter-institutional cooperative efforts aimed at improving the college experience for students, particularly in the first year.

HUMPHREY TONKIN is President Emeritus of the University of Hartford and University Professor of the Humanities. He also serves as Vice-President for Program Evaluation and Research at the IPSL. His international activities have included service as chair of the Council for International Exchange of Scholars, the Canadian Fulbright Commission, and the American Forum for Global Education. He currently serves on the board of World Learning and represents the Universal Esperanto Association at the United Nations.

He holds undergraduate degrees from Cambridge University and a Ph.D. from Harvard and publishes and teaches in English literature and linguistics.

JOHN M. WHITELEY is professor of social ecology at the University of California Irvine. He holds a doctorate in education from Harvard University and is particularly interested in the moral development of young people. His published work includes essays and books on character development in college students, on counseling psychology, and on peace studies. He is currently conducting research on conflict prevention in the Caucasus region of the former Soviet Union.

# Index

# Also available from the IPSL Press:

### Visions of Service
#### edited by Linda A. Chisholm

This book introduces students to five of the world's great religions—Hinduism, Buddhism, Judaism, Christianity, and Islam—with a special emphasis on each religion's philosophy of service and call to serve. It excerpts regarding service and social responsibility from the sacred writings of each tradition, followed by questions for study and reflection. 2004.

### Understanding the Education—and through It the culture—in Education Abroad
#### by Linda A. Chisholm and Howard A. Berry

Based on the premise that an educational system both reflects and shapes a culture, this book is a guide for students going abroad to study. It leads them step-by-step through an in-depth investigation of the university they attend overseas and higher education in their host country. The study will help them both to be a successful student and to come to a deeper knowledge of their host culture. 2002.

### Charting a Hero's Journey
#### by Linda A. Chisholm

Based on the work of Joseph Campbell and using excerpts from the journals of such people as Jane Addams, Langston Hughes, Octavio Paz, Samuel Johnson, Mary Kingsley, and Kathleen Norris, *Charting a Hero's Journey* is a guide to the writing of a journal for college students engaged in study abroad, off-campus study, and/or service-learning. 2000.

---

**For more information about IPSL publications,
visit www.ipsl.org or e-mail publications@ipsl.org.**

### Portrait of a Partnership
by Mora Dickson

This book, the last of many written by Mora Dickson, documents her life with Alec Dickson, founder of Voluntary Service Overseas, the British organization upon which John F. Kennedy modeled the U.S. Peace Corps. 2004.

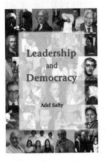

### Leadership and Democracy
by Adel Safty

How do leadership and democracy intersect, and what are the qualities of leadership in a world of democratic empowerment? Professor Adel Safty, Permanent UNESCO Chair in International Leadership and a superb observer of the world political scene, offers a panoramic view of the state of democracy across the world. 2004.

### Service-Learning in Higher Education Around the World: An Initial Look
a report by Howard A. Berry and Linda A. Chisholm

This report, supported by the Ford Foundation, is the first international survey of service-learning. In addition to describing models of service-learning programs, it gives examples of service-learning from over 100 institutions in 33 countries. 1999.

### How to Serve & Learn Abroad Effectively: Students Tell Students
by Howard A. Berry and Linda A. Chisholm

Based on the experiences and reflections of over 1,000 students who served and learned through The International Partnership for Service-Learning, the authors have organized the students' advice into a lively and readable book that helps current students to choose a study abroad and/or volunteer program that is right for them and then give and get the most through their community service at home or abroad. It is also useful to those who advise, orient, and re-enter study abroad students. 1992.